A JURISPRUDENCE OF CONVERSATIONS

How do feminists, as lawyers and activists, think about, and do law, in a way that makes life more meaningful and just? How are law and feminism called into relation, given meaning, engaged with, used, refused, adapted and brought to life through collaborative action? Grounded in empirical studies, this book is both a history of the emergence of feminist jurisprudence in post-colonial India and a model of innovative legal research. The book inaugurates a creative practice of scholarly activism that engages a new way of thinking about law and feminist jurisprudence, one that is geared to acknowledge and take responsibility for the hierarchies in Indian academic practices. Its method of conversation and accountability continues the feminist tradition of taking reciprocity and the time and place of collaboration seriously. By bringing legal academics and sex worker activists into conversation, the book helps make visible the specific ties between post-colonial life and law and joins the work of refusing and reimagining the hierarchical formation of legal knowledge in a caste-based Indian society. A significant contribution to the history and practice of feminist jurisprudence in post-colonial India, *A Jurisprudence of Conversations* will appeal to both an academic and an activist readership.

Debolina Dutta is a Research Fellow at Melbourne Law School's ARC Centre of Excellence for the Elimination of Violence Against Women (CEVAW). She has a long-standing association with the sex workers' movement in India and is the co-director of the award-winning documentary film *We Are Foot Soldiers* (2011) on the activism of sex workers' children in Kolkata.

LAW IN CONTEXT

Since 1970, the Law in Context series has been at the forefront of a movement to broaden the study of law. The series is a vehicle for the publication of innovative monographs and texts that treat law and legal phenomena critically in their cultural, social, political, technological, environmental and economic contexts. A contextual approach involves treating legal subjects broadly, using materials from other humanities and social sciences, and from any other discipline that helps to explain the operation in practice of the particular legal field or legal phenomena under investigation. It is intended that this orientation is at once more stimulating and more revealing than the bare exposition of legal rules. The series includes original research monographs, coursebooks and textbooks that foreground contextual approaches and methods. The series includes and welcomes books on the study of law in all its contexts, including domestic legal systems, European and international law, transnational and global legal processes, and comparative law.

Books in the Series

Acosta: *The National Versus the Foreigner in South America: 200 Years of Migration and Citizenship Law*
Alaattinoğlu: *Grievance Formation, Rights and Remedies*
Ali: *Modern Challenges to Islamic Law*
Alyagon Darr: *Plausible Crime Stories: The Legal History of Sexual Offences in Mandate Palestine*
Anderson, Schum & Twining: *Analysis of Evidence, 2nd Edition*
Ashworth: *Sentencing and Criminal Justice, 6th Edition*
Barton Douglas: *Law and Parenthood*
Baxi, McCrudden & Paliwala: *Law's Ethical, Global and Theoretical Contexts: Essays in Honour of William Twining*
Beecher-Monas: *Evaluating Scientific Evidence: An Interdisciplinary Framework for Intellectual Due Process*
Bell: *French Legal Cultures*

Bercusson: *European Labour Law, 2nd Edition*
Birkinshaw: *European Public Law*
Birkinshaw: *Freedom of Information: The Law, the Practice and the Ideal, 4th Edition*
Blick: *Electrified Democracy: The Internet and the United Kingdom Parliament in History*
Broderick Ferri: *International and European Disability Law and Policy: Text, Cases and Materials*
Brownsword & Goodwin: *Law and the Technologies of the Twenty-First Century: Text and Materials*
Cane & Goudkamp: *Atiyah's Accidents, Compensation and the Law, 9th Edition*
Clarke: *Principles of Property Law*
Clarke Kohler: *Property Law: Commentary and Materials*
Collins: *The Law of Contract, 4th Edition*
Collins, Ewing & McColgan: *Labour Law, 3rd Edition*
Corrias, *Law and Inhumanity: Dehumanization, Silent Claims and Atrocity Crimes*
Cowan: *Housing Law and Policy*
Cranston: *Making Commercial Law Through Practice 1830–1970*
Cranston: *Legal Foundations of the Welfare State*
Darian-Smith: *Laws and Societies in Global Contexts: Contemporary Approaches*
Dauvergne: *Making People Illegal: What Globalisation Means for Immigration and Law*
David: *Kinship, Law and Politics: An Anatomy of Belonging*
Davies: *Perspectives on Labour Law, 2nd Edition*
Dembour: *Who Believes in Human Rights?: Reflections on the European Convention*
de Sousa Santos: *Toward a New Legal Common Sense: Law, Globalization, and Emancipation*
Diduck: *Law's Families*
Douglas-Scott: *Brexit, Union, and Disunion: The Evolution of British Constitutional Unsettlement*
Dowdle: *Transnational Law: A Framework for Analysis*
Dupret: *Positive Law from the Muslim World: Jurisprudence, History, Practices*
Dutta: *A Jurisprudence of Conversations: Law, Life and Feminism in Post-colonial India*
Emon: *Jurisdictional Exceptionalisms: Islamic Law, International Law, and Parental Child Abduction*
Estella: *Legal Foundations of EU Economic Governance*
Fortin: *Children's Rights and the Developing Law, 3rd Edition*
Garnsey: *The Justice of Visual Art: Creative State-Building in Times of Political Transition*
Garton, Probert & Bean: *Moffat's Trusts Law: Text and Materials, 7th Edition*
Ghai & Woodman: *Practising Self-Government: A Comparative Study of Autonomous Regions*
Glover-Thomas: *Reconstructing Mental Health Law and Policy*
Gobert & Punch: *Rethinking Corporate Crime*
Goldman: *Globalisation and the Western Legal Tradition: Recurring Patterns of Law and Authority*
Haack: *Evidence Matters: Science, Proof, and Truth in the Law*
Harlow & Rawlings: *Law and Administration, 4th Edition*
Harris: *An Introduction to Law, 8th Edition*
Harris, Campbell & Halson: *Remedies in Contract and Tort, 2nd Edition*
Harvey: *Seeking Asylum in the UK: Problems and Prospects*

Herring: *Law and the Relational Self*
Hervey & McHale: *European Union Health Law: Themes and Implications*
Hervey & McHale: *Health Law and the European Union*
Holder & Lee: *Environmental Protection, Law and Policy: Text and Materials, 2nd Edition*
Hommes: *The Convention and the Kingdom: How the Netherlands Received the European Convention on Human Rights*
Jackson & Summers: *The Internationalisation of Criminal Evidence: Beyond the Common Law and Civil Law Traditions*
Jeutner: *The Reasonable Person: A Legal Biography*
Kennedy: *Inducing Intimacy: Deception, Consent and the Law*
Kostakopoulou: *The Future Governance of Citizenship*
Kreiczer-Levy: *Destabilized Property: Property Law in the Sharing Economy*
Kubal: *Immigration and Refugee Law in Russia: Socio-Legal Perspectives*
Lewis: *Choice and the Legal Order: Rising Above Politics*
Likosky: *Law, Infrastructure and Human Rights*
Likosky: *Transnational Legal Processes: Globalisation and Power Disparities*
Lixinski: *Legalized Identities: Cultural Heritage Law and the Shaping of Transitional Justice*
Loughnan: *Self, Others and the State: Relations of Criminal Responsibility*
Lunney: *A History of Australian Tort Law 1901–1945: England's Obedient Servant?*
Maughan & Webb: *Lawyering Skills and the Legal Process, 2nd Edition*
McGaughey: *Principles of Enterprise Law*
McGlynn: *Families and the European Union: Law, Politics and Pluralism*
Mertens: *A Philosophical Introduction to Human Rights*
Miller: *An Introduction to German Law and Legal Culture: Text and Materials*
Moffat: *Trusts Law: Text and Materials*
Monti: *EC Competition Law*
Morgan: *Contract Law Minimalism: A Formalist Restatement of Commercial Contract Law*
Morgan & Yeung: *An Introduction to Law and Regulation: Text and Materials*
Nash: *British Islam and English Law: A Classical Pluralist Perspective*
Ng: *Political Censorship in British Hong Kong: Freedom of Expression and the Law (1842–1997)*
Nicola & Davies: *EU Law Stories: Contextual and Critical Histories of European Jurisprudence*
Norrie: *Crime, Reason and History: A Critical Introduction to Criminal Law, 3rd Edition*
Norrie: *Rethinking Criminal Justice: Punishment, Abolition and Moral Psychology*
O'Dair: *Legal Ethics: Text and Materials*
Oliver: *Common Values and the Public–Private Divide*
Oliver & Drewry: *The Law and Parliament*
Palmer & Roberts: *Dispute Processes: ADR and the Primary Forms of Decision-Making, 1st Edition*
Palmer & Roberts: *Dispute Processes: ADR and the Primary Forms of Decision-Making, 3rd Edition*
Picciotto: *International Business Taxation*
Pieraccini: *Regulating the Sea: A Socio-Legal Analysis of English Marine Protected Areas*

Probert: *The Changing Legal Regulation of Cohabitation, 1600–2010: From Fornicators to Family, 1600–2010*
Qiao: *The Authoritarian Commons: Neighborhood Democratization in Urban China*
Radi: *Rules and Practices of International Investment Law and Arbitration*
Reed: *Internet Law: Text and Materials*
Richardson: *Law, Process and Custody*
Roberts & Palmer: *Dispute Processes: ADR and the Primary Forms of Decision-Making, 2nd Edition*
Rowbottom: *Democracy Distorted: Wealth, Influence and Democratic Politics*
Sauter: *Public Services in EU Law*
Scott & Black: *Cranston's Consumers and the Law*
Seneviratne: *Ombudsmen: Public Services and Administrative Justice*
Seppänen: *Ideological Conflict and the Rule of Law in Contemporary China: Useful Paradoxes*
Siems: *Comparative Law, 3rd Edition*
Stapleton: *Product Liability*
Stewart: *Gender, Law and Justice in a Global Market*
Tamanaha: *Law as a Means to an End: Threat to the Rule of Law*
Taylor: *Fortin's Children's Rights and the Developing Law, 4th Edition*
Tuori: *Properties of Law: Modern Law and After*
Turpin & Tomkins: *British Government and the Constitution: Text and Materials, 7th Edition*
Twining: *General Jurisprudence: Understanding Law from a Global Perspective*
Twining: *Globalisation and Legal Theory*
Twining: *Human Rights, Southern Voices: Francis Deng, Abdullahi An-Na'im, Yash Ghai and Upendra Baxi*
Twining: *Jurist in Context: A Memoir*
Twining: *Karl Llewellyn and the Realist Movement, 2nd Edition*
Twining: *Rethinking Evidence: Exploratory Essays, 2nd Edition*
Twining & Miers: *How to Do Things with Rules, 5th Edition*
Varney: *Disability, Human Rights and Contract Law*
Wan: *Film and Constitutional Controversy: Visualizing Hong Kong Identity in the Age of 'One Country, Two Systems'*
Ward: *A Critical Introduction to European Law, 3rd Edition*
Ward: *Law, Text, Terror*
Ward: *Shakespeare and Legal Imagination*
Watt: *The Making Sense of Politics, Media, and Law: Rhetorical Performance as Invention, Creation, Production*
Wells & Quick: *Lacey, Wells and Quick: Reconstructing Criminal Law: Text and Materials, 4th Edition*
Woodhead: *Caring for Cultural Heritage: An Integrated Approach to Legal and Ethical Initiatives in the United Kingdom*
Yeung & Ranchordás: *An Introduction to Law and Regulation: Text and Materials, 2nd edition*
Young: *Turpin and Tomkins' British Government and the Constitution: Text and Materials, 8th Edition*
Zander: *Cases and Materials on the English Legal System, 10th Edition*
Zander: *The Law-Making Process, 6th Edition*

International Journal of Law in Context: A Global Forum for Interdisciplinary Legal Studies

The *International Journal of Law in Context* is the companion journal to the Law in Context book series and provides a forum for interdisciplinary legal studies and offers intellectual space for ground-breaking critical research. It publishes contextual work about law and its relationship with other disciplines including but not limited to science, literature, humanities, philosophy, sociology, psychology, ethics, history and geography. More information about the journal and how to submit an article can be found at http://journals.cambridge.org/ijc

A JURISPRUDENCE OF CONVERSATIONS

Law, Life and Feminism in Post-colonial India

Debolina Dutta

Melbourne Law School

CAMBRIDGE
UNIVERSITY PRESS

CAMBRIDGE
UNIVERSITY PRESS

Shaftesbury Road, Cambridge CB2 8EA, United Kingdom

One Liberty Plaza, 20th Floor, New York, NY 10006, USA

477 Williamstown Road, Port Melbourne, VIC 3207, Australia

314–321, 3rd Floor, Plot 3, Splendor Forum, Jasola District Centre, New Delhi – 110025, India

103 Penang Road, #05–06/07, Visioncrest Commercial, Singapore 238467

Cambridge University Press is part of Cambridge University Press & Assessment, a department of the University of Cambridge.

We share the University's mission to contribute to society through the pursuit of education, learning and research at the highest international levels of excellence.

www.cambridge.org
Information on this title: www.cambridge.org/9781009581561

DOI: 10.1017/9781009581554

When citing this work, please include a reference to the DOI 10.1017/9781009581554

First published 2026
Cover image: Woodcut print by Pratima Dutta

A catalogue record for this publication is available from the British Library

Library of Congress Cataloging-in-Publication Data
Names: Dutta, Debolina, author.
Title: A jurisprudence of conversations : law, life, and feminism in post-colonial India / Debolina Dutta, Melbourne Law School.
Description: Cambridge, United Kingdom ; New York, NY : Cambridge University Press, 2025. | Includes bibliographical references and index.
Identifiers: LCCN 2025024745 (print) | LCCN 2025024746 (ebook) | ISBN 9781009581561 (hardback) | ISBN 9781009581523 (paperback) | ISBN 9781009581554 (epub)
Subjects: LCSH: Feminist jurisprudence–India. | Women–Legal status, laws, etc.–India. | India–Politics and government–History.
Classification: LCC KNS516 .D88 2025 (print) | LCC KNS516 (ebook) | DDC 346.5401/3082–dc23/eng/20250522
LC record available at https://lccn.loc.gov/2025024745
LC ebook record available at https://lccn.loc.gov/2025024746

ISBN 978-1-009-58156-1 Hardback

To Ma and Baba. . .
always and forever. . .

Contents

Illustrations

Acknowledgements

Before I begin to acknowledge my debts to those who inspired and enabled me to think and write this book, I must recollect a conversation where the process of making *this* book truly began.

In 2012, at a sex workers' conference in Kolkata, a conversation that I was facilitating was disrupted. At this conference, I had co-organised a panel with another feminist lawyer. We organised the panel with an awareness that knowledge production was a hierarchical practice in general. In the case of sex workers, in particular, there was a long history of knowledge production through exclusionary practices. Particularly in a specialised field such as law, knowledge was produced by excluding sex workers voices from conversations about their own lives and livelihood despite a robust movement being in existence for more than three decades.[1] Our panel, therefore, was curated in consultation with sex worker groups so that we discussed something that would be relevant to their context; a sex worker was included on the panel as a speaker; a colleague was requested to act as interpreter to enable conversation across the three languages (Hindi, Bangla and English) that were being spoken in the room; even the seating arrangement in the room was altered by moving the panellists' seats down from the podium and placing on the same ground while facing the audience.

[1] A response to this exclusionary practice of knowledge production gave rise to a slogan of the global sex workers' movement, 'nothing about us, without us'. Nadia Van der Linde, 'Nothing About Us, Without Us: Reversing the Power Dynamics of Philanthropy' (*Open Democracy*, 18 March 2014), www.opendemocracy.net/en/transformation/nothing-about-us-without-us-reversing-power-dynamics-of-philanthr. Accessed 24 April 2024.

However, mid-way through the discussions, just before my turn to speak, sex workers took over the conversation. I had to give up my turn to speak and was forced to listen in silence. For my feminist friend and me, social movements have been our training grounds alongside our academic learning. We were allies of the sex workers' movement and were armed with all the political correctness born out of critical legal research. We were highly critical of the exclusionary practices that disadvantaged sex workers. And yet, our inclusionary methods failed to generate a meaningful conversation and were rejected and disrupted.

At the time, I did not know what to make of this experience. But not speaking and having to listen in silence troubled me. I felt as if a relationship that I had carefully built over a long period of time had fractured. Over the years, I have come to see this experience as a metaphor for productive disruption. It was perhaps what Spivak would call an 'affirmative sabotage'. It has set me on a path of rethinking my place in academia and what I do with my knowledge of law and feminism. It has slowly brewed inside to take the form of the ethical dilemma that this book is about. Being an academic and a researcher, I know that *I* ought to speak, I need to find my voice, my place. The question is how to speak, and more importantly, how to listen, to those who are placed differently from me. In short, how to train oneself in the art of ethical conversations across divides. I do not claim to have worked it out, but must acknowledge this event that provided the initial provocation that has taken the shape of this book more than a decade later.

Since its inception, with me this book has been on a considerably long and arduous journey. Its writing happened alongside the ebb and flow of profound joy and grief. The book has lived through the catastrophic COVID pandemic. I have befriended and found the support of a wide network of loving, nurturing people through the process of its birthing. The ideas in the book, its research and writing came to life at my institutional homes across three different continents.

Our daughter Misha's arrival coincided with the completion of the first draft of the book. Its final stages coincided with the loss of my mother, my life force. My mother (Ma), Pratima Dutta, was a rare combination of fragility and fearlessness. She was the fountain of joy and inspiration in my life. And there I was one dark morning in a cold hospital ICU room holding her hands, staring blankly at a beeping machine, seeing the light go out of her eyes and my life. Nothing in my life was meaningful, if it could not be shared with her. But even in death, she held me together and lifted me up through her lust for life that will now be living forever in my memories. Ma's fighting spirit, her aesthetics, her passion towards her work while battling chronic illnesses and her multifaceted creativity provided much inspiration while growing up. Most importantly, her kindness, love, unquestioning belief in me and single-handed dedication towards the fulfilment of my dreams are what have brought me to this day. Although strong-willed, she never took it upon herself to influence my decisions in life, for which I am forever grateful to her. I cannot help but wish that she was less duty-bound to the life of others and had got the chance to live the life she deserved without experiencing such burnout of her health and talents.

Ma's passing left me in a state of such acute shock and sadness that I felt completely empty of life, emotions and words. Some days carried a semblance of normalcy, some days were just unliveable. Having to see my labour of love come to fruition during this time of heartbreak was extremely hard. I thank our little daughter Misha for gently piecing my head and heart together. With her love, laughter, drama, relentless talking and creation of chaos, ironically, she slowly worked her magic to put things back in order. Misha is my precious gift that keeps on giving.

I was always sceptical of my abilities to finish this book. Oishik believed not only could I write this one, but I could also become a space traveller or even Sherlock Holmes, if I so desired. The burden of his unrealistic and unshakeable faith in me sometimes gets difficult to carry. But it does make my life easier for finding a large share of the joys and inspiration necessary for pursuing my dreams right next to me. His gentle presence and unconditional love make life, and the things that I do in pursuit of it, worthwhile. My mother and Oishik shared a friendship and camaraderie that drove them to long-drawn arguments on art, life and politics every night at the dining table. Their joie de vivre and passion for debate and disagreements fuelled and flexed my intellectual muscles. Oishik read and reread drafts of the chapters when I couldn't bear to look at them myself. Ma made delicious food to provide comfort and motivation as I juggled the birthing of this book with full-time motherhood and teaching. It is her artwork – representing the scales of justice – that adorns the cover of this book. Make whatever sense of it you will. For me, it is a way of imprinting my labour of love with her touch, in her physical absence. I thank Hamsini Marada for taking a photograph of the artwork which appears on the cover.

Since the time I was little, every year on his birthday, my father, Ajit Dutta (Baba) gifted me a book. These books were on an unusual and eclectic mix of subjects, hardly considered appropriate for a child, such as magic, witchcraft, reincarnation, philosophy, UFOs, photography, religion and mystery. Eight months before he passed, Baba told me that it was time for him to leave, and as it turned out, he was right. I lost Baba much before I had anything to do with this book. We seldom agreed on anything, but he instilled in me my intellectual curiosity and the original inspiration to pursue a life of the mind. Baba's ability to find morbid things funny or the image of him sitting in front of a chessboard contemplating a move or working his magic with his Nikon camera trying to preserve life in black and white, provided sustenance whenever I struggled with ideation and writing. Ma and Baba were two very different people, albeit united in their unconventional ways of looking at the world and their love for conversations with an openness and hospitality towards anyone and everyone. Owing to their natures, passions and professions, our house was the haunt for regular adda by a motley group of people with varied interests and vocation. Many of my parents' friends and acquaintances were talented artists, musicians, writers and other professionals; some of them were social misfits; almost all of them were individuals with quirks and queer habits; and none of them was alike. Growing up amidst these endless conversations facilitated by my parents has been a rare privilege that has shaped me and my world. I feel sad to think that Ma and Baba are not there to see their daughter become the author of a book that, among other things, is about conversations. But drawing on Baba's faith in magic and the otherworldly, I see the signs that they are around somewhere celebrating and cheering me on, as always. I dedicate this book to them, my loving Ma and Baba, two incredibly different and interesting people. I also dedicate it to the undying human spirit that searches and researches to find the light through loss, fractures, failures, genocide, war, displacement, injustice, catastrophes and the everyday rigmarole of life.

—

This project came full circle at the Melbourne Law School (MLS). I began researching for this book here as a doctoral student, went away in between to do full-time teaching, and then came back as a Research Fellow to finish the book at MLS, which is located on the lands of the Wurundjeri People of the Kulin Nation to which their sovereignty has not been ceded. I pay my respects to their elders – past, present and future.

I always feel a little overwhelmed speaking about Ann Genovese and Shaun McVeigh, my mentors at MLS. It is with Shaun and Ann that I have discovered my love for research and the aesthetics of serious academic scholarship. They made me believe in the worth of my own project and patiently guided me through all stages of this book, both intellectually and emotionally. I could not have found more generous and humorous role models. Ann's vibrant energy, intellectual discipline, the kindness with which she encouraged me at every step to speak my mind and hold my ground, and her endless wisdom about life and relationships, kept me going through some very tough times. Shaun's intellectual brevity, precision and the calm with which he understood what I wanted to communicate even before I could put it in words for him was inspiring. His generosity with time and practical sensibility, and careful attempts to help build my self-confidence have deeply influenced me.

Dianne Otto has been a source of inspiration through her scholarship and activism. Long before I went to Melbourne, I knew about Di's work through my sexual rights activist community in India. I may not have ended up at MLS if it wasn't for her encouragement, help and guidance. Sundhya Pahuja's ever-smiling sunny presence and her professional and personal guidance have sustained me at every step throughout my stay in Melbourne. I thank her for her brilliant sense of humour, support and generosity.

Jenny Morgan, Tim Lindsey, Peter Rush and Farrah Ahmed have also always been very welcoming with their support and advice. The administrative staff at the Institute for International Law and the Humanities are a very special group of people who run the show from their place in the backstage. I am grateful to Domingo Cordoba, Vesna Stefanovski,

Rebecca Croser, Mas Generis, Andrew Dalziel and Ade Suharto for their support.

—

I am immensely thankful to the Institute of Global Law and Policy (IGLP) at the Harvard Law School that gave me a residential fellowship to help transition this project from a doctoral thesis to a book. I would like to especially thank David Kennedy at IGLP for providing me with the time, resources and research support to carry out the bulk of the writing. David was also very generous with his time to offer feedback on my research.

My time as a faculty at the Jindal Global Law School (JGLS) enriched the book. The 'Jurisprudence' and 'Feminist Legal Research Methods' courses that I taught, the engagement of my students in class, and the insights from my teaching and research assistants, kept alive a connection with the book even when I wasn't writing. I especially thank C. Rajkumar, the Vice Chancellor, S. G. Sreejith, the Vice Dean and all my colleagues at JGLS for fostering a truly generative and interdisciplinary space for critical legal research in India.

I thank Heather Douglas and and all my colleagues at the ARC (Australian Research Council) Centre of Excellence for the Elimination of Violence Against Women (CEVAW) for making available the support and resources that were necessary for bringing this project to its closure at MLS, the very place where it started.

Doing the research for this book has been made possible due to the intellectual and financial support extended to me by various institutions. The generous scholarships, fieldwork grants and travel funds from the University of Melbourne helped me live in Melbourne and travel for my research. I received the Emerging Scholars International Research Fellowship from the International Association for the Study of Sexuality, Culture and Society (IASSCS), which covered the expenses for my fieldwork in India. I am also thankful to the School of Law, University of Texas at Austin, for giving me the Audrey Rapoport Prize for Scholarship on Gender and Human Rights 2017. The prize, for a version of a chapter in the book, came at an especially low phase and provided me the encouragement to spring back to writing soon after getting out of hospital from a major surgery and amidst the onslaught of mind-numbing medications.

Aruna Ramachandran, with her eye for detail, read and helped me finalise the initial stages of this book for which I am thankful to her.

Someone who I do not know in person, but whose work I have read and reread, whose work is unrelated to mine but has greatly inspired me to write this book is Siddhartha Mukherjee, an oncologist-physician and academic. His style of storytelling, merging cutting edge-scientific research, personal history and thousands of years of the history of human health and medicine, is truly magical. I envy his ability to mix in-depth research with the vastness of a field and then present it with the lightness of a master storyteller. Three other people to whom I am similarly indebted are Satyajit Ray, Alfred Hitchcock and Toni Morrison. Thank you for your gifts of imagination, craft and daring.

—

It would not have been possible to write this book if the people at DMSC and VAMP and Upendra Baxi and Ratna Kapur had not agreed to share their time and knowledge with me. I am very thankful to them for making the experiences of their lives known to me. I especially thank Meena Seshu, Pintu Maity, Bharati Dey, Shantilal Kale and Kiran Deshmukh for facilitating my meetings with the members of DMSC and VAMP. Long before this book, DMSC and VAMP had been instrumental in shaping my activist sensibilities and the practical understanding of law, for which I am immensely grateful to each one of its members.

I am thankful to have had the opportunity of interacting closely with Raju Naik and Kamlabai Pani at VAMP and Dr Smarajit Jana and Mrinal Kanti Datta at DMSC during my fieldwork. They passed on soon after I completed my research.

—

The intellectual acumen and camaraderie of an amazing group of co-travellers kept my spirits high through some of the most gruelling phases of my research. All members of the Feminist Reading Group and the Jurisprudence Reading Group at MLS provided the intellectual nourishment that was necessary, apart from thinking about cake and beer at Last Jar, to keep my focus on my research. For this, I am thankful to Claire Opperman, Julia Dehm, Sara Dehm, Samia Khatun, Tayechelem Moges, Cait Storr, Corrine Tan, Maria Elander, Robyn Honey, Tsegaye Regassa Ararssa, Rose Parfitt, Sophie Rigney, James Parker, Tom Andrews, Ben Silverstein, Jordy Silverstein, Madeline Chiam, Monique Cormier, Laura Petersen, Luis Eslava, Jake Goldfien, Marie Aronsson, Adrian Storrier, Joseph Kikonyogo, Sadaf Aziz, Florence Adora, Dudi Rulliadi, Gashahun L. Fura, Robi Rado, Dolly Kikon, Josh Paine, Sandeep Kirpalani, Bina Fernandez, Maddy Clarke, Rajdeep Roy, Shakira Hussein, Shantanu Mehra and Rajgopal Saikumar.

Joan Nestle, Claire Opperman, Ananya Baskin and Adil Hasan Khan are the special people in Melbourne from whose company I derived great joy. Joan, my 'little sister', born only forty years before me, is an epitome of love and wisdom with whom I share a connection from another life. Claire is the person with whom I have spent some of the most comforting times. Her support and care towards my emotional sustenance has been incredible. Ananya, my tiny friend, was four when I first met her. I enjoyed my time with her so much that it sometimes made me wonder if my mind had achieved its age-appropriate growth. Adil is a never-ending source of silly humour. I often don't get his jokes, but they do make me laugh nonetheless.

—

At Melbourne, Boston, Oldenburg and Hamburg, which I visited while researching and writing this book, many people invited me into their families, offered their homes for me to stay in, and charmed me with their culinary wizardry. This made it possible for me to happily settle into new places away from familiar faces and my loved ones in India. For sharing such warmth and hospitality, I am very thankful to Dianne Otto, Sundhya Pahuja, Joan Nestle, Claire Opperman, Sylvia Pritsch, Jeremy Baskin, Paul Ronfeldt, Samantha Ronfeldt, Joseph Ronfeldt, Mangesh Padmawar, Priti Tagalpallevar, Om Pahuja, Asha Pahuja, Monika Pahuja,

Amitabh Mattoo, Brian Gangemi, Aditi Chakrabarty, Divyam Shroff, Faizan Jawed Siddiqi and Bedatri D. Choudhury.

—

A wonderful group of friends, former colleagues and mentors helped me find my way into researching the combined pleasures and struggles of activism and scholarship, which forms the foundation of this book. This list is indeed endless, but I need to mention Janaki Nair, Anchita Ghatak Gitanjali Misra, Bishakha Datta, Shohini Ghosh, Vinita Sahasranaman, Pramada Menon, Meenu Pandey, Sanjana Gaind, Sunita Kujur, Chaitali Bhatia, Meena Seshu, Smarajit Jana, Flavia Agnes, Elsa Oliviera, Laura Murray, Sonia Correa, Wendy Harcourt, Dawn Cavanagh, Cynthia Rothschild, Rosalind Petchesky, Jaime Todd Gher and Sarah Hawkes. They provided inspiration, guidance and made available the opportunities that were necessary to get to this book.

—

I am lucky to have a group of friends from my childhood and beyond whose existence and wisdom give me the resources to move through life. They provide the inspiration and joy for doing whatever it is that I do. This is a lot that I know will show up, no matter what: Shayanti Sinha, Priyanka Ganguly, Srabani Paul, Suparna Banerjee, Sakyadeb Choudhury, Sarmistha Mazumdar and Deepti Mohan.

—

A significant portion of the writing of this book happened under difficult circumstances. This was a period of serious illness, a surgery and emotional upheavals that would have made things very tough, if it were not for the warmth and friendships of a new group of people I met in Sonipat while working at JGLS. Innumerable evenings were spent laughing, chatting, grumbling, complaining, eating, drinking and playing Jenga with Rohini Sen and Saptarshi Mandal. Their friendship is very special to me. At other times, there were Mimi Roy, Shubhasree Bhattacharya, Shilpi Bhattacharya and Arpita Saptarshi Mandal Gupta whose camaraderie sustained me through the harsh Sonipat times. Rajshree Chandra,

Dipika Jain, Deblina Dey and Sannoy Das welcomed me into their homes and fed me delicious food. Tapati Chouwdhury and Toya were no less than emotional anchors. Their care and hospitality are irreplaceable.

I thank Dipali Das, Mamta Rani, Kabita, Asha and Jhuma Khatun for helping me manage my household and sharing my care work, which allowed me to continue my intellectual pursuits.

Along with thousands of others living in the Indian sub-continent, my family hails from a generation of displaced people whose existence was reduced to nothing overnight due to the partition of India-Pakistan in 1947. As refugees, their gift to the world have been the knowledge of resilience and an ability to find friendship in unlikely places for the co-creation of life from ashes. There are some people in my family who passed on these lessons of sustenance and survival into their future generations, making me a beneficiary of their wisdom. Notable among them is my maternal grandmother, Suruchi Chakraborty, my Didima. She was an exceptional woman and I reap the benefits of the strength she built in her daughter. She sent her daughter, my mother, away from home in Assam to Santiniketan at the age of sixteen to pursue an education and career in the fine arts. This was at a time and age when most of her contemporaries only invested in planning for their daughters' marriages. Unlike many women in her generation, Didima, despite her own lack of higher education, was extremely forward thinking, and it is on her shoulders that I stand today. Purnima Bhattacharya was a bookworm and a living encyclopaedia who instilled in me an admiration for women who wanted to know and read. While growing up, Sudhish Senapati, barrister, judge and lawyer extraordinaire, turned his courtroom experiences into fairy tales for me. It is due to him that I cherished a dream of becoming a lawyer from the time I was ten!

Over the years, Ranjit Chakrabarty, Tapan Dutta Purkayastha, Prithvish Nag, Arun Bhattacharya, Ashima Choudhury, Sucharoo Nag, Sutapa Nag and Rajshekhar Deb have provided much support and encouragement that was necessary for me to have come this far. I am also extremely thankful to Suneeta Dutta and Siddhartha Dutta for their support and guidance at an especially stressful phase during my mother's illness.

To Nayantara Nag, Vaibhav Kothari and little Viraj Nag Kothari, I owe a special thank you. Along with Oishik and me, they welcomed Misha into the warmth of their home with open arms. Although younger than me, like a seasoned elder, Nayantara provided the much-needed support, care and wisdom that was necessary when we knew nothing about how to sustain a tiny life. She provided the confidence to bring an infant into our lives on a day's notice.

—

Through Oishik, I have found a set of loving relations in-law who have acted as my cheer leaders and support group at various stages of my life and this book: Roma Sarkar (Thia), Ishika Sircar (Raka), Sayak Datta, Veer Datta, Kanishka Basu, Ratna Gangopadhyay, Amal Sinha, Manjula Chatterjee and Ashima Saxena.

Swapna Sinha's keen emotional intelligence and selflessness has made her the go-to person in times of major distress. During my mother's illness and after her passing, the period through which I completed writing this book, she provided a kind of support, love and care that I have no words to describe. Anjana Sircar and Anjan Sircar are always a friendly source of love and support. In them, I am truly lucky to have found a second set of loving, nurturing parents. Shayak Sircar, by hatching an ingenuous plan, goaded and encouraged me to go back to Harvard for the second time during the peak of the COVID pandemic, which is when I wrote the long-delayed introduction of this book. Who else could have helped me facilitate a productive alliance between the deadly COVID virus and this project!

—

A bunch of people from Misha's world, real and imaginary, became my interlocutors on most days during our bedtime storytelling sessions at night: Ayansh dada, Ishaan, Toya didi, Nannan Star, Tisha baby, Dhwani baby, Sunayana Ma'am, Gola dada, Gungun didi, Viraj dada, Goldilocks, Max, Liddy, Sophie, Gini didi, Anvi didi, Ricco dada and Mapi. In one of the stories, I told her, there was a character who struggled to finish writing a book because she was distracted by demons and monsters. For every hurdle that the writer encountered, Misha offered help along with the assistance and support of her people who possessed various powers of rescue, including the ability to combat with rotten candies. I thank Misha's people for keeping the humour and imagination alive during a very hard time.

—

I can never truly account for the debts that I have incurred through the book. Lately, I was beginning to think that this project will never get to see the light of day. But look how far I have come. As I write these acknowledgements, I feel overwhelmed with an immense sense of gratitude towards life itself and all of you who have accompanied me on this journey of seeing my book through to its end. You have provided me with intellectual, emotional and the spiritual sustenance necessary to get to this point. You have also made me aware of the finitude of life, knowledge and all things good and bad. To all of you, once again, thank you for humouring me!

I am grateful to the three anonymous reviewers whose generous and insightful suggestions helped me revise and complete the book for publication. A big thank you to the editorial team at Cambridge University Press for all their help through every step of the publication process.

Abbreviations

AIIHPH	All India Institute of Hygiene and Public Health
BPTA	Bombay Public Trust Act, 1950
CFLR	Centre for Feminist Legal Research
DMSC	Durbar Mahila Samanwaya Committee
IAWS	Indian Association for Women's Studies
ITPA	Immoral Traffic (Prevention) Act, 1956
NCW	National Commission for Women
NGO	non-governmental organisation
SRA	Societies Registration Act, 1860
SRB	Self-Regulatory Board
VAMP	Veshya Anyay Mukti Parishad
WBCSA	West Bengal Co-operative Societies Act, 1983
WBSRA	West Bengal Societies Registration Act, 1961

PART I

SETTING THE STAGE

CHAPTER 1

Law and Its Relations

Ethics are not a problem of knowledge but a call of relationship.[1]

How do feminists, as lawyers and activists, think about and do law in a way that it makes life more meaningful and just, in a specific context? How are law and feminism called into relation, given meaning, engaged with, used, refused, adapted, and brought to life through collaborative action? How is feminist jurisprudential knowledge collectively lived with at a place and time? *A Jurisprudence of Conversations* shows how life, law and feminism are lived in and through conversations. In this book, conversations, performed by a diverse set of interlocutors, become a site, and a means, for calling law and feminism into mutual relations with life. As an interlocutor myself, I work to weave a historicised account of such conversations, joining a multitude of interlocutors, locations and temporality, to demonstrate how these, in turn, generate a field of feminist jurisprudence in post-colonial India.

Predominantly, accounts of law as a site of power, how it causes or magnifies social marginalisation, and how it may be resisted and reformed, abound in feminist jurisprudential scholarship in the common law world.[2] This book is not invested in developing a similar

[1] Gayatri Chakravorty Spivak, 'Echo', in Gayatri Chakravorty Spivak, *The Spivak Reader*, ed. Donna Landry and Gerald MacLean (Routledge, 1996), 175–202, 190.

[2] See generally Katharine Barlett (ed.), *Feminist Legal Theory: Readings in Law and Gender* (Avalon Publishing, 1991); Patricia Smith (ed.), *Feminist Jurisprudence* (Oxford University Press, 1993); Ratna Kapur (ed.), *Feminist Terrains in Legal Domains: Interdisciplinary Essays on Women and Law in India* (Kali for Women, 1996).

critique of law and jurisprudence from a feminist perspective.[3] From underneath the shadows of major feminist jurisprudential thought that reveals how law wields power over post-colonial lives, this book is interested in drawing out the traditions of mutuality and reciprocity of law–life relations. It foregrounds how we wield agency to work with law, befriend it and do things with it to organise our life and relationships with others.

The aim of this book is not to reveal how we can transcend social hierarchies through conversations. In and of themselves, conversations are not a solution to the existence of inequalities and that is not the claim I am making. Conversations are a form of art that requires practise. As much as they enable alliances, conversations are often a site of contestations, disagreements and failures that tell us where a dissociation may be necessary. This book invigorates conversation as a method to accentuate the work that feminists do, as scholars and activists, to bring law into a relationship of mutuality with life, given our differences, inequalities and deep fissures, through co-creation. I activate a less acknowledged feminist tradition in law that works to reimagine a lived and relational form of jurisprudential knowledge based on an interdependence between life, law and feminism.

The feminist thrust of this book lies in taking up the question of method as central to its jurisprudence. A bulk of feminist scholarship in law and other disciplines, and in many different times and places, is animated by conversations on the question of method. Such as what suffices as feminist method, or how method and the content of knowledge are related and jointly qualify to be termed 'feminist', or how it is method that makes a particular form of knowledge feminist or not.[4]

[3] Scholars, across disciplines, have envisaged the relationship between critique and knowledge. As a mode of engagement with knowledge, critique has been largely conceived as involving repair or exposing error or having a better understanding or a fixing and improving, of knowledge. See Wendy Brown, 'Introduction', in Talal Asad, Wendy Brown, Judith Butler and Saba Mahmood, *Is Critique Secular? Blasphemy, Injury, and Free Speech* (University of California Press, 2009), 9; Michel Foucault, 'Practicing Criticism', in *Politics, Philosophy, Culture: Interviews and Other Writings, 1977–1984*, trans. A. Sheridan et al., ed. L. D. Kritzman (Routledge, 1988), 152–58; Davies, *Asking the Law Question*, 199.

[4] See generally Sandra Harding (ed.), *Feminism and Methodology* (Indiana University Press, 1988); Andrea Doucet and Natasha S. Mauthner, 'Feminist Methodologies and

In alignment with such traditions of enquiry, but explored more imaginatively, method is understood to mean not just the tools of interpretation and analysis but also a practical way of shaping law's mutual relations with people and place.

This book comprises a series of interrelated and situated conversations amongst a wide array of people, lawyers and non-lawyers, that take place in varied contexts in post-colonial India. Through this I argue that knowledge production about law in India is not solely the domain of legal academics but has been developed in relationship with non-lawyer activists. I illustrate how crafting a mutual relationship with law, and not just being in opposition to it, has been crucial to the formations of activist and scholarly lives in contemporary post-colonial India. Rather than writing a criticism of law, the book thus illuminates the coming into of law's mutuality with post-colonial life.

My argument is grounded in fieldwork with the help of which I draw into conversation two very diverse sets of interlocutors. These are legal academics Upendra Baxi and Ratna Kapur; and sex worker activist groups Durbar Mahila Samanwaya Committee (DMSC) and Veshya Anyay Mukti Parishad (VAMP). I read a select set of materials authored by the sex workers' collectives and the legal academics, two groups that are engaged in varied life activities that are, however, concerned with law.

The nature and form of the materials are as diverse as their authors. These include activist documents such as a manifesto, a statement, a legal petition, posters, pamphlets, organisational brochures, announcements, annual reports and newsletters, all of which have been collectively authored by sex worker groups from 1995 to 2016. There is 'An Open

Epistemology', in C. D. Bryant and D. L. Peck (eds), *Handbook of 21st Century Sociology* (Sage, 2006), 26–32; Martin Hammersley, 'On Feminist Methodology' (1992) 26(2), *Sociology*, 187; Bartlett, 'Feminist Legal Methods'; Catharine A. MacKinnon, 'Feminism, Marxism, Method, and the State: An Agenda for Theory' (1982) 7(3), *Signs*, 515; Kathryn Abrams, 'Feminist Lawyering and Legal Method' (1991) 16, *Law and Social Inquiry*, 373; Maithree Wickramasinghe, *Feminist Research Methodology* (Zubaan, 2015); Gayatri Spivak, 'Feminism and Critical Theory' (1978) 1(3), *Women's Studies International Quarterly*, 241; Carol Smart, 'Shifting Horizons: Reflections on Qualitative Methods' (2009) 10(3), *Feminist Theory*, 295; C. Smart, J. Hockey and A. James (eds), *The Craft of Knowledge: Experiences of Living with Data* (Palgrave Macmillan, 2014).

Letter to the Chief Justice of India', co-authored by Upendra Baxi and three other law professors, Vasudha Dhagamwar, Raghunath Kelkar and Lotika Sarkar, in 1979. There is also a book published in 1996 called *Subversive Sites: Feminist Engagements with Law in India*, which is co-authored by feminist legal scholars Ratna Kapur and Brenda Cossman.

I draw on a localised practice of *adda* – which means a meeting place and is also a Bengali quotidian activity of mutual conversation and sociality – to rejuvenate and adapt such art of discourse into a scholarly method. I shape and perform adda as a shared activity to interpret the meanings of these literatures in conversation with the authors. As method, adda is both an oral and a textual practice. It is a way of conceiving and engaging in the discursive field of feminist jurisprudence as a relational practice of legal knowledge production. It is also a means of conducting empirical research for reading and interpreting the texts that shape its body of scholarship, in conversation with those who have produced them. Post-colonial thinkers in the humanities have previously used adda as a method for historicising and representing critical thought and texts. The book joins in that tradition to shape it as a method for representing a critical feminist jurisprudence that is emplaced in lived traditions and texts, produced in the historical context in post-colonial India.

I call into relation literatures of diverse genres, authored by people who are disparately located, both socially and in terms of the field of legal knowledge production per se. For instance, the book juxtaposes a reading of activist pamphlets, petitions, by-laws and other organisational documents of the sex workers' collectives alongside the readings of scholarly books, letters and journal articles by well-known legal academics. The reading and interpretation of these texts is performed in conversation with the authors as a shared activity by means of which its meanings are grounded in lived experience. This makes visible how legal wisdom and meaning-making are tied to everyday speech, proximate forms of cohabitation and relational forms of living, of which the texts are a part.

I read the texts in dialogue with their authors. I simultaneously locate my reading at the specific places from where the texts emerged, namely the university and the collectives. I conduct oral conversations with authors about the experiences that informed the writing of these texts, the ideas presented in the texts and the place and time at which the texts were written. I draw out the conversations that the authors were engaged in, and those that informed the practices of collectivisation and scholarly writing in their different contexts at the time. This is how, as you will see, I work to weave a narrative by relating the sex workers' practices of collectivisation and the academics' practices of scholarly writing, as well as the locations where these practices took place.

WHY ADDA?

Adda is an everyday term and lived practice in India. It is tethered to a place and people. In Hindi, which is spoken in parts of north India, adda is a *noun* and denotes a place of gathering. In Bangla, adda is a *verb* and denotes a particular kind of action or an activity of reciprocal conversations amongst people.[5] Adda is thus understood to mean both a form of conversations and a meeting place. Indian post-colonial scholars located in the disciplines of history and literature have already brought adda into academic discourse.[6] Their understanding of the practice is not identical, but they have used it as a mode of knowing and analysing the discursive productions of critical thought as post-colonial thinkers.

My use of adda in this book is ontological. Broadly speaking, ontology is the branch of philosophy that is concerned with questions of our being and experience in the world in relation to knowledge.[7] This makes the question of how we engage in knowledge production, and by undertaking what particular role and responsibilities, an ontological exercise. Australian feminist legal scholar Margaret Davies argues that theoretical

[5] Dipesh Chakrabarty, *Provincializing Europe: Postcolonial Thought and Historical Difference* (Princeton University Press, 2008), 187.

[6] Chakrabarty, *Provincializing Europe*; Gayatri Chakravorty Spivak, 'Can the Subaltern Speak?', in Cary Nelson and Lawrence Grossberg (eds), *Marxism and the Interpretation of Culture* (University of Illinois Press, 1988), 271–313. I undertake a detailed discussion of these specific works in Chapter 2 of this book and outline how my use of adda is both similar and distinct from them.

[7] Peter van Inwagen and Meghan Sullivan, 'Metaphysics', in Edward N. Zalta (ed.), *Stanford Encyclopedia of Philosophy* (Spring 2018), https://plato.stanford.edu/entries/metaphysics.

knowledge production about law or the theories of law, which is what jurisprudence is generally understood to mean, is a contextual and embodied activity that is not external to ourselves and/or our being.[8] For Davies, 'law and knowledge exist only in everyday reality, and are a product of life and culture'.[9] Contrary to a more conventional understanding of jurisprudence, even in analytical terms law cannot be thought to be 'conceptually separate from the human lives who have created it, who apply it, who criticise it, and who relate to it'.[10]

I engage in adda in order to actively experience feminist jurisprudential knowledge production, which is related to my being and mode of doing this research.[11] Through my method, I materialise my role and its incumbent responsibilities as a feminist researcher of law from India, in relation to jurisprudence and the people whose wisdom I draw from and build on.[12] The practice of adda, for me, is an act and activity of reciprocal conversations for conducting lawful relations and grounding these at a place and time.[13] I see 'lawful' neither as an antonym of 'lawless', nor as

[8] Margaret Davies, *Asking the Law Question*, 3rd ed. (Thomson Lawbook Co., 2008), 3–4. The first edition of this book was published in 1994.

[9] Ibid., 5.

[10] Ibid., 4. Raymond Wacks provides a general definition of jurisprudence: '"jurisprudence" concerns the theoretical analysis of law at the highest level of abstraction'. See Raymond Wacks, *Philosophy of Law: A Very Short Introduction* (Oxford University Press, 2014), xiii.

[11] In another article, Margaret Davies argues that the mark of a critical researcher is the lack of the belief that research is an objective and detached activity in which the researcher engages merely as an 'observer or discoverer of knowledge' from a distance. For a critical researcher, method is a path that s/he consciously chooses and charts in response to her specific subjectivity. Margaret Davies, 'Ethics and Methodology in Legal Theory: A (Personal) Research Anti-Manifesto' (2002) 6, *Law Text Culture*, 23.

[12] There is an existing feminist critique of how ontological enquiries have worked to essentialise the experiences of womanhood and have negatively impacted the feminist project. My performance of adda works to guard against any kind of essentialism precisely because it is time and place specific and is *not* generalisable or universally applicable. As I will show, my performance of adda is shape shifting and attains different forms in Chapters 3–5. See, generally, Maria Drakopoulou, 'Revisiting Feminist Jurisprudence: A Rehabilitation' (2013) 3(2), *Feminists@Law*.

[13] I draw my understanding of the conduct of lawful relations from the works of Australian jurisprudents Shaun McVeigh and Ann Genovese. McVeigh and Genovese understand lawful relations as a tradition and conduct of life for practising a belonging and a mutuality with law respectively. McVeigh and Genovese were my doctoral supervisors,

a synonym of 'legal'. The conduct of lawful relations is a situated ethical practice of reciprocity with my interlocutors as I take up the responsibility of relating their lives and law, through a reading and interpretation of texts authored by them. Thus, I work to bring adda into my disciplinary location of law as a practical method for *doing* feminist jurisprudence relationally with my interlocutors.

The work of Canadian feminist legal scholar Jennifer Nedelsky particularly talks about the importance and significance of adopting a relational approach to law and jurisprudence. Nedelsky looks at how law structures and constitutes our relations in life, and argues that such relational experiences amongst people are crucial for our understandings of law and jurisprudence.[14] She demonstrates how, to give an example from the book, the relationship between children and their parents and how they experience and understand autonomy while growing up cannot be divorced from the knowledge of autonomy as a legal concept.[15]

The relational approach to law that I practise through adda is distinct from Nedelsky's argument in her book. The focus of my method is on developing a practical mode of establishing a relationship *with* law, and not illuminating that/how it has *already* structured our relations in the world. While I agree that, as Nedelsky shows us, law has a pre-existing

and my thesis took shape through my experiences of actual conversations with them. I provide a detailed discussion of how I draw from the works of both scholars in Chapter 2. There are resonances in the way Davies, McVeigh and Genovese understand jurisprudence, which is as an experiential body of knowledge. However, their approaches to jurisprudence are also distinct. In my view, McVeigh and Genovese understand jurisprudence itself to be an embodied scholarly activity and a living means for thinking about and conducting the relations between life and law. See Shaun McVeigh, 'Afterword: Office and the Conduct of the Minor Jurisprudent (2015) 5, *University of California Irvine Law Review*, 499, 501; Ann Genovese, 'On Australian Feminist Tradition: Three Notes on Conduct, Inheritance, and the Relations of Historiography and Jurisprudence' (2014) 38(4), *Journal of Australian Studies*, 430, 431; Ann Genovese and Shaun McVeigh, 'Nineteen Eighty-Three: A Jurisographic Report on *Commonwealth v Tasmania*' (2015) 24(1), *Griffith Law Review*, 68; Shaunnagh Dorsett and Shaun McVeigh, *Jurisdiction* (Routledge-Cavendish, 2012).

[14] Jennifer Nedelsky, *Law's Relations: A Relational Theory of Self, Autonomy, and Law* (Oxford University Press, 2013).

[15] Ibid., 4.

role in organising our collective lives, I show how relationships are formed amongst people and between their lives and law, through conversations about law.

From a performative aspect, the joining of a multitude of voices, enabled in adda, bears the potential to show how a diverse cohort of actors – with and without formal academic training in law – co-create a chorus of collective wisdom about law and how it is lived and known. In this way, the dividing lines between the bearers and recipients of legal wisdom may get shifted. Not just amongst the people engaged in adda, but also between their lives and law. Although the class, caste, gender, educational or other social hierarchies remain, the thoughts and ideas of each person that contributes to the discourse may be brought to rest on a common ground. The social and educational differences may be made to lose intensity as determinants of the status and value of our legal wisdom. Adda can become a common ground for calling into relation the legal wisdom of the 'learned' and the so-called uneducated. In terms of a jurisprudence, conceptualised and performed in this way, adda enables a play with the academic norms around who can speak about law with authority or whose account of law can be deemed as a source of legal knowledge.

Method is a path and a conduit of knowledge production.[16] My practice of adda is both an *act* and a form of *activity* by which I stage and experience the shaping of the feminist jurisprudential knowledge in this book.[17] The performances of adda take place in two ways.

[16] Davies, 'Ethics and Methodology in Legal Theory', 23.

[17] My understanding and performance of adda is akin to a Marxist notion of praxis. In 'Theses on Feuerbach' (1845), a collection of eleven short philosophical notes, Karl Marx articulates a theory–practice relationship in which the two exist in a form that is mutually enhancing. Theory, for Marx, is a set of ideas about the world that are connected to questions of justice through the transformation of social relations. But for him, such ideas can only change the world when they are translated into material practices; and the worth of such ideas can also only be evidenced through the material practices that reflect such thinking. Practice, in his understanding, is not any random activity, but rather a form of consciously intended actions that are undertaken, or not, for changing social relations. Therefore, for Marx, praxis encapsulates a theory–practice relationship where each is the source of the other and in unison they work to change social relations. Karl Marx, 'Theses on Feuerbach', in Robert C. Tucker (ed.), *The Marx-Engels Reader*, 2nd ed. (W.W. Norton and Co., 1978), 143–45.

They are both oral and through texts. I draw published texts into conversation, thereby drawing different authors and their ideas posited in scholarship, into dialogue with each other. Then, by performing adda quite literally as a conversation with sex workers and legal academics, I do the research and fieldwork for this book.

That is how I use adda for calling into relation the sex workers' practices of collectivisation and the legal academics' practices of scholarly writing with the field of Indian feminist jurisprudence. In this way I show that adda works as a method for recognising the diverse experiences, and locations, of mutual law–life relations that produce a field of Indian feminist jurisprudence. Thus, the method and argument of this book share a relationship of interdependence.[18]

The interdependent method and argument are especially pertinent in relation to knowledge production in the Indian context, which has historically been a fraught terrain. In India, the academic pursuit of intellectual labour per se, and the question of who has a right to engage in it, is historically embedded in the caste system.[19] People's relationship with intellectual labour is determined and mediated by their standing in the graded social hierarchy of caste.[20] The caste system also has implications for why the practices of certain people would count as knowledge, while those of certain others would not.

[18] The questions of method and substance in feminist jurisprudence are held inseparable by scholars who have worked in the field in non-Indian contexts. The knowledge that a feminist jurisprudence seeks to produce, and how it produces it, are considered so mutually interdependent that the field itself is often understood as a method of legal knowledge production. See generally Katharine T. Bartlett, 'Feminist Legal Methods' (1990) 103(4), *Harvard Law Review*, 829.

[19] B. R. Ambedkar, 'Castes in India', in Valerian Rodrigues (ed.), *The Essential Writings of B. R. Ambedkar* (Oxford University Press, 2010), 241; Surinder S. Jodhka, *Caste in Contemporary India* (Routledge, 2014).

[20] In India, surnames are an easy determinant of a person's caste status. It can be asserted from the surnames of academics in India, especially those who are internationally renowned for their scholarly works, that a large majority of them belong to upper castes. With regard to this, names of popular scholars who form part of the Subaltern Studies group are some notable examples: Partha Chatterjee, Ranajit Guha, Dipesh Chakrabarty, Gayatri Chakravorty Spivak. See Raja Jayaraman, 'Personal Identity in a Globalized World: Cultural Roots of Hindu Personal Names and Surnames' (2005) 38 (3), *Journal of Popular Culture*, 476.

A number of Dalit-Bahujan[21] and feminist scholars/activists have argued that the organising logic of caste is written into the systems of academic education and expertise-driven practices of knowledge production in India.[22] The field of intellectual labour and academic practices is a hierarchical experience for people who have no formal education, or those who speak and write in the vernacular, or those who do not engage in a certain kind of theoretical work. Consequently, the academic field of law and jurisprudential knowledge production, and my own practices of it, are not immune to such hierarchies by virtue of being located within the larger context of intellectual labour in India.[23]

The objective of my method and argument is to speak to the location of Indian feminist jurisprudence within a caste-based hierarchical field of intellectual labour. I take responsibility for working out my method and argument in a manner that speaks meaningfully to the existence of the logic of a caste-based hierarchy in Indian academic practices.[24] I do not address the question of hierarchy through a socio-legal enquiry into the caste composition of the two groups of interlocutors. I also do not engage with the human rights discourse on the caste-based social

[21] 'Dalit' means oppressed or broken. It is a term used to refer to people belonging to the formerly untouchable castes in India. Dalit-Bahujan signifies political solidarity between non–upper caste communities. See Gopal Guru and V. Geetha, 'New Phase of Dalit-Bahujan Intellectual Activity' (2000) 35(3), *Economic and Political Weekly*, 30.

[22] See references to the works of Kumud Pawade, Chandra Bhan Prasad, Pragnya Daya Pawar and Meena Kandasamy in Sharmila Rege, 'Education as "Trutiya Ratna": Towards Phule-Ambedkarite Feminist Pedagogical Practice' (2010) 45 (44–45), *Economic and Political Weekly*, 88. See also Braj Ranjan Mani, *Debrahminising History: Dominance and Resistance in Indian Society* (Manohar, 2005); Gopal Guru and Sundar Sarukkai, *The Cracked Mirror: An Indian Debate on Experience and Theory* (Oxford University Press, 2017); Kancha Ilaiah, *Why I Am Not a Hindu: A Shudra Critique of Hindutva Philosophy, Culture and Political Economy* (Bhatkal & Sen, 2005).

[23] Sumit Baudh has narrated how it was more difficult for him to come out as Dalit than queer even in the progressive space of the National Law School of India University, Bangalore, where he studied. Mentioned in Nivedita Menon, 'Sexuality, Caste, Governmentality: Contests over "Gender" in India' (2009) 91, *Feminist Review*, 94. See, generally, Chirayu Jain, Spadika Jayaraj, Sanjana Muraleedharan, Harjas Singh and Marc S. Galanter, 'The Elusive Island of Excellence: A Study on Student Demographics, Accessibility and Inclusivity at National Law School 2015–16' (2016), https://papers.ssrn.com/sol3/papers.cfm?abstract_id=2788311.

[24] I belong to an upper caste.

discriminations faced by sex workers.[25] Both these enquiries – about the human rights of sex workers and the socio-legal dimensions of caste – are significant and inform my understanding of the relationship between knowledge and caste. However, based on such understanding, my intent and scholarly engagement are distinct.

The focus of this book lies in staging a performance of how a field of Indian feminist jurisprudence is experienced and produced relationally in conversations.[26] My specific intent is to demonstrate how knowledge productions within this field result from the experiences of mutual relations amongst people and between people's lives and law, which happen at specific places and times. To this end, I undertake the practice of research in this book as a creative and an imaginative exercise to form reciprocal ties with, and amongst, my interlocutors; and between their lives and law. Simultaneously, I work against a structural disparity that

[25] It is a widely prevalent understanding amongst many feminist scholars that there is a direct link between sex work, poverty and the lack of access to education. It is believed that women are forced to sell sexual services because they have not experienced formal education, due to which they are driven into conditions of poverty that force them into sex work in which commercial transactions can take place based on the selling of the kind of bodily services that, in a patriarchal society, become a readily marketable product for women. See Geetanjali Gangoli, 'Sex Work, Poverty and Migration in Eastern India', in Sadhna Arya and Anupama Roy (eds), *Poverty, Gender and Migration* (Sage, 2006), 214–35.

[26] Throughout this book, as I draw considerable attention to the question of how feminist jurisprudential knowledge production is experienced by diverse groups of people, I am mindful of what American feminist historian Joan Scott warns us against: of taking experience categorically as an unquestioned arbiter of truth, which can then foreclose possibilities of a critical engagement with the processes through which experience comes to be. I attend to the question of experience not as a category for truth telling but to illuminate two things. One, that the experiences of law are also constituted of the conscious actions through which one thinks about and practises law. Two, that a multitude of people, and their diverse ways of thinking about and practising law, make the scholarly field of Indian feminist jurisprudence. Joan Scott, 'The Evidence of Experience' (1991) 17(4), *Critical Inquiry*, 773. For a feminist counter to Scott's critique of experience and the importance of holding on to it as feminist epistemology, see Johanna Oksala, 'In Defense of Experience' (2014) 29(2), *Hypatia*, 388. For a similar conversation on the category of experience in the context of caste and gender in India, see Gopal Guru, 'Dalit Women Talk Differently' (1995) 30(41–42), *Economic and Political Weekly*, 2548; Sharmila Rege, 'Dalit Women Talk Differently: A Critique of "Difference" and Towards a Dalit Feminist Standpoint Position' (1998) 33(44), *Economic and Political Weekly*, WS39.

exists in the field of legal knowledge production with respect to whom can be counted as knowledgeable or experienced in law, and by speaking from where.

The practices of academics and activists are engaged with in tandem because of the apparent disparity amongst them vis-à-vis legal knowledge production. The academic discipline of law, and legal imagination and practice, are commonly regarded as a realm of specialised and professional knowledge in India. Thus, in popular perception, legal academics are readily recognisable as interlocutors and contributors of a jurisprudence. Sex worker activists, however, are not.

In common perception, sex workers are rendered non-recognisable as contributors to the field of legal knowledge owing to their social and educational differences from those of us who are related with academia. The sex workers not only have no academic training in law, but a majority also possesses no formal education. Moreover, their socio-legal status in India is marked as criminals by the state. These compounding circumstances locate sex worker activists at the bottom of the hierarchy vis-à-vis those of us who have ties with the legal academy and whose practices qualify as producing jurisprudential knowledge.

The inability to recognise activists as bearers of their own legal wisdom arise from a disparity in how we evaluate the understanding of law gained at university and through experiences other than these, such as collectivisation. For feminist practices of legal knowledge production in India, by implication, such non-recognition can inadvertently carry another meaning. It can work to privilege the mind and intellectual labour of the academic/scholar/researcher when it comes to producing legal meaning. This can then reproduce caste-based hierarchy in scholarship by setting a preferential precedent regarding whose experiences of law, and gained from where, are invested with the authority to count as knowledge in scholarly feminist discussions about law.

This kind of hierarchy vis-à-vis feminist practices of jurisprudence potentially impedes our engagements with the field and its rich repertoire of knowledge comprising a diversity of the meanings and experiences of law in India, which is what the method of this book helps to work against. The book makes a specific methodological argument and contribution to Indian feminist jurisprudence that helps to recognise how the practices of people who *do not* appear knowledgeable, and those who *do*, together produce the field. The scholarship in this book is directed at inverting the hierarchical logic of the caste system that is embedded in how we perceive non-academic practices of knowledge production vis-à-vis academics' practices of scholarly writing.

I obviously do not seek to demonstrate that academic and sex worker experiences of law are one and the same. Rather, I develop a method that can help to think from my disciplinary location in law, and at the same time speak to the specific historical context of the field of knowledge this book engages in. By using a localised practice as my method, I am able to show how sex workers' collectivisation *and* the scholarship of academics, albeit different, are both equally valuable practices. Both are folded together and contribute to the productions of a field of Indian feminist jurisprudence.

Adda assists in reworking the disparate locations of my interlocutors *in relation to* the field of Indian feminist jurisprudence. It first helps me acknowledge that people with very limited, or no, formal education, and from within and outside the legal academy, have the right to engage in intellectual labour; and then demonstrate how such diverse groups of people together shape a field of Indian feminist jurisprudence. For example, the legal academics – Upendra Baxi and Ratna Kapur – are different from each other in terms of their scholarship. However, both are renowned scholars, and therefore, their practices carry greater authority with respect to the academic field of legal knowledge production in relation to me and the sex workers.[27] By engaging with texts authored by academics and sex workers, and by practising reciprocity in the conversations with both groups, I make them speak as my interlocutors who carry equal authority in this book's account of the field of Indian feminist jurisprudence.

Through my mode of engagement with the materials, I call the practices of sex worker activists and legal academics into relation and

[27] On the practice of academic authority, see Erica McWilliam, 'Performing between the Posts: Authority, Posture, and Contemporary Feminist Scholarship', in William G. Tierney and Yvonna S. Lincoln (eds), *Representation and the Text: Re-framing the Narrative Voice* (SUNY Press, 1997) 219–32.

position the authors as my interlocutors. I accord equal value to sex workers' conversations that inhabit their practices of collectivisation and the academics' conversations that inhabit their practices of scholarship. In doing so, I position both groups on a par with each other and as bearers of their own insights for the productions of feminist jurisprudential knowledge. Thus, I work to demonstrate how both sets of conversations, although these are disparately located vis-à-vis Indian feminist jurisprudence, can be seen as jointly contributing to the productions of its body of knowledge. In performing adda as my method, I take up the responsibility of demonstrating how people who are disparately located experience mutual relations with law in their specific place and time through the active practices of collectivisation and scholarship.

Having provided a glimpse into what the reader can expect to unfold in the later chapters, I will further elucidate some of this book's key aspects and situate them in relation to feminist jurisprudential scholarship in India. This chapter is meant to do two things. One, to familiarise the reader with the established convention of diversity in the field of Indian feminist jurisprudence, which I will join with and expand. Two, to explain the relevance of this book's method and argument to the caste question.

Next, I will offer an illustration of the field by introducing the body of literature that the book is drawing from and contributing to. I will foreground that there are different voices in the field, each of which speaks from a different locus both within and outside Indian legal academia. My purpose here is not to provide an exhaustive summary of the field but relay the contents of some of the literature that makes the scholarly field of Indian feminist jurisprudence a diverse body of knowledge. I will then move on to clarifying my understanding of caste and its relationship with intellectual labour in India. I will elaborate on how such an understanding informs my decision to do adda with sex worker activists and legal academics *together*.

FEMINISM AND LAW IN INDIA: AN OVERVIEW OF THE FIELD

In the common law world, the field of feminist jurisprudence, in general, is argued to have originated through the interventions of feminist scholars who were part of legal academia.[28] In these places, feminist jurisprudence developed as a named form of legal knowledge at the end of the twentieth century as feminists engaged with the foundations and formulations of law in conventional jurisprudence/legal theory and practices of adjudication.[29] Although the field in all of these places is not uniform, or restricted only to legal academia, they share one thing in common. They are all concerned with the experiential dimensions of law, or how law is lived.[30]

Likewise, the field of feminist jurisprudence in India is also concerned with the experiences of law, but its body of knowledge did not solely originate in conversations amongst feminists from legal academia.[31] In India, a place that borrows the term 'feminist jurisprudence' from its non-Indian counterparts, the field did not begin as an interrogation of the gendered foundations of jurisprudence/legal theory. It constituted adjudicatory practices concerning women as its entry point of enquiry.[32] It is only very recently that the relationship between feminist jurisprudence and Indian legal academia has come to be formally established.

Feminist jurisprudence found its way into legal academia as a named field of legal study when, in 2003, the National Commission for Women

[28] Margaret Thornton, 'The Development of Feminist Jurisprudence' (1998) 9(2), *Legal Education Review*, 171.

[29] See, generally, Ann C. Scales, 'Towards a Feminist Jurisprudence' (1981) 56, *Indiana Law Journal*, 375; Regina Graycar and Jenny Morgan, *The Hidden Gender of Law*, 2nd ed. (Federation Press, 2002); Ann Genovese and Margaret Thornton, 'On *The Liberal Promise*: A Conversation' (2015) 41(1), *Australian Feminist Law Journal*, 3; Carol Smart, *Feminism and the Power of Law* (Routledge, 2002).

[30] See, generally, Frances E. Olsen, *Feminist Legal Theory I: Foundations and Outlooks* (New York University Press, 1995); Frances E. Olsen, *Feminist Legal Theory II: Positioning Feminist Theory Within Law* (New York University Press, 1995); Margaret Davies and Vanessa E. Munro (eds), *The Ashgate Companion to Feminist Legal Theory* (Routledge, 2013); Robin West, 'Women in the Legal Academy: A Brief History of Feminist Legal Theory' (2018) 87(3), *Fordham Law Review*, 977.

[31] For an account that argues that the field of feminist jurisprudence in Australia also did not solely originate in feminist conversations in legal academia, see Genovese, 'On Australian Feminist Tradition'.

[32] 'The terms "feminism" and "jurisprudence" first came together at a conference organised by women from Harvard Law School in April 1978 in celebration of the 25th anniversary of another first, that of female graduates from its hallowed halls.' Drakopoulou, 'Revisiting Feminist Jurisprudence'.

(NCW)[33] began advocating for its inclusion in the law curriculum.[34] Based on the efforts of the NCW, the Bar Council of India (a statutory body that regulates the conduct of the legal profession) decided that feminist jurisprudence was an important area of legal studies that needed to be included as part of jurisprudence courses in the LLB and LLM degrees. It took much longer to implement this decision and replace the precursor of feminist jurisprudence, a subject that was commonly taught at public university law schools by the name of 'Women and Law and Law Relating to the Child'. This subject was about the special legislations, case law and constitutional provisions that applied to women and children. Although 'women and law' as a subject of legal study worked to set up correlations between the categories of women and law *within* the legal academy, it was not practised as a feminist intellectual project of/in law.

To date, there has not been a consolidated effort in the Indian legal academy to develop a systematic theory and practice of law from a feminist standpoint.[35] Understandably, there is no specific body of scholarship that self-identifies its intellectual practices under the name of either 'feminist jurisprudence' or 'Indian feminist jurisprudence'. For this reason, the field is not clearly bounded by a demarcated inside and an outside, and the term 'feminist jurisprudence' cannot be simply applied to a given body of literature. There is no *explicit* understanding amongst the practitioners in the field, which has been arrived at through conversations, as to what kind of engagements with law qualifies to be called 'Indian feminist jurisprudence' and what does not. This leaves the understanding and organisation of the field open to multiple interpretations. To provide a brief introduction to the field, I have organised my

[33] The NCW is a policy-oriented official organisation formed in 1992 by the Government of India to liaise between the state and the Indian women's movement. Prabha Kotiswaran, 'Governance Feminism in the Postcolony', in Janet Halley, Prabha Kotiswaran, Rachel Rebouché and Hila Shamir, *Governance Feminism: An Introduction* (University of Minnesota Press, 2018), 81.

[34] National Commission for Women, http://ncwapps.nic.in/frmreportFeministJurists1.aspx.

[35] Archana Parashar, 'Feminism in Indian Legal Education', in Amita Dhanda and Archana Parashar (eds), *Engendering Law: Essays in Honour of Lotika Sarkar* (Eastern Book Company, 1999), 89–116.

account by relying on a range of published literature that correlates law and feminism from an Indian perspective, or engages with law in the Indian context, from a stated feminist position.

The scholarly field of feminist jurisprudence in India may be loosely described as a contemporary body of knowledge consisting of a repertoire of feminist socio-legal literature spanning more than four decades.[36] Feminist legal scholar Archana Parashar describes feminist jurisprudence in the Indian legal academic context as 'contemporary debates about the relationship between law and society'.[37] Methodologically, from the perspective of this wide-ranging scholarship about law that originates in feminist thought and practice, the experiences of law primarily map onto social experiences. This means that in India the field is thought and practised in terms of law's relationships with the differing and interlocking social experiences of gender, class, caste, sexuality and religion.[38] Consequently, this way of thinking about and practising law's relations has established a close proximity between the field of Indian feminist jurisprudence and movements for social justice.[39] This proximity has primarily resulted from the intimate ties between Indian feminisms and social justice movements.[40]

36 Pratiksha Baxi, 'Feminist Contributions to Sociology of Law: A Review' (2008) 43(43), *Economic and Political Weekly*, 79.

37 Parashar, 'Feminism in Indian Legal Education', 108.

38 Vrinda Narain, *Reclaiming the Nation: Muslim Women and the Law in India* (University of Toronto Press, 2008); Kalpana Kannabiran (ed.), *Women and Law: Critical Feminist Perspectives* (Sage, 2013); Srimati Basu, *She Comes to Take Her Rights: Indian Women, Property, and Propriety* (SUNY Press, 1999); Geetanjali Gangoli, *Indian Feminisms: Law, Patriarchies and Violence in India* (Routledge, 2007); Kriti Singh, *Separated and Divorced Women in India: Economic Rights and Entitlements* (Sage, 2013); Jaya Sagade, *Child Marriage in India: Socio-legal and Human Rights Dimensions* (Oxford University Press, 2012); Archana Parashar, *Women and Family Law Reform in India: Uniform Civil Code and Gender Equality* (Sage, 1992).

39 Menon, 'Sexual Violence and the Law in India', 208.

40 Samita Sen, 'Toward a Feminist Politics? The Indian Women's Movement in Historical Perspective', Policy Research Report on Gender and Development, Working Paper Series No. 9, World Bank, Development Research Group/Poverty Reduction and Economic Management Network, April 2000, http://unpan1.un.org/intradoc/groups/public/documents/apcity/unpan051009.pdf; Maitrayee Chaudhuri, 'Feminism in India: The Tale and Its Telling' (2019) 1(209), *Revue Tiers Monde*, 19, www.cairn.info/revue-tiers-monde-2012-1-page-19.htm#.

Speaking of Indian feminisms, in *The History of Doing* (1993), feminist scholar Radha Kumar has argued that Indian feminisms are not focused on demanding women's 'equality with men'.[41] Kumar documents the history of the feminist and women's rights movements in India from 1800 to 1990 and clarifies that the feminisms emerging from the practices of the Indian women's movement are not founded on an inherent opposition between men and women. Kumar argues that feminists have opposed the areas in which men exercised control over women's lives, and the practices that accorded superiority to men over women; and in doing so, Indian feminisms have also simultaneously acknowledged a 'complementarity between the two distinct biologically defined areas of masculine and feminine'.[42] For Kumar, Indian feminisms, that are founded on concerns with unequal relations of gender have not been preoccupied with questions of sameness/differences amongst men and women. Rather, the debates and discussions amongst feminists have focused equally on the differences amongst women.[43]

Feminist political scientist Nivedita Menon has also argued that Indian feminisms are founded on an understanding of woman as a subject who is a sum total of her gender, caste, class, and religious status and conditions.[44] Menon argues that from the 1990s onwards, conversations in the women's movement underwent a systematic shift in terms of its subject of enquiry. This happened when 'woman' as a category of study and analysis shifted to a broader understanding of gender in order to accommodate the experiences of sexually marginalised men and women, such as gay men and sex working women.[45] Menon traces this shift in articulation to the women's movement's conversations with two other social justice movements in India, namely the sex workers' and the queer rights movements (I discuss the sex workers' movement in Chapters 3 and 4). Both the sex workers' and queer rights movements, which began in the early 1990s, made gendered experiences of sexuality

[41] Radha Kumar, *The History of Doing: An Illustrated Account of Movements for Women's Rights and Feminism in India, 1800–1990* (Zubaan, 1993), 4.

[42] Ibid. [43] Ibid.

[44] Nivedita Menon, 'Is Feminism About "Women"? A Critical View on Intersectionality from India' (2015) 50(17), *Economic and Political Weekly*, 37.

[45] Menon, 'Sexuality, Caste, Governmentality'.

a part of the conversations of the women's movement, leading to a shift in its focus and terminology.[46]

In a piece titled 'Legitimately Ours: The Parallel Systems of Feminist Jurisprudence' (2018), feminist activist Abha Bhaiya demonstrates that the relationships between feminisms and social movements themselves form a locus for engagements with law and questions of jurisprudence in the Indian context.[47] Bhaiya provides an account of the activist Indian tradition of feminist jurisprudence. By way of illustration, she discusses the Nari Adalats, the community-based, women-led tribunals/courts. These were established in Gujarat in the 1990s to address women's experiences of violence that did not find representation in formal law and legal institutions.[48] She refers to these courts as informal legal institutions that acted as a link between state and non-state actors. Bhaiya uses the illustration to argue that the Indian feminist jurisprudential tradition is a field of engagement with law that is not conceived solely in relation to the state and what it authorises as 'legal' or 'illegal'. Instead, Indian feminist jurisprudence is a field of feminist engagements with questions of law in relation to women's experiences of community relations and social life.[49]

When the feminisms of the Indian women's movement began to interact with law in the 1980s and 1990s, two things happened. First, the amalgam of law and feminism was conceived largely as a project of social justice. Second, the focus of this project came to be directed primarily at the state through the demands for law reform and new legislations. Menon argues that after the independence of India from colonial rule, feminists reposed trust in the state and its institutional mechanisms, which dissipated with the declaration of the Emergency and the accompanying political events in the 1970s.[50] Thus, according to Menon, post the 1970s, in the aftermath of the declaration of Emergency (this event is discussed in Chapter 5 in relation to the writing of the

[46] Nivedita Menon, 'Outing Heteronormativity: Nation, Citizen, Feminist Disruptions', in Nivedita Menon (ed.), *Sexualities* (Women Unlimited, 2007).

[47] Abha Bhaiya, 'Legitimately Ours: The Parallel Systems of Feminist Jurisprudence', in Poonam Kathuria and Abha Bhaiya (eds), *Indian Feminisms: Individual and Collective Journeys* (Zubaan, 2018), 46–64.

[48] Ibid., 57. [49] Ibid. [50] Menon, 'Sexual Violence and the Law in India', 206.

Open Letter),[51] there was a shift in the way feminists engaged with the state and its institutions.[52]

In *Subversive Sites: Feminist Engagements with Law in India* (1996), feminist legal scholars Ratna Kapur and Brenda Cossman argue that throughout the 1980s, from the standpoint of the women's movement, law has either been conceived as a corrective tool for undoing experiences of hierarchy and discrimination, or it has been an object of criticism for contributing to these experiences (I discuss this book in Chapter 5).[53] Speaking in relation to a similar context about contemporary feminist legal scholarship in India, in *Engendering Law: Essays in Honour of Lotika Sarkar* (1999), Archana Parashar laments the absence of a legal project from an Indian feminist standpoint.[54] According to her, legal thought and jurisprudence carry a positivist account of law in India that is primarily interested in law's doctrinal conceptions.[55] A positivist understanding of law as a command of the sovereign was the most conducive for colonial rule, and was thus followed by the British administration in India.[56] A similar conception of law – as command of the state – dominates contemporary legal scholarship, even after colonialism ended and a change was implemented in India's political system. For Parashar, it is such narrow academic engagements with law in general that have led to a dearth of scholarly theorisations of law from the specific context and experiences of Indian women.[57]

Nonetheless, there is indeed a discursive body of scholarly and activist feminist engagement with law that is produced from both within and

[51] See U. Baxi et al., 'An Open Letter to the Chief Justice of India'.

[52] Kuldip Nayar, *The Judgment: Inside Story of the Emergency in India* (Vikas, 1977).

[53] This argument can be evidenced from a host of feminist writings published through this period about the women's movement's incessant demands for law reform or new legislations. See generally, Flavia Agnes, 'Protecting Women Against Violence: Review of a Decade of Legislation, 1980–89' (1992) 27(17), *Economic and Political Weekly*, WS19; Ruth Vanita and Madhu Kishwar, 'Using Women as a Pretext for Repression: The Indecent Representation of Women (Prohibition) Bill' (1987) 37, *Manushi*, https://feministlawarchives.pldindia.org/wp-content/uploads/the-indecent-representation-of-women-prohibition-bill-manushi-no-37-1987.pdf.

[54] Archana Parashar and Amita Dhanda, 'Introduction', in Amita Dhanda and Archana Parashar (eds), *Engendering Law: Essays in Honour of Lotika Sarkar* (Eastern Book Company, 1999), 1–32, 3.

[55] Ibid. [56] Ibid. [57] Ibid.

outside Indian legal academia. The scholarly and activist conversations that have worked to shape the field of Indian feminist jurisprudence by forming law's relations with social experiences, based on which I have organised my discussion, appear in the form of published texts. The conversations have taken place in writings and publications in the English language whereby scholars/activists/litigators have shaped the field by agreeing, disagreeing or drawing and building on each other's ideas.

I see the field of Indian feminist jurisprudence as comprising a set of conversations amongst three kinds of people who are either academics or possess advanced academic qualifications. They are feminists who are academically trained and based in the discipline of law;[58] feminists who are academically trained and based in the humanities and social sciences, particularly in the disciplines of sociology,[59] history[60] and political science;[61] and feminist activists and litigators.[62] Conversations amongst

58 Ratna Kapur, *Erotic Justice: Law and the New Politics of Postcolonialism* (Routledge-Cavendish, 2005); Upendra Baxi, 'From Human Rights to the Right to Be a Woman', in Amita Dhanda and Archana Parashar (eds), *Engendering Law: Essays in Honour of Lotika Sarkar* (Eastern Book Company, 1999), 275–90; Lotika Sarkar, 'Rape: A Human Rights Versus a Patriarchal Interpretation' (1994) 1(1), *Indian Journal of Gender Studies*, 69; Parashar, *Women and Family Law Reform in India*; Kalpana Kannabiran and Vasanth Kannabiran, *De-eroticizing Assault: Essays on Modesty, Honour and Power* (Popular Prakashan, 2002); Prabha Kotiswaran, *Dangerous Sex, Invisible Labor: Sex Work and the Law in India* (Princeton University Press, 2011).

59 Pratiksha Baxi, *Public Secrets of Law* (Oxford University Press, 2014); Raka Ray, *Fields of Protest: Women's Movements in India* (University of Minnesota Press, 1998); Basu, *She Comes to Take Her Rights*.

60 Janaki Nair, *Women and Law in Colonial India: A Social History* (Kali for Women, 1996); Lata Mani, 'Contentious Traditions: The Debate on Sati in Colonial India' (1987) 7, *Cultural Critique*, 119; Anupama Rao (ed.), *Gender and Caste* (Zed Books, 2005); Prem Chowdhry, *Contentious Marriages, Eloping Couples: Gender, Caste, and Patriarchy in Northern India* (Oxford University Press, 2009).

61 Nivedita Menon, *Recovering Subversion: Feminist Politics Beyond the Law* (University of Illinois Press, 2004); Anupama Roy, *Gendered Citizenship: Historical and Conceptual Explorations* (Orient BlackSwan, 2013).

62 Flavia Agnes, *State, Gender and the Rhetoric of Law Reform* (Research Centre for Women's Studies, Shreemati Nathibai Damodar Thackersey Women's University, 1995); Indira Jaising (ed.), *Men's Laws, Women's Lives: A Constitutional Perspective on Religion, Common Law and Culture in South Asia* (Women Unlimited, 2005); Nandita Haksar, *De-mystification of Law for Women* (South Asia Books, 1996).

these people who are based inside and outside the university, both within India and elsewhere, resulted in shaping a body of literature that, I think, can be organised around two overlapping thematic areas.

Substantively, the scholarly literature that shapes the field of Indian feminist jurisprudence may be divided according to the areas of women's/gendered experiences of *violence* and *difference*.[63] Feminist legal literature on the gendered experiences of violence have addressed issues such as rape, dowry deaths, domestic violence, *sati* or widow burning, obscenity and sexual harassment.[64] Scholarship in the area of the gendered experiences of difference has addressed issues such as sexuality, Muslim women's right to divorce, Hindu women's succession rights, and the Uniform Civil Code versus personal laws debates.[65] Amongst all of these issues, law's pertinence in relation to women's experiences of rape and sexual violence has remained the most prominent and recurring topic of conversation amongst feminists up until very recent times.[66] Engagements with rape law reform have been fundamental to the activism of the Indian women's movement.[67] The women's movement's engagements in law reform and the demands for protective legislations for women have been a primary topic of the conversations that took place in the field of Indian feminist jurisprudence through scholarship in the 1980s.[68]

A document that has played an indirect role in the rape law reform of the 1980s, and is widely regarded as one of the first programmatic feminist engagements with law, is the 1974 report titled *Towards*

[63] For a discussion on how difference has become an important category of analysis in Indian feminist thought, see Rege, 'Dalit Women Talk Differently'.

[64] See generally Agnes, 'Protecting Women Against Violence'.

[65] Flavia Agnes, *Law and Gender Inequality: The Politics of Women's Rights in India*, in *Women and Law in India* (Oxford University Press, 2016).

[66] As Prabha Kotiswaran argues, 'Rape law reform defines the very core of the [Indian women's movement].' Kotiswaran, 'Governance Feminism in the Postcolony', 77.

[67] Ibid.

[68] Janet Halley, Prabha Kotiswaran, Rachel Rebouché and Hila Shamir, *Governance Feminism: An Introduction* (University of Minnesota Press, 2018); Kalpana Kannabiran and Ritu Menon, *From Mathura to Manorama: Resisting Violence Against Women in India* (Women Unlimited, 2007).

Equality.[69] The report played an important part in 1980s activism around rape law reform that took shape through the writing of the Open Letter in 1979 by Upendra Baxi and his colleagues.[70] Lotika Sarkar, a co-author of the report, was also a co-author of the Open Letter, a crucial document that set in motion the Indian women's movement's engagement with rape law reform (I discuss the Open Letter in Chapter 5).[71]

The publication of the *Towards Equality* report was the result of a government-commissioned project, which set up a committee to review the status of women in Indian society. This report, almost 500 pages long, was co-authored by the members of the committee, which included a diverse and eminent group of political activists and/or academics who were associated with social justice movements.[72]

The report has a dedicated chapter titled 'Women and the Law', which mainly looks at women's standing in personal laws such as those relating to divorce, inheritance and adoption.[73] In their prefatory note addressing the minister for education and social welfare, the authors point at the inequalities in all aspects of women's lives thus: 'our investigation has revealed that large masses of women in this country have remained unaffected by the rights guaranteed to them by the Constitution and the laws enacted since independence'.[74] The report

69 Government of India, *Towards Equality: Report of the Committee on the Status of Women in India* (Ministry of Education and Social Welfare, Department of Social Welfare, New Delhi, December 1974) http://pldindia.org/wp-content/uploads/2013/04/Towards-Equality-1974-Part-1.pdf.

70 For a range of feminist and academic writings on the importance of this report and how it shaped a feminist discourse in India, see generally Mary John (ed.), *Women's Studies in India: A Reader* (Penguin India, 2008); Parashar, 'Feminism in Indian Legal Education'; Upendra Baxi, 'Unlearning the Law with Lotika Sarkar', Lotika Sarkar Memorial Lecture (2014) 2 *Journal of the Campus Law Centre* 1, http://clc.du.ac.in/JCLC/JCLC%20Vol_2.pdf.

71 For an account of how the Open Letter impacted the women's movement's activism around rape law reform, see P. Baxi, *Public Secrets of Law*; Kumar, *The History of Doing*, 4; John, *Women's Studies in India*.

72 The other members of the committee were: Phulrenu Guha (politician), Maniben Kara (activist), Savitri Shyam, Neera Dogra, Vikram Mahajan (activist and social entrepreneur), Leela Dube (academic), Sakina A. Hasan (academic), Urmila Haksar and Vina Mazumdar (academic).

73 'Women and the Law', chapter 4 in Government of India, *Towards Equality*, 102–47.

74 Ibid.

highlighted the differing status *amongst* women by noting that the experiences of poor and rural women were different from those of middle-class women.[75] In effect, it suggested that 'woman' was not a homogeneous group, and further that the constitutional provisions of equality touched the lives of different groups of women differently, in comparison to each other. The authors of the report thus argued that women's standing within law, and in society, was unequal not just in relation to men, but also in relation to each other.

On the question of women's political participation, and on what measures could address this aspect of inequality in status, there was a difference of opinion amongst the authors. Lotika Sarkar and Vina Mazumdar disagreed with the rest of the group and wrote a note of dissent at the end of the report where they stated, 'our investigations have proved that the application of the theoretical principle of equality in the context of unequal situations only intensifies inequalities, because equality in such situations merely means privileges for those who have them already and not for those who need them'.[76] Through their dissent, Sarkar and Mazumdar asserted that constitutional equality's lack of uniform jurisdiction over women's lives was caused by the inadequate translation of its theoretical assumptions into practice. According to the report, the operation of constitutional legal provisions took place in the context of social inequalities of caste, class and gender, for which reason it was unable to reach and benefit all women. The report thus established the correlations between women's experiences of law and their experiences of a discriminatory and unequal social life.

In the aftermath of the report, since the early 1980s, women's experiences of rape have been a dominant topic of conversations in the

[75] According to feminist scholar Mary E. John, it is this aspect of the report, as well as the report as a whole, that changed the dominant course of the relationship between women and academic research in India from the mid 1970s and led to the setting up of the new field of study called women's studies in academic institutions. The report led to the realisation that the lives of poor rural women needed to be recognised and transformed, which set in motion a shift in thinking about women and institutional education. From 'women as subjects to be educated', the discourse turned to '"women" as new subjects of investigation and study'. John, *Women's Studies in India*, 5.

[76] Lotika Sarkar and Vina Mazumdar, 'Note of Dissent by Lotika Sarkar and Vina Mazumdar', Government of India, *Towards Equality*, 355–57, 357.

women's movement as well as amongst feminist scholars. Rape has not just been understood as a form of gender-based oppression that is intimately related with sexuality, class and caste, but also as a form of state oppression.[77] This understanding emerged from the fact that many of the incidents of rape around which the women's movement had mobilised, concerned women from marginalised class and caste communities, and those who were raped by the police in custody.[78] This was also a period during which the country was recovering from the police brutality unleashed during the Emergency (1975–77), and all progressive forces, including some voices within the women's movement, were very sceptical of the state entity and its institutions.[79]

Indian feminisms' relations with law have been thought and practised largely through engagements with the state. In the 1980s, Lotika Sarkar cautioned against the women's movement's demand to shift the burden of proof from the state to the accused in cases of rape.[80] She argued that vesting more power in the state in the prosecution of rape was not wise given its capacity to stifle dissent, as witnessed during the Emergency.[81] Writing in the late 1990s, feminist sociologist Raka Ray, in a discussion on the role of the state in the activism of the women's movement, argued that the relationship between feminists and the Indian state has been marked by 'ambivalen[ce]'.[82] Ray noted that some feminists believed that the state was 'both friend and foe'.[83] However, according to Ray, feminists largely recognised that the state was biased not just in favour of men, but also people who belonged to the upper castes, upper classes and majoritarian religions.[84] Joining in this discussion, feminist lawyer and activist Flavia Agnes criticised the possibilities of a friendship between the women's movement and the Indian state. She argued that the women's movement's constant reliance on law reform as a means of

[77] Kannabiran and Menon, *From Mathura to Manorama*; Debolina Dutta and Oishik Sircar, 'India's Winter of Discontent: Some Feminist Dilemmas in the Wake of a Rape' (2013) 39(1), *Feminist Studies*, 293.

[78] Ibid. [79] Menon, 'Sexual Violence and the Law in India', 206.

[80] Kotiswaran, 'Governance Feminism in the Postcolony', 90–91.

[81] Rajeswari Sunder Rajan, *The Scandal of the State: Women, Law and Citizenship in Postcolonial India* (Duke University Press, 2003), 242.

[82] Ray, *Fields of Protest*, 13. [83] Ibid. [84] Ibid., 14.

gaining protection from violence had, in fact, resulted in giving more power to the institution and strengthened the scope for state-authorised violence.[85]

The scholarship of Flavia Agnes exemplifies conversations between people who are not located in academia, but have nonetheless shaped the field of Indian feminist jurisprudence. Agnes, who has been active in the women's movement, founded the feminist litigation organisation called Majlis in Mumbai, and has been practising law as a women's rights lawyer since the late 1980s. Her conversations with the women clients she represents in court, and with the women's movement, have informed her scholarship on law's relationship with gender, minority rights, domestic violence and the women's movement.[86]

To give an instance of Agnes's conversations with her clients that shaped her scholarship on law and sexuality:[87] in 2005, the Government of Maharashtra banned the operation of dance bars. These bars were a form of adult entertainment where women danced to popular Bollywood music to entertain customers in beer-selling bars.[88] The control of prostitution and trafficking was stated as the reason for instituting this ban.[89] The bar owners protested the ban and filed a writ petition in the Bombay High Court.[90] On the request of the Bar Girls Union, Agnes agreed to legally represent them and filed an intervener application in the writ petition filed by the bar owners. In her writings

[85] Agnes, 'Protecting Women Against Violence'.

[86] Agnes, *State, Gender and the Rhetoric of Law Reform*; Flavia Agnes, 'Women's Movement within a Secular Framework' (1994) 29(19), *Economic and Political Weekly*, 1123; Flavia Agnes, *Family Law*, vol. II: *Marriage, Divorce and Matrimonial Litigation* (Oxford University Press, 2012); Agnes, *Law and Gender Inequality*.

[87] Flavia Agnes, 'Hypocritical Morality: Mumbai's Ban on Bar Dancers' (2005) 149, *Manushi*, www.manushi-india.org/html_articles/hypocritical_morality_mumbais_ban_on_bar_dancers.htm.

[88] According to Flavia Agnes, the proliferation of dance bars in Maharashtra is 'linked not only to the restaurant industry and the entertainment business, but also to the state policy on the sale of liquor'. All of these businesses saw changes post the economic liberalisation of India in the 1990s and the government's development agenda that was set in motion during this time. See ibid.

[89] Ibid.

[90] *State of Maharashtra* v. *Indian Hotel and Restaurants Association* WP No. 2450/2005 (Bombay High Court), https://indiankanoon.org/doc/38033723.

about her experiences of this litigation, Agnes has referenced her conversations with the bar dancers as the source of her arguments in courts.[91]

Agnes has written about how, through her conversations with the women bar dancers, she understood that the feminist issue at stake in this litigation was women's right to livelihood and their oppression by a patriarchal state.[92] Through her conversations with the bar dancers she had learnt that their main concern was police harassment.[93] Agnes perceived her role as a means for the experiences of bar-dancing women, many of whom belonged to lower castes and had received very minimal formal education, to become a part of the legal discourse on matters relating to *their* lives and livelihood.[94] For this reason, Agnes conceived of the litigation as an extension of her feminist engagements, both scholarly and otherwise, against state violence.

In scholarly literature on the role of the state and the issue of rape/sexual violence, a non-Indian scholar who has often been cited is American feminist legal scholar Catharine MacKinnon.[95] In this regard, a notable example of scholarly work that has been in conversation with MacKinnon is Nivedita Menon's *Recovering Subversion: Feminist Politics*

91 Flavia Agnes, 'The Bar Dancer and the Trafficked Migrant: Globalisation and Subaltern Existence', in Sibaji Pratim Basu (ed.), *The Fleeing People of South Asia: Selections from Refugee Watch* (Anthem, 2009), 355–66.

92 Ibid. 93 Agnes, 'Hypocritical Morality'.

94 Speaking about a research study that Majlis had conducted with other women's groups in Bombay before the litigation, Agnes noted, 'Contrary to the official statement that more than 75 percent of the dancers are Bangladeshis and constitute a security risk, the sample study revealed that only 2 of the 153 girls who were interviewed were outsiders – they were Nepalis. Around 20 percent of the women were either from Mumbai or came from poverty-stricken districts of Maharashtra. 50 percent of the women who were interviewed were from backward castes, marginalized communities and notified tribes of Madhya Pradesh, Uttar Pradesh and Rajasthan – Bedia, Chari, Rajnat, Dhanawat, etc. The literacy levels were low – 50 percent were illiterate and only 25 percent had studied beyond the primary level. They had no training in any other skills.' Ibid.

95 Catharine MacKinnon, *Toward a Feminist Theory of the State* (Harvard University Press, 1989). Indian feminist scholars who have referred to MacKinnon in their scholarship are: Kannabiran and Kannabiran, *De-eroticizing Assault*; Menon, *Recovering Subversion*; P. Baxi, *Public Secrets of Law*; Ratna Kapur, 'Sexcapades and the Law' (2001) 505, *Seminar*, http://cscs.res.in/dataarchive/textfiles/textfile.2012-03-12.1317951631/file; Kotiswaran, 'Governance Feminism in the Postcolony'.

Beyond the Law, published in 2004.[96] Menon, in her discussion on rape law reform, in fact disagrees with MacKinnon. For MacKinnon, making a distinction between rape and consensual sexual intercourse between men and women is inconsequential under the conditions of patriarchy.[97] In response to this, Menon argues that if that were the case, then it would be impossible to prosecute for rape. She asks, if all sex is violence how can you single out sexual assault and call it a crime? Menon thus argues that MacKinnon's position on women's subordination is so totalising that it not only forecloses possibilities for women to assert their sexuality, but also for feminist critique. In her book, which is not specifically about rape law but is a much broader engagement with 'law and the state as engaged with by feminist practices', Menon makes an argument for an emancipatory feminist political imagination. She argues in favour of a feminist engagement that is able to look beyond both law and the woman subject as its matter of discourse. For Menon, law is a universal and normative domain composed of rules, which has dissonances with feminist emancipatory politics that must be both subjective and susceptible to shifting goals.[98]

As rape and sexual violence continue to be the central concerns in feminist conversations about law in India, I offer the following instances by way of illustrating an ongoing set of conversations amongst feminists on this subject. In *Public Secrets of Law: Rape Trials in India* published in 2014, feminist sociologist Pratiksha Baxi carries out a study of rape trials to look at the 'relationship between law and public secrecy'.[99] In the book, Baxi presents her feminist ethnographic study of a trial court, which she had carried out over a period of two years, to argue that rape trials are a performance of secrecy rather than a public articulation of women's experiences of rape.[100] Baxi contends that a disqualification of women's testimonies at various sites of state law, such as the police

96 Menon, *Recovering Subversion*, 35–36.

97 MacKinnon, *Toward a Feminist Theory of the State*.

98 'I understand emancipation as a process without closure, it is not a goal that we can reach . . . To move away from legal and state-centred conceptions of political practice is to recognize political practice as the perpetual attempt to eliminate oppression rather than the achievement of this elimination.' See Menon, *Recovering Subversion*, 20.

99 P. Baxi, *Public Secrets of Law*, xxiii. 100 Ibid.

station, court or the forensic laboratory, renders rape trials a violent experience for victims/survivors.[101] Baxi argues that her ethnographic study reveals that a rape victim as a juridical subject holds multiple subjectivities in rape trials because there is no fixed legal norm that is applied to the understanding of rape. She shows how the legal norm is actually a shifting one that plays out in ways that are far from what is written as law and also work to conceal women's lived experiences of rape from the public.[102]

In a piece published in 2018, feminist legal scholar Prabha Kotiswaran provides a detailed account of Indian feminisms' encounters and alliances with the post-colonial state around the issue of rape law reform since the late 1980s.[103] Kotiswaran has developed her account in a co-authored book titled *Governance Feminism,* in conversations with her non-Indian colleagues and feminist legal scholars, Janet Halley, Rachel Rebouche and Hila Shamir.[104] Kotiswaran argues that historically, Indian feminisms have had close ties with the state. This has given rise to what she terms 'governance feminism in the postcolony', a form of regulatory feminism that acts as a handmaiden in the Indian state's mode of governance.[105] This form of feminism, Kotiswaran argues, manifests through an overdependence on criminal law, an extremely gendered understanding of sexual violence and a less antagonistic approach to state power.[106] Kotiswaran is critical of this form of feminism that, as she argues, participates in a governing of women who are sexually marginalised, and also enables feminism to walk the corridors of power.

Nivedita Menon, in her 2019 article 'Sexual Violence and the Law in India', has expressly stated her disagreements with Kotiswaran's application of a 'governance feminism' framework for understanding the feminist experiences of law in India. The use of this framework, Menon notes, yields arguments that are untenable in the Indian context. She argues that Kotiswaran is extrapolating a framework that has been 'developed in the West', and is unproblematically applying it to the Indian context. Such an application of a theoretical explanation, for Menon, is

[101] Ibid., xxix. [102] Ibid. [103] Kotiswaran, 'Governance Feminism in the Postcolony'.
[104] Halley et al., *Governance Feminism.*
[105] Kotiswaran, 'Governance Feminism in the Postcolony'. [106] Ibid., 76.

inappropriate for fully understanding the Indian experience of feminist legal engagements, which is far from wielding any kind of power alongside, or in relation to, the state.[107]

Kotiswaran is careful to declare that her articulation is but an attempt at tracing shifts in feminist legal engagements in India that appear to bear points of both convergence and divergence with similar trends in the western context.[108] In a methodological sense, this articulation indicates a lack of mere extrapolation and application of a foreign theoretical tool. Moreover, for the scholarly field of Indian feminist jurisprudence an east/west positioning of methodological frameworks is untenable (I will illustrate this point in my discussion of *Subversive Sites* in Chapter 5).[109] That is because Indian feminist jurisprudence and its body of knowledge, in fact, has developed much of its theory and practice through conversations across what Menon calls 'different spatio-temporal locations'.[110]

This overview of the scholarship in the field thus illustrates that, methodologically, its body of knowledge is organised around law's relationships with the differing social experiences of gender, class, caste, sexuality and religion. The scholarly practices of a diverse group of people have collectively established and authorised these relations. In terms of substance, women's/gendered experiences of *violence* and *difference* are two organising themes or trajectories of feminist jurisprudential scholarship in India. Both themes have also been addressed by my interlocutors, as will appear in later chapters, suggesting a convergence of their thoughts and practices with the scholarly field of Indian feminist jurisprudence.

I will now discuss the relationship between caste and academic practices of knowledge production. I will then explain how the performances

[107] Menon, 'Sexual Violence and the Law in India', 209.

[108] Kotiswaran, 'Governance Feminism in the Postcolony', 76–77.

[109] See Kapur and Cossman, *Subversive Sites.*

[110] Menon, 'Sexual Violence and the Law in India', 209. Menon herself, for instance, draws extensively from the work of Michel Foucault to develop her own feminist engagements with law and politics. See Nivedita Menon, 'Foucault and Indian Scholarship: History, Governmentality, Modernity', in Franson Manjali (ed.), *Trajectory of French Thought* (Rupa, 2004), 63–81.

of adda with the sex workers and the academics is both a continuation of the conversations in the scholarly field of Indian feminist jurisprudence as well as a counter-action to caste-based hierarchy in the field of academic intellectual labour in India.

THE CASTE OF KNOWLEDGE

The fourfold caste system, the *chaturvarna*, is a practice of social classification authorised by Hindu religious scriptures.[111] Its elementary aspect is the classification of people into four castes, or *varnas*, namely Brahmin, Kshatriya, Vaishya and Shudra. The Dalits, or former untouchables, are outside this graded hierarchy and are excluded from the social order. Each varna is categorised based on the form of labour that was assigned to them at birth. The Brahmins 'should cultivate knowledge ... the Kshatriya should bear arms ... the Vaishya should trade and ... the Shudra should serve'.[112] However, as B. R. Ambedkar, legal scholar and one of the pioneers of the anti-caste movement in India, has argued, the caste system is not a division of labour alone. It is also a classification of the lives of people who were ordained to perform such labour into a hierarchical value system.[113]

The caste system operates through a mind–body hierarchy that attributes superiority to intellectual labour (and those who do it) and devalues various forms of bodily labour (and their doers) by considering them to be inferior. At the top of a caste-based value system is the Brahmin whose duty is to possess and practise intellectual labour. At the bottom is the Shudra who is prohibited from practising intellectual labour, and, instead, is duty-bound to be at the service of those who are higher up in the caste order. The logic of caste shapes perceptions of

[111] Bhimrao Ramji Ambedkar, 'Castes in India: Their Mechanism, Genesis, and Development', *Dr. Babasaheb Ambedkar: Writings and Speeches*, vol. 1 (Education Department, Government of Maharashtra, 1979), 3–22, www.columbia.edu/itc/mealac/pritchett/00ambedkar/txt_ambedkar_castes.html; Jodhka, *Caste in Contemporary India.*

[112] B. R. Ambedkar, 'Annihilation of Caste', in Valerian Rodrigues (ed.), *The Essential Writings of B. R. Ambedkar* (Oxford University Press, 2010), 263–305, 281.

[113] Ibid., 263.

intellectual labour as a superior activity and of bodily labour as a relatively inferior one. Subsequently, the lives of those who engage in intellectual activity are perceived to be superior in relation to those who engage in other forms of labour. This value system informs how different experiences of labour have historically come to bear a relation to the productions of knowledge.

Political scientist Gopal Guru argues that there is a 'lack of egalitarian conditions' in the academic practices of the social sciences in India because intellectual superiority is attributed to those who do theoretical work, as opposed to those who do empirical research.[114] According to Guru, this works to devalue the experiential basis of knowledge and is representative of the hierarchy between 'theoretical Brahmins and empirical Shudras'.[115]

As a countermeasure to such hierarchies, Guru advocates the use of 'the egalitarian principle' for a reorganisation of academic practices in the social sciences.[116] He argues that the egalitarian principle is a means by which the practitioners of social sciences can be instilled with a 'sense of moral responsibility' to justify their modes of knowledge production.[117] In other words, it places a knowledge practitioner under obligation to explain why a particular theory is accorded a privileged position within knowledge in relation to a descriptive account of the same.[118] What Guru seems to be primarily critical of through his foregrounding of such a theory/experience divide is how this makes academic knowledge production an exclusionary field dominated by experts and specialists who are accorded the privilege of knowing experience by theorising it. Guru argues that academia presupposes 'an intellectual position that some fields of enquiry must be left free for the specialists', which the egalitarian principle can work against, since it carries an obligation to consider experiential accounts as a form of knowledge.[119] Moreover, Guru argues, it offers a 'promise' to groups 'whose entry into the intellectual field has been historically prohibited by social forces in India'.[120]

[114] Gopal Guru, 'Egalitarianism and the Social Sciences in India', in Guru and Sarukkai, *The Cracked Mirror*, 9.

[115] Ibid., 10. [116] Ibid., 19. [117] Ibid., 11. [118] Ibid. [119] Ibid., 12. [120] Ibid.

The caste-based prohibition of access to intellectual fields has come to bear a correlation with law in contemporary India due to law's desired role in the organisation of an egalitarian post-colonial society. The common law tradition, as a legal system and a field of academic study, was instituted in India through colonialism, and is therefore a colonial inheritance.[121] In the past, law had worked as an instrument in the hands of colonial authorities for commanding native Indian subjects. It was used for subjugating and ruling a people, and for ordering and enacting unjust forms of coloniser–colonised relations.[122] With the advent of colonial rule, the centuries-old caste system underwent alterations, but even after independence caste remains very much a part of people's lives, although caste-based discriminations were made illegal in India after the enactment of the Indian Constitution in 1950.[123]

In the framing of the Indian Constitution, a conception of social equality informed by anti-caste thinking was considered to be a marker for instituting a break with India's colonial and Brahminical past.[124] B. R. Ambedkar, the chairman of the committee that drafted the Constitution of independent India, was one of the foremost proponents of anti-caste constitutional legal thought.[125] He argued that a complete 'annihilation of caste' was necessary for constituting a post-colonial sovereign nation-state as an independent legal entity.[126] The attempt was to create a state

[121] Parashar and Dhanda, 'Introduction'; Amita Dhanda and Archana Parashar (eds), *Decolonisation of Legal Knowledge* (Routledge, 2009); Aakash Singh Rathore and Garima Goswamy, *Rethinking Indian Jurisprudence: An Introduction to the Philosophy of Law* (Routledge, 2018).

[122] Parashar and Dhanda, 'Introduction', 7.

[123] Nicholas B. Dirks, *Castes of Mind: Colonialism and the Making of Modern India* (Princeton University Press, 2002), 10. Article 15 of the Indian Constitution prohibits discriminations based on caste; Article 17 declares the practice of untouchability to be illegal. In 1955, India enacted the Untouchability (Offences) Act (renamed in 1976 as the Protection of Civil Rights Act).

[124] Upendra Baxi, 'Postcolonial Legality: A Postscript from India' (2012) 45(2), *Law and Politics in Africa, Asia and Latin America*, 178; Upendra Baxi, 'Emancipation as Justice: Babasaheb Ambedkar's Legacy and Vision', in Upendra Baxi and Bhikhu Parekh (eds), *Crisis and Change in Contemporary India* (Sage, 1995), 122–49.

[125] Anurag Bhaskar, *The Foresighted Ambedkar: Ideas That Shaped Indian Constitutional Discourse* (Penguin, 2024).

[126] Ambedkar, 'Annihilation of Caste'.

formation that was built on equality amongst its citizens, unlike the inequality that existed amongst the colonised for centuries based on a notion of *dharma*, the divinely ordained duty prescribed in ancient Hindu law, or the Dharmashastra.[127] Dharma is thus an understanding of legal duty derived from Hindu religious scriptures that individuals carry, and must perform, based on the role assigned to them by their caste status at birth.[128] Ambedkar argued that 'what the Hindus call religion is really Law or at best legalized class-ethics'.[129]

The equality principle in the Indian Constitution, which is predicated on non-discrimination, counters the imposition of such an eternally fixed caste-based understanding of duty, including a duty not to engage in education, in the case of those who are Dalits or belong to lower castes. In countering such authoritative conceptions of duty, the enactment of the Constitution in 1950, among other things, opened access to locations from where some people had historically been excluded due to their caste affiliations.[130] Public educational institutions have since been made subject to affirmative legal action – such as reservations – with the intent of a redistribution of the field of intellectual labour.[131] However, although this measure has created access, there is documentary evidence which shows how caste-based exclusion is still prevalent in academia and

[127] Ludo Rocher, *Studies in Hindu Law and Dharmasastra*, ed. Donald R. Davis (Anthem Press, 2013); Patrick Olivelle and Donald R. Davis (eds), *Hindu Law: A New History of Dharmasastra* (Oxford University Press, 2017).

[128] Scholars have argued that this understanding of dharma, or a divine duty, is fundamental to Hindu law and jurisprudence, and the Dharmashastra is 'an intellectual tradition associated with Brahmin communities and worldviews'. See Donald R. Davis, Jr, 'Introduction', in Olivelle and Davis, *Hindu Law*, 4.

[129] Ambedkar, 'Annihilation of Caste', 299.

[130] Article 15 of the Constitution: the state shall not discriminate against any citizen on the basis of religion, race, caste, sex, place of birth. Article 15(4) imposes an obligation on the state to pass positively discriminatory laws to achieve the end of non-discrimination for caste-based minorities. This provision has been interpreted to extend affirmative action or reservations in educational institutions for caste-based minorities. See Central Government Act, Article 15 in the Constitution of India, 1949, https://indiankanoon.org/doc/609295.

[131] See Ashwini Deshpande, *Affirmative Action in India*, Oxford India Short Introductions (Oxford University Press, 2013); Marc Galanter, *Competing Equalities: Law and the Backward Classes in India* (University of California Press, 1984).

attains further discriminatory proportions through its interlocking with gender, sexuality, religion and class.[132]

In the legal discipline, a notable example of how the practice of feminist legal knowledge is made to speak to the privileges of academic location vis-à-vis that of sex workers is found in the work of Prabha Kotiswaran. Kotiswaran develops a feminist account of labour law in India based on her conversations with sex workers' activist groups, her research participants.[133] She provides an account of sex workers' engagements with the 'work position' which, as she argues, has long been a concern for feminists.[134] She shows how, for instance, by fashioning their position as self-employed actors, sex workers alter tenancy relations in the sex market and institute an alternative conception of labour relations.[135]

Kotiswaran characterises her empirical research with sex workers as socio-legal scholarship, as opposed to 'ethnography'.[136] In doing so, her work joins a long-standing feminist jurisprudential scholarly field that is predominantly constituted by socio-legal scholarship. Kotiswaran notes that during her research, she grappled with the fact that her position as an academic researcher carried the hierarchies of privilege into her conversations with sex workers.[137] She addressed this hierarchy by sharing her 'professional expertise as a lawyer' with her participants during fieldwork, which was motivated by her commitment to feminist advocacy and praxis.[138]

Thus, my adda with sex workers is not the first instance of such a conversation in the field of Indian feminist jurisprudence. But the juxtaposition of this conversation alongside a conversation with academics, and consequently my demonstration of how both groups co-create the knowledge that produces the field, are new. My project is to make visible the privilege and superiority that the notions of academic expertise work

[132] See Samson K. Ovichegan, *Faces of Discrimination in Higher Education in India: Quota Policy, Social Justice and the Dalits*, Routledge Research in Educational Equality and Diversity (Routledge, 2015); Varsha Ayyar, 'Caste-Gender Matrix and the Promise and Practice of Academia' (2017) 52(50), *Economic and Political Weekly*.

[133] Kotiswaran, *Dangerous Sex, Invisible Labor.* [134] Ibid., 10.

[135] Ibid., chapter 5, 'Born Unto Brothels: Sex Workers in a Kolkata Red-Light Area', 137.

[136] Ibid., 19. [137] Ibid.. [138] Ibid.

to activate by distancing legal wisdom from everyday experiences and living. My unease with that arises from the fact that such notions of expertise are tied to caste hierarchy, as well as make legal wisdom and knowledge captive within legal academia and a product of academic methods alone.

A key outcome of the logic of caste is a mind–body hierarchy. The mind–body hierarchy, simply put, results in the privileging of theoretical analysis of law over empirical data.[139] A conventional understanding of theory is that it is the framework by which we explain and give meaning to data through interpretation. It is analysis that turns data or information into knowledge – requiring the application of the legal mind. Subsequently, the analytical or knowing mind takes precedence over the experiencing body and the researcher gains primacy over her subjects. Therefore, by virtue of this ordering, the researcher gains superiority over those whose experiences they come to know and shape as knowledge through their research. This is the logical structure of our expertise-driven research culture and practices underlined by caste.

As feminists and lawyers, questions of justice and fairness in law and in the world are things that we care about. So, we often worry about hierarchies in social relations and their legal implications. Similarly, the underlying mind–body hierarchy in research practices warrants our attention since it orders research relations hierarchically – and we become agents of it – because we carry out such relations. And this hierarchy is written into the performance of our role – it has nothing to do with being a bad researcher, it is the default condition of intellectual labour. The question is should we worry about it? Yes, we do, if we think it is worth worrying about unjust structures.

This book, therefore, aims to show how the practices of people who *do not* appear knowledgeable or as thinking minds, and those who *do*, together produce the field. So, rather than engaging in a critique of how the caste system marginalises sex workers, my engagement is directed at inverting the hierarchical value system of caste that embeds how we perceive sex worker practices of collectivisation vis-à-vis

[139] Gopal Guru and Sundar Sarukkai, *The Cracked Mirror: An Indian Debate on Experience and Theory* (Oxford University Press, 2017).

academics' practices of scholarly writing in imaginative and performative terms.[140] I show that the activist thoughts and practices of sex worker groups that inform their engagements with law through collectivisations are on a par with academic discourses of law, and collaborate in the productions of Indian feminist jurisprudence. With this, sex workers emerge as bearers of their own thoughts and practices of law and not only as subjects of discourses belonging to others, such as myself or other academic researchers.

I engage in adda with sex workers about their practices of collectivisation, and with academics about their practices of scholarship, to work out how their experiences at particular locations inform their diverse ways of thinking about and practising their relations with law. Thus, the fieldwork consists of conversations with both scholars and activists. The academics and the sex workers are disparately located. My obligation is to work out a practice of engagement with research participants so that neither the position of the researcher, nor those of sex workers and academics, can be assumed to have any more understanding and experience of law than others. This is necessary so that every participant is an interlocutor and can speak with the same degree of authority. As you will see, the performances of adda that take place in this book institute a mode of *speaking* and *listening* with the research participants, which enables a sharing of authority in the field of intellectual labour and enables our relations to be founded on a counter-hierarchical method of collaborative conversations.

[140] Historically, the segregation and distancing of Dalits and people of oppressed castes from academia and practices of knowledge production have been intrinsically related to the acts of extreme violence carried out against them by people of the oppressor castes. Simply put, the lack of access to education is closely tied to the continuance of social, cultural, economic and legal structures that enable, condone and exacerbate violence against Dalits and people of lower caste, in ways which are both physical and psychic. See generally, Anand Teltumbde, *The Persistence of Caste: The Khairlanji Murders and India's Hidden Apartheid* (Zed Books, 2010); Praveen Donthi, 'How Caste Shaped the Experience of Rohith Vemula and Other Students at the University of Hyderabad', *Caravan*, 24 August 2016, https://caravanmagazine.in/vantage/caste-shaped-experience-rohith-vemula-students-university-hyderabad; *Scroll.in*, '2016 Una Flogging Incident: Dalit Victim Writes to President, Asks for Mercy killing', 28 November 2018, https://scroll.in/latest/903757/2016-una-flogging-incident-dalit-victim-writes-to-president-asks-for-mercy-killing.

A ROADMAP FOR THE BOOK

The book is divided into two parts. Part I, 'Setting the Stage', prepares the reader for the performances of my method. It comprises Chapters 1 and 2. Chapter 2 explains how I have conceived adda as a method by drawing from and combining post-colonial, feminist and jurisprudential thought. Part II is titled 'Performing Adda'. It comprises Chapters 3–5, which demonstrate the performances of adda with sex workers and legal academics. The adda with sex workers is presented first (Chapters 3 and 4), followed by a presentation of the adda with academics (Chapter 5). These chapters draw out the distinct forms of jurisprudence that are born out of the activist and academic practices of life and law. The performances of adda in these chapters work to present sex workers' collectivisation and the academics' scholarship as a conjoined set of experiences that together produce a field of Indian feminist jurisprudence.

An in-depth engagement with the sex workers' activist literature is not yet available in a scholarly discussion of Indian feminist jurisprudence, so I discuss the entire gamut of activist publications produced by DMSC and VAMP, and dedicate two separate chapters to the reading of these materials. By doing this, I have organised the book according to a non-linear timeline. This means that although the publication of the Open Letter by Baxi and others (in 1979) precedes the temporality of the writing of the sex workers' activist documents, which happened much later (1995 onwards), a discussion of the activist documents appear first. The discussions of the Open Letter and *Subversive Sites* have been combined in one chapter to assert how academics, although they speak from within academia, think and act differently in relation to law and their own specific times and places.

The performances of adda in Chapters 3–5 unfold in two interrelated threads. In the first, I follow the pattern of correlations between law and social experiences that have received explicit attention in the works of scholars that make up the field of Indian feminist jurisprudence.[141] I have, therefore, attended to how the legal academics

[141] 'Pattern of correlations' here refers to what Shaun McVeigh, borrowing from C. F. Black, calls a patterning of lawful relations, i.e., as he explains: 'patterning might be thought of as a way of finding, or finding yourself in, relations of law'. Shaun McVeigh, 'Conditions of Carriage: Finding a Place' (2017) 21, *Law Text Culture*, 165, 167.

and sex workers have correlated law and the social experiences of gender/class/caste/sexuality/religion. The second thread develops the methodological argument of this book by carving out how the sex workers and academics actively experience mutual relations between their lives and law through collectivisation and scholarship respectively.

A note on why I have chosen these particular groups of sex workers and academics, and not others, may seem necessary. Even as I say 'academics' and 'sex workers', taking them to be a collective entity, I do not mean to suggest that these are homogenous groups or that my select set of people are representatives who can speak for all members of their group. On the contrary, my choice of interlocutors has to do with foregrounding the differences between the groups.

The DMSC and VAMP are both sex worker–led collectives, but they are very different in terms of their composition, scale and approach to law. The choice of Baxi and Kapur has to do with the fact that, although they are established legal scholars, both have shared a tenuous relationship with Indian feminisms: Baxi, because he is a man and is known more for his work on constitutional and human rights law, is seldom identified as a feminist scholar; Kapur, because she has been based outside of India for several years, is recognised more as a post-colonial legal scholar than as an 'Indian' feminist. The differences amongst the sex worker groups, and amongst the academics, help to make visible the diversities amongst the locations and experiences of all my interlocutors and the specificities of their practices of life and law.

ON STYLE

The book is a documentation or a record of my practice of adda and is written in the form of a report. As the author, I am reporting to the reader how, as I learnt and wrote about Indian feminist jurisprudence, I trained myself to practise a method that is, rather than an analysis, an enactment of a relational form of being and knowing.[142] The author–

[142] This description of my project is borrowed from Margaret Davies who provided me with some of the expressions and language to communicate my project to the reader in this way. She was a reader and examiner of my PhD thesis, from which this book emerges.

reader relationship that I envision through the reporting, therefore, is not didactic. As you will see, adda as in the method of this book is not a set of instructions for righteous engagement in the field of feminist and legal research.

Adda as a method of research is neither generalisable nor formulaic. In and of itself, adda is not readily available as a method for research, for it requires its doers and practitioners to bring it to life. With the change of place, and its doers, the content of adda varies. Even as adda is pragmatic, it is not programmatic, since the relations that found adda are always contextual, and therefore, dynamic. There is no perfect adda. Adda's training lies in its doing and redoing. Thus, it requires consistent training and practise in context to work it out as a method for research.

I adopt this experimental method to tell a story about how a field of legal knowledge comes to be formed in the context of a particular place and its history. The tone set by this book is in line with the style and genre of report writing. The book is an invitation to its reader to take on the role of an attentive listener. The invitation is a request for tuning-in to a style of scholarship that is enacted through adda and is about being receptive to relational engagements as much as about conceptual grip and clarity on a field.

CHAPTER 2

Adda as Method

> True conversation demands both listening and speaking skills. It requires open-mindedness, patience, a degree of safety and a willingness to change. To listen to others means sometimes to quiet oneself. To speak to others means sometimes to feel unsure, vulnerable.[1]
>
> ... adda, that favourite Bengali activity of energetic debate and raucous dissent.[2]
>
> The politics of the world says: grab; the politics of our adda says, let go.[3]

In the context of a Bengali post-colonial life, adda belongs to an artistic and literary genre where it is neither solely text-based nor only about public or published texts, but is embedded in a linguistic tradition in oral or *moukhik* form. Moukhik, in Bangla, refers to that which is tied to speech and what is spoken, as well as the expressional.[4] In other words, adda is as much about the content of speech as it is about the style, manner, gestures or conduct of its participants.

[1] Penny Weiss, 'Conversation as Method', in *Conversations with Feminism: Political Theory and Practice* (Rowman & Littlefield, 1998), 3.

[2] Chakraborty, 'Being Bengali', 5. For another account in a popular feature film depicting the role of adda as integral to Bengali-ness and an educated, middle-class Bengali culture, see Satyajit Ray, *Agantuk* ('The stranger'), released in 1991, https://en.wikipedia.org/wiki/Agantuk.

[3] Buddhadeva Bose, 'Adda' (Rosinka Chaudhuri, trans.), in Amit Chaudhuri (ed.), *Memory's Gold: Writings on Calcutta* (Penguin Viking, 2008), 276.

[4] Sailendra Biswas, *Samsad Bengali–English Dictionary* (3rd ed., Sahitya Samsad, 2000), 885; see generally Shabnam Virmani and Ajab Shahar Team, 'Maukhik Parampara: Oral Traditions' (*Ajab Shahar*, 15 March 2021), http://ajabshahar.com/words/details/66/Maukhik-Parampara. Accessed 15 March 2021.

Adda is an integral part of Bengali life and literature. It has been widely talked about and depicted in literature, art and cinema. Adda is both a place of assembly and an art of conversation. Although linguistic variations may somewhat alter its meaning, these are the two ways in which the term is primarily understood. In the northern parts of India, where people mostly speak Hindi, adda is a noun and denotes a place of gathering, like a bus station (bus adda). In Bengal, where I am from, adda is a verb. It denotes a very particular kind of action or activity or an occurrence of friendly, mutual conversation that is usually carried out between multiple actors.

All the different grammatical iterations and uses of adda share a sense of reciprocal exchange between participants, which is grounded in a place and time. No participant, insofar as conducting the actual activity of adda is concerned, need be either inferior or superior to the others, and some shared ground would have to exist among them to be a part of such conversations. In the way that it is practised in an everyday context, adda enables relations among people through engaged and pointed deliberations that are interpersonal in nature, and consist of wide-ranging subjects. As an oral tradition, it rests on the ability of its practitioners to engage in it cordially and skilfully as an art, and is a source of communal pleasure.[5] Adda is thus an act of coming together or a meeting of people for a reciprocal exchange of ideas and engagement in pleasurable dialogue with one another, freely and without any fixed or predetermined end in view.[6]

The Bengali preoccupation with adda is well illustrated in the following scene from Satyajit Ray's film *Agantuk* (The stranger).[7] The scene takes place in a living room where, over a cup of tea, two men – an anthropologist and an actor – are debating the role of adda in shaping the world of arts and culture of the educated Bengali middle class. It is a conversation *about* adda that is taking place as the two characters engage

[5] Dipesh Chakrabarty, *Provincializing Europe: Postcolonial Thought and Historical Difference* (Princeton University Press, 2007), 205.

[6] Buddhdeva Bose, 'Adda', in Amit Choudhary, *Memory's Gold: Writings on Calcutta* (Penguin, 2008), 273.

[7] Satyajit Ray, *Agantuk* (1991), https://en.wikipedia.org/wiki/Agantuk. Accessed 15 March 2021.

in adda themselves. Even as the two characters ascribe meaning to adda and try to trace its source, they do it in and through adda.

R: Football, and one other thing, that you must be missing abroad, are the Bengalis' lifeblood.

M: What is that thing which I am missing?

R: Bengalis have a monopoly in that, you can also call it their invention.

M: *Rashogolla*?[8]

R: Adda! Unadulterated adda. Adda in the coffee house, near the lake, at the tea stall ... without which Bengalis are unable to digest their food. Adda-made-in-Bengal.

M: Allow me to contradict you, Mr. Rakshit. Do you know about the *akhra*, or Gymnasium, that existed in Greece almost two thousand five hundred years ago?

R: Oh, that place for physical exercise?

M: Not only for physical exercise. The Gymnasium was also the place to exercise the mind. In the *akhras* of Athens, Socrates, Plato, Alcibiades and other well-known intellectuals of their time would gather together and engage in intellectual conversations. They spoke about philosophy, politics, mathematics, art, literature ... *Dialogues*, which you can read even today. What will you call this?

R: Oh, this is nothing but one kind of adda ...[9]

As an everyday art of conversation that is devoid of a fixed agenda, adda is not useless banter. Through the act of meeting with others and engaging in adda, one's own knowledge about the world comes into being, in a pleasurable and leisurely manner. However, this leisurely aspect of adda is sometimes also identified with idleness, which is personified in the *adda-baaj*, one who is wasteful and whiles away valuable time. M, in the above instance from the film, is making a similar distinction between productive and unproductive adda. M, by his own

[8] 'A beloved confection of fresh milk curd and sugar syrup, rosogolla is most closely associated with the West Bengal sweets-making tradition.' Ishita Dey, 'Rosogolla', in Darra Goldstein (ed.), *The Oxford Companion to Sugar and Sweets* (Oxford University Press, 2015), 580.

[9] Translated from Bangla to English by the author.

admission a Marxist, is alluding to a decadent Bengali-ness that tends to pass off unproductive adda as an expression of high culture, whereas it is merely an excuse for irresponsibility. Although there can be no denying the fact that adda need not be idealised, it is a distinction between work and play that precedes the separation of productive adda from its non-productive counterpart.

The contest between work and play, as well as valuation of adda on these terms, does nothing to alter its intrinsic place in Bengali artistic and cultural life. For Bengalis, many scholars and literary writers have noted, the practice has nothing to do with its social benefits. Adda occupies a very special place by virtue of its role in shaping creativity, cultural consciousness and an aesthetic sensibility.

As is evident, adda is an act of collective and pleasurable immersion in the aesthetics of life and learning. Mere speaking *to* others does not qualify as adda. Rather, it is a particular manner of speaking *with* others that is embedded in a place and time as well as generates pleasure. Adda is a means of experiencing knowledge, that is gaining a worldview, by engaging in mutual speaking and listening that is physically and emotionally pleasurable. In terms of being an artistic expression, adda defies homogeneity and the dominance of any singular way of thinking, expressing and experiencing knowledge. Adda, performed aesthetically, shapes the habits of the mind and the senses. Adda is born out of forms of life and living that are a melting pot of different religions, languages and gastronomy. The appreciation of such aesthetics requires an appreciation for expressions and entanglements of diverse ideas, however much they may appear contradictory, unrelated or even irrelevant.

THE TRADITION OF ADDA

Adda is a recognised method of knowledge production in post-colonial theory that has been developed by scholars in the humanities. I work with adda and adapt it to perform, and thus experience, the relations that produce a field of feminist jurisprudence in India.[10] I performed

[10] French philosopher and sociologist Pierre Bourdieu argues that 'to think in terms of field is to think relationally'. Quoted in Ray, *Fields of Protest*, 6.

adda to do the fieldwork for this book. My practice of adda as an act and an activity for relating life and law involves three things. One, the discussions in this chapter about how I bring post-colonial, feminist and jurisprudential thought into conversation to shape and adapt my thinking of the practice of adda. Two, informed by my thinking, the performances of reciprocal conversations that I carry out with my interlocutors to interpret their texts and learn about how their lives and law mutually correlate. Three, the written presentations of such conversations through the discussions of the texts authored by my interlocutors (in Chapters 3–5). All of these activities together consist of the fieldwork, which is done to engage with/in the field of Indian feminist jurisprudence.

My articulation of the practice of adda in this book and its subsequent performance as a method – what I understand as fieldwork – is distinct from legal ethnography.[11] Through ethnographic fieldwork, anthropologists and ethnographers have productively engaged with the question of knowledge and its relationship with the conduct and experiences of everyday life.[12] In this respect, anthropologists and ethnographers share their concerns with jurisprudents who question and relate the

[11] Legal ethnography, which draws on the field of anthropology, can be loosely described as a method which has been developed by researchers to study the combined operations of law, society and culture. See Eve Darian-Smith (ed.), *Ethnography and Law* (Routledge, 2017).

[12] For anthropological and ethnographic works that have dealt with the question of the relationship between everyday life and knowledge, see Veena Das, 'What Does Ordinary Ethics Look Like?', in Michael Lambek, Veena Das, Didier Fassin and Webb Keane, *Four Lectures on Ethics: Anthropological Perspectives* (University of Chicago Press, 2015); Veena Das, 'Public Good, Ethics, and Everyday Life: Beyond the Boundaries of Bioethics' (1999) 128(4), *Daedalus*, 99; Veena Das, 'Ethics, the Householder's Dilemma, and the Difficulty of Reality' (2014) 4(1), *HAU: Journal of Ethnographic Theory*, 487; Veena Das, 'Ethics, Self-Knowledge, and Life Taken as a Whole' (2018) 8(3), *HAU: Journal of Ethnographic Theory*, 537; Deborah Bird Rose, *Reports from a Wild Country: Ethics for Decolonisation* (University of New South Wales Press, 2004); Deborah Bird Rose, *Hidden Histories: Black Stories from Victoria River Downs, Humbert River and Wave Hill Stations* (Aboriginal Studies Press, 1991); Annelise Riles, *The Network Inside Out* (University of Michigan Press, 2001); Annelise Riles, 'An Ethnography of Abstractions?' (2000) *Cornell Law Faculty Publications*, 781, https://scholarship.law.cornell.edu/facpub/781; Annelise Riles, *Collateral Knowledge: Legal Reasoning in the Global Financial Markets* (University of Chicago Press, 2011).

experiences of law and life.[13] Understandably, for the productions of feminist socio-legal scholarship, which is what Indian feminist jurisprudence primarily comprises, ethnography is increasingly being used by scholars/researchers. It is regarded as an effective mode of engaging in fieldwork for the purpose of understanding the lived experiences of law.[14] Although well established, the ethnographic method is neither in tune with the intent of my project, nor adequate for my argument.[15]

As a method, ethnography exclusively belongs in academia in terms of both its origin and use in practices of knowledge production. A corollary to its sole academic belonging is that the performance of ethnography might proceed with implicit assumptions of an academic researcher's expertise or specialised knowledge vis-à-vis such method, owing to her location in the scholarly world.[16] For the practical purposes of staging

[13] Jurisprudents: 'those who care for the conduct of lawful relations'. See McVeigh, 'Conditions of Carriage', 165.

[14] For examples of feminist legal ethnographic research in the Indian context, see Pooja Parmar, *Indigeneity and Legal Pluralism in India: Claims, Histories, Meanings* (Cambridge University Press, 2015); Srimati Basu, *The Trouble with Marriage: Feminists Confront Law and Violence in India* (University of California Press, 2015); Baxi, *Public Secrets of Law*; Gopika Solanki, *Adjudication in Religious Family Laws: Cultural Accommodation, Legal Pluralism, and Gender Equality in India* (Cambridge University Press, 2011). For an example of legal ethnography in another Southern context (but not feminist), see Luis Eslava, *Local Space, Global Life: The Everyday Operation of International Law and Development* (Cambridge University Press, 2015).

[15] As I mentioned in Chapter 1, Prabha Kotiswaran, who is also engaged in conversations with sex workers, has noted that the fieldwork she has conducted for her research is not a form of ethnography but socio-legal scholarship. Her argument for not calling her research ethnography is as follows: 'Anthropologists have critically reflected on what constitutes the "field" and fieldwork, and its importance for the professional identity of anthropologists ... Yet given the common understanding of ethnography as "the collection of information on the behavior of actors in a particular context over an extended period of time" ... I do not claim the status of ethnography for my empirical work, settling instead for the more legible but not always legitimate (within law schools anyway) category of "sociolegal" scholarship.' See Kotiswaran, *Dangerous Sex, Invisible Labor*, 19. However, in another article Kotiswaran describes her method as 'legal ethnography'. See Prabha Kotiswaran, 'Born Unto Brothels: Toward a Legal Ethnography of Sex Work in an Indian Red-Light Area' (2008) 33(3), *Law and Social Inquiry*, 579.

[16] In the context of indigenous communities, feminist scholars have put forth sharp critiques of anthropological ethnographic research by arguing that its use for studying non-western and indigenous societies and cultures is embedded in a discriminatory

the performances of adda, such an assumption, even if implicit, would establish hierarchy amongst the interlocutors within this book and be counterproductive to its objectives.

This book shows how the field of feminist jurisprudence is experienced and produced relationally in conversations. To counter the caste-based hierarchy in the field of intellectual labour, I seek to *also* demonstrate that the body of knowledge that constitutes Indian feminist jurisprudence is one that is shared amongst people belonging to the scholarly world and those who are commonly perceived to be outside of it. This is not an easy task. It requires a method that is both recognisable as scholarly and is commonly known so that the method may be jointly owned and shared by all participants, with academic affiliations and otherwise. Only through a shared ownership of the means of production can each of us hold positions within the field of feminist jurisprudence whereby our contributions will assume equal value.

The interlocutors in this book would have to speak in a similar capacity as co-owners of the means of knowledge production, because only then will I be able to meaningfully argue, through my conversations, that both groups jointly produce the field. This can happen if I am able to let go of my sole authority of interpretation and meaning making and perform my method as a shared activity along with my interlocutors. The reciprocal exchanges with my interlocutors, which is incumbent on my performances of adda, make it possible to consider the place and role of every participant as an interlocutor. This method also makes it possible for me to participate in adda and shape and experience my own position of researcher *as* interlocutor in the conversations that produce the field. Adda, in its everyday sense, is particularly helpful for the purposes of my argument because it is already grounded in the conduct of daily life and relations. As a living/lived discourse, the practice of adda is, therefore, potentially known and shared by all. This would not be the case for a method like ethnography, which is exclusively known and performed by

politics of knowledge production. They have argued that the history of this methodology is embedded in the history of colonialism and discriminations against aboriginal/indigenous people. See Linda Tuhiwai Smith, *Decolonizing Methodologies: Research and Indigenous Peoples* (Zed Books, 2012).

those in academia and/or engaged in scholarly practices of knowledge production.

The remainder of this chapter is organised so as to draw out the meaning and practices of adda, and how I have adapted it to demonstrate the productions of a field of Indian feminist jurisprudence. First, I will elaborate on the tradition of adda and its significance within post-colonial feminist thought and everyday life in India. Next, I will explain how I join adda with a jurisprudential tradition of the conduct of lawful relations to adapt the practice of adda as a particular method for doing Indian feminist jurisprudence. Finally, I will describe how I arranged for my adda with sex workers and legal academics. This section is an account of the modalities that I put in place to set up adda with my interlocutors in order for the performance of my engagement with their texts to materialise, which I report and document through Chapters 3–5.

ADDA IN POST-COLONIAL THOUGHT

One of adda's foremost proponents, novelist, playwright and journalist Buddhadeva Bose, described adda as an everyday art of conversation that leads to collaborative learning and knowledge production. In his essay 'Adda', Bose wrote that the practice was instrumental in shaping his consciousness of the world and played a major role in his emergence as a learned and literary figure. That is why, he noted, he was not a mere 'devotee' of adda but would be a 'priest' who would assume the task, in the essay, of speaking about 'its virtues'.[17] Bose's view of adda finds resonance in the words of prominent Bengali graphic artist, and member of the Communist Party of India, Debabrata Mukhopadhyay, who wrote, 'my education, whether in art or culture generally, is largely a contribution of adda'.[18]

In this book, however, I do not practise adda as a mode of consciousness raising, whether of my own or that of others.[19] Neither do I claim

[17] Bose, 'Adda', 272. [18] Chakrabarty, *Provincializing Europe*, 201.

[19] Consciousness raising has attained a place of prominence for law as a feminist method, particularly in feminist jurisprudence, through the work of American feminist legal scholar Catharine MacKinnon. See MacKinnon, *Toward a Feminist Theory of the State*. For a critique of MacKinnon's feminist standpoint and method, see Angela P. Harris, 'Race and Essentialism in Feminist Legal Theory' (1990) 42(3), *Stanford Law Review*, 581.

that it is an archetype for gaining a worldview or knowledge. Adda is *not* an idealised mode of engaging in feminist jurisprudential knowledge production that is applicable in all contexts. My performances of adda as a method are an adaptation of the everyday practice and not simply a replication of it.[20] I do adda as a practical method for relating the experiences of life and law in India. This means that I do adda as a particular activity of actual conversations with my interlocutors for reading and interpreting texts; and as an imagined, creative act or a staging of reciprocal relations through the conversations. I perform adda as a method for the specific purpose of taking up the responsibility of rendering reciprocal ties with, and amongst, my interlocutors, and between their lives and law.

In Indian academia, although not yet for the purposes of engaging with law, adda is already regarded as a scholarly method. Historian and post-colonial studies scholar Dipesh Chakrabarty uses adda to draw the linkages between everyday life and historicised discourses of post-colonial modernity. In his view, adda worked to close the gap between 'the word and the world' of historical discourses.[21]

Chakrabarty's account of adda is a point of origin for a historicised production of a discourse of modernity/modern thought out of the everyday operation of life at a post-colonial location.[22] He historicises

[20] The practice of adda in the everyday context is a means of conversation without a pre-decided end, and therefore can potentially flow in any direction. Gayatri Chakravorty Spivak has pointed out that the meaning and purpose of adda as 'free form chat with many focuses [where] no one tells anybody how long they will speak', gets defeated when the practice is put to the task of achieving a definitive end, within a fixed duration of time. My practice of adda in this book is an adaptation of a 'living discourse' and not merely a replication of its everyday conventions and protocols in entirety. I conduct adda with my interlocutors for the particular purpose of reading and interpreting the texts authored by them in order to write this book. Thus, the performance of adda in this book proceeds with a particular end in view and is time bound with respect to the completion of the writing of this account of Indian feminist jurisprudence. See Gayatri Chakravorty Spivak, 'Envisioning an Aesthetic Education in the Era of Globalisation', TLHEC8: Workshop with Prof. Gayatri Spivak, Teaching & Learning TV by UTLO (2014), www.youtube.com/watch?v=iMTzutBH5eM&feature=youtu.be.

[21] Chakrabarty, *Provincializing Europe*, 'Preface to the 2007 Edition: Provincializing Europe in Global Times', ix.

[22] Chakrabarty explains his choice of material as a deliberate gesture of engaging with 'material from the history of the social group [he] came from'. Ibid., xvi.

the experiences of the middle-class Bengali adda as a dialogue between tradition and modernity. He argues that the modernity born out of European life traditions was both similar and different from the confluence of non-European tradition and modernity that materialised in, and through, adda.[23] It was so on account of being shaped by a group of people whose notions of the traditional and the modern were produced through the intermingling of a European culture with their own as a result of colonialism.[24]

In Chakrabarty's account, adda was a tradition, as well as a point of origin for a unique Bengali post-colonial modernity. This form of modernity was both different from its European counterpart as it was not a mere imitation, and also similar as it was formed due to the colonial contact and the interconnections with Europe.[25] In showing adda as a collective practice that was responsible for birthing another kind of discourse about modernity by post-colonial subjects, Chakrabarty demonstrates how a different form of modernity was actively inhabited at a location other than Europe. This works to decentre Europe as *the* only source of modernity both in the sense of a period and an origin for historical thought. It also works to cast a post-colonial location, the *other* of Europe which is generally understood only as a site of traditions, as a site of the production of modern thought.

Chakrabarty, through his account of adda, blurs the demarcations between tradition and modernity to successfully perform his task of 'provincialising Europe'.[26] By showing how ideas of modernity and tradition met in, and through, Bengali adda, Chakrabarty illustrates its usefulness for bringing into conversation varied, even disparate,

[23] Ibid., chapter 7: 'Adda: A History of Sociality'. [24] Ibid.

[25] Social historian and cultural anthropologist Badri Narayan describes Chakrabarty's account of adda as a form of 'double-consciousness' marked by a joining of tradition and modernity. Badri Narayan, 'Margins and Politics: Introduction', in *The Making of the Dalit Public in North India: Uttar Pradesh, 1950–Present* (Oxford University Press, 2016), 5.

[26] In his preface to the book, Chakrabarty outlines the premise based on which he engaged in the scholarly task of provincialising Europe. He writes, 'To "provincialize" Europe was precisely to find out how and in what sense European ideas that were universal were also, at one and the same time, drawn from very particular intellectual and historical traditions that could not claim any universal validity.' Chakrabarty, *Provincializing Europe*, 'Preface to the 2007 Edition', xiii.

traditions of thoughts and practices. Chakrabarty's account is an imaginative take on the dwellings of scholarly discourse in the form of everyday adda, a way of social life specific to a location and its history.

Chakrabarty makes a note of certain concerns that have found a firm place in feminist thought. He elucidates that the separation between the private and public spheres operational in Bengali life at the time was mapped onto the everyday practices of adda and the discourses of modernity that it was instrumental in shaping.[27] Women's social inscription in the domestic sphere hindered their participation in public life, which they were not able to do as freely as their male counterparts.[28] So, the discourses of modernity that adda shaped in early twentieth-century colonial Bengal carried an overtly male point of view, because women were not its active participants as often as men.[29]

Taking up Chakrabarty's work on adda is helpful as it assists in thinking about the practice as a scholarly method for correlating the lived and the written discourses of Indian feminist jurisprudence, as well as historicising them.[30] But how does the thinking and practice of adda become a feminist method that is adequate for demonstrating the experiences and productions of Indian feminist jurisprudence? I draw the intellectual resources to think about the practice of adda as a feminist method from the work of Indian literary thinker Gayatri Chakravorty Spivak, particularly from her article 'Can the Subaltern Speak?',

27 Ibid., 207.

28 Chakrabarty notes that this separation of the public and private spheres of life meant that women, whose socially legitimate place at the time was within the private realm, had separate addas of their own. But because that is not his subject of study in the book, Chakrabarty's account of adda does not elaborate on how Bengali women's modernity was shaped through their own adda. See ibid.

29 According to Ann Genovese, 'The feminist … must pay attention to how relations are experienced, how they came to be one thing rather than another, for in that contingent space, drama, conflict and agency, reside. This includes being clear that questions of method and source are not separate.' Genovese, 'On Australian Feminist Tradition'. Chakrabarty's account of adda is informed by sources that are based on male experiences alone. As a method, this makes his account of adda a limited understanding of how the practice was/can be experienced across relations of gender.

30 For Chakrabarty, adda helped him close the gap between the lived and the written discourses of history. Chakrabarty, *Provincializing Europe*, 'Preface to the 2007 Edition', ix.

published in the 1980s.[31] I go to Spivak because she helps me think closely about research that, in any field, entails a representative task, and the nature of the performances of this task determine the replication or reorganisation of hierarchical relations and structures of knowledge. In a more concrete sense, she helps me see how adda, essentially an oral tradition, can be also envisioned as a textual practice.

Spivak posits reciprocal *speaking* and *listening*, as one must also do in adda, to be a feminist ethic and method of knowledge production. For her, speaking and listening between a scholar/thinker and her subject or the people she is writing about are a metaphor for a relational practice of taking up scholarly responsibility as a feminist.[32] In her account, conversation is an intellectual practice by which a critical scholar/thinker is able to relate with, and thus ethically narrate the experiences of, others who may be very different/similar to herself.[33] Speaking and listening are thus a practice of reciprocal relations, enabling the experiences of other people to be adequately represented within critical discourses even if these are the farthest from those of the person who is representing them, such as in case of subaltern subjects.

[31] The essay was published for the first time in 1985 in a journal called *Wedge*. It was titled 'Can the Subaltern Speak? Speculations on Widow Sacrifice'. In 1988, the essay was reproduced in an edited volume called *Marxism and the Interpretation of Culture* by Cary Nelson and Larry Grossberg. This time, the essay was simply titled 'Can the Subaltern Speak?' In 1999, Spivak revised the essay and published it as a chapter in her book, *A Critique of Postcolonial Reason: Toward a History of the Vanishing Present* (Harvard University Press, 1999).

[32] 'Subaltern as female cannot be heard or read.' Spivak, 'Can the Subaltern Speak?', 308; Gayatri Chakravorty Spivak, 'Subaltern Talk: Interview with the Editors', in Gayatri Chakravorty Spivak, *The Spivak Reader*, ed. Donna Landry and Gerald MacLean (Routledge, 1996), 287–308, 289. See also Gayatri Chakravorty Spivak, 'An Interview with Gayatri Spivak', by Sara Danius, Stefan Jonsson and Gayatri Chakravorty Spivak (1993) 20 (2), *boundary 2*, 24; Gayatri Chakravorty Spivak, 'An Interview with Gayatri Chakravorty Spivak: New Nations Writers Conference in South Africa', by Leon de Kock (1992) 23 (3), *Ariel: A Review of International English Literature*, 29, 46.

[33] Spivak's understanding of knowledge formation through conversation has strong resonances with the work of Italian feminist philosopher Adriana Cavarero. Cavarero speaks about how narrating the other's experiences through the relational means of friendship and dialogue can work against establishing discursive norms of identity and bring out the uniqueness of who we are. Adriana Cavarero, *Relating Narratives: Storytelling and Selfhood* (Routledge, 2014).

The term 'subaltern' refers to a social group that has no representation in democratic institutions, such as the state. It is a group whose subaltern status is predicated upon a lack of access to social mobility across class, caste and gendered structures, due to the non-representation of their interests and desires within democratic structures.[34] My interlocutors – sex worker activists and legal academics – are not subaltern in this sense because they are already in conversation with institutional structures such as the state, which is a part of what I will document in the rest of the chapters. Still, Spivak's account of adda is useful for two reasons.

One, it helps to demonstrate how adda can be thought as a method and a practice of reciprocal conversations with my interlocutors for relating with and narrating their experiences of life and law. Two, it demonstrates how a doing of adda can facilitate a relationship between disparate ideas and practices that are historically not on a par with each other in so far as their contributions to knowledge production are concerned (namely, the activism of sex workers and the scholarship of legal academics vis-à-vis the productions of Indian feminist jurisprudence).

Representations of the 'Third World woman' in critical discourses, contrary to their promise, often worked to alienate her from her own experience.[35] In doing so, the intellectual labour of critical scholars/thinkers, and their means of discourse, relegated the Third World woman to the status of a subaltern subject, serving the ends of the colonial project.[36] Spivak argues that it is only when a subaltern as woman is called into relation through careful listening that her speech becomes audible, and a meaningful representation of her experiences, comprising both her experiential similarities and differences, becomes possible.[37]

[34] See Swapan Chakravorty, Suzana Milevska and Tani E. Barlow, *Conversations with Gayatri Chakravorty Spivak* (Seagull Books, 2006), 62; Spivak, 'An Interview with Gayatri Chakravorty Spivak', by Leon De Kock, 45.

[35] Spivak, 'Can the Subaltern Speak?', 280.

[36] Spivak writes, 'Western intellectual production is, in many ways, complicit with Western international economic interests.' Ibid., 271.

[37] Spivak, 'Subaltern Talk', 287–308.

Spivak's concern is not limited to the accuracy of representations of gendered experiences; neither is it limited by an intention to expose inappropriate modes of intellectual productions about the experiences of a subaltern woman. Spivak demonstrates that the subaltern as woman is shaped based on how, and the positions from where, she is spoken for and/or of, and represented. The subaltern as woman, or as gendered subject, is shaped and inflected not just by an existing social male/female binary, but also due to the way in which her speech is represented within discourses.

On the question of representation, 'Can the Subaltern Speak?' is particularly insightful. Spivak draws attention to how the scholarly task of relating the experiences of others or representing them in discourses may be understood as a relational activity. For her, representations are of two kinds – *Vertreten* and *Darstellen*.[38] *Vertreten* is 'representation as "speaking for", as in politics', and *Darstellen* is '"re-presentation", as in art or philosophy'.[39] The former is in the nature of a narration, which is a direct account of experiences, or relating what *is*. The latter is a rendering of an image, one that is more imaginative and is shaped by relating with the experiences of others in a manner that is desirable (politically and ethically).[40] Moreover, while a 'speaking for' tends to relay the other's experiences through substitution, 're-presentation' is a mode of relating and recounting other people's experiences whereby the relationship between oneself and others (who may be similar/different) is acknowledged.

Spivak argues that feminist knowledge production that is enabled through conversations is a mode of representation that 'entails both a standing-in-the-other's-shoes and an imaginative and aesthetic re-presentation, a staging in the theatrical sense'.[41] Conversations, thus, are a specific kind of feminist practice for Spivak; while they are a means of learning about and relaying others' concrete experiences by acting as

[38] Spivak, 'Can the Subaltern Speak?', 276. [39] Ibid., 275.

[40] Ibid., 275, 276; see Sarah Harasym (ed.), *Gayatri Chakravorty Spivak: The Post-colonial Critic – Interviews, Strategies, Dialogues* (Routledge, 1990), 108; Gayatri Chakravorty Spivak, *The Spivak Reader*, ed. Donna Landry and Gerald MacLean (Routledge, 1996), 16.

[41] Spivak, *The Spivak Reader*, 16.

a substitute for them (proxy), they are simultaneously an imaginative rendering (portrait) of such experiences in an ethical or relational way.

Spivak's notion of conversations resonates with Chakrabarty's account of adda in one significant way. Their point of convergence is that both make it possible to think of the practice as a scholarly method for correlating divergent and disparate experiences. What Spivak specifically argues, and what proves useful for me, is that reciprocal conversation is a means of representing other people's experiences, and a feminist mode of ethically engaging in intellectual practices, by relating and reading texts.[42] She helps me think of adda as reciprocal acts of speaking and listening and as a way of taking responsibility for one's feminist worldview through the representations of others. Spivak helps me think of adda as an act and an activity for taking up the responsibility to read and interpret other people's texts through reciprocal conversations with them for the purpose of relating with, and representing, their experiences.

I perform adda, drawing from Spivak, in the senses of both proxy and portrait. This means that I do adda as an act and activity of relating the experiences of my interlocutors by both recounting and reimagining these. In the following chapters, the performances of adda through which the activist and academic texts are read will unfold in two interrelated threads. In the first, I relate how legal academics and sex workers articulate the correlations between the experiences of law and the social categories of gender/class/caste/sexuality/religion (a representation through proxy); in the second thread, I develop the methodological argument of the book, through an imaginative rendering of how sex workers' practices of collectivisation and the scholarly practices of legal academics may be acknowledged as related activities that jointly produce

[42] In this context of the ethics of critical legal scholarship's engagement with other people's worlds and experiences, Margaret Davies writes, 'The key to world travelling . . . is that it is not done imperialistically to appropriate or assimilate the other's world. It must be done openly, with an attitude of playfulness, creativity and acceptance towards the other: this is an attitude which, however, cannot be practised in hostile worlds.' Adda, for me, enables a mode of working through hostility even if it may not repair hostility. Margaret Davies, 'Ethics and Methodology in Legal Theory: A (Personal) Research Anti-manifesto', 6 *Law Text Culture*, 7 (2002) 19.

a field of Indian feminist jurisprudence (a representation through portrait).

So far, adda has come to mean a way of imagining a reciprocal relationship with others through a reading and interpretation of the others' text. The relationship pertains to a reciprocity of ideas between one who is engaged in knowledge production and the others whose experiences she is representing or documenting. This, however, does not automatically make adda an adequate method for demonstrating the experiences and productions of a feminist jurisprudence. It is this question that I will address next.

HOW ADDA MEETS WITH JURISPRUDENCE

The performances of adda in the later chapters of this book pertain to the practices of the sex worker activists, a group of persons who mostly do not have any formal educational training; the other part pertains to the practices of two renowned legal academics. This means that there already exists a disparity between the two groups, and consequently the texts they have authored do not lend themselves to be read as equally meaningful for understanding the mutual ties between life and law in post-colonial India. So, just engaging in a conversation with them about their texts does not enable me to accord equal value to the diverse thoughts and practices by which they accord meaning to law. Unless further attention is paid to working out how I can take the responsibility of calling them into a different relation with law/jurisprudence, a feminist understanding of adda, as derived from Spivak, becomes only partially viable as a method.

JURISPRUDENCE AS CONDUCT OF LIFE AND LAW

I will now turn to works of jurisprudence that I find useful for shaping and adapting adda for the specific purpose of relating the disparate experiences of life and law of my interlocutors. I particularly draw on the works of Australian jurisprudents Ann Genovese and Shaun McVeigh for whom, as I understand, jurisprudence has to do with how we think about law and organise everyday life and conduct our relations, lawfully. Among other things, doing jurisprudence means to care for law by taking responsibility for law's hierarchies and engaging in its reorganisation through a lawful conduct in everyday lived relations. The understanding and practice of the conduct of lawful relations are not identical for McVeigh and Genovese. However, both scholars understand the conduct of lawful relations as a tradition that is both lived and may be practised as a method for knowledge production about the relationship between life and law. Binding adda with their legal thought, I shape it as a method that is adequate to my task.

OFFICE

In *Jurisdiction*, where McVeigh writes with Australian feminist legal historian Shaunnagh Dorsett, they speak about the conduct of lawful relations in the everyday context of one's relations at work or in office. They speak of one's duties and responsibilities of office as in public life at a particular location and time.[43] This would mean that thinking in jurisprudential terms relates to the exercise of authority as a legal scholar and as one occupying a particular office that entails the task of caring for law and attributing meaning to it by conducting lawful relations in public life.[44] Here, the exercise of authority assumes meaning not as an enactment of power but of responsibility. To exercise authority as a jurisprudent in this case denotes the act of speaking authoritatively about law in such a way that it can create an ethical relationship between oneself, others and law.

Dorsett and McVeigh argue that in the western common law tradition, jurisdiction is a technology and a practice by which a law, any law, attains meaning and authority at a place; and it is simultaneously a means of drawing a limitation on law's authority at that place. They argue that 'to approach law through jurisdiction is to approach law as an activity and a conduct of life'.[45] Conduct of lawful relations thought through jurisdiction works as a reminder particularly for those who work within a common law tradition. Jurisdiction helps to think about legal representation as a limited exercise of authority to speak in the name of law.[46] Jurisdiction ties law and authority to a place. Thus, thinking through jurisdiction helps in tethering and limiting law, and the understanding of

[43] Dorsett and McVeigh, *Jurisdiction*. [44] Ibid., 139. [45] Ibid. [46] Ibid., 4.

law carried by a subject who speaks as its representative, to the specific location of such a subject from where she speaks and conducts her life.

The conduct of lawful relations becomes a method of jurisprudence via the office and role of *a* jurisprudent, when the duties of such a role are shaped and inhabited in a particular way.[47] When, in the role of a jurisprudent, one adopts an ethic of care in fulfilling the responsibility of conducting relations lawfully at a place, such action takes on meaning as an activity and method of jurisprudence. In material terms, lawful relations are formed when, through one's conduct of everyday relations, her conceptions of life and law form a belonging with each other.[48]

As I see it, by writing about office, the authors respond to common law's historical ties with life in settler-colonial Australia, the location of the university at which they perform their official role and responsibilities in public life. It is, among other things, a way of assuming responsibility for the relationships that are enacted through common law's hierarchical relations with Australian Aboriginal land and its native people. It is a way of taking responsibility for common law's historical ties with a place and the hierarchical relations it has produced, to make them more lawful through one's conduct of relationships, whether at a university or any other institutional location. Thus, assuming one's role and duties in office as a jurisprudent is a way of caring for law and caring for others. And this is done by taking responsibility for the lawful participation and conduct of relations with others in public institutional life.

PERSONAE

In a related context, writing about what the conduct of lawful relations might mean, not just as a jurisprudent but also as feminist, Ann Genovese's work is insightful.[49] For Genovese, women's lived

[47] Ibid., 27. [48] Ibid., 16.

[49] The disparate set of scholarship by Ann Genovese that I draw from throughout this book has culminated into a book authored by her called *Feminist Jurisography: Law, History, Writing*. In her book, Genovese names her relational practice of jurisprudential knowledge production, 'feminist jurisography'. For an account of what it means to engage oneself in writing about law, feminism and history, as well as to bring these disciplines and their obligations into relation in context, see Ann Genovese, *Feminist Jurisography: Law, History, Writing* (Routledge, 2023).

experiences present a more complex scenario for thinking about one's institutional role and responsibilities as feminist. In general, women's marginal place within public life makes it difficult to think about the official responsibilities of a feminist or jurisprudent since, historically, women did not have a rightful place within public office/institutions. In Genovese's work, an account of feminist jurisprudence as a conduct of lawful relations becomes available, which is shaped specifically by thinking through the role and performances of a feminist persona. For Genovese, feminist jurisprudence denotes a law–life relationship of mutuality, shaped through the lawful conduct of the persona of a feminist and jurisprudent both in private and in public life.[50]

McVeigh, like Genovese, speaks about the conduct of lawful relations shaped through personae in 'Afterword: Office and the Conduct of the Minor Jurisprudent'.[51] McVeigh argues that the persona of a minor jurisprudent is like that of feminists who undertake work to create a new kind of feminist persona for experiencing public life. The minor jurisprudent, according to McVeigh, is also engaged in working out a juridical persona for participating in a public life not only shaped by the traditions of office and official role.[52] Both Genovese and McVeigh draw on the work of French philosopher Pierre Hadot to make their respective arguments about the conduct of personae as a method for jurisprudence by way of caring for law and relationships lived with others.[53] For Hadot, a philosophy of everyday life is concerned with asking the question, 'how should I conduct a life?'[54] What they imbibe from the tradition of philosophy that Hadot speaks about is a way of thinking about the responsibilities involved in the everyday conduct of life and relations as a jurisprudent and feminist.

The conduct of such a role, for them, consist of practical exercises that enable the shaping of the persona of a feminist or a minor jurisprudent, and acting and engaging in the world by taking responsibility

[50] Genovese, *Feminist Jurisography*, 95–121. [51] McVeigh, 'Afterword'. [52] Ibid., 501.

[53] Ibid.; Genovese, 'On Australian Feminist Tradition', 431; Genovese and McVeigh, 'Nineteen Eighty Three'.

[54] Ann Genovese, 'Inheriting and Inhabiting the Pleasures and Duties of Our Own Existence: *The Second Sex* and Feminist Jurisprudence' (2013) 38(1), *Australian Feminist Law Journal*, 41.

accordingly.[55] To put it simply, as I understand, McVeigh and Genovese join Hadot's philosophy of the conduct of life with their jurisprudential thinking on the conduct of lawful relations. Thus, by attaching what they see as the persona of a jurisprudent and the responsibilities and mode of engagement in public life required to be practised by such a persona, with Hadot's thinking on the philosophy of life, McVeigh and Genovese shape jurisprudence as a vocation.

They turn jurisprudence into a practical activity and a means of caring for law and its lived relations at a place, through such activity. In doing so, to me, they provide a means of thinking about my own performance of adda as a way of conducting and fulfilling my role as a feminist jurisprudent in India and taking up the responsibility of forming reciprocal relations with my interlocutors, and between their lives and law.

Genovese demonstrates what thinking about and practising the conduct of lawful relations might mean for a feminist project in law in a settler-colonial Australia.[56] She draws attention to the fact that thinking about how to conduct oneself and one's relations lawfully is significant for practising a feminist jurisprudence that is tied to a place and its lived traditions and history.[57]

For Genovese, conduct is a philosophical tradition, and a distinct feminist tradition. She argues that when conduct, jointly as a philosophical and a feminist tradition, is brought to a doing of jurisprudence, it helps to understand how law is experienced in place and time.[58] In the tradition of conduct, everyday practices as they attach to a disciplinary location or status or role or office, denote experiences of 'conscious and productive activity' that are undertaken for changing one's ways of knowing and living in the world.[59] This means that the daily practices undertaken as the feminist, the legal academic, the sex worker, the jurisprudent, attain meaning and significance for shaping and experiencing knowledge.

[55] Pierre Hadot, *Philosophy as a Way of Life: Spiritual Exercises from Socrates to Foucault* (Wiley-Blackwell, 1995).

[56] Genovese, 'On Australian Feminist Tradition'.

[57] Ibid.; Genovese, *Feminist Jurisography*, 122–38.

[58] Genovese, 'On Australian Feminist Tradition'; Genovese, 'Inheriting and Inhabiting'.

[59] Genovese, 'Inheriting and Inhabiting', 42.

Genovese argues that the doing of feminism and jurisprudence in the tradition of conduct involves consciously taking up roles and duties towards others *as* someone or something, and undertaking activities to fulfil such roles. The self, in Genovese's articulation, who is both a feminist and a jurisprudent, is not a persona that is formed *only* by external institutions and structures such as the state, patriarchy, colonialism, academia, the judiciary and so on. Such a persona is *also* shaped by one's worldview and the execution of role and duties that are consciously taken up in alignment with one's lawful imaginations of a life in a context. By performing a consciously chosen role and duties towards others as, say, a jurisprudent, feminist, researcher, teacher or activist, one is able to form relations ethically, or lawfully, for engaging in the productions of feminist knowledge about the experiences of law.

Genovese, and Dorsett and McVeigh, think about and practise the conduct of lawful relations differently, but broadly speaking they use it as a particular form of jurisprudence. In their accounts, conduct of lawful relations is a method of caring for and shaping law through lived activities at a place and time. It is a means of relating oneself and others with law by conducting one's life in a way such that responsibility may be taken for its hierarchical inheritances. In thinking about jurisprudence through conduct, one thinks of it in a way that is integral to oneself, the world and their own intimate and official relations, in a specific location and shaped by particular histories.

The way that Genovese and McVeigh make their arguments in their respective works through questions of role and persona in place and time, is particularly useful. What I learn and imbibe from them is a way of thinking about my practice of adda and taking up responsibility through such activity to fulfil my role as a researcher of feminist jurisprudence from India. For me, such responsibility involves two things. One, to make law and its particular experiences in the context of India visible through my representations of the practices of my interlocutors by way of both proxy and portrait. Two, to show that my interlocutors carry their own different roles/personae and responsibilities when they speak about law, which resonate in their conversations with me, but are also embedded in their texts and in relations outside the adda that I am reporting. This is how my performance of adda takes the shape of a scholarly method for doing and actively experiencing the productions of a feminist jurisprudence in India.

A significant aspect of how I execute my responsibility through the performances of adda is that it is not an identical activity in every location. My performance takes different forms based on the specific locations of my interlocutors, from where they speak about law. By doing this, I am also able to account for my own practice of listening, which is attuned to the distinctiveness of every location and how my interlocutors speak about and from them. Therefore, although my practice of adda remains similar at all four locations in terms of my intent to fulfil a particular kind of responsibility to demonstrate my argument, adda attains different forms based on where the reciprocal speaking and listening are conducted.

I have previously noted in this chapter that my understanding of fieldwork consists of the discussions in this chapter; the reciprocal oral exchanges that I carry out with my interlocutors in person to interpret their texts; and my written report of such conversations in Chapters 3–5. These activities together comprise the work that I do to engage with/in the field of Indian feminist jurisprudence and demonstrate how this body of knowledge is experienced and produced relationally in conversations. In the following sections, I will describe what preceded my performance of adda with my interlocutors. I will discuss how I arranged for the particular conversations with the sex workers of DMSC and VAMP, and with legal academics Ratna Kapur and Upendra Baxi, about their texts. With this, I complete the task of setting the stage and preparing the reader for my performances of adda, which will unfold through the next three chapters.

CONVERSATIONS WITH MY INTERLOCUTORS

My interlocutors in this book are a group of people with whom I have very different levels of familiarity and relationships. Growing up in Kolkata, I have known DMSC and its members personally since my first year of law school, which was about two decades ago. I did my first internship with the organisation on their anti-trafficking programme where, as a legal intern, my job was to conduct training workshops for sex workers on the constitutional rights of citizens in India. Ever since, I have remained a close associate with the sex workers' movement in Kolkata led by DMSC in various capacities as a researcher, filmmaker and friend. I was introduced to VAMP much later, after finishing my law degree, during my first job with a feminist, human rights organisation in Delhi where I worked as a research and advocacy officer. While DMSC's orientation was known to be predominantly Marxist, VAMP's orientation was overtly feminist and queer. Both DMSC and VAMP have played a major role in introducing me to feminist, queer and socialist thinking.

It is during my time as a law student, as I got introduced to DMSC, that I also came to know about both Upendra Baxi and Ratna Kapur, although their scholarship was never taught as part of my law school curriculum. I came to know about Kapur through my engagement with the sex workers' movement. She has been one of the key figures to have brought queer thought to build alliances between feminism and sex work, which is a very polarised and fraught discursive terrain in the Indian context and globally. It is only later that I met Kapur personally at conferences and other academic events and was introduced to her through common friends. Unlike all the other interlocutors, I met Upendra Baxi for the first time when I visited him at his residence in New Delhi to conduct my adda with him.[60] He is one of the most well-known legal scholars in India and anybody who has studied law in this country would know him by name, if not through his intellectual

[60] During the time of my visit, I was suffering from a serious illness and was about to undergo surgery. On the day that I conducted my conversation with him, I was especially unwell. On hearing this, and that I had travelled a long distance to come to their house, Prema Baxi, Upendra Baxi's partner and wife, took the trouble of preparing food that I was able to have in that condition. She said, 'if my daughter had travelled such a long distance to come to my house, wouldn't I have made something for her to eat?' Prema also informed me that my conversation with Baxi could not go on for too long owing to a health condition from which he was still recovering. In conventional feminist accounts, Prema's caring gestures towards me, a complete stranger, and her husband would lend itself to being read as a form of unpaid female domestic labour in the service of the professional pursuits of her male partner. But in my view, it *also* spoke of a practice of care in relating with others that was prevalent in their shared household. Prema's presence is peripheral to my adda, but my encounter with her bears testimony to the caring environment in Baxi's private life. This would have nurtured and sustained his scholarly productions and relations in public life, which are the focus of my enquiry.

contributions to the field. However, I came to know of Baxi through my activist circles outside of law school, where he was known for having skilfully crafted a bridge between his teaching, scholarship and activism. He was also known for his flamboyance in the law classroom and consistent engagement with the everyday life of law with a commitment to social justice.[61]

My conversations for this book with the sex workers and the legal academics were spread out over a period of four years from 2014 to 2017. I conducted them in two batches after acquiring ethics approval for these batches separately. I conducted conversations with sex worker activists from August 2014 to January 2015, after I received clearance from the Ethics Committee at the University of Melbourne. During these six months, I divided my time between Kolkata (West Bengal) and Sangli (Maharashtra), where DMSC and VAMP are respectively based. The months of November and December in 2014 were spent in Sangli, and the rest of the time was spent in Kolkata.

The confidentiality rule that is conventionally applied in research, particularly with marginalised communities, was not relevant in the present research. This is because the subject matter of the conversations, in the cases of sex workers and academics alike, pertained to published texts or texts that are made available in the public domain by the authors themselves. Although there were references to aspects of their private lives on account of the latter's significance in shaping their role/persona in public life, these were not the focal point of the conversations. Moreover, in the case of sex worker members of the DMSC, in particular, disclosure of identity is a crucial aspect of their practices of collectivisation. They do this to ensure that sex worker members of the collective are able to shape, and publicly present in conversations with others, a notion of a sex worker self that is not ashamed to be who she is. Thus, a university standard of research ethics had to be altered for conducting my conversations with the sex worker groups.

To be able to converse with sex workers who are part of the organisations, I had to seek ethics clearance from DMSC's and VAMP's own

[61] Arvind Narrain, Sitharaman Kakarala, Lawrence Liang and Sruti Chaganti, *Of Life and Law: Upendra Baxi in Conversation* (Orient Blackswan, 2024).

internal ethics committees. The committees consist of sex worker members and also non–sex workers who are part of their organisations. This process of ethical clearance has to be followed by any researcher who wishes to interview sex workers who are part of the two organisations. This measure has been put in place to guard against incidents of malpractice by researchers, such as misrepresentation of sex workers' views.[62]

I began by collecting all activist documents the organisations had produced. After familiarising myself thoroughly with these documents, I interviewed sex workers who hold leadership positions within the organisations. Both organisations put me in touch with one of their staff as a contact person. I discussed my plans with them in detail and prepared a list of names of activists who I wanted to interview, based on my own knowledge of the organisations' activities, as well as their suggestions.

Each one of my participants spoke to me as an official representative of their respective organisations, and of their collective activism. My conversations benefited immensely from my prior associations with the sex workers at these organisations forged through other research work that I have done with them.[63] Due to my long-term association with the sex workers of DMSC and VAMP, I did not experience difficulties in gaining access and setting up conversations with the sex workers.[64] My level of familiarity with DMSC members, however, was greater than that with members of VAMP.

The conversations were mostly held within the two organisations' office premises, which were always buzzing with activity. One could hear sounds of laughter and a lot of talking going on. At DMSC, sex workers

[62] See generally, 'VAMP Protests against *Prostitutes of God*', https://directorsnotes.com/2010/10/12/vamp-protests-against-prostitutes-of-god (VAMP protest video against the documentary film *Prostitutes of God*); *Telegraph*, 'What Are Little Girls Made Of? Nightmares on Celluloid', Letters to the Editor, 15 March 2005, www.telegraphindia.com/opinion/letters-to-editor-15-03-2005/cid/1022371 (DMSC protest letter against documentary film *Born into Brothels*).

[63] See generally, Oishik Sircar and Debolina Dutta, 'Beyond Compassion: Children of Sex Workers in Kolkata's Sonagachi' (2011) 18(3), *Childhood*, 333; Debolina Dutta and Oishik Sircar (dir.), *We Are Foot Soldiers* (PSBT India, 2015), www.youtube.com/watch?v=Bfm06qBo4c4; Debolina Dutta, 'Brushstrokes: The Sound of Laughter', *In Plainspeak*, 18 January 2016, www.tarshi.net/inplainspeak/brushstrokes-the-sound-of-laughter.

[64] See, generally, Kotiswaran, *Dangerous Sex, Invisible Labour*, 17.

were always coming and going from their offices, appearing to be in a rush, wearing a more official demeanour than those at VAMP. Sex workers at VAMP had the appearances of homely, rural women and the pace of their activities was much more leisurely. I also conducted conversations with sex workers and staff members of the organisations between meetings, and while travelling from one place to another. This was the case especially at VAMP where I was unfamiliar with the area, and the organisation's offices were located far away from each other, so someone from the organisation usually accompanied me to the next meeting. For instance, I travelled to Miraj, a nearby district of Sangli, to conduct some of my interviews.

At both organisations, I noted the prevalence of a similar ritual that contributed to the shaping of my researcher position in the sex workers' view prior to my conversations with them. When non–sex workers from outside visit the sex workers, they are expected to drink tea served and prepared by sex workers, or at least drink tea *with* them. This is a practice that sex workers use to decide upon their own manner of engagement in conversations with an outsider.

For DMSC, this practice is an explicit strategy for determining the attitude of their visitor towards sex workers. To them, sharing food symbolises breaking the barriers of stigma and establishing respect for the women. So a refusal to drink tea with sex workers is read as prejudicial. Given my prior knowledge of the significance of this practice, this ritual became an integral part of the way in which I conducted my conversations with the sex workers. During my conversations with sex workers both at DMSC and at VAMP, I thus sipped on many more cups of tea than I desired, no matter the time of day.

At DMSC, I spoke with seven sex worker activists and three non–sex worker members who are integral to DMSC's activist work. This includes their two advocacy officers, the son of a sex worker who was one of DMSC's founding members, and the person they call their technical advisor, a medical doctor who was instrumental in the formation of the organisation. All the interviews were individual conversations, and with some of the participants I spoke more than once. All the sex workers interviewed at DMSC identified as female; transgender members were not available during my visit.

At VAMP, I conducted conversations with thirteen members: ten sex worker activists and three non–sex worker members of the organisation. Two of the three non–sex worker participants were sons of sex workers and had been associated with the sex workers' movement for a long time. The other person was a well-known feminist activist who, along with the sex workers, was instrumental in founding VAMP. I also held three group discussions. One of these was done with a group of three transgender sex workers who were members of an allied organisation called Muskaan. It was formed under the aegis of VAMP, especially for representing the unique needs and demands of the transgender sex worker community. All three, right at the start of the conversation, insisted that they be identified as a third gender that denoted *both* male and female, and needed to be distinguished from male *to* female transgender, or trans-women.[65] The point of distinction here was an assertion that their gendered position did not represent a transitioning from one to the other, but held the qualities and essence of both in equal measure. One of them introduced herself also as a *jogappa*, or a man-woman who was married to the Hindu goddess Yellamma.[66]

Most of the sex workers at VAMP asked me to introduce myself first and wanted to listen to why I had come to speak with them. It was the sex workers themselves who, on it being explained to them that my intent was to understand, among other things, how their collective was formed, urged me to conduct conversations with groups and not just individuals. The rationale they provided to me for following this practice was this: because their activism is carried out as a community of sex workers, it was important that they conversed with me also as a group, and not just individually. They explained that VAMP didn't believe in having individual leaders. Whoever wanted to take leadership at any given point of time could do so; it was not a fixed role and certainly not an individual one. Moreover, I was told, because my intent was to understand the processes

[65] See generally, Gayatri Reddy, *With Respect to Sex: Negotiating Hijra Identity in South India* (University of Chicago Press, 2005).

[66] Nicholas J. Bradford, 'Transgenderism and the Cult of Yellamma: Heat, Sex, and Sickness in South Indian Ritual', in Gary David Comstock and Susan E. Henking (eds), *Que(e)rying Religion: A Critical Anthology* (A&C Black, 1997), 294–310.

behind their collective formation, my research would benefit from speaking with them collectively.

I had ethics approval to have only individual conversations and not group discussions, so listening to them would be a deviation from what had been authorised by the ethics committee. Moreover, my consent forms were not designed to record their permission for using the content of what they spoke collectively. However, I still decided to listen to their proposition. If I did not comply with their decision about how *they* wished to grant me consent to use the information that *they* shared about *their* activism, it would be a breach of my own responsibility of conducting adda lawfully as a reciprocal exchange of mutual speaking and listening. For positioning sex workers as my interlocutors, it was important to arrive at a mutual consensus and not impose my decision on them. Otherwise, it would interfere with my performance of adda. Sharing the decision-making process between myself and them in this matter would only work to make the conversations more ethical.[67]

My discussion sessions with sex workers at DMSC were carried out in Bangla, and with sex workers at VAMP, in Hindi. Bangla is my mother tongue and Hindi is India's national language. I am fluent in both. On some occasions when the sex workers at VAMP spoke a word or a sentence in their native languages, Marathi or Kannada, translations were readily made available by their sex worker peers. Some of VAMP's activist materials are also written in Marathi, which was translated to me by VAMP's office staff member who looks after their communications.

The use of the two different languages in which I spoke with sex workers, or performed adda with them, is of consequence. For instance, the Bangla word for sex worker that DMSC members used to refer to themselves is 'jouno kormi'. It literally translates into 'sex worker'. In Bangla, 'jouno' refers to sex, and 'kormi' is one who works. The Hindi term which VAMP members used to refer to

[67] For the university ethics board, I dealt with this breach of protocol by explaining in my report to the ethics committee the importance of listening to the propositions of my research participants about how they wished to carry out the conversations. I explained to the committee that this mutual working out of the mode in which conversations proceeded bore a relation to my argument as well as my understanding of the materials that shaped this book.

themselves was 'dhandhewali'. In Hindi, *dhandha* is business, which when used as a prefix to *wali* means a woman who does business, or a businesswoman. The differences in their meanings informed the way in which sex workers conducted their conversations and shaped their roles/personae and took responsibilities in their relations with others within their community and outside. This became visible only when I paid attention to the specific languages in which I spoke with my interlocutors, which carried distinct meanings of 'sex worker' at the two locations.

The length of my conversations varied between one and three hours, and the sessions were audio recorded with permission from each participant. I translated the consent forms into Bangla and Hindi, because none of the sex workers could read and write in English. To a few of the participants who could not even read Bangla or Hindi, I read out the consent form and explained each and every clause. Once they had understood it fully, they put their signatures/initials on the forms. At VAMP, where I conducted group discussions, the participants decided that one member of the group, on behalf of the others present, would sign it. I completed adda with sex workers in one stretch and did my adda with the legal academics a year later.

For my conversations with the legal academics, I had to seek ethics clearance from the university separately. The procedures followed for doing the conversations were similar for both groups of people, except for the fact that I interacted with sex workers for a much longer duration, which included the time required to collect activist materials. The texts produced by academics, around which I organised my conversations with them, were more readily available.

My conversation with Ratna Kapur was done via Skype in 2016, while she was in Geneva. This was the only conversation that was not done in person. To mitigate this fact, Kapur insisted that we do the conversation through a video call to have a sense of the physical presence and being of the person on the other side of the conversation. I sent a description of my research and a set of indicative questions to her prior to the interview. Our conversation was carried out in English and I spoke to her for an hour and a half, which was digitally recorded. I sent her another set of questions based on my first Skype conversation with her, which she answered very promptly on email. She signed the consent form and emailed it to me after the Skype conversation was done.

Upendra Baxi, like Ratna Kapur, readily agreed to have a conversation with me despite having just recovered at that time from a severe illness. I spoke with Baxi at his New Delhi residence in 2017. My adda with him lasted for two hours, and like all the other conversations, was digitally recorded and he consented to the use of all information for this book.

During the interim period before my conversation with him at his residence, an email exchange with Baxi had begun. Baxi directed me to other materials, interviews and articles that were related to the Open Letter. One of these was an interview with feminist historian Janaki Nair, professor at the Centre for Historical Studies, School of Social Sciences, Jawaharlal Nehru University. This audiovisual material was directly relevant for my discussions as it pertained to Baxi's experiences of crafting the letter. On asking Nair, she made the recordings available to me, which proved to be crucial for working towards and preparing for my conversation with Baxi.[68] I conducted my adda with Baxi in English. During my adda with Baxi, I picked up on threads that were part of his conversation with Nair. Subsequent to my adda with Baxi, I have continued to be in conversation with him over email, where I have discussed my research with him and he has directed my attention to other relevant academic literature.

Now having set the stage for the conversations to take place, I will proceed to the second part of the book, which is titled 'Performing Adda'. In this part, I will perform my method and demonstrate how the field of Indian feminist jurisprudence is produced through the diverse formations of mutual law–life relations at a time and place. I demonstrate how adda can be practised as a counter-hierarchical, shared method of knowledge making for learning about the diverse experiences and locations of the field of Indian feminist jurisprudence.

[68] Available with me on file. I have a prior relationship with Prof. Janaki Nair. She was my MPhil supervisor at the Centre for Studies in Social Sciences, Kolkata and I have been a consistent beneficiary of her intellectual care. It is due to our existing relationship that I was able to reach out to her and request the material that was her research work.

The account of Indian feminist jurisprudence that I present in the next part is a montage of a multiplicity of conversations amongst diverse people at diverse locations. My account of the field is a collected work of my performance of adda with my interlocutors, which is the method of this book, and the conversations between my interlocutors and other people that I learned about through my method. Thus, the demonstration of my argument entails two parallel conversations in Chapters 3–5. One, my own performance of adda with my interlocutors; and two, my accounts of with whom, when and where my interlocutors engaged in conversations outside of my adda with them, which worked to inform their own thoughts and practices of collectivisation and scholarship. The accounting of the two parallel conversations has shaped the next part of this book and my demonstration of the argument that adda helps us understand how sex workers and legal academics jointly contribute to the productions of the field of Indian feminist jurisprudence. As you will see, through the next three chapters, where adda has been performed, I add more texture to the form and meaning of my method.

PART II

PERFORMING ADDA

CHAPTER 3

Sex Worker Feminist Jurisprudence I

DMSC

Amra adda mari, adda mara-i amader kaaj, adda mere amra manusher chinta bhabna bodlai.[1]

(We have friendly conversations with people, that is our job, it is through conversations that we change the way people think.)

DMSC, popularly known as Durbar, is an organisation *of* sex workers located in Kolkata, West Bengal.[2] With a membership of around 40,000 male, female and transgender persons, it is governed and managed by sex workers. The offices of the organisation are located in a place called Sonagachi, which is a zoned red-light area in north Kolkata. Sonagachi was earlier known as 'Sonagaji', named after a Muslim preacher called Gazi Sonaullah Shah Chisti Rahamatullah who came from Iran and settled in that area sometime before the nineteenth century.[3] Sex workers demarcate the houses in Sonagachi as *familybari,* or residential houses of non–sex workers,

[1] Conversation with Bishakha Nashkar, sex worker and DMSC member, Kalighat, Kolkata, 21 January 2015.

[2] While I do not track this connection, it is necessary to mention that DMSC's growth as a collective took place through the years when West Bengal had a communist government in power. West Bengal had the world's longest-running democratically elected communist regime, which lasted 34 years, ending in 2011. See generally Ross Mallick, *Development Policy of a Communist Government: West Bengal since 1977* (Cambridge University Press, 2007). For an account of DMSC's collectivisation, see, generally, Shohini Ghosh (dir.), *The Tales of the Nightfairies* (Mediastorm Collective, 2002), www.youtube.com/watch?v=Ystke5m8now&t=168s.

[3] Sumanta Banerjee, *Dangerous Outcast: The Prostitute in Nineteenth Century Bengal* (Seagull Books, 1998), 73n5, 203.

and *linebari*,[4] houses of sex workers used for both commercial and residential purposes.

Within the busy and narrow lanes of present-day Sonagachi where sex workers both live and work, the office of Durbar is situated in a three-storey building. The self-funded initiatives are housed in this building on Nilmoni Mitra Street.[5] The sex workers' bank, called USHA Cooperative, is housed on the second floor. On the third floor is a short-stay home for women who are rescued from the red-light areas through the Self-Regulatory Boards (SRBs), a community-based anti-trafficking mechanism. On the first floor is the office of Durbar's elected general secretary. Each room on this floor is used for various official activities, such as for a health clinic, or official meetings. The donor-funded projects are housed in another building located in a nearby area, popularly referred to as the Project Office. This building is populated with sex workers and non–sex worker staff who are employed to work on various activities funded by external agencies for the empowerment of sex workers. The offices also house Durbar's partner organisations, which are groups comprising sex workers' lovers, clients and children.[6]

The activist texts authored by Durbar that I read in this chapter were published between 1995 and 2016 and are all written in either Bangla or English. These materials include a manifesto, posters, pamphlets, petitions, organisational by-laws, brochures, announcements and newsletters.[7] The documents are addressed to both Durbar members and

[4] In colloquial Bangla, the word 'line' refers to any kind of profession: musician, doctor, lawyer etc. *Bari* is house. Thus, in this context, 'linebari' refers to a house where sex work is carried out as a profession.

[5] The DMSC's office on Nilmoni Mitra Street was acquired in 2000 with a loan from a nationalised bank.

[6] Komol Gandhar is the performing arts division of DMSC, comprising sex workers and their children. Sathi Sangathan, or the Companions' Collective, is a collective of the non-paying partners of sex workers, who form a part of sex workers' families and communities. Amra Padatik is a collective of the children of sex workers, formed in response to a provision in the Immoral Traffic (Prevention) Act, 1956, which prohibits anybody above the age of eighteen years, including sex workers' children, to live on the earnings of sex work. Anandam is an organisation for lesbian, gay, bisexual and transsexual people who do sex work, or are associated with the sex worker community.

[7] The specific documents are listed in the Bibliography at the end of this book.

outsiders. Documents not meant for internal organisational purposes are addressed to a more general audience, or to the society at large.

This chapter is organised around three key conversations – between sex workers and public health practitioners, state officials and members of the judiciary. Through my adda with the members of Dubar, I draw out how these conversations work to inform sex workers' ideas and practices of collectivisation from the 1990s in post-liberalisation India.[8] During this time, with the advent of the privatisation of the economy, foreign funding for HIV/AIDS programmes and anti-trafficking work increased manifold, and the sex worker emerged in public and legal discourses as a subject of new forms of state regulation.[9]

These three sets of conversations illustrate how Durbar's distinct feminist jurisprudential discourse is produced through sex workers' interactions with representatives of public institutions, which inhabit their collective activist ideas and practices of 'cooperation' and 'reinhabitation'. Through 'cooperation' and 'reinhabitation', sex workers shape their collective role in public life as jounokormi/sex workers, to form mutual relations with other people and with law. Sex workers have achieved this mutuality by reorganising the hierarchical relations of gender, class and caste experienced by them. Mediated by such alteration of hierarchies, sex workers have also reorganised their relation with the Indian state, and altered the criminalised status and conditions accorded to them by the state. Thus, in this chapter, you will see how

[8] In 1991, the Indian government liberalised its economy and implemented a model of economic reforms popularly called LPG (liberalisation privatisation globalisation). Among other things, it allowed foreign funders and private entities to invest in the public sector to enable the country to emerge out of a debt trap, and as a pathway to becoming a fast-growing developing economy on a par with the economic powers of the world. With the boom in jobs and the migration to cities that accompanied the availability of opportunities that came with private investment, sex workers came to be understood as a threat to the health of the workforce that was now in demand. Moreover, their collective identity formation was happening at a time when the state, through economic reforms, was espousing individualised notions of responsibility of the self, and formally withdrawing from its role as a welfare state. See generally, Economic and Political Weekly, *Quarter Century of Liberalisation in India: Essays from Economic & Political Weekly* (Oxford University Press, 2018).

[9] See generally Kotiswaran, 'Introduction', in Kotiswaran, *Sex Work*, xi–lxii.

sex workers' experiences of activism in Kolkata have produced a mode of non-adversarial feminist jurisprudence.

I begin this chapter with the conversations that took place amongst sex-working women in Sonagachi; and between the women and the public health practitioners who were representatives of a state-run institution called the All India Institute of Hygiene and Public Health (AIIHPH). The conversations initiated the collectivisation of sex workers in the red-light areas of Sonagachi and in the formation of DMSC in 1995, followed by its registration in 1997 as a society under the West Bengal Societies Registration Act, 1961 (WBSRA).

I then move to the conversations that took place between sex workers and state officials. The conversations led to the formation of USHA, a sex workers' cooperative bank in 1995, and a local anti-trafficking mechanism called the Self-Regulatory Boards in 1999. I also describe the statute, Immoral Traffic (Prevention) Act, 1956 (ITPA), that regulates sex work in India and forms a part of the backdrop in which sex workers' conversations and collectivisation take place.

The chapter closes with my discussion of the conversations between sex workers and the judiciary that led to the organisation of the Hindu religious festival of Durga Puja by Durbar within the red-light area of Sonagachi in 2013. Through these key conversations, alongside which sex workers are also in conversations amongst themselves, a consolidation of activist thinking and practices of 'cooperation' and 'reinhabitation' takes place, producing a non-adversarial mode of feminist jurisprudence.

SEX WORKERS AND PUBLIC HEALTH PRACTITIONERS

The period of the early 1990s was a significant time for India. The economy of the country was formally privatised and globalisation was embraced. The advent of privatisation and globalisation made way for foreign funds to be used for the development of marginalised communities. An increased interest amongst development practitioners to control the spread of HIV/AIDS gave rise to the flow of funds for the regulation of sexually transmitted diseases through public health programmes. These programmes focused on sex workers as a vector of the disease and as a high-risk population because of their multiple sexual partners.[10] During this time, the AIIHPH, which was a state-run institution, initiated its STD and HIV prevention programme in Kolkata with support from the World Health Organization. This state-administered public health initiative was started under the leadership of Smarajit Jana, a medical doctor and epidemiologist.[11] The public health initiative under Jana came to be popularly known as the Sonagachi Project.[12]

What was unique about the Sonagachi Project was that a state-run institution recruited sex workers from Sonagachi to train them to work as peer educators.[13] This meant that a group of sex workers, whose relations with the Indian state had been hitherto largely determined by criminal law, were now employed by a state-run agency to carry out a state agenda. The women would be trained in safe sexual practices for the purposes of training other sex workers, their peers. Because peer educators were also sex workers, it was assumed they would have easier access to the community and have greater understanding of how to engage with sex workers.[14]

I met Jana one afternoon in Durbar's office to hear about how his conversations with the sex workers began. He shared that he and his team started the process of recruiting sex workers for the Sonagachi Project with only one criterion. They decided to hire women who possessed good communication skills. However, the women who arrived for the job interview carried such shame and stigma that most of them had their faces completely covered and barely looked the interviewers in the eye.[15] For the recruiters, this made the process of hiring sex workers for

[10] Kotiswaran, 'Introduction', xi–lxii.

[11] Smarajit Jana passed away in 2022 after contracting the novel coronavirus.

[12] John Restakis, *Humanizing the Economy: Co-operatives in the Age of Capital* (New Society Publishers, 2010), 135–60 (chapter 7).

[13] Durbar Mahila Samanwaya Committee, www.durbar.org/html/history.html.

[14] Conversation with Smarajit Jana, Chief Advisor, DMSC, at Girish Park, Kolkata, 30 January 2015.

[15] This is in sharp contrast to Sumanta Banerjee's account of sex workers in colonial Bengal. Banerjee narrates that prostitutes in colonial Bengal time and again resisted the dominant discriminatory gendered practices of their times: prostitutes were the first women to have taken to the theatre and perform female roles on stage along with male actors (p. 119); prostitutes regularly wrote letters to newspapers in which they were

the peer educator roles very difficult. As a consequence, Jana and his team decided that whoever looked the interviewers in the eye – let alone had a proper conversation – would be hired to work as a peer educator.[16]

Bishakha Nashkar, a sex worker and a member of DMSC since its early years, recalled in our adda that the AIIHPH recruited around twelve sex workers from Sonagachi.[17] Both active and retired sex workers were officially appointed as peer educators for the Sonagachi Project. The women's specific task in the role of peer educator was to go into the brothel areas and speak with sex workers, establish friendships with them, educate them about sexual health and HIV/AIDS, and distribute condoms.[18] To do this, after their recruitment, each peer educator was made to go through a training programme that equipped them with knowledge of sexual health and HIV/AIDS.[19]

In the 1990s, having conversations with sex workers outside the bounds of a red-light area was socially forbidden, even for officials of a government-approved programme. It was not easy even for an established state-run institution such as the AIIHPH to hire a venue where trainings for sex workers could be held.[20] For training the first group of peer educators, a place was hired in the College Street area of north Kolkata. An official letter was sent from the AIIHPH and a booking amount was also paid. However, just a day before the training, the authorities called Jana and informed him that the booking had to be cancelled because sex workers could not be allowed into their premises.

critical of existing social practices in their lives, like evictions from brothels, practices of child marriage, deceit and adultery within marriage (pp. 117–18); there were literary writings by prostitutes like the well-known theatre actress Binodini, who wrote against the practices of Bengali *bhadralok* (elite) society that attempted to keep prostitutes and their children ostracised from the society by opposing the admission of their children into educational institutions (p. 120); prostitutes resisted the requirement of registration under the Contagious Diseases Act and often defended themselves in court and got themselves acquitted by playing on the gaps in the law. Banerjee, *Dangerous Outcast*, 154–55.

[16] Ibid. [17] Conversation with Bishakha Nashkar, above n 1.

[18] 'Durbar Mahila Samanwaya Committee (DMSC) & The Usha Multipurpose Cooperative Society Ltd', www.nswp.org/sites/nswp.org/files/DMSC%20short%20history.pdf.

[19] Conversation with Smarajit Jana, above n 14. [20] Ibid.

To compensate for the cancellation, the authorities offered to double AIIHPH's deposit.[21]

Jana noted that, at that time, speaking with sex workers within the bounds of Sonagachi was not easy either. When the Sonagachi Project had just begun, he and a few other members of his team from AIIHPH visited sex workers' homes along with the peer educators. During these visits, sex workers offered tea and refreshments to the AIIHPH members to extend their hospitality, as well as to see how these people from non–sex worker communities responded to sex workers. If they did not drink the tea or eat the food offered by sex workers, this was read as an endorsement of societal stigma that segregated sex workers from the rest of the community. Jana recounted (as I also noted in Chapter 2 about my own experience of participating in this practice) that the tea-drinking exercise was an informal protocol used by sex workers for knowing in advance if a mutually respectful conversation could be carried out with an outsider.[22]

Speaking about her experiences of the Sonagachi Project, Nashkar who was part of the programme shared that being a state-run initiative, it was able to earn a certain amount of credibility among the sex worker community.[23] In those days, it was not common for brothel owners to allow women working for them to speak with other sex workers and brothel owners, or just generally with people residing in the locality.[24] Brothel owners seldom gave permission to sex workers to travel to another red-light area, lest they decided to work for someone else. Once sex workers became peer educators, they had to travel outside of their brothel areas. This provided sex workers with the opportunity to converse with others, including other women like them who resided in the neighbouring localities.[25]

When the women began speaking amongst themselves, Nashkar noted, they learnt about each other's lives and the commonalities in

21 Conversation with Smarajit Jana, above n 14.

22 Ibid.; the same was mentioned by Bishakha Nashkar, sex worker and member of DMSC, above n 1.

23 Conversation with Bishakha Nashkar, above n 1. 24 Ibid.

25 Conversation with Smarajit Jana, above n 14.

their experiences.[26] For example, almost every sex worker had been arrested by the police for soliciting, often only for being physically present in a public place. The police and local gangsters extorted a monthly fee from all sex workers for working in an area that they had marked as their jurisdiction. Sex workers' family members, who survived on their income, disrespected and disowned them because of their occupation. Many sex workers had been abused by the police and guards at shelter homes where they were sent after being rescued from a brothel. For a majority of sex workers, growing up as girls meant that more attention was paid to their marriage, rather than education, and a lot of them who were married off at a very early age joined sex work to escape an abusive domestic life.[27]

Bharati Dey, sex worker and former elected general secretary of Durbar, told me that the women learnt from speaking with each other that their most common experience was that a large number of their children were school dropouts. Their children were expelled from educational and boarding institutions when school authorities learnt about their mothers' occupations. Assuming that marriage and domesticity would cast a safety net and undo the stigma in such situations, sex worker mothers got their daughters married at a very young age without disclosing their occupation to their daughters' in-laws.[28] In most cases, the in-laws eventually found out the reality and sent the girls back to their mothers. With their sons, most sex workers shared a hostile relationship. A majority of sex workers' sons blamed their mothers for being treated as social outcasts by other people in the neighbourhood.[29] They became abusive and joined local gangster groups to extort sex workers.[30]

When women learnt about their lives by conversing amongst each other, they realised that their experiences *of* sex work arose from the fact of their being women and poor.[31] The women's social status and

[26] Conversation with Bishakha Nashkar, above n 1.

[27] Ibid.; conversation with Bharati Dey, sex worker and former elected general secretary of DMSC, Nilmoni Mitra Street, Kolkata, 14 January 2015.

[28] Conversation with Bharati Dey, above n 27. [29] Ibid.

[30] Ibid.; conversation with Purnima Chatterjee, sex worker and member of DMSC, Nilmoni Mitra Street, Kolkata, 10 October 2014.

[31] Conversation with Bishakha Nashkar, above n 1.

conditions of class and gender allowed sex work to be controlled by a nexus of pimps, madams, police, politicians, traffickers and moneylenders.[32] This placed sex workers at the bottom of gender- and class-based power relations with very little capacity for negotiation and self-reliance.[33] As a result, their work as peer educators became less effective. The objective of the Sonagachi Project was to implement ways to control the transmission of HIV and STD among sex workers and their partners. To this end, the task of the peer educator was to motivate sex workers to get their clients to use condoms in order to protect their own health as well as that of their clients and partners.[34]

When the women began to assemble in a local park for their evening chat sessions after finishing their day's work as peer educators, Nashkar shared, they realised how their task of condom distribution was not as simple as it seemed.[35] They were confronted with challenges pertaining to their experiences *as* sex workers that caused an impediment in the execution of their job as peer educators.[36] How could a sex worker, a poor and uneducated woman, ensure that her client, a man, would want to learn from her about how and why to alter his sexual practices? How could a sex worker, living in extreme poverty, afford to lose clients by insisting that they use condoms? Being in a competitive profession meant that the woman next door might agree to take him as her client and not insist on using a condom. How would the refusal of a sex worker to have sexual relations without a condom be meaningful unless each and every sex worker in the locality could be convinced to do the same for every single sexual act? How could a sex worker, who was able to refuse services to her clients for not using condoms, also refuse sexual relations with her husband, lover or *babu* (permanent client) for the same reasons? More importantly, in a context where for most people sexual relations with a sex worker meant an irresponsible and unsafe act, how could sex workers

[32] Restakis, *Humanizing the Economy*, 135–60.

[33] DMSC, *Sex Workers' Manifesto*, First National Conference of Sex Workers in India, 14–16 November 1997 (published by DMSC for distribution at the conference) (on file with author). The manifesto is seven pages long. A version is available at www.nswp.org/sites/nswp.org/files/Sex%20Workers%20Manifesto%20-%20Meeting%20in%20India.pdf.

[34] Ibid. [35] Conversation with Bishakha Nashkar, above n 1. [36] Ibid.

convince clients to exercise responsibility and care within such a relationship?[37]

The women began to deliberate on these challenges facing their work as peer educators. In doing so, they concluded that to confront these challenges, first and foremost, they needed to build a positive role for themselves by which they could gain a sense of self-worth and confidence.[38] Without doing so, peer educators would never be able to motivate sex workers to develop an interest in improving their own lives and investing in their health.[39] Soon afterwards, peer educators started to take on tasks that were not restricted to condom distribution alone. They acted as arbitrators in disputes between sex workers and madams; fought violent clients and pimps; fought the local mafia and moneylenders; made regular appearances at police stations on behalf of sex workers for unlawful arrests; and also ensured that ailing sex workers got proper medical care.[40]

As a result of women's conversations with the public health practitioners of AIIHPH, and the internal conversations that ensued amongst the women, sex workers realised that unsafe sexual practices were an issue that intersected with larger disparities of class, caste and patriarchal power relations in society.[41] Sex worker peer educators realised that their lives were 'enmeshed in ... powerful dominant ideologies which shape ... moral ethical values', and a discriminatory worldview was what sustained social disparities.[42] For this reason, sex workers decided that they needed a forum for reorganising disparities by replacing the discriminatory worldview with ideas and practices that would enable the women to create mutual relations within their immediate community.[43]

Sex workers also identified a need for attaching a new meaning to their lives through the formation of a 'self-defined and self-conscious identity *as* sex workers in the public sphere'.[44] A reference to the need for shaping an identity *as* sex workers, and not *of* sex workers, suggests

[37] DMSC, *Sex Workers' Manifesto*, above n 33; conversation with Bishakha Nashkar, above n 1.

[38] Conversation with Bishakha Nashkar, above n 1.

[39] Restakis, *Humanizing the Economy*.

[40] Conversation with Bishakha Nashkar, above n 1.

[41] DMSC, *Sex Workers' Manifesto*, above n 33.

[42] Ibid.

[43] Conversation with Bishakha Nashkar, above n 1.

[44] DMSC, *Sex Workers' Manifesto*, above n 33.

that such a role did not already exist and had to be crafted. It became apparent to me during the conversations that this assertion of crafting a new identity *as* sex workers was the crucial intellectual work that the sex workers performed to transform their role in public life through practices of collectivisation.

The women realised that as sex workers they were 'of course not uncontaminated by the ideologies of the society … [they] live in'.[45] In this context, the creation of a sex worker self that was contrary to dominant societal values, while sex workers were also located within and informed by those very values, would be difficult. Based on discussions amongst each other, the women came to an understanding that the working out of their own meaning of 'sex worker' would have to be done collectively.[46] An individual sex worker who was at the very bottom of the social hierarchy and with very low self-esteem would not be able to craft a positive role for herself, without the friendship and support of others like her.[47]

Nashkar explained to me that for the women, shaping a new role in public life as sex workers was aided by their intermediate role as peer educators in a state-authorised programme.[48] The transition of the women's role in relation to a public from peer educators to sex workers began with the interactions and sharing of experiences amongst the women in Sonagachi.[49] These interactions, Nashkar continued, on account of emerging from women's conversations with public health practitioners and having gained their friendship, enabled sex workers to come to a twofold realisation.[50]

First, what made it possible for sex workers to challenge the unequal and discriminatory practices within their community was the strength of a collective voice and affiliation to a formal institution with proper rules and regulations. Second, sex workers, who were a stigmatised group and consisted mostly of poor and illiterate women, needed to gain non–sex worker allies in the community. Thus, if the women were to assume a role in public life as sex workers, they

[45] Ibid. [46] Ibid.; conversation with Bishakha Nashkar, above n 1.
[47] Conversation with Bishakha Nashkar, above n 1. [48] Ibid. [49] Ibid. [50] Ibid.

needed to formalise their organisational activities and form friendships with non–sex worker allies.[51]

After further deliberations, the sex workers decided to officially register their collective organisation under WBSRA.[52] This law, enacted by the West Bengal Legislative Assembly in 1961, provides for the registration of non-governmental organisations whose primary offices are in West Bengal.[53] Under WBSRA, societies may be formed through a memorandum of association amongst seven or more members who have decided to come together for literary, cultural, scientific, political, charitable or even religious purposes.[54]

Rama Debnath, a sex worker and former elected president of Durbar, shared during our adda that a group of nine sex workers, with the help of Jana and others from AIIHPH, made an application to officially register their collective.[55] Jana recounted that the women wanted to register their collective as a sex workers' organisation and wanted to give it a name that represented their indomitable fighting spirit.[56] In the application for registration, the women jointly decided to call the organisation Durbar, which in Bangla means 'unstoppable'. The application was thus submitted in the name of Durbar Jounokormi Samanyaya Committee (Unstoppable Sex Workers' Coordination Committee). With this, sex workers' conversations with state officials began.

SEX WORKERS AND STATE OFFICIALS

In 1995, the sex workers submitted their formal application to the Office of the Registrar mandated under WBSRA. Once the application was submitted, the registrar's office rejected the application without formally

[51] Ibid.; DMSC, *Sex Workers' Manifesto*, above n 33.

[52] West Bengal Societies Registration Act, 1961 (WBSRA), www.wbja.nic.in/wbja_adm/files/The%20West%20Bengal%20Societies%20Registration%20Act,%201961.pdf.

[53] Prior to the passing of this legislation, organisations could be formed under the Societies Registrations Act, 1860, which was originally passed by the British in order to encourage like-minded people to form associations for any literary, scientific or charitable purposes. See Societies Registration Act, 1860, https://indiankanoon.org/doc/1700055.

[54] WBSRA, above n 52.

[55] Conversation with Rama Debnath, sex worker and member of DMSC, Nilmoni Mitra Street, Kolkata, 18 October 2014.

[56] Conversation with Smarajit Jana, above n 14.

stating any reasons.[57] During verbal communications, the officials indicated their discomfort with the use of 'sex worker' in the name of the organisation.[58] Due to this, the women decided to exclude the words 'jouno kormi' (sex worker) from the name of their organisation and replaced it with the more generic *mahila* (woman). The application was then sent back to the registrar for re-evaluation. This time, the application did not get rejected. The sex workers' collective organisation came to be officially formed and known as Durbar Mahila Samanwaya Committee (Unstoppable Women's Coordination Committee). Although the words 'sex worker' were dropped from the name of the organisation, the memorandum of association explicitly stated that *only* sex workers could be members of DMSC.[59]

Through the process of registration under WBSRA, the women officially initiated a new role in public life as sex workers, which was distinct from the role that had been deemed to be inhabited by prostitutes as per ITPA.[60] Through adda with the activists, more generally, it became apparent that DMSC's collective activism, the initiation of which emerged from sex workers' specific conversations in the context of the 1990s, was taking place in relation to women's experiences that had resulted largely from the provisions and implementation of ITPA (see Fig. 3.1).[61] I will now outline the provisions of ITPA, which, in different measures, provided a backdrop for women's conversations with state officials and their formation of a new role in public life as sex workers through collectivisation.

[57] Ibid. [58] Ibid. [59] WBSRA, above n 52.

[60] Immoral Traffic (Prevention) Act, 1956 (ITPA), https://indiankanoon.org/doc/69064674.

[61] In 2006, the Ministry of Women and Child Development introduced the Immoral Traffic (Prevention) Amendment Bill, 2006, in the lower house of Parliament with the inclusion of new provisions, such as the criminalisation of clients. In response, the National Network of Sex Workers, of which DMSC is a part, mobilised thousands of sex workers from around the country to march to the Indian Parliament in Delhi and register a public protest. The DMSC acquired permission from the Ministry of Railways to organise an exclusively designated train for sex workers from West Bengal to travel to Delhi, which was called the Durbar Express. This event is a big milestone in the history of the sex workers' movement and women's mobilisation in India. See, generally, Shohini Ghosh, 'Decriminalizing Sex Work' (March 2008) 583, *Seminar*, www.india-seminar.com/2008/583/583_shohini_ghosh.htm.

Figure 3.1 DMSC booklet calling for the repeal of ITPA. *Source*: DMSC, Kolkata.

THE IMMORAL TRAFFIC (PREVENTION) ACT, 1956

In India, sex workers' relationships in their public/private lives – with partners, family members, neighbours, clients, co-workers – are ordered by the state through the ITPA.[62] Scholarly historical accounts of sex work have traced the origin of the ITPA's mode of ordering to colonial rule by

[62] See, generally, Ratna Kapur, 'India', in *Collateral Damage: The Impact of Anti-trafficking Measures on Human Rights Around the World* (Global Alliance Against Traffic in Women,

pointing out how, in the mid-nineteenth century, 'prostitution' became a part of official discourses in a form that resonates with the contemporary moment.[63] The resonance, among other things, lies in how the state segregates sex workers from the public by imposing punitive measures to regulate their lives and livelihood through the ITPA. While the focus was on disease control under colonialism, the post-colonial state's attention has shifted to the crime of trafficking, which is the sole framework through which prostitution is currently understood and proscribed by the state.

The person of the 'common prostitute' entered the legal vocabulary of the colonial state with the identification of a subject whose sexual relations with British soldiers needed to be regulated in order to control the spread of venereal diseases among British populations.[64] The scare of venereal diseases prompted the colonial administration to pass the Cantonment Act, 1864, and the Contagious Diseases Acts of the 1860s–1880s with the intention of regulating prostitution in India.[65]

The Cantonment Act specifically targeted a certain section of women who practised prostitution within the jurisdiction of the cantonment areas, while the Contagious Diseases Acts covered 'common prostitutes'. The women who were left out of the Cantonment Act were ordinary working-class women who resided outside the cantonment areas and were officially not deemed fit to be sexual partners for British soldiers. These women violated official rules and carried out sexual relations with the soldiers, rendering 'disease control' through the Cantonment Act impossible.[66] The Contagious Diseases Acts were thus enacted to bring such practices of prostitution under the regulation of the British administration.[67]

2007), 114; Ashwini Tambe, *Codes of Misconduct: Regulating Prostitution in Late Colonial Bombay* (Zubaan, 2009), xx, xxii; Banerjee, *Dangerous Outcast*, 59.

63 Tambe, *Codes of Misconduct*, xx, xxii; Banerjee, *Dangerous Outcast*, 59.

64 Tambe, *Codes of Misconduct*, xx, xxii.

65 Ibid.; Banerjee, *Dangerous Outcast*, 59; see also Judith R. Walkowitz, *Prostitution and Victorian Society: Women, Class and the State* (Cambridge University Press, 1980).

66 Banerjee, *Dangerous Outcast*, 65–66.

67 The Contagious Diseases Acts carried stricter provision for Indian prostitutes compared to their British predecessors. Indian prostitutes were compulsorily required to register themselves with the administration, undergo regular medical checkups, were prohibited

In 1949, the United Nations General Assembly adopted the Convention for the Suppression of Traffic in Persons and of the Exploitation of the Prostitution of Others. The Government of India, which was now a free and sovereign state, ratified this international convention in 1953 and enacted the Suppression of Immoral Traffic in Women and Girls Act, 1956.[68] In 1986, the name of the legislation was changed to the present-day Immoral Traffic (Prevention) Act through an amendment. The term, 'woman' was replaced with the word 'person' in order for the provisions of ITPA to be more responsive to non-female sex workers who were also identified as victims of prostitution.[69]

The inclusion of 'person' as victim under ITPA did not significantly alter the gender binary on which the legislation was founded. Even though in some sections 'he/she'[70] or 'his/her'[71] is used as the corresponding pronoun to refer to the victim subject, the use of 'her' is more rampant in the sections relating to the 'rescue of person'[72] from prostitution. Sections dealing with the handing over of such persons into the safe hands of 'parents', 'guardian' or 'husband' use only a female pronoun to refer to the rescued person. This formulation reveals a state imagination whereby the subject in need of guardianship/regulation remains predominantly a woman, under the control and supervision of others, even if she is an adult.

The ITPA makes 'prostitution in or in the vicinity of public place' a criminal offence.[73] In doing so, it assigns culpability to 'any person who carries on prostitution and [even] the person with whom such prostitution is carried on'.[74] The notion of 'public place' held within ITPA's legislative provisions denotes not just a place but also people, because it is defined as 'any place intended for use by, or accessible to, the public and includes any public conveyance'.[75] The *people* constituting a public is not further characterised, but as *place*, it is said to include an 'educational institution', a 'hospital', a 'nursing home', 'any place of public religious worship' and also

from entering certain specified areas, and could even be incarcerated if found infected with venereal diseases. See ibid., 67.

[68] Rakesh Shukla, 'A Walk Through the Labyrinths of Sex Work Law', in Murthy and Seshu, *The Business of Sex*, 212–42, 229.

[69] Ibid. [70] ITPA, above n 60, Sec. 5(b). [71] Ibid., Sec. 5(c). [72] Ibid., Sec. 16.

[73] Ibid., Sec. 7. [74] Ibid., Sec. 7(1). [75] Ibid., Sec. 2(h).

an area that is within 'two hundred meters' distance of such places.[76] In effect, these provisions work to sever sex workers' being and belonging from a public – as place and people – almost in its entirety.

A sex worker's non-commercial familial relationships, likewise, are also ordered: anybody, including a husband, 'living with, or to be habitually in the company of, a prostitute', is a trafficker;[77] a sex worker's child 'over the age of eighteen years who knowingly lives' on her earnings is also a trafficker.[78] The provisions of the ITPA make almost all aspects of sex workers' lives the subject matter of criminal law. This precludes 'prostitutes' from engaging in any kind of shared community life mutually with other people at the places where they live and work. Sex workers' relationships formed within the institution of marriage are also not recognised, because even non-commercial relationships with husbands and children are included in the ambit of the ITPA.[79] Such characterisation resonates with the popular and patriarchal descriptions of the sex worker as *rasta-r meye* (woman of the streets), *bajari meye* and *bazaru aurat* (woman of the market)[80] – both street and market being constitutive aspects of a public.

This means that the ITPA locates sex workers outside of a legitimate notion of people contained in its category of 'public', and works to separate them from those whom it includes in this category. Such a hierarchical ordering of sex workers' lives vis-à-vis other people within the community provided the backdrop against which sex-working women carried out their conversations not only with state officials but also with the judiciary.

[76] Ibid., Sec. 7(1b). [77] Ibid., Sec. 4(2a). [78] Ibid., Sec. 4(1).

[79] In *Subversive Sites*, Ratna Kapur and Brenda Cossman examine how the Indian state conceives female subjectivity based on contradictory divisions of the private and public spheres of women's lives. The authors argue, based on what is an established feminist position in many different places, that a 'familial ideology' informs the ways in which women's lives are perceived by the state and falsely divided into separate domains of private and public spheres. According to them, the formulation of the ITPA points to the fact that it is not the location at which sexual practices are carried out, but rather the perceived public nature of sexuality performed outside the institution of marriage, as in the case of sex work, which has caused the latter to be brought within the ambit of criminal law. Kapur and Cossman, *Subversive Sites*, 124.

[80] These are everyday expressions in Bangla and Hindi for referring to sex workers in the vernacular.

COOPERATION

I now return to my description and reporting of adda with my interlocutors regarding the registration of DMSC. Bharati Dey told me that with the official registration of DMSC, sex-working women could now assemble in public places without the interference of the police, which was made permissible by the ITPA.[81] They could also legitimately carry out activities in public places.[82] In order to actualise a collective, or think and act collectively as sex workers in such public places, the women, however, still needed to create mutual relations amongst themselves, and with the larger sex worker and non–sex worker community.[83] My conversations with sex workers made it apparent how the registration of DMSC as a formal organisation constituted *only* by sex workers worked towards this end. Sex workers were able to assume a role in public places that was very different from their legal status of 'public women' that ITPA attached to its 'prostitute' subjects; and it provided sex workers a legitimate place to think and act collectively and form relations with other people living in Sonagachi.

My engagement with DMSC's activism through adda has helped me understand that sex workers envisage a collective in relation to a public that comprises both a place and a people. In 1995, the same year in which DMSC was officially registered, sex workers also decided to form a cooperative bank of their own that would be located in Sonagachi and work to alter sex workers' relations with other people who lived in that place.[84] Jana recounted during our adda that the reason why sex workers decided to form a cooperative bank was because it would alter their prevalent hierarchical economic relations with the pimps and moneylenders of Sonagachi. More importantly, by virtue of being collectively owned, the financial institution would also train women to think and act collectively vis-à-vis the community of people with whom they shared their lives in Sonagachi.[85]

The state-authorised provisions through which people could form a cooperative financial institution resonated with DMSC's thinking to

[81] Conversation with Bharati Dey, above n 27. [82] Ibid. [83] Ibid.
[84] Conversation with Smarajit Jana, above n 14. [85] Ibid.

facilitate mutual relations with the legal worldview contained in the provisions.[86] The provisions allowed the members of a cooperative bank to have joint ownership of such an institution, which could also be used for other community-based activities.[87] The West Bengal Co-operative Societies Act, 1983 (WBCSA), which contained this provision, was a product of a cooperatives movement in India.[88] It was enacted for the purpose of financially uplifting poorer communities through the democratic principles of cooperation.[89] During the colonial period, and also after independence, the cooperative movement gained momentum among political thinkers as an alternative set of ideas and practices that could counter the capitalist economic system of production that left the vast majority of people in India poor and exploited. During colonial rule, the Bengali poet, philosopher and educationist Rabindranath Tagore was one of the most vocal proponents of the cooperative movement. He saw cooperative thinking as a way of challenging the exploitation meted out to the Indian farming communities by the British and the native ruling classes.[90]

Tagore's idea of cooperation included the understanding that the relationship between farmers and their lands was not a relationship of exploitation, but of care and subsistence. In 1928, he wrote *Samabaya Niti*, which was later published in English as *The Co-operative Principles.*[91]

[86] Ibid. [87] Ibid.; Restakis, *Humanizing the Economy*, 144–45.

[88] West Bengal Co-operative Societies Act, 1983 (WBCSA), www.wbja.nic.in/wbja_adm/files/The%20West%20Bengal%20Societies%20Registration%20Act,%201961.pdf.

[89] Sharit Kumar Bhowmik, 'Ideology and the Co-operative Movement: Worker Co-operatives in the Tea Industry' (1988) 23(51), *Economic and Political Weekly*, 2703; Satyendra Nath Sen, *Cooperative Movement in West Bengal* (Bookland, 1966); Ranabir Samaddar, *Passive Revolution in West Bengal, 1977–2011* (Sage, 2013); Anil Bhuimali, *Rural Cooperative and Economic Development* (Sarup & Sons, 2003).

[90] In 1916, Tagore wrote *Ghare Baire* (*The Home and the World*), where he was extremely critical of the exploitation of farmers by both the British and nationalist leaders of the Swadeshi Movement who justified the sacrifice of the interests of poor farmers for the greater good of India's independence. Through the character of Nikhil, a *zamindar* (landowner), Tagore brought out the conflict between the duties of the public office of the landowner towards his subjects and the private commitment of the same individual towards the cause of India's independence. Rabindranath Tagore, *The Home and the World* (Penguin, 2005).

[91] Published in 1963 by Visva Bharati, the resident publication house at Santiniketan (literally, Abode of Peace), the liberal arts school founded by Tagore in West Bengal.

Samabaya means cooperation, while the term *niti*, which has its origin in the Sanskrit language, denotes a path, behaviour or means of conduct.[92] In *Samabaya Niti*, Tagore suggests that the conduct of cooperation amongst poor and exploited farmers was an effective means of achieving a just and equitable life for themselves.[93]

DMSC's thinking on cooperative banking, with an intent to craft a new role and responsibilities for women as sex workers in public life, was shaped by drawing on Tagore's worldview. I found extracts from Tagore's *Samabaya Niti* in a monthly vernacular magazine called *Durbar Bhavna* (Durbar's Worldview) published by DMSC.[94] The magazine carries articles that not only pertain to sex workers' lives and activism, but also topics that are of contemporary social relevance, such as climate change (see Fig. 3.2). A 2014 edition of *Durbar Bhavna* states how Tagore's thinking on cooperatives influenced and also inspired sex workers' cooperative thought. Tagore's belief in the importance of developing internal community strength for tackling problems, rather than a reliance on external help and charity, is significantly incorporated into Durbar's activism.[95] Although Tagore's writings pertained to the specific conditions of farmers in pre-independent India, they draw upon these ideas to use it as a means for sex workers' collective organisation.

The WBCSA reflects the idea that the collective power of the working-class poor could be consolidated through cooperative action amongst them. According to this law, cooperatives are envisaged as a third sector

[92] Indian economist Amartya Sen, in the introductory chapter 'A Classical Distinction in Indian Jurisprudence' of his book *The Idea of Justice*, alludes to a similar meaning of the word 'niti'. According to Sen, niti in Indian jurisprudence is an ethical idea representing justice. He writes, 'among the principal uses of the term niti are organizational propriety and behavioural correctness'. Amartya Sen, *The Idea of Justice* (Harvard University Press, 2011), 20; see generally Rajendra Prasad, *A Conceptual-Analytic Study of Classical Indian Philosophy of Morals*, vol. 12, part I (Concept Publishing Company, 2008), 6.

[93] Rabindranath Tagore, *The Co-operative Principles* (Visva-Bharati, 1963) (originally published in Bangla in 1928 as *Samabaya Niti*).

[94] Rabindranath Tagore, 'Samabyay', *Durbar Bhavna*, nos 5–6 (Durbar Prakashani, September–October 2014), 27–34.

[95] Smarajit Jana, 'Editorial', *Durbar Bhavna*, nos 5–6 (Durbar Prakashani, September–October 2014), 3–6.

Figure 3.2 *Durbar Bhavna*, DMSC's magazine. *Source*: DMSC, Kolkata.

of the economy along with the private and public sectors.[96] The 'thirdness' of the cooperative, as per the state, lies in the fact that it is neither driven by the objectives of the state, nor intended for individual profit. Rather, 'the cooperative' exists for the benefit of a community through

[96] See, generally, Bhowmik, 'Ideology and the Co-operative Movement'.

cooperation amongst its members and responsibility and care for others.[97] There are clear mutual alignments between the objectives of the WBCSA and DMSC's thinking, which, Jana told me, made the sex workers decide to form a cooperative bank under WBCSA.

Durbar made an application under WBCSA to officially create a sex workers' cooperative financial institution. Just like their first attempt at registration, the application was rejected by the West Bengal government's Department of Cooperation. The authorities opposed the application on the ground that the statute specified that applicants were required to be of good moral character.[98] Jana recounted that the officials were generally sympathetic towards DMSC.[99] Because it was mentioned that the women were engaged in sex work, an activity which is posited as immoral in the ITPA, DMSC's application got rejected.[100] The members of the newly formed DMSC, a group of women who believed they were unstoppable, took up the matter by engaging in conversations with the state officials.[101]

During one such conversation, one of the officials suggested to the sex workers that the impediment posed by the wording in the statute around 'moral character' could be circumvented if the women identified themselves in the application as 'housewives'.[102] The sex workers immediately urged the official to define what the latter understood by 'moral character'. Sex workers explained that they did not steal from anyone, did not kill anyone, did not take bribes from anyone unlike most politicians, so there was no question of their being immoral.[103] The officials appeared unconvinced even after a heated debate. This was when one of the sex workers told the minister that she would state in the application form that she was a housewife only if he agreed to marry her right away

97 'We act consistently with the mission of the organization, being honest and transparent in what we do and say, and accept responsibility for our collective and individual actions.' DMSC, *Durbar: A Brief Profile*, 4th ed. (Durbar Prakashani, 2011), 8.

98 Jana, 'Editorial', *Durbar Bhavna*, above n 95.

99 Conversation with Smarajit Jana, above n 14.

100 The ITPA characterises 'prostitution' as an 'immoral' act, resulting in the characterisation of a prostitute as an immoral person. Jana, 'Editorial', *Durbar Bhavna*, above n 95.

101 Conversation with Bishakha Nashkar, above n 1.

102 Conversation with Smarajit Jana, above n 14.

103 Jana, 'Editorial', *Durbar Bhavna*, above n 95; Restakis, *Humanizing the Economy*, 135–60.

and attached that status to her name. Otherwise, she argued, it would make her a liar, an immoral person.[104]

The cooperatives minister, Saral Deb, was genuinely interested in the expansion of cooperative societies.[105] The existing provision in the legislation on the moral character of the applicant, however, remained a ground on the basis of which other government officials raised objections. Unable to act in the presence of such opposition from his own colleagues, and because of the debates that ensued with DMSC members, Minister Deb took up the issue for debate in the state legislative assembly. This resulted in the removal from the act a provision that required an applicant to be of good moral character.[106]

In *Humanizing the Economy: Co-operatives in the Age of Capital*, community organiser and philosopher John Restakis documents the formation of DMSC's cooperative bank.[107] Restakis argues that the approach of establishing mutual trust within the community adopted by the Sonagachi Project pivoted the formation of DMSC as an organisation of, and for, sex workers. It was then that the formation of a sex workers' cooperative bank right in the middle of a red-light area became possible.[108] Restakis argues that DMSC intended the bank to be registered as a sex workers' cooperative bank because the motives driving sex workers were self-ownership and autonomy within a financial institution.[109]

During the course of adda with sex workers, it became evident that the collective ownership of a financial institution 'of, for and by ... sex workers'[110] was tethered to women's imagination of new roles and relationships in public life as sex workers. The formation of the bank, inclusive of its rules and regulations, speaks of sex workers' intentions of fostering mutual ties within their community, and with the place where they live and work.

In 1995, DMSC members formed the cooperative bank called USHA Multipurpose Cooperative Society Limited. The membership and administration of the bank are designed to ensure that its ownership rests entirely with sex workers (see Fig. 3.3). Mrinal Kanti Dutta, the son of a sex worker

[104] Conversations with Smarajit Jana, above n 14; Bishakha Nashkar, above n 1.

[105] Conversation with Smarajit Jana, above n 14.

[106] Jana, 'Editorial', *Durbar Bhavna*, above n 95.

[107] Restakis, *Humanizing the Economy*, 146. [108] Ibid., 144. [109] Ibid.

[110] DMSC, *Durbar: A Brief Profile*, above n 97, 25.

Figure 3.3 Brochure for USHA Multipurpose Cooperative Society Ltd, run by DMSC.
Source: DMSC, Kolkata.

and an active member of DMSC since its inception, noted that only sex workers could become members of the cooperative and were vested with decision-making powers.[111] The board of directors of USHA, comprising nine members, consists only of sex workers, and is re-elected every five years through secret ballot. The USHA Cooperative Society provides loans to equip sex workers to participate in community life through activities such as children's education, healthcare, festivals, house repairing and buying property.[112] These practices are meant to enable women to assert their place as sex workers amongst other people in the community.[113]

Dutta pointed out to me that USHA also administered a practice of daily collection in the red-light areas that necessitated that its members made door-to-door visits and spoke with sex-working women in the locality who were not necessarily members of DMSC or USHA.[114] Sex workers visited every household and spoke with women to encourage them to become members of the bank. This system was devised not only to ensure financial security for sex workers, but also to secure communications and alliances amongst sex workers living and working in Sonagachi.

REINHABITATION

A clear statement of how sex workers envision their relations with other people and their place of work is available in the *Sex Workers' Manifesto.*[115] The manifesto was first published and circulated in 1997 at the Sex Workers' Festival as a theme paper for the event (see Fig. 3.4). The document was published both in English and Bangla to reach out to a wider audience.[116]

111 Conversation with Mrinal Kanti Dutta, founding member of DMSC, Girish Park, Kolkata, 30 January 2015. Dutta died in June 2015, six months after I interviewed him at DMSC's office. He was the son of a sex worker and a founding member of DMSC. He had written many books in Bangla on *hijras* and *kotis* (transgender persons) in Bengal.

112 By-laws of Usha Multipurpose Co-operative Society Limited (n.d.) (on file with author).

113 Conversation with Mrinal Kanti Dutta, above n 111.

114 Ibid.

115 DMSC, *Sex Workers' Manifesto,* above n 33.

116 Soon after DMSC came into formal existence, they organised the first national conference of sex workers in Calcutta in 1997 as a way of asserting public visibility and reaching out to people. The conference was organised in the form of a festival with dance, music and theatre performances, lectures, debates and food stalls. This was DMSC's first big public event. It was the first time in India that almost 3,000 sex workers

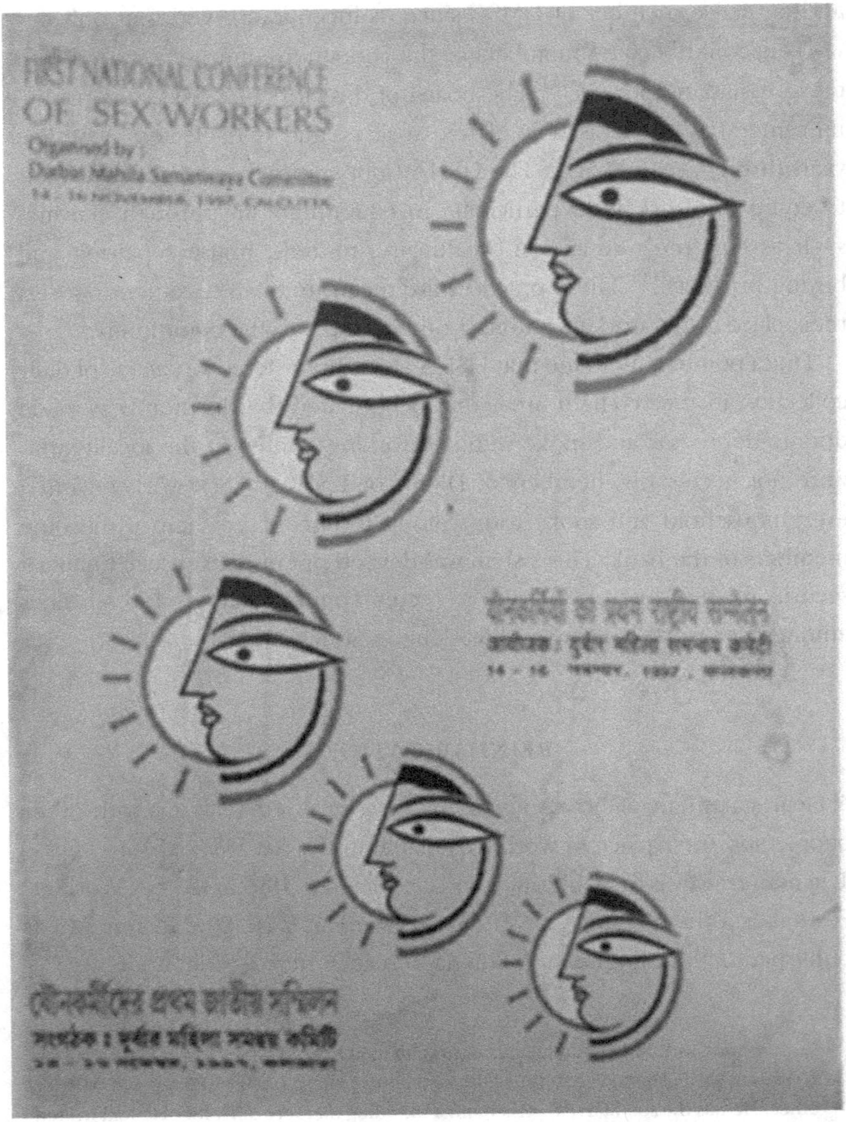

Figure 3.4 Booklet issued to mark the First Sex Workers' National Conference, Calcutta, organised by DMSC in 1997. *Source*: DMSC, Kolkata.

from all over the country had come together to talk collectively about their lives and demand rights publicly. The rallying cry at this conference was *gawtar khatiye khai, sramik-er adhikar chai* (we work our bodies, we want workers' rights). DMSC, *Durbar: A Brief Profile*, above n 97, 59; see generally Moni Nag, 'Sex Workers in Sonagachi' (2005) 40(49), *Economic and Political Weekly*, 5151.

Dutta noted that even though the *Sex Workers' Manifesto* was in English, a language that a majority of DMSC's members could not speak, read or write, the sex workers of DMSC were its co-authors, and the document was key for understanding the experiences of sex workers' collectivisation.[117] Making a distinction between *bhasha* (language) and *bhaab* (expression/meaning), he explained that the words were indeed chosen and put together by friends and allies, but the words derived their meaning from sex workers' lived experiences and DMSC's activist struggles.[118] For Dutta, the words could only make sense to a reader when they were related with sex workers' lived experiences of exploitation and the collective struggles against it.

The *Sex Workers' Manifesto* would only make sense if one looked for the correlations between the ideas posited in it and DMSC's larger practices of collectivisation. In doing so, it becomes apparent how the manifesto, and other activist publications like it, are a part of DMSC's cooperative mode of engagement within a public.[119] These publications are written for an external audience, to invite readers into friendly conversations with sex workers. A majority of DMSC's pamphlets and other published documents meant for public circulation are therefore addressed to a 'dear companion',[120] 'comrades'[121] or 'friends'.[122] Some of these documents end with a call for participation and cooperation of the reader,[123] 'not merely as a spectator or listener . . . [but] as comrade, [and] as organizer participants'.[124]

The *Sex Workers' Manifesto* ends with a clarion call: 'We have to win this battle and the war too – for a gender just, socially equitable, emotionally fulfilling, intellectually stimulating and exhilarating future for men,

[117] Conversation with Mrinal Kanti Dutta, above n 111. [118] Ibid.

[119] DMSC, *Durbar: A Brief Profile*, above n 97, 42.

[120] DMSC, '20 Years of USHA Multipurpose Cooperative Society' (January 2015) (on file with author; title translated from the Bangla).

[121] Secretary's Address, Third State Conference of Sex Workers (report published by DMSC, May 2005) (on file with author), 15.

[122] DMSC, *All India Conference of Entertainment Workers* (pamphlet published by DMSC, March 2007, on file with author).

[123] DMSC, '20 Years of USHA Multipurpose Cooperative Society', above n 120.

[124] DMSC, *All India Conference of Entertainment Workers*, above n 122.

women and children.'[125] For sex workers, the enemy in this 'battle' for gender justice is not men, or particular people, but certain 'ideologies' that dictate and govern people's actions. The DMSC argues that the responsibility for discriminatory actions should not be imposed only on individuals. Instead, it should be imposed on a discriminatory worldview that, in fact, makes certain discriminatory actions possible in a given society. Therefore, locating responsibility in individuals fails to shake the foundations of such actions, or the worldview of permissibility that enables the oppression of sex workers.[126]

This approach, which considers clients/buyers of sex work also as victims of an exploitative worldview, works to produce a different account of sex workers' relations with other people than what is espoused by the ITPA. For DMSC, clients, pimps and madams are admittedly abusive, but they are also the victims of an 'ideology' that permits the abuse and discriminatory treatment of sex workers. The *Sex Workers' Manifesto* points out to its readers that it 'is important to remember that there is no uniform category as men. Men like women are differentiated by their class, caste, race and other social relations'.[127] Moreover, in 'most cases this male client himself may be a poor, displaced man. Is he in a position to value his own life or has he enough motivation to protect his own health?'[128]

Although the *Sex Workers' Manifesto* states the specific problems facing sex workers, it does not propose that there are definitive solutions to the problems raised, or that the answers are known to sex workers. Rather, there is an admission of the fact that no authentic solutions are known to sex workers because they are themselves steeped in the ideologies they identify as the source of their exploitation.[129] Nonetheless, the document makes one point very clearly. It argues that sex workers experience the world in a particular way that is both similar to other marginalised

[125] DMSC, *Sex Workers' Manifesto*, above n 33.

[126] 'Conditioned by patriarchal gender ideologies both men and women in general approve of the control of sex trade and oppression of sex workers as necessary for maintaining social order. The power of this moral discourse is so strong that we prostitutes too tend to think of ourselves as morally corrupt and deprived. The men who come to us as clients are victims of the same ideology too.' Ibid.

[127] Ibid. [128] Ibid. [129] Ibid.

groups and different from others with respect to the sexual nature of their work.[130] Moreover, the use of 'we' and 'us' throughout the text, as opposed to 'you' and 'them', works to impose responsibility for the plight of sex workers on others as well as on sex workers themselves. In doing so, the *Sex Workers' Manifesto* creates a sex worker who assumes responsibility for her own life in the relations that are formed with others.

The *Sex Workers' Manifesto* has been widely read and interpreted by feminist scholars/academics/researchers.[131] Feminist economist Swati Ghosh traces the similarities and dissimilarities between the manifesto and its 'near-namesake the Communist Manifesto'.[132] In her reading of the manifesto, however, Ghosh identifies more differences than similarities in the content and approaches of the two texts. According to Ghosh, the *Sex Workers' Manifesto* identifies patriarchy, rather than class, as the cause of sex workers' oppression. Arguing that the *Sex Workers' Manifesto* is critical of patriarchy, Ghosh proceeds to evaluate whether the analysis in 'the sex workers' manifesto is feminist',[133] and if it is able to conceive of 'a gender-just society that would not marginalize sex workers'.[134] At the end of her essay, Ghosh concludes that the *Sex Workers' Manifesto* is, in fact, not feminist.[135] By reading the *Sex Workers' Manifesto* as a standalone text independent of the activism that manifested it, Ghosh argues that the DMSC's position on gender is not informed by a feminist tradition that conceives male/female relations as a binary opposition.[136]

My engagement with the field of Indian feminist jurisprudence more broadly, and my specific method of engaging with the *Sex Workers'*

[130] Ibid.

[131] See generally DMSC, *Sex Workers Manifesto*, in Kotiswaran, *Sex Work*, 268; DMSC, *Sex Workers' Manifesto*, in *Sarai Reader 05: Bare Acts*, http://archive.sarai.net/files/original/fccac16766a1acc2cd3ee2956fe9e03c.pdf.

[132] Swati Ghosh, 'Elusive Choice and Agency: A Feminist Re-reading of the Sex Workers' Manifesto', in Rohini Sahni, V. Kalyan Shankar and Hemant Apte (eds), *Prostitution and Beyond: An Analysis of Sex Workers in India* (Sage, 2008) 54–72, 56.

[133] Ibid., 66. [134] Ibid.

[135] 'The declared radical content of the manifesto nearly evaporates at a closer scrutiny ... The power relation was not reversed in the least. The basic paradigm of the manifesto continued to stick to the liberal frame intact, presuming away the imperative of dependence and domination.' Ibid.

[136] Ibid.

Manifesto through adda, reveals a different account and forces me to differ with Ghosh. My method of interpreting the *Sex Workers' Manifesto* presents the text in a continuum with the field of Indian feminist jurisprudence that I outlined in Chapter 1. The position on the inseparable nature of gender and class that is held in the *Sex Workers' Manifesto* is, in fact, reminiscent of an Indian feminist tradition that is not conceived singularly on the basis of a male/female binary opposition.[137] The account of class and gender relations that emerges from sex workers' experiences of collectivisation and cooperative thinking, as reflected in the *Sex Workers' Manifesto*, has significant implications for how sex workers mutually relate with law. This will become more evident when I discuss DMSC's anti-trafficking mechanism called Self-Regulatory Boards later in this section.

The *Sex Workers' Manifesto* places male–female relations in a hierarchy, as well as in a continuum of oppression. The text acknowledges male privilege, alongside sex workers' vulnerability in comparison to other women. It juxtaposes such understanding with an acknowledgment of the additional vulnerability experienced by male sex workers in comparison to women who are engaged in the same profession.[138] For me, as noted earlier, sex workers' thinking on the interrelated nature of class and gender is clearly in conversation with the scholarship that shapes the field of Indian feminist jurisprudence.

Adda makes visible the work that the text does by linking sex workers' experiences with 'the labourer from Bihar who pulls a rickshaw in Calcutta, or the worker from Calcutta who works part time in a factory in Bombay'.[139] The articulation of experiential commonalities between sex workers and these other migrant, marginalised groups of men works to show how 'woman' is understood as a relational category not just in terms of gender or class, but also place. Perceiving the sex worker in these terms further works to clarify the rationale behind the practical workings of USHA, which I will discuss now.

The DMSC's organisational documents state that the USHA cooperative bank was not formed for the purpose of economic *rehabilitation* of sex

[137] Refer to my discussion in Section 1.2 in Chapter 1.
[138] DMSC, *Sex Workers' Manifesto*, above n 33. [139] Ibid.

workers active in the profession. Rather, it was designed to provide financial support to sex workers in situations of crisis, and to 'minimize economic desperation by creating a space for negotiation'.[140] The DMSC argues that state-sanctioned rehabilitation programmes that attempt to remove sex workers from their occupation 'through meager income generation activities' are 'unable to erase the social stigma carried by sex workers'.[141] Even if sex workers are taught different activities, these skills are rendered useless because of the stigma associated with sex work, due to which people do not access their services. The DMSC's position on rehabilitation is further explained in the *Sex Workers' Manifesto*, which states, 'is rehabilitation a feasible or even desirable option for us? In a country where unemployment is of such gigantic proportions, where does the compulsion of displacing millions of women and men who are already engaged in an income earning occupation which supports themselves and their extended families come from?'[142]

The ITPA stipulates the 'removal' of sex workers from where prostitution is carried out in order to 'rescue' women from trafficking.[143] After rescuing her, the police are supposed to present a sex worker to a magistrate. The magistrate is then supposed to determine the 'prospects of her rehabilitation'.[144] Based on what the magistrate deems fit, the sex worker is either sent home or kept in institutional care under the guardianship of the state. Once rescued, the act does not permit adult sex workers to decide where they want to go, or with whom they want to live. Against this backdrop, the ownership of a financial institution by sex workers not only provides them with financial support, but also enables them to claim their belonging to their occupation, and the place where it is carried out.

Sex workers' belonging to their occupation and place of work is firmly established through the formulation of USHA's by-laws.[145] The latter

[140] DMSC, *Durbar: A Brief Profile*, above n 97, 25 (emphasis in original); by-laws of USHA Multipurpose Co-operative Society Limited (n.d.) (on file with author).

[141] DMSC, *Sex Workers' Manifesto*, above n 33. [142] Ibid.

[143] ITPA, above n 60, Sec. 2(f) and Sec. 16. [144] Ibid., Sec. 17(2).

[145] By-laws of Usha Multipurpose Co-operative Society Limited (n.d.) (on file with author). This document was originally in Bangla, because none of the sex workers speaks English, but was later translated into English by a non–sex worker staff of DMSC.

state that the 'economical [*sic*] development and social *rehabitation* of Sex Worker'[146] is USHA's primary objective. The use of 'rehabitation', a term that is not part of common parlance, yet sounds similar to reinhabitation, is telling. The online version of the *Oxford English Dictionary* defines 'rehabitation' as 'the action or an act of *reinhabiting* a country, area, house, etc.'[147] The term has a particular conceptual usage in the works of American ecologists Peter Berg and Raymond F. Dasmann. In the late 1970s, the concept was used by Berg and Dasmann to articulate a practice of responsible living at a place by caring for it and through its restoration.[148] The authors explain: 'reinhabitation means learning to live-in-place in an area that has been disrupted and injured through past exploitation ... It involves applying for membership in a biotic community and ceasing to be its exploiter.'[149]

What Berg and Dasmann understood by 'reinhabitation' is reflected in DMSC's activism. The use of *rehabitation* in the by-laws of the society, as one of USHA's objectives, speaks to sex workers' desire for cooperation amongst the members of their community for undoing exploitation. It is suggestive of an assertion of sex workers' relationship to their place of occupation and living. It is also suggestive of a desire to make that very place liveable, rather than get 'displaced', or be removed or *rehabilitated* to another place and another occupation. In such a formulation, DMSC echoes Berg and Dasmann's idea of living-in-place as a practice of living responsibly by forming a relationship with 'place' and caring for it. The DMSC's reinhabitation of place is realised through USHA, since it enables women to continue to work as sex workers and fosters mutual ties with those who inhabit Sonagachi, where the women live and work.

Adda with members of DMSC made it evident that the activist practice of reinhabitation tied back to the question of the role and responsibilities that sex workers decided to carve out for themselves when the women

146 Ibid., By-law 4(a); emphasis added.

147 *Oxford English Dictionary* (my emphasis), www.oxforddictionaries.com/definition/english/rehabitation.

148 Peter Berg and Raymond F. Dasmann, 'Reinhabiting California', in David Pepper, Frank Webster and George Revill (eds), *Environmentalisms: Critical Concepts* (Routledge, 2002), vol. 2, 231.

149 Ibid., 232.

first started organising in Sonagachi in the early 1990s. What became apparent as I engaged in adda with sex workers was how the sex workers' intellectual and practical processes of organisation, through which DMSC materialised as a collective, simultaneously involved the formation of mutual relations with law. This kind of relationship with law, which was set in motion by officially designating DMSC as a *sex workers' collective* through registration under the WBSRA, is actualised, for instance, by way of an internal mode of organising mutual relations amongst sex workers.

ELECTIONS

The formation of mutual relations amongst sex workers, which is at the heart of DMSC's organising force, can be understood in terms of its membership structure. The sex worker members of DMSC can be classified into two kinds. One, those who hold leadership positions within the organisation through a process of election and look after its overall workings. Two, those who are known as *shadharon* jouno kormi, or ordinary sex workers, and are responsible for specific funded and non-funded organisational activities. The DMSC's leadership positions – secretary, president and treasurer – have been created as a result of its official registration under the WBSRA, which requires every organisation to fill these three positions. The DMSC's members decided to institute an elaborate electoral process, even though it is not mandated under the act, to create a sustainable leadership structure based on rotation. Elections in the DMSC, as Nashkar mentioned to me, are a means of self-training in how to take up responsibilities in the role of sex worker activist, and of learning how to execute such responsibilities by thinking collectively and not for individual gain.[150]

Seema Fokla, sex worker and member of DMSC who follows the election process closely, recounted in our adda that DMSC elections are conducted every three years and at two levels – branch committees and the central committee. These committees work to demarcate DMSC's jurisdiction and determine the nature of authority that its members can wield in relation to one another.

[150] Conversation with Bishakha Nashkar, above n 1.

The central committee is located in Sonagachi. The secretary, president and treasurer of each branch committee elects the central committee, which consists of the secretary, assistant secretary, president, vice president and treasurer. In order to maintain the democratic structure at the central level, a working committee is formed with a total of fourteen elected members who represent different constituencies within the sex worker community.[151] Fokla told me that the branch committees at the field level and the working committee were meant for jointly putting in place a leadership structure that would not allow any individual leader to assume absolute power.[152]

In a detailed internal document that lays down the guidelines for contesting DMSC elections, it is stated that a candidate has to be a female sex worker, and a member of DMSC with at least two years of organisational work experience.[153] She must have good relationships with sex workers in her locality and be able to protest abusive actions by her *babu* (partner/permanent client). An elected person can serve only for two terms and cannot stand for election after that. She must be able to declare publicly that she is a sex worker, even on television and in the print media. Those who have an employee status with the DMSC by virtue of working on its donor-funded projects have to resign from their paid positions in order to contest elections.[154]

Once a candidate gets elected as leader, she has to make herself available for organisational work at any time of the day or night, whenever there is any emergency. For this reason, a sex worker who has a chronic illness that requires her to be in bed most of the time, as well those who have little children between one and five years, cannot contest elections. However, if a sex worker gives birth or adopts a child after she is elected, she will still be required to fulfil the responsibilities of her leadership role. A sex worker who is unable to deliver on her responsibilities even after six months of getting elected will have to step down from her position of community leader.

151 DMSC, *Codes of Conduct for Durbar Leaders and Members* (pamphlet published by DMSC, n. d., on file with author) (title translated into English by author).

152 Conversation with Seema Fokla, sex worker and DMSC member, Kalighat, Kolkata, 24 September 2014.

153 Detailed list of internal rules and regulations for elections (on file with author).

154 Conversation with Seema Fokla, above n 152.

Although DMSC intended to foster mutual relations between sex workers, it is evident from some of the organisational guidelines that this was not the sole intention. The organisational practices of DMSC are conceived with a view to inculcating a sense of fairness and an unbiased worldview in sex workers' minds. The DMSC's activism is also interested in building mutual relationships with those who are not sex workers. For instance, DMSC lays down in its guidelines that in case of any dispute between sex workers and others, or between sex workers, they would generally support a sex worker, but come to a conclusion only after listening to both parties.[155] The DMSC's members decided to make friends with sex workers and learn about their needs and conditions, and also build friendship with those who were outside of the sex work context in order to let them know about sex workers' lives.[156] Members of the DMSC forbid the use of any kind of foul language or verbal abuse against another person, sex worker or not. A non–sex worker member and employee of the DMSC, Mahashweta Mukherjee, told me that the penalty imposed for such action was that the person would have to treat everyone else to a cup of tea at her own expense.[157] Thus, the atonement for such actions is not conceived in terms of singling out and ostracising the guilty member from the community. Rather, it has been designed to foster inclusion and mutual ties within the community.

The DMSC's electoral process is an elaborate system by which women are positioned in the public and in relation to public institutions as sex workers by placing them in decision-making roles within the sex worker community. This process also provides a nuanced mechanism for power sharing amongst sex workers who assume leadership positions within the organisation. The design of the electoral process is attentive to power differences between female sex workers and male partners and clients, as well as amongst female sex workers – in particular, between sex workers who occupy decision-making roles and others who do not.

Sex workers' relations within the sex worker community, and with the non–sex worker staff who are employed by DMSC to assist in its work, are

[155] Conversation with Bishakha Nashkar, above n 1. [156] Ibid.

[157] Conversation with Mahashweta Mukherjee, non–sex worker advocacy officer, DMSC, Girish Park, Kolkata, 12 October 2014.

founded on 'three "R"s – Respect, Reliance and Recognition'.[158] This refers to 'Respect towards sex workers, Reliance on their potential and knowledge to run the programme and the Recognition of their professional and human rights'.[159] There are gender, class, caste and educational differences between sex workers and their staff. In order to prevent such differences from translating into hierarchies between them within DMSC, 'the 3 Rs' act as principles of self-regulation. These principles are meant to regulate the conduct of each and every DMSC member to ensure that they remain accountable to their larger collective ideal of cooperation.[160]

By formulating community interest as that which does not benefit sex worker members of the organisation alone, DMSC broadens the concept of community for sex workers. The formulation of these rules suggests that community does not consist of sex workers alone. It is constituted of a network of people with whom sex workers interact and share their lives and livelihoods. It includes sex workers who are not yet members of DMSC, non–sex workers residing in the locality, children and partners of sex workers, as well as clients, pimps and madams.

Sex worker Purnima Chatterjee shared that DMSC's regulatory practices, likewise, were not limited to only sex workers.[161] Self-regulation refers to a reorganisation of relations amongst sex workers. It also refers to a practice of the reorganisation of sex workers' relations with state representatives *by* sex workers themselves. This aspect of DMSC's activism becomes evident on engaging with their conception and implementation of the anti-trafficking mechanism called the Self-Regulatory Boards (SRB).

SELF-REGULATORY BOARDS

With the liberalisation of the Indian economy in the 1990s, foreign funding started to arrive for developmental issues, including for women's uplift. Out of this, a state and NGO regime emerged with a shared

[158] DMSC, *Durbar: A Brief Profile*, above n 97, 10. [159] Ibid.

[160] Conversations with Bishakha Nashkar, above n 1; Mrinal Kanti Dutta, above n 111.

[161] Conversation with Purnima Chatterjee, above n 30.

anti-trafficking agenda, which fused with the HIV/AIDS-related interventions that targeted sex workers as a high-risk group. The inflow of funds coincided with the 1995 World Conference on Women in Beijing, where India renewed its commitment to the combat of trafficking. In this scenario, a state-authorised anti-trafficking agenda, which already existed and was being carried out through ITPA, got strengthened.[162]

Against this backdrop of state-authorised anti-trafficking measures, DMSC created the SRBs in Sonagachi in 1999 (see Fig. 3.5). This localised intervention was specifically meant for tackling 'the problem of underage and unwilling girls trafficked into sex work sites, and of unwilling women duped/coerced/forced into sex work'.[163] Purnima Chatterjee explained to me that SRBs focus on women and girls because in the brothels in Kolkata, only female sex workers provide their sexual services, therefore, only women and girls could get forced to work there.[164]

The SRBs consist of a committee of nine or ten members, of which sex workers and their children comprise 50 per cent of the membership.[165] The SRBs' anti-trafficking model is based on what DMSC describes as a 'public–private partnership', because it is instituted through 'collaborative efforts of sex workers and of people from the rest of the society'.[166] Jana noted during our adda that the SRBs were a means of creating local partnerships between sex workers and state officials who held institutional positions.[167] Debnath mentioned to me that the inclusion of government representatives in the functioning of SRBs was a way of making officials who had institutional resources execute their duties of addressing the issue of trafficking jointly *with* sex workers.[168]

162 See, generally, Kapur, 'India', in *Collateral Damage*, 114.

163 DMSC, *Self Regulatory Board: A Rolling Success in Anti-trafficking Program, Lessons Learnt From DMSC* (Durbar Prakashani, 2007), 8 (on file with author).

164 Conversation with Purnima Chatterjee, above n 30.

165 The rest of the committee includes a member of the state legislative assembly, a member of parliament, a local counsellor, a medical doctor, a lawyer, a person from the Ministry of Women and Social Welfare, and a person working in a local women's rights NGO. DMSC, *Community Led Anti Trafficking and Child Protection Program* (Durbar Prakashani, 2013), 19 (on file with author).

166 DMSC, *Self Regulatory Board*, above n 163, 13.

167 Conversation with Smarajit Jana, above n 14.

168 Conversation with Rama Debnath, above n 55.

Figure 3.5 DMSC booklet on the Self-Regulatory Board. *Source*: DMSC, Kolkata.

Debnath noted that the state would never repeal the ITPA, no matter how assertively sex workers argued that it was discriminatory and ineffective for putting an end to trafficking.[169] Because of this, sex workers themselves had to take the responsibility of putting in place an alternative model that might actually be useful in the situation and create a dialogue with the state. Otherwise, the state would never be willing to involve sex workers in its own discourses on this issue.[170] Chatterjee told me that even if DMSC's model was not perfect, it was useful for starting public discussion, debate and a contemplation on trafficking based on sex workers' activist experiences. Most importantly, SRBs were able to challenge the foregone conclusion about the effectiveness of punitive measures as the only possible means of addressing trafficking.[171]

Dey recounted that sex workers needed to present an alternative model that was able to speak to the anti-trafficking discourse of the state, albeit differently, and only then could the state be drawn to carry out mutual discussion with sex workers.[172] For sex workers, the state was an important public institution.[173] It was necessary for instituting structural changes in sex workers' lives that were not possible through small-scale interventions. The state machinery is also considered to be an important catalyst for undoing social stigma, provided sex workers are themselves able to make the institution and its laws work to their own advantage as their friends (see Fig. 3.6).[174]

DMSC's intention of making the state work in their favour is accompanied by methods that are distinct from the state-sanctioned anti-trafficking approach to sex work. Their method is distinct in two ways. First, rather than aiming for the penalisation of traffickers, the focus of SRBs is on trafficked persons. Greater importance is given to privacy, confidentiality and respect for the decision-making capacity of the trafficked person. The SRBs focus on providing 'career building opportunities

[169] Ibid. [170] Ibid.

[171] Conversations with Purnima Chatterjee, above n 30; Smarajit Jana, above n 14.

[172] Conversations with Bharati Dey, above n 27; Purnima Chatterjee, above n 30; Smarajit Jana, above n 14.

[173] Conversation with Bharati Dey, above n 27.

[174] Conversations with Bharati Dey, above n 27; Bishakha Nashkar, above n 1.

Figure 3.6 'Law as a friend of sex workers': A DMSC booklet on sex workers' legal rights. *Source*: DMSC, Kolkata.

[to the trafficked person] instead of taking decisions on her behalf'.[175] The rescued person's preference is also given priority for deciding whether she would be sent to her own residence or kept in institutional care.[176] The DMSC believes that long-term institutionalisation of a rescued person amounts to a prison-like condition in which a person's need for a shared life and livelihood is not met.[177]

Second, SRBs attempt to tackle trafficking 'by making it non-viable … [for] madams and brothel owners to recruit underage or trafficked persons as sex workers'.[178] This means that DMSC believes in convincing pimps and madams that employing underage and unwilling persons is a harmful practice. Dey noted during our adda that convincing madams so that they willingly cooperated with DMSC, rather than punishing them, could ensure long-lasting systemic change.

So far, my adda with the sex workers shows that cooperative thinking and the reinhabitation of Sonagachi are the two primary collective organisational practices that amalgamate the formation of DMSC. The SRBs, USHA and the official registration of DMSC, all of which are founded on 'cooperation' and 'reinhabitation', shape the role of a sex worker and a form of mutual engagement in women's relations in public life. I will now attend to how DMSC addresses issues of caste in their conversations with the judiciary, and continues its consolidation of a new role of the sex worker in legal discourse, which was initiated with the formation of DMSC in 1995.

SEX WORKERS AND THE JUDICIARY

The reinhabitation of Sonagachi where the sex workers live and work, and cooperation amongst sex workers and other people, is also experienced by DMSC members through the organisation of public festivals. Public festivals have been a crucial aspect of DMSC's activism since the early days of its formation.[179] The DMSC's members argue that festivals are a popular form of social life, and the celebratory mode of interaction at festivals makes for an effective backdrop for public engagement in

[175] DMSC, *Community Led Anti Trafficking*, above n 165, 19. [176] Ibid. [177] Ibid.
[178] Ibid., 18. [179] DMSC, *Durbar: A Brief Profile*, above n 97, 52.

which ordinary people, including sex workers themselves, can partake with pleasure.[180]

Dey noted that the form of interaction at such events was an effective way in which sex workers were able to engage in conversations with common people and secure a place amongst them.[181] Through participation in public festivals, sex workers are able to challenge the negative perception that exists in people's minds about them and undo the stigma that engulfs their lives.[182]

In 2013, the DMSC tradition of organising public festivals was extended to the celebration of the Durga Puja, a major Hindu festival in Bengal. In popular understanding, this festival is regarded as a marker of the victory of good over evil and celebrates the mythological defeat of the half-man half-buffalo demon, Mahishasura, by the goddess with ten hands, *dashabhuja* Durga, an epitome of positive female power.[183] By virtue of being a Hindu festival, the celebration of the Durga Puja is interconnected with caste practices ordained by the religion.[184]

Durga's four children, who are also worshipped along with her during the festival, represent the four tiers of graded caste hierarchy within Hinduism.[185] Saraswati, the goddess of learning, represents the Brahmins; Kartikeya, the god of power, represents the Kshatriyas;

[180] See Debolina Dutta and Oishik Sircar, 'Sex, Work and Pleasure', *Times of India*, 10 April 2007, http://timesofindia.indiatimes.com/edit-page/Sex-work-and-pleasure/articleshow/1881189.cms; Debolina Dutta and Oishik Sircar, 'From Entertainment Worker to Sex Worker: Strategic Politics of DMSC' (2008) 4(3), *Global South*, 3–5.

[181] Conversation with Bharati Dey, above n 27.

[182] Ibid.; conversation with Purnima Chatterjee, above n 30.

[183] Gopal Sengupta, 'Meaning of Durga Puja', *Daily Star*, 6 October 2011, http://archive.thedailystar.net/newDesign/news-details.php?nid=205286.

[184] Some scholars argue that the celebration of the festival in the city of Kolkata takes on an urban secular nature. However, through the festival's caste connotations, its religious aspect very much lives on. This is not to argue against the secular nature of the festival in Bengal, but to assert that the creation of a binary opposition between religion and secularism is not helpful for understanding how ideas of religion and secularism may be more interrelated than distinct from each other. See generally Anjan Ghosh, 'Spaces of Recognition: Puja and Power in Contemporary Calcutta' (2000) 26(2), *Journal of Southern African Studies*, 289–99; Tapati Guha-Thakurta, *In the Name of the Goddess: Durga Pujas of Contemporary Kolkata* (Primus Books, 2015).

[185] For an accessible introduction to the system of caste in India, see Surinder S. Jodhka, *Caste* (Oxford University Press, 2013).

Lakshmi, the goddess of wealth, represents the Vaishyas; and Ganesh, the elephant god of labour, represents the Shudras.[186] The meaning that may be read into this practice of worshipping this cluster of gods/goddesses is rather telling: in the worship of the goddess Durga, a religious figure, these four castes are made to stand united and form a harmonious social order that is then able to fight and defeat an outside, evil force.

As a matter of tradition, to make the idol of the goddess the potters require *punya mati*, or sacred mud from a brothel, a sex worker's home (see Fig. 3.7). A popular belief that sustains this age-old mud ritual is the idea that the threshold of a sex worker's house is most pious because men who enter the place shed all their virtues at this point, making the soil where such virtues accumulate pure and sacred.[187] There are competing stories originating from different sources that explain this ritual in different ways; however, in DMSC's understanding, this practice is an inheritance of the caste order.[188]

The DMSC argues that in the past, in Bengal, the worship of the goddess's children ensured that the four main castes into which a traditional Hindu society was divided were represented through the festival.[189] There were certain occupations in society that did not find representation in the 'chaturvarna', the fourfold caste system, and which were left out of the composition of the gods/goddesses worshipped during Durga Puja. In the festival, the outcastes also had to be included in the social fold. This led to the practice of collecting mud from the houses of people who were otherwise kept outside of the caste system: *beshya* (prostitute), *dom* (those who cremate dead bodies), *muchi* (cobbler), *myathor* (manual scavenger, sweeper), *kamar* (iron worker).[190] According to DMSC, this discriminatory practice is still continued only with sex workers in the name of religious tradition. This becomes possible because, unlike in case of the others, sex workers' segregation from

[186] June McDaniel, *Offering Flowers, Feeding Skulls: Popular Goddess Worship in West Bengal* (Oxford University Press, 2014), 225.

[187] DMSC, *Smarakpatra*, 17 (on file with author); see Banerjee, *Dangerous Outcast*, 24.

[188] DMSC, *Sex Workers' Durga Puja Will Now Reach Your Neighbourhood From Sonagachi: Are You with Us?* (DMSC pamphlet, n.d., on file with author; translation of title by author).

[189] Ibid. [190] Ibid.

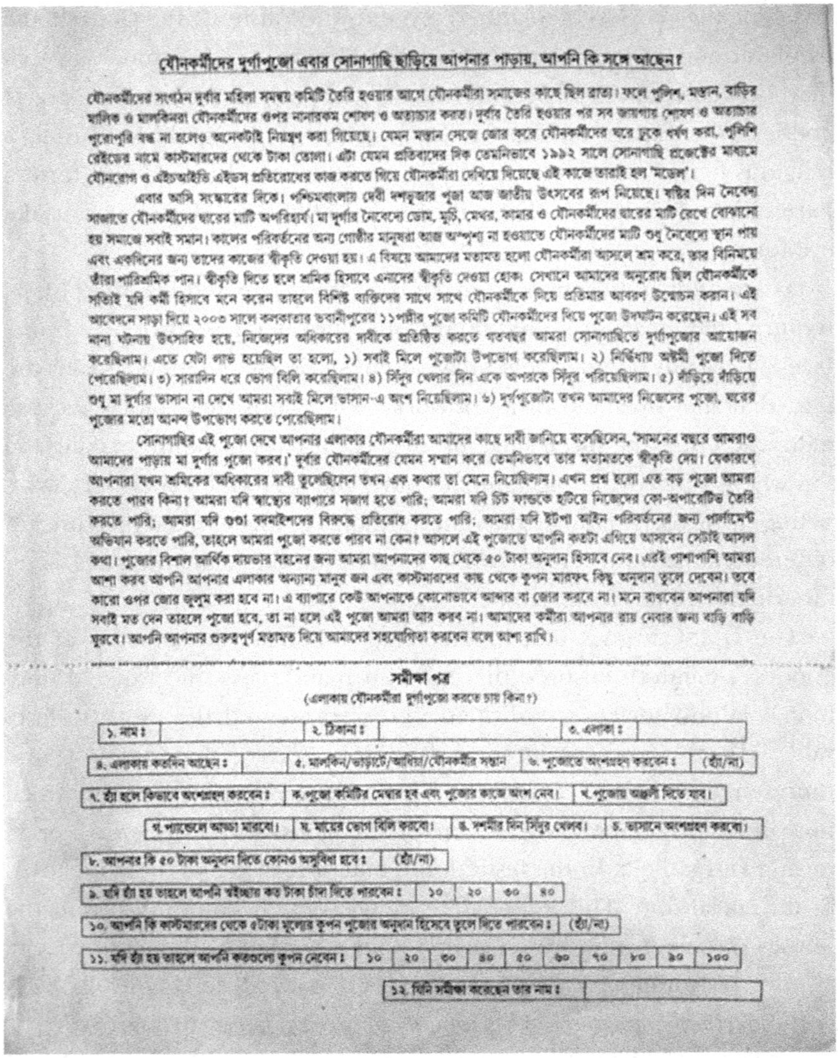

Figure 3.7 DMSC pamphlet explaining the caste-based exclusion of sex workers from Durga Puja. *Source*: DMSC, Kolkata.

the rest of the society is legitimised by the criminalisation of their life and occupation.[191] With the aid of criminal law, the religious practice

[191] Although, in theory, there may be some truth to this claim, in practice, the segregation of lower-caste people from participating in the festival still continues. In 2010, a leading daily newspaper article in West Bengal reported an incident where thirty families living

continues to preserve discriminatory caste-based social relations and constructs the sex worker as an inferior subject compared to other women because of her occupation.

Dey recounted to me that to work against sex workers' segregation from community life through the organisation of public festivals, DMSC deployed a simple method.[192] The DMSC's public events are open for everyone to attend and are organised by obtaining written permission from state authorities for the use of public places. This gives confidence to sex workers in asserting their public presence. For sex workers, as Dey shared with me, this practice of obtaining state permission works to make a legitimate claim to public life. It helps them gain official evidence that attests to the fact that sex workers are like other citizens. That is, sex workers are neither inferior to others, nor do they claim to be above the rules that every other ordinary citizen has to follow.[193]

In 2013, the sex workers of DMSC decided to organise the Durga Puja in Sonagachi. As Dey noted, the women made an application to the local police station seeking permission to use an area in the locality for constructing the *pandal*, a temporary shaded structure within which the goddess is placed. Before doing so, discussions were held amongst sex workers on whether organising the festival would be opposed to DMSC's activist practices.[194] The DMSC had earlier resisted the mud ritual as a way of protesting sex workers' social segregation, so it was a concern whether organising the festival would be in conflict with their belief.[195] But given that a majority of sex workers experienced exclusion from participating freely in celebrations of the festival because of social stigma, DMSC decided to organise the festival.

in Murshidabad belonging to the Muchi caste were not allowed to take part in the Durga Puja celebrations in the village. Alamgir Hosain, 'Caste Bar on Puja Festivity', *Telegraph*, 16 October 2010, www.telegraphindia.com/1101016/jsp/bengal/story_13063416.jsp.

[192] Conversation with Bharati Dey, above n 27.

[193] Ibid.; conversation with Mahashweta Mukherjee, above n 157.

[194] Conversation with Mahashweta Mukherjee, above n 157.

[195] Sujoy Dhar, 'RIGHTS-INDIA: Sex Workers Draw the Line on Religious Rites', *Inter Press Service*, 5 September 2002, www.ipsnews.net/2002/09/rights-india-sex-workers-draw-the-line-on-religious-rites.

The Kolkata Police Department is the authority that grants permission to people who wish to publicly organise the Durga Puja. The police refused to grant permission to DMSC for organising the festival in Sonagachi, stating that the refusal could only be overturned by a court order.[196] In general, litigation was not a preferred method of activism for sex workers. Being a process that is both money- and time-consuming, for a group of poor women it seldom yields results that are comparable to the resources that are invested.[197] In this case, however, DMSC decided to go to court because there was no other effective way of ensuring that the festival could be organised by sex workers with the cooperation of the police and local residents in Sonagachi, which was essential for holding the large-scale event of the Durga Puja successfully.[198]

The sex workers filed a writ petition in the Calcutta High Court 'against the refusal … [or] in-action on the part of the State Administration' for not allowing sex workers 'to perform Durga puja, the annual festival of … [the] State'.[199] Because sex workers were social 'outcasts' who were 'not allowed to have free access to any Public Puja Pandal',[200] the denial of permission attained a different meaning for them. It amounted to a violation of the constitutional guarantee that confers on every citizen of India the right 'to profess, practice and propagate religion'.[201]

In the Calcutta High Court, the matter was presided over by a two-judge bench that was surprised at the fact that despite their marginalised status, the petitioners 'did not feel shy to call themselves … sex workers'.[202] The bench noted that it realised that the petitioners were

196 Conversation with Bharati Dey, above n 27.

197 Prabha Kotiswaran has characterised the Indian sex workers' movement as 'litigation-shy'. Prabha Kotiswaran, 'Sword or Shield? The Role of the Law in the Indian Sex Workers' Movement' (2013) 15(4), *Interventions: International Journal of Postcolonial Studies*, 530–48.

198 Conversation with Bharati Dey, above n 27.

199 *State of West Bengal & Ors* v. *Durbar Mahila Samanwaya Committee & Ors*, M.A.T. 1493 of 2013, High Court of Calcutta Appellate Side, Banerjee HJ and Chaudhuri HJ, 26 September 2013, https://indiankanoon.org/doc/63503501.

200 Ibid.

201 The Constitution of India, 1949, Article 25, https://indiankanoon.org/doc/631708.

202 *State of West Bengal* v. *Durbar Mahila Samanwaya Committee*, above n 199.

'asking for their recognition[, which] is a debatable issue' and so it would be appropriate 'for the legislature to give a thought over it' instead.[203]

However, because the case related to the rights of a historically marginalised group, the judges felt that it was a significant matter and ordered the formation of a joint committee consisting of all parties involved in the dispute to mutually find a solution to the problem. A committee was thus formed consisting of three lawyers appointed by the court, the sub-inspector of the local police station, representatives of DMSC and the other groups whose applications were also allegedly rejected by the police.[204] The committee, after discussions, decided that the festival would be jointly organised, although a majority share of the expenses would be borne by the DMSC and that the latter would take the lead.[205]

DMSC's Durga Puja celebration was unique in many respects.[206] Never before, anywhere in West Bengal, had this annual festival been officially and publicly celebrated by sex workers. The event was widely reported in the newspapers and many people visited the site just to witness this fact.[207] At the festival, the idol of the goddess Durga and the demon Mahishasura looked like any other ordinary idols. The goddess held the different weapons in her ten hands, impaling Mahishasura with a trident, and her four children stood next to her, two on each side. But, in a very subtle way, DMSC publicised its demand for the repeal of the ITPA that criminalised sex workers' lives.[208] A placard was hung around the neck of Mahishasura with 'ITPA' written on it (see Figs. 3.8 and 3.9), signifying

[203] Ibid.

[204] In 2016, due to police harassment, DMSC could not organise the festival. See PTI, 'Kolkata: Sex Workers Complain About Police Harassment, Stop Holding Durga Puja', *Indian Express*, 7 October 2016, http://indianexpress.com/article/india/india-news-india/sex-workers-in-kolkata-stop-holding-durga-puja-3070859.

[205] *State of West Bengal* v. *Durbar Mahila Samanwaya Committee*, above n 199.

[206] Conversation with Mahashweta Mukherjee, above n 157.

[207] See IANS, 'Finally, Kolkata Sex Workers Get Their Own Durga Puja', *Business Standard* (online), 9 October 2013, www.business-standard.com/article/news-ians/finally-kolkata-sex-workers-get-their-own-durga-puja-113100900907_1.html; *Outlook*, 'Kolkata Sex Workers Host Their First Own Durga Puja', 11 October 2014, http://test.outlookindia.com/newswire/story/kolkata-sex-workers-host-their-first-own-durga-puja/813238.

[208] In Kolkata, there is a vibrant tradition of using the Durga Puja to raise awareness around contemporary events of societal concern. See generally IANS, 'Durga Puja Pandals to

Figure 3.8 DMSC's Durga Puja, 12 October 2013. *Source*: *India Today*, 'Sex-Workers in Kolkata Are Being Trained to Work at Food Stalls for Durga Puja Celebrations', 22 September 2017, www.indiatoday.in/lifestyle/people/story/sex-workers-sonagachi-red-light-area-durga-puja-training-govt-food-stalls-lifest-1050139-2017-09-22.

Figure 3.9 Mahishasura: Law as demon incarnate. *Source*: Hemchhaya De, 'Is Consensual Sex Work a Crime?', *Telegraph*, 23 October 2013, www.telegraphindia.com/1131023/jsp/opinion/story_17483745.jsp#.WFy8bLZ96Rs.

Touch Upon Controversial Global Issues', *Hans India*, 3 October 2015, www.thehansindia.com/posts/index/National/2015-10-03/Durga-Puja-pandals-to-touch-upon-controversial-global-issues/178993; *India Today*, 'Kolkata Durga Puja Harps On Various Social Issues With Theme Puja', 19 October 2015, http://indiatoday.intoday.in/education/story/durga-puja-pandals/1/502282.html.

the defeat of the demonic ITPA in the hands of the collective power of sex workers.[209] This form of representation, for Mukherjee, also symbolised the defeat of the exploitative police force that routinely abused its powers by using ITPA to harass, exploit and extort from sex workers.[210]

The adda with sex workers helped me understand that in DMSC's Durga Puja, because permission was sought from official sources, the police were, in fact, made to cooperate with and assist sex workers towards a smooth organisation of the event. This new relationship of cooperation with the police that was enacted by way of sex workers' conversations with the judiciary worked to alter the state dismissal of sex workers' will and decision-making capacity through ITPA in matters concerning their own lives and livelihood. Because as a method adda helps to focus on relations, and modes of their organisation and reordering, I have been able to recognise how DMSC's act of going to court with this matter was significant. Such action worked to draw the state, through its representatives, into an alternative legal relationship with sex workers that was based on the practices of cooperation and reinhabitation of Sonagachi.

The performance of adda makes apparent that the organisation of the festival also acts against a caste-based segregation of sex workers from the general category of women to instil a sense of mutuality amongst them. This is done through an activist practice of the traditional ritual of *shidoor khela,* from which sex workers used to be otherwise socially barred. The ritual of shidoor khela, performed on the last day of the festival, is a public ritual in which only married women, not widows, can participate. To perform this ritual, women smear vermillion, a symbol of their married status, on each other's foreheads and engage in friendly play with one another.

Mukherjee noted that in DMSC's activist practice of shidoor khela, sex workers and non–sex workers – married, unmarried, widowed, male, female, transgender, young, old and disabled – were all equally

[209] There is a counter-story from an Adivasi vantage that reveals how the characterisation of the ITPA as the Mahishasura reproduces racism and casteism. See, Debolina Dutta, 'Of Festivals, Rights and Public Life: Sex Workers' Activism in India as Affirmative Sabotage', *Australian Feminist Law Journal* 44 (2) (2018), 221–43.

[210] Conversation with Mahashweta Mukherjee, above n 157.

welcomed.[211] DMSC did not consider the shidoor khela as an endorsement of a religious tradition, or an adherence to social norms.[212] For sex workers, whose familial and marital ties are shrouded in illegality, the ritual symbolises a complex gesture devoid of a singular meaning.[213] For Dey, the meaning that is of foremost significance for all sex workers is that the practice helps to reclaim a caste-based tradition that segregates sex workers from other women.[214]

Thus, my performance of adda as a method of engagement with DMSC's activism made visible how, for sex workers, their practice of shidoor khela makes it possible to experience mutual ties with a larger community of women in Sonagachi *as* sex workers. The organisation of the festival, including its rituals, makes it possible for sex workers to experience community life through a practice of its traditions, yet also disrupting its discriminatory form. The DMSC's activism produces a sex worker in legal discourse who is able to experience a public life in cooperation with her community members and is able to reinhabit the place where she lives and works.

Most importantly, the adda in this chapter helps to understand how DMSC's activism constitutes sex workers' practices of intellectual labour, and inhabits a particular sex worker feminist jurisprudence. The DMSC's collective activist conduct shapes a distinct feminist and legal subject of the sex worker. This subject is a product of the practices of sex-working women's intellectual labour informed by their experiences of conversations in Sonagachi, Kolkata.

How exactly was the adda performed with DMSC members? I participated in adda by reading and interpreting DMSC's activist texts in reciprocal conversations with their members. A shared meaning of the contents of activist documents through my discussions and interactions with members emerged, which I grounded at the organisational site of DMSC in Sonagachi. I spoke to sex workers about their experiences of collectivisation that were mentioned in the texts. I invested in a careful

211 Ibid.

212 Conversations with Rama Debnath, above n 55; Purnima Chatterjee, above n 30.

213 Conversations with Bharati Dey, above n 27; Purnima Chatterjee, above n 30.

214 Conversation with Bharati Dey, above n 27.

listening to what my interlocutors had to say about their collective practices and the thinking behind these, to understand the significance of the arguments made by DMSC through its activism. I paid attention to how sex workers explained their own experiences of collectivisation and its interconnections with the place at which the collective is formed. Based on this adda, I correlated the contents of DMSC's activist texts, sex workers' experiences of collective activism and the place at which the activism is conducted.

Through a performance of adda, I have drawn out three aspects in this chapter. First, the formation of DMSC inhabits sex workers' conversations with representatives of public institutions, which were carried out from the 1990s through the mid 2000s. These conversations – between sex workers, public health practitioners, state officials and the judiciary – led to women's understanding of their practices as *jouno kaaj* or sex work, based on which they crafted a new role for themselves in their daily public life. Simultaneously with the conversations with these official figures, sex workers also carried out internal conversations amongst each other in which the women did the conscious work of formulating their new sex worker role and activist practices.

Second, in the process of crafting a new role as sex worker, and the responsibilities associated with it, the women shaped their two tenets of activist conduct: 'cooperation' and 'reinhabitation'. These principles were practised by means of the official registration of DMSC as a society under WBSRA in 1995; the formation and registration of a cooperative bank called USHA in 1995; the formation of a local anti-trafficking mechanism called SRBs in 1999; and the organisation of the Durga Puja in 2013.

Third, the formation of SRBs, USHA, the official registration of DMSC, and the organisation of Durga Puja, are two-pronged activities. On the one hand, these develop an account of gender, class and caste based on the specific activist experiences of sex-working women in Sonagachi, which are then brought by DMSC to its engagements with law or legal issues, such as trafficking. On the other hand, these activities inhabit and perform a representation of a sex worker self in legal discourse who is shaped by practising 'cooperation' and 'reinhabitation'. The sex worker shaped by DMSC is thus developed as distinct from the state-authorised criminal subject of the ITPA, who is not accorded any decision-making power over her life and livelihood and is also not considered to be a responsible person.

Through 'cooperation' and 'reinhabitation', sex workers of DMSC shaped their collective role in public life as sex workers, to form mutual relations with other people and with law. In so doing, I have worked to argue that the performance of adda helps to understand how DMSC's processes of collectivisation in Kolkata are not just a form of activism. They are sex workers' experiences of intellectual labour that work to produce a non-adversarial mode of feminist jurisprudence. Therefore, in this chapter, my method enables an understanding and recognition of sex workers' activism in Kolkata as one of the many diverse experiences and locations of mutual law–life relations, which contribute to the productions of a field of Indian feminist jurisprudence.

The next chapter engages with the activist texts produced by the sex workers' collective called VAMP, which is located in Sangli, Maharashtra. Through my adda with VAMP members, I will draw out the specific conversations that inform the collectivisation of sex workers in Sangli and the formation of the organisation. I will show how VAMP contributes to the shaping of another form of sex worker jurisprudence based on mutual law–life relations in the context of the specific experiences and location of the activism of sex-working women in Sangli.

CHAPTER 4

Sex Worker Feminist Jurisprudence II

VAMP

Hum apas mein baat cheet karte hain, vichaar karte hain, aur apna mamla suljhate hain.[1]

(We talk amongst ourselves, think through, and resolve matters on our own.)

This chapter revolves around a sex worker jurisprudence of another kind that is based on the activism of the sex workers' collective called VAMP. Based in Sangli and Miraj in Maharashtra, VAMP has a membership of over 5,000 sex-working women. Originating in Sangli, it later branched out to Miraj when a large number of women there started to play an active role within the organisation.[2] Not all of VAMP's members live in Sangli/Miraj. Many of them live in other places in Maharashtra, or in the neighbouring state of Karnataka.[3] At VAMP, for some of the women, sex work is their only source of livelihood, while others also work as vegetable vendors or as domestic help.[4] The women who live in Karnataka are also migrant workers who travel across state borders to ply their occupation in various cities in Maharashtra.

Sangli and Miraj are district towns in southern Maharashtra. Sangli boasts the highest sugar production in India, with a large number of sugarcane factories which cause an influx of migrant workers from around the region.[5] Miraj, on the other hand, is a major railway junction

[1] Conversation with Kamlabai Pani, sex worker and VAMP member, Miraj, Sangli, 10 December 2014.

[2] Conversation with Kiran Deshmukh, sex worker and VAMP member, Balajinagar, Sangli, 6 December 2014.

[3] Conversation with Kamlabai Pani, above n 1. [4] Ibid.

[5] Earlier known as South Satara, the place came to be called Sangli in 1961.

connecting smaller towns and districts in the region to big cities such as Mumbai, the commercial capital of India and the capital of the state of Maharashtra. This makes it convenient for women who reside in Sangli and Miraj to travel to different locations for work. The primary constituency of DMSC is women who live and work in Sonagachi, whereas VAMP is constituted of essentially a mobile group of women who live and work across many places in the states of Maharashtra and Karnataka.

VAMP works in partnership with five other collectives of marginalised groups in Sangli. These collectives have been initiated and consolidated by VAMP, and work as sex workers' allies. These are: VAMP Plus, a collective of HIV-positive sex workers; Muskaan (Smile), a collective of male and trans sex workers; Mitra (Friend), a collective of children of sex workers; Vidrohi Mahila Manch (Rebellious Women's Platform), a collective of rural women; and Nazariya (Point of View), a collective of Muslim women.[6]

I engage with VAMP's collectivisation through a reading and interpretation of activist materials authored by VAMP, like I did in the case of DMSC. I do so by way of conducting reciprocal conversations regarding the meanings and significance of the contents of these texts with my interlocutors from VAMP. By engaging in adda, I draw out a set of three key conversations, beginning in the early 1990s, between sex workers and representatives of other social movements, which resulted in the formation of VAMP.

I show how these conversations informed the collectivisation of sex workers in Sangli and the formation of VAMP, an NGO jointly registered as a charitable society under the Societies Registration Act, 1860 (SRA), and as a public trust under the Bombay Public Trust Act, 1950 (BPTA). In the form of an NGO of this kind, VAMP has crafted a collective role for women in public life as businesswomen, or dhandhewali. The primary thrust of women's role in public life as dhandhewali is the principle of non-regulation/non-governance of their lives either by VAMP or by any external authority such as the state, to develop the faculties of judgement and mutual trust in and/or amongst women.

[6] Conversation with Shantilal Kale, staff member of Sangram, Balajinagar, Sangli, 5 December 2014.

By working for the non-governance of women's lives, VAMP is able to reorganise women's hierarchical gender, class and caste relations in Sangli, as well as sex workers' hierarchical relations with the Indian state, which considers them to be both criminals and superstitious or irrational. My adda in this chapter helps show how, in the form of an NGO, VAMP shapes women's mutual relations with other people, and with law, at the place where it is located.

The activist materials produced by VAMP are distinct from DMSC's materials discussed in the previous chapter. The activist literatures of VAMP, apart from their organisational annual reports meant for donors, are mostly in the nature of short advocacy documents. While DMSC's documents are addressed to both DMSC members and others, VAMP's documents are primarily meant for an external audience. For instance, the texts are mostly written as recommendations for law and policy reform related to trafficking, and are addressed to UN bodies, national and international human rights organisations, funding organisations and the Indian government. One particular advocacy document, which was written in 1995, is akin to DMSC's *Sex Workers' Manifesto*. It is addressed to feminists and is a statement of VAMP's views on sex work and the lived experiences of sex workers.

The activist documents produced by VAMP are written in English and Marathi. In this chapter, I read only VAMP's activist texts written in English.[7] I spent some time with VAMP's staff members to understand the content of the texts written in Marathi.[8] On listening to them, it appeared that these documents carried nothing in them that was not also included in the English documents that I had already read for my research.

This chapter is organised around three specific conversations – between sex workers in Sangli and a non–sex worker women's organisation, and Dalit and non-Dalit feminist and men's groups. I open the chapter with a discussion of the conversations between a women's organ-

[7] As I mentioned in Chapter 2, I cannot read or write Marathi, but I have elementary conversational understanding of the language.

[8] Conversation with Shantilal Kale, above n 6.

isation based in Sangli called Sangram. Sangram started working with sex workers on the initiative of feminist activist Meena Seshu, and the women's conversations with her began in the early 1990s. These conversations motivated sex workers to shape VAMP as an NGO through registrations under SRA and BPTA. I then move to discuss the conversations between sex workers and Dalit/non-Dalit feminist groups in Maharashtra. The chapter closes with a discussion of the conversations between sex workers and local Dalit/non-Dalit men's groups in Sangli. Alongside these conversations, sex workers are also in conversation amongst themselves, and all of these inform women's collectivisation.

SEX WORKERS AND A NON-SEX WORKER WOMEN'S ORGANISATION

Started in 1995, VAMP was an offspring of the Sampada Grameen Mahila Sanstha, or Sangram, an organisation that works for rural women. Sangram, which literally means 'struggle', is an NGO headed by feminist activist Meena Seshu. In the early 1990s, Sangram started its work of preventing HIV/AIDS and raising awareness amongst sex workers in Sangli about the disease. At that time, Sangli was one of the locations with the highest prevalence of HIV/AIDS in the region.[9]

Meena Seshu is a key figure at VAMP. Sex worker and senior member of VAMP Kamlabai Pani described Seshu as the primary catalyst for building women's shared understanding of their lives, and also leading their collectivisation in Sangli.[10] According to Pani's description, Seshu's role is that of a leader in the sex worker community in Sangli.

Seshu is a professionally trained social worker and one who has worked as a community organiser with workers' unions in the region.

[9] Sangram/VAMP Team, *The VAMP/Sangram Sex Worker's Movement in India's Southwest*, AWID, 3, www.awid.org/sites/default/files/atoms/files/changing_their_world_2_-_vamp_-sex_workers_movement_in_indias_southwest.pdf.

[10] Conversation with Kamlabai Pani, above n 1. Kamlabai passed away two months after I interviewed her. See the obituary by Meena Seshu, 'Kamala Maushi: Salute to a Proud Devadasi', 15 February 2015, www.sangram.org/resources/Kamala-Maushi-Salute-to-a-proud-Devadasi.pdf.

After completing her degree, her first employment was with a *bidi*[11] workers' union in Nipani, Karnataka, where her role was that of a community organiser and a liaison officer between female bidi workers and the workers' union.[12] Seshu told me that, as a feminist, her work with the union was a first-hand learning in how progressive male intellectuals dictate to women, whom they deem incapable of thinking and acting for themselves, how to be free.[13] When she met the sex workers in Sangli, she realised that women in sex work experienced the worst kind of treatment at the hands of the progressive members of society.[14]

Seshu's conversations with the sex workers began in the early 1990s when she left her job with the union in Nipani and started working in Sangli. Gradually, Seshu's relationship with sex workers turned into a close friendship.[15] Seshu recounted that Sangram was set up sometime in the early 1980s, but was formally revived in 1994 by a group of academics and activists who lived in Sangli.[16] In the beginning, sixteen sex workers

[11] A type of local cigarette made with unprocessed tobacco.

[12] Conversation with Meena Seshu, General Secretary of Sangram, Balajinagar, Sangli, 2 December 2014.

[13] Ibid.

[14] Ibid. While in Nipani, through her work with the union, Seshu met bidi workers who belonged to a local *devadasi* community. The union worked on the rehabilitation of these women. The union believed that the women's rehabilitation would be possible only if they gave up their matted hair, a marker of their devadasi identity that distinguished them from other women. The women's matted hair, according to the union, was also a marker of irrationality and superstitious thinking, so the union forced the women to give up practices attached to their devadasi identity. The term 'devadasi' refers to a religious tradition of dedicating young women to the service of the goddess Yellamma for their entire lifetime. The dedication involves a marriage-like practice, and once a woman becomes a devadasi, she cannot marry a mortal. Traditionally, devadasis were women who were trained in classical Indian music and dance and held the social status of artistes. See Lucinda Ramberg, *Given to the Goddess: South Indian Devadasis and the Sexuality of Religion* (Duke University Press, 2014); Muvalur Ramamirthammal, Kalpana Kannabiran and Vasanth Kannabiran (eds), *Web of Deceit: Devadasi Reforms in Colonial India* (Kali for Women, 2003).

[15] Meena Seshu and Laxmi Murthy, 'The Business of Sex: An Introduction', in Murthy and Seshu, *The Business of Sex* (Zubaan, 2014), 17.

[16] The group of academics and activists included Ms Prabha Kulkarni, Dr Usha Udgaonkar, Dr Vandana Dandekar, Ms Ujjwala Paranjape, Dr Rajalaxmi Barve, Ms Shital Pratap and Meena Seshu.

were recruited to work as peer educators in the HIV/AIDS prevention programme.[17] Sangram believed that 'insiders [were] more effective than outsiders in reaching out to a community, and that women in sex work can enforce condom use for their own protection'.[18] Just like the peer educators in DMSC's Sonagachi Project, Sangram recruited sex workers to make door-to-door visits to sex worker households to educate them about HIV/AIDS. Sangram prioritised the protection of sex workers and did not see them 'as vectors of HIV, or urge them to take steps to protect others from HIV infection'.[19]

Pani told me that Sangram's attitude towards sex workers was unique right from the start, which is what drew sex-working women into Sangram's HIV/AIDS work.[20] However, even though Sangram was successful in involving sex workers in its HIV/AIDS prevention programme, it faced difficulties in achieving its other goal. Sangram actively tried to 'build a community-based organization of sex workers' in Sangli, but it was unable to make the women act together and trust each other outside of the peer educators' programme.[21]

Around this time (in the early 1990s), when sex workers were yet to come together as a group, a sex worker was raped and murdered in Sangli.[22] There was neither any protest held by the women's movement to condemn the incident, nor was the incident properly reported in the media.[23] The public apathy towards the incident made Seshu realise that violence faced by sex-working women was an issue that the state, feminists as well as the society did not care for (see Fig. 4.1).[24]

[17] Conversation with Meena Seshu, above n 12.

[18] Sangram/VAMP Team, *The VAMP/Sangram Sex Worker's Movement in India's Southwest*, above n 9, 3; see generally Sangram, *Sangram Bill of Rights*, www.sangram.org/resources/sangram_billof_rights.pdf.

[19] Sangram/VAMP Team, *The VAMP/Sangram Sex Worker's Movement in India's Southwest*, above n 9, 4.

[20] Conversation with Kamlabai Pani, above n 1.

[21] Sangram/VAMP Team, *The VAMP/Sangram Sex Worker's Movement in India's Southwest*, above n 9, 4.

[22] Conversation with Meena Seshu, above n 12. [23] Ibid.

[24] Ibid.; Sangram/VAMP Team, *The VAMP/Sangram Sex Worker's Movement in India's Southwest*, above n 9, 4.

November 2002

OF VESHYAS, VAMPS, WHORES AND WOMEN

Challenging preconceived notions of prostitution and sex work

Rights or Wrongs? | Unzipped | Action Update | Reality Bites | Fact File | Making History | New!

SANGRAM • POINT OF VIEW • VAMP

Turning a Blind Eye

WHEN A POLICEMAN rapes a tribal woman, everyone is outraged. But if that same woman happens to be in prostitution, nobody considers it rape. If a dalit woman is murdered, it is considered murder. But if that same woman is in prostitution, it is considered 'natural', almost as if murder is an accepted outcome of being in prostitution. The question then is this: Why isn't violence against women in prostitution seen as violence against women?

The reasons for this are deeply embedded in the structures of society. They include the patriarchal division of women into 'good' and 'bad' women, the 'whore stigma' that separates women in prostitution from all other women; and the belief that prostitution itself is inherently violent. This societal paradigm expresses itself as the violence of stigmatization.

'Good' and 'bad' women

Women who follow the norms of a patriarchal society are viewed as 'good women' and it is their status as 'good women' (rather than their status as women) that entitles them to certain rights in the eyes of society. The Indian Penal Code still allows a woman's sexual history to be heard during a rape trial, a clause that ends up branding single, lesbian, prostitute and other women as 'bad' women who have sex outside of marriage, for pleasure or to earn a living. When a 'bad woman' is raped or assaulted, society does not view it as rape-a transgression against a transgressor is not viewed as a crime.

The whore stigma

Women in prostitution fall squarely into the category of 'bad women'. Interestingly, although prostitutes are considered to be victims, they are also viewed as wanton (liberated sexual beings), debauched (making valueless money from sex) and morally weak. The whore stigma emphasizes the 'evil influence' of such 'base' women on the 'good' moral character of society, deeming them deviant; women who have transgressed the norms of 'acceptable' social behaviour. The concept of the fallen, debased and deviant woman has always governed public opinion, policy and law. Women have therefore been policed, coerced and raided, to be rescued, reformed and rehabilitated by a society that would like to order and control their life styles.

Prostitution as violence

The concept of 'prostitution as violence' also prevents society from viewing the day-to-day violence within prostitution as violence. Kathleen Barry[1] has elaborated on the manner in which prostitution is inherently violent, whether women are kidnapped, purchased, fraudulently contracted through organized crime syndicates or procured through love and befriending tactics.

This perspective assumes that all prostitutes are forced into the institution, and that trading money for sex is synonymous with sexual exploitation - and sexual violence. There is no doubt that any form of force in any situation - whether sexual or not - is violence. But the viewing of all prostitution as forced and inherently violent prevents the viewing of what happens within prostitution as violence. When every sexual encounter between a woman and her client is viewed as rape, there is no room for a woman in prostitution to actually be raped.

The violence of stigmatization

The issue is not one of choice or force. The issue is one of socialization. The good woman/bad woman discourse is the socialization of mainstream morality. And this is the choice that women in prostitution are forced to make. To be 'good' or to be 'bad'. Once they have chosen the 'bad' (to overthrow societal norms and morality) there is no going back for them. There is also a sense of liberation, a reality that fights for recognition. But they have violated the sacred space of womanhood as enshrined in mainstream morality. Thus the punishment is stigmatization. Therefore VAMP says "the violence of stigma we dare to survive, of dignity we dare to dream."

contd. on last page

Figure 4.1 VAMP's newsletter, *Of Veshyas, Vamps, Whores and Women* (November 2002). *Source*: VAMP, Sangli.

Shabana Kazi, sex worker and member of VAMP, told me that even though the rape and murder of sex workers was not uncommon in those days, it hardly ever caught the attention of even the sex workers in Sangli.[25] However, she added, gradually when more and more women came to work with Sangram, they started to take notice of this occurrence.[26]

By 1995, the number of women who were associated with Sangram as peer educators had increased from 16 to 150.[27] The increased participation of sex workers in the peer educators' programme happened because it was able to generate interest in their own lives. As a result of this, sex workers' conversations with Seshu took a different turn.[28]

Pani shared that one day, during this time when the peer educators' programme was gaining momentum, sex workers went to Seshu's house to express their interest in starting an organisation that would be collectively run by the women.[29] The women wanted their organisation to be modelled on Sangram, which was an NGO and not like the cooperative societies that they saw around them.[30] Kiran Deshmukh, sex worker and member of VAMP, explained that the women's dislike for cooperatives was born out of their knowledge of the corrupt workings of the powerful sugar cooperatives in the region.[31]

Sex workers' decision to organise themselves as an NGO and not as a cooperative carries meaning for women's engagement with law and within a community of people in Sangli. Pani told me that when the sex workers decided to organise as a group on the model of Sangram, they also decided that VAMP's relationship with Sangram was going to be

[25] Conversation with Shabana Kazi, sex worker and member of VAMP, Miraj, Sangli, 8 December 2014.

[26] Ibid.

[27] Sangram/VAMP Team, *The VAMP/Sangram Sex Worker's Movement in India's Southwest*, above n 9, 4.

[28] Ibid.

[29] Conversation with Kamlabai Pani, above n 1. This is also noted in *Of Veshyas, Vamps, Whores and Women*, www.sangram.org/upload/resources/of_veshyas_vamps_whores_and_women_part_I.pdf.

[30] Sangram/VAMP Team, *The VAMP/Sangram Sex Worker's Movement in India's Southwest*, above n 9, 5.

[31] Ibid.

Figure 4.2 Brochure of a play, performed by sex worker members of VAMP, which tells the story of their collectivisation. *Source*: VAMP, Sangli.

one of friendly companionship and not regulatory (see Fig. 4.2).[32] She clarified that the women decided that VAMP would carry out its work independently through its own administrative processes, but would seek ‘guidance and advice’[33] from Sangram whenever necessary. The women felt confident of managing their community work by themselves, but they realised that they ‘needed help with back-office work such as writing proposals, managing accounts, and dealing with the Charity Commission’.[34]

[32] Conversation with Kamlabai Pani, above n 1.

[33] Sangram/VAMP Team, *The VAMP/Sangram Sex Worker's Movement in India's Southwest*, above n 9, 5.

[34] Ibid.

The Charity Commission is an official body that regulates the management and administration of organisations that are formed for a charitable purpose, or for the welfare and benefit of the general public. Charitable societies are registered under the SRA, as mentioned earlier. The powers vested in the commission by the SRA include the regulation, management and dissolution of societies.

The formation of charitable organisations, or societies, is both a federal and a state subject. After India's independence from colonial rule in 1947, under the new Constitution, societies came to be listed as a state subject whereby different measures could be put in place by individual states to regulate their formation and functioning.[35] In the state of Maharashtra where VAMP is located, the formation of societies also falls under the stipulations of the BPTA. It is mandated under BPTA that societies that are formed for charitable purposes within the state of Maharashtra are required to be registered under both SRA and BPTA.

The procedure for registration confers two separate registration numbers for such organisations registered under both acts. This means that an organisation that is jointly registered under the two acts, such as VAMP, takes the legal form of a charitable society as well as that of a public trust. According to BPTA, the purposes for which a charitable organisation may be formed include poverty alleviation, medical relief, education or any other activity that is for the welfare of the public and for its utility.[36] VAMP was formed for the welfare of the sex worker community and with the intention of preventing HIV/AIDS amongst them.[37] The women specifically intended to work against the devaluation of human lives as a result of the stigma associated with sex work and the contraction of HIV/AIDS.[38]

In 1995, under both SRA and BPTA, VAMP was first registered in the name of Veshya Aids Muqabla Parishad (Council for Sex Workers' Struggle Against AIDS).[39] In 1998, the organisation changed its name

[35] Constitution of India, Seventh Schedule, List II (State List), entry 32, www.mea.gov.in/Images/pdf1/S7.pdf.

[36] Bombay Public Trust Act, 1950, Sec. 9(1), https://charity.maharashtra.gov.in/Portals/0/Files/B.P.T.Act,1950.pdf.

[37] Conversation with Kamlabai Pani, above n 1. [38] Ibid.

[39] Sangram/VAMP Team, *The VAMP/Sangram Sex Worker's Movement in India's Southwest*, above n 9, 5.

to Veshya Anyay Mukti Parishad (Council for Sex Workers' Freedom from Injustice).[40] The change of name marks an important shift in the meaning of the organisation of sex workers in Sangli. The organisational agenda transitioned from a 'struggle against AIDS' to an intention to form a collective that actively sought the liberation of sex workers from oppression and injustice.[41] Deshmukh noted that sex workers initiated VAMP's transition from *AIDS muqabla* (fight against AIDS) to *anyay mukti* (freedom from injustice) by starting to work on the overall well-being of women in prostitution and their children.[42]

COMMUNITY AND COLLECTIVE

The approach to an organisational form that VAMP adopted through its registration as a charitable society *and* a public trust is distinct from the organisation of DMSC. The primary distinction lies in the fact that DMSC was shaped as a collective self-regulatory body by, for and of sex workers, which was built on 'cooperation' and 're-inhabitation'. VAMP, on the other hand, worked to shape an organisation of women in prostitution who were opposed to any kind of regulation of their lives and livelihood both by VAMP, their own collective body, or any other authority.

A foundational common law doctrine that governs public trusts carries the understanding that certain resources are not for individual ownership, and are meant to be shared amongst people or used for public gain.[43] VAMP's organisational thoughts and practices bear a reflection of this legal principle. I learnt that the women believe that their collective is a repository of wisdom, a common resource that is equally owned by all members within the organisation, and for which women must trust each other to take wilful responsibility in the absence of any regulatory authority.

Pani told me that for VAMP members, it was of the utmost importance that their organisational practices should encourage mutual trust between individual members for whose gain the collective was formed.[44]

[40] Ibid. [41] Ibid. [42] Conversation with Kiran Deshmukh, above n 2.

[43] See Michael C. Blumm, 'The Public Trust Doctrine: A Twenty-First Century Concept' (2010) 16, *Hastings West-Northwest Journal of Environmental Law and Policy*, 105.

[44] Conversation with Kamlabai Pani, above n 1.

She noted that the women thought that their relationships with each other could not be regulated through forced allegiance to a collective form of life. Rather, it had to be based on mutual trust amongst sex workers, which was born out of each individual sex worker's interest in shaping and sharing a public life that was not discriminatory for women and people of all genders.[45] That is why, Pani told me, VAMP adopted a 'volunteer-based' structure that was a 'loose collective' without well-defined, stringent rules and regulations.[46]

Deshmukh believes that an individual sex worker is located within a network of relations in a community consisting of sex workers and non–sex workers.[47] Nonetheless, a sex-working woman's individual interests may not be the same as those of others in the community. For this reason, Deshmukh added, sex workers decided that their organisation should be structured in a way that individual interests did not become subservient to community interests.[48] Moreover, Deshmukh noted, the relationship that bound an individual sex worker to the collective was a voluntary association. The essence of this relationship was an individual sex worker's sense of trust in others with whom she shared her life, and a willingness to care for them.[49]

Adda with my interlocutors at VAMP makes it apparent how sex workers see *community* and *collective* as two distinct associations that shape their understanding of, and conduct in, a public life as dhandhewali/businesswomen. The significance and meaning of sex workers' role as dhandhewali/businesswomen in relation to VAMP's activism will become evident in the next section. Now I will focus on an interrelated subject that pertains to how women's notions of community and collective inform the legal imperatives of an NGO through which women nurture a sense of trust amongst themselves.

Deshmukh told me that the women could form a community with other people even if they did not trust or care for sex workers in return.[50] A collective, however, could be formed only amongst those who were

[45] Ibid.

[46] Sangram/VAMP Team, *The VAMP/Sangram Sex Worker's Movement in India's Southwest*, above n 9, 5.

[47] Conversation with Kiran Deshmukh, above n 2. [48] Ibid. [49] Ibid.

[50] Ibid. Also repeated by Shabana Kazi, above n 25; and Kamlabai Pani, above n 1.

bound by a mutually caring and trusted relationship.[51] It thus becomes evident that the women's notions of community and collective are shaped through their own as well as other people's experiences of discrimination.

Both Kazi and Pani recounted how their sense of a collective emerged from seeing the discriminatory experiences of people suffering from HIV/AIDS.[52] Kazi became conscious of the need for collective activism when she witnessed the death of a man who was suffering from AIDS and whom she considered as her brother.[53] She admitted him into a hospital when she came to know that his family members refused to take care of him because he had contracted AIDS. Kazi herself had also experienced discriminatory behaviour from people who rejected her as an immoral woman because of her occupation.

When the man eventually died, even those who performed last rites as their occupation refused to cremate his body because it was contaminated with what they considered to be an immoral disease.[54] Kazi, a Muslim by faith, believed that anyone who was born as a human being had a right to be cremated according to their religion, or as they desired. For Kazi, it was a birthright inherent to human existence, and so she decided to assume the responsibility to ensure that her brother's body was cremated as per his religious beliefs.[55] This incident instilled in her a collective feeling based on common experiences of discrimination faced by sex workers and those who were suffering from HIV/AIDS.[56]

Pani recounted how she came to be considered as an angel of last rites by many within the local community of stigmatised HIV/AIDS-infected people in Sangli.[57] Sex workers and non–sex workers came to Pani with their wishes pertaining to how they wanted their burial, funeral or cremation to happen after their death. One person, abandoned by his blood relations due to the fact that he had HIV/AIDS, requested her to organise a procession of musicians and drummers when he passed away. Pani believed that those who are alive had a responsibility to ensure that

[51] Conversation with Kiran Deshmukh, above n 2.

[52] Conversations with Shabana Kazi, above n 25; Kamlabai Pani, above n 1.

[53] Conversation with Shabana Kazi, above n 25. [54] Ibid. [55] Ibid. [56] Ibid.

[57] Conversation with Kamlabai Pani, above n 1.

for those who were dead, the end of their life's journey must happen well.[58] So, to honour a dead man's wish, as someone who had herself experienced discriminations in her life for being a sex worker, she took on the responsibility of arranging for the procession to take place.[59]

COLLECTIVE CONSCIOUSNESS

The women's close encounters with the experiences of stigma and discrimination due to HIV/AIDS made sex workers feel the need for inculcating a sense of mutual trust and care in their relationships with each other. How sex workers formed such relations can be understood by paying attention to two interconnected aspects of their activism: first, the choice of a *voluntary* organisational structure; and second, an investment in the development of sex workers' *collective consciousness.* These two organisational aspects of sex workers' intra-group relations are tethered to how the women authorise their more public role and responsibilities as dhandhewali by taking on the form of a non-governmental structure. At VAMP, the thinking and practices regarding non-governmental organisation are not so much about shaping an entity that is distinguishable from the government/state as much as about putting in place a non-regulatory mode of collectivisation.

In a document that narrates a history of VAMPS's formation, it is stated that the organisation is officially 'governed by a board of peer educators'.[60] Seshu told me that these were sex workers who became peer educators for Sangram, and at the time of VAMP's registration as an NGO, they constituted its board of directors.[61] It was this same group of women, Deshmukh noted, who assumed leadership positions within VAMP.[62] Even though this board of peer educators dictates VAMP's governance in terms of its daily functioning and activities, by listening

[58] Ibid.

[59] Group discussion with Kamlabai Pani, Kiran Deshmukh and Shantilal Kale at Miraj, Sangli, 10 December 2014.

[60] Sangram/VAMP Team, *The VAMP/Sangram Sex Worker's Movement in India's Southwest,* above n 9, 5.

[61] Conversation with Meena Seshu, above n 12.

[62] Sangram/VAMP Team, *The VAMP/Sangram Sex Worker's Movement in India's Southwest,* above n 9, 5.

to the sex workers I was enabled to see that the women's manner of assuming leadership worked to deter them from dictating or regulating the conduct of others in the collective and/or in the wider community.

A recurring assertion that emerges through adda is that VAMP is organised as a *sangathan* (collective) and not as a workers' union. On being asked what they meant by this, Deshmukh, Kazi and Pani pointed out that a union works as a formal system bound by a fixed agenda and rules. A sangathan, on the other hand, is a loose structure formed by the coming together of a group of persons who trust, and care for, each other, and are concerned with whatever is relevant to the lives of those who are part of it.[63] The basis of a sangathan, Deshmukh noted, was that each individual must be trusted to think and act for the benefit of others and not be directed to do so by anyone.[64]

Pani recounted that when sex workers started VAMP, they realised that a sangathan could only be formed through voluntary participation, and when individual sex workers perceived themselves to be equivalent to the collective structure.[65] This means that collective consciousness cannot be formed amongst sex workers if they experience the collective–individual relationship as one of dominance and/or subordination. It is by giving value to the individual and trusting her to assume a leadership role within the organisation that VAMP will be able to inculcate a sense of collective interest amongst its members.[66] As a voluntary organisation, VAMP takes care not to compel women to be answerable to one another. Rather, it fosters self-reliance amongst sex workers by trusting their commitment to the consolidation of a sex workers' collective consciousness.[67]

What I gather by speaking with Pani is that to develop collective allegiance, women had to be *trusted* by each other and could not be told how to think and act, because otherwise their participation in VAMP would not remain voluntary. In my understanding, the rationale behind the organisation of VAMP as this kind of a voluntary, collective NGO is

[63] Conversations with Kiran Deshmukh, above n 2; Shabana Kazi, above n 25; Kamlabai Pani, above n 1.

[64] Conversation with Kiran Deshmukh, above n 2.

[65] Conversation with Kamlabai Pani, above n 1. [66] Ibid. [67] Ibid.

significant in terms of how sex-working women have shaped their public life in Sangli. VAMP's activism gets consciously directed at the non-governance of sex-working women's lives. But what does non-governmental organisation mean for the women at VAMP?

Unlike DMSC, which considers itself to be a self-regulatory mechanism for the exercise of sex workers' collective authority in Sonagachi, VAMP envisages its role vis-à-vis sex workers differently. Seshu told me that VAMP's activism held back from a regulation of women's thoughts and actions, even through the exercise of a collective authority of sex-working women.[68] The distinction that sex workers make between a *member* of a union and a *volunteer* of a collective is particularly useful for the purpose of understanding VAMP's practices of non-governance. During our adda, Deshmukh noted that a member of a union thinks and acts according to a set of predetermined rules that are issued by the collective, thus locating the collective above the individual sex worker.

In the absence of predetermined rules that bind thoughts and actions, one has to use her own faculties of *vichaar* (judgement) and *buddhi* (intelligence). A strong collective is formed, Deshmukh observed, only when there is room within it for every individual sex worker to disagree with others, voice their conflicting views strongly and take decisions independently.[69] This can happen when individual sex workers have worked to develop the faculties of their minds – to apply their own intelligence and decide for themselves – which can be achieved when participation in the collective is not regulated by anyone and made completely voluntary.[70]

At VAMP, unlike at DMSC, designations such as secretary or president are attached to the names of some sex workers who constitute the governing body as mandated under the SRA and do not signify any

[68] Conversation with Meena Seshu, above n 12.

[69] 'The effects of decentralization are most evident among VAMP board members, who are strong, thinking individuals with diverse, often conflicting views and opinions, rather than cardboard cutouts echoing identical thoughts and ideas.' Sangram, *Of Veshyas, Vamps, Whores and Women*, 9, www.sangram.org/upload/resources/Of_veshyas_vamp_whore_and_women_II.pdf.

[70] Conversation with Kiran Deshmukh, above n 2.

added responsibility.[71] The creation of these positions primarily serves a legal requirement for registration under the SRA, without carrying any further meaning for sex workers' organisational practices.[72] At DMSC, these designations denote leadership positions with added obligations for individual sex workers vis-à-vis the collective. This became evident through my adda with Seshu where she told me how sex workers performed their leadership roles. At VAMP, leaders are not invested with any additional power or obligations. These designations signify no more than an acquired wisdom regarding the ways of living and organising relations within a community in Sangli.

VAMP holds *mohalla* (neighbourhood) meetings in Sangli every week.[73] These meetings are for discussing issues concerning the community of sex workers dispersed across the two states of Maharashtra and Karnataka where VAMP carries out its activities. Women attend the meetings to share information about matters relating to their particular locality and for discussing problems that they have been unable to solve. These women then go and report back to the others in their area whom they represent at the mohalla meetings, to ensure that there is no information gap amongst sex workers.

How, and how much, a member will involve herself in organisational activities is subject to individuals' own decisions. Unlike in the case of DMSC, the taking up of collective obligations in VAMP is voluntary and not channelled through the institutionalisation of a leadership structure. Speaking about the voluntary nature of VAMP's leadership structure, Pani told me that attendance at these meetings was not compulsory for anyone.[74] Anybody from the sex worker community where VAMP carries out its activities is free to attend the mohalla committee meetings and can 'make a complaint, or [seek] help in arbitration of community

[71] As I discussed in Chapter 3, at DMSC leadership positions signify positions of power and have added obligations attached to them. The DMSC follows an electoral system to put in place a democratic system of leadership, which may otherwise be difficult for a group constituted of 65,000 members.

[72] Societies Registration Act, 1860, Sec. 2 and 16, www.mca.gov.in/Ministry/actsbills/pdf/Societies_Registration_Act_1860.pdf.

[73] Conversation with Meena Seshu, above n 12.

[74] Conversation with Kamlabai Pani, above n 1.

disputes'.[75] Thus, on any given day, anyone can assume a leadership role within the discussions that are held.

The conception and formation of VAMP as a non-governmental organisational form were motivated by women's learnings from the work of Sangram and the involvement of Seshu in their activism. Its formation was also simultaneously developed in conversations with a Dalit activist tradition in Maharashtra. Sex workers' activist mode of crafting a role in public life as dhandhewali is reflective of a discourse of Dalit feminism that gained a foothold in Maharashtra in the 1990s. This discourse emerged from a combined anti-caste and anti-prostitution position on gender, espoused by B. R. Ambedkar. Sex workers at VAMP craft their role of dhandhewali in public life by aligning with Ambedkar's anti-caste thinking on the formation of sangathan or a collective consciousness, while rejecting his anti-prostitution stand. This will become evident in the next section where I discuss sex workers' conversations with Dalit women's groups, and a women's movement that primarily comprises non-Dalits.

SEX WORKERS AND DALIT/NON-DALIT FEMINIST GROUPS

The 1990s were preceded by events through which the issue of caste gained new visibility in public life. In 1979, the government set up the Mandal Commission to identify communities that were socially and educationally backward.[76] The commission's recommendations in its report, which suggested increased reservations in government jobs and public universities, led to violent protests by upper castes across India.[77] The backlash continued throughout the 1990s.[78]

[75] Sangram/VAMP Team, *The VAMP/Sangram Sex Worker's Movement in India's Southwest*, above n 9, 5.

[76] See generally, Zoya Hasan, *Politics of Inclusion: Castes, Minorities, and Affirmative Action* (Oxford University Press, 2011).

[77] See generally, K. Balagopal, 'This Anti-Mandal Mania' (1990) 25(40), *Economic and Political Weekly*, 2231.

[78] In Delhi, two university students attempted self-immolation; the protests also caused road blockades and strikes, with government services, transportation services, schools, colleges and even businesses remaining shut in many places throughout India. See

The 1990s also saw the rise of religious Hindu fundamentalist groups. In 1992, the Babri Masjid, a sixteenth-century mosque, was demolished in Ayodhya, Uttar Pradesh. The demolition was carried out by the volunteers of several Hindu right-wing political outfits in order to claim what they argued was the birthplace of the Hindu god Ram.[79]

The demolition of the mosque was carried out on 6 December, the anniversary of Ambedkar's death, which is observed as a sacred day among Dalit communities. Wandana Sonalkar argues that the demolition of the mosque was a deliberate move against the emerging consolidation of anti-caste politics.[80] She writes, 'The choice of this date indicates that the right-wing Hindus were hitting out at the Dalits also, by contesting their space in the political calendar.'[81]

Against this larger backdrop, throughout the 1990s Dalit women were organising themselves in Maharashtra and Karnataka. Dalit and labour rights activist Ruth Manorama founded the National Federation of Dalit Women in 1993. The same year, Manorama was involved in organising a public hearing on Violence Against Dalit Women in Bangalore. In 1995, another Dalit women's organisation called the Dalit Mahila Sanghatana was formed, and the Maharashtra Dalit Women's Conference was organised. In Delhi, the All India Democratic Women's Association's Convention Against Untouchability and Dalit Women's Oppression was held in 1998. These Dalit women's groups in the 1990s made it possible for the collective voices of Dalit women to be publicly heard.[82]

Anti-caste scholar Gopal Guru characterises this emerging voice through which Dalit women were seeking to define themselves as a voice of *difference*.[83] Sonalkar argues that Dalit women's processes of self-

Christophe Jaffrelot, *India's Silent Revolution: The Rise of the Lower Castes in North India* (C. Hurst & Co., 2003), 347.

79 See Brenda Cossman and Ratna Kapur, *Secularism's Last Sigh? Hindutva and the (Mis)rule of Law* (Oxford University Press, 2001).

80 Wandana Sonalkar, 'Translator's Introduction', in Urmila Pawar and Meenakshi Moon, *We Also Made History: Women in the Ambedkarite Movement* (Zubaan, 2008), 8.

81 Ibid. 82 Ibid., 11. 83 Guru, 'Dalit Women Talk Differently'.

definition through the assertion of difference in the 1990s occurred in relation to both Dalit men and non-Dalit women. She writes:

> Since the 1990s we have seen dalit women asserting themselves politically in a new surge of consciousness. They are trying to define themselves in relation to the dalit movement in contemporary society, still largely dominated by men, and to a women's movement largely initiated and sustained by upper-caste women; and raising questions for both.[84]

The shaping of a collective role as dhandhewali by sex-working women in Sangli, who are mostly Dalit, is a similar process of self-definition in relation to not just Dalit men and non-Dalit women, but also a non-sex-working Dalit women's movement in Maharashtra in the 1990s.

Seshu recounted that in 1995, sex workers of VAMP participated at an event of public hearing.[85] It was organised by international women's and human rights organisations and was part of a series titled 'Public Hearings on Crimes Against Women in the Asia-Pacific Region'.[86] The hearing was meant to be a platform for women to speak about their experiences of violence that had resulted particularly from the idea of development embraced by the government and the development projects it had undertaken after economic liberalisation in 1991.

The women from VAMP participated at this event to speak about their exclusion from the human rights discourse that did not take into consideration the experiences of violence faced by women in sex work.[87] At this public hearing, sex workers of VAMP read out a document titled 'A Statement of Women in Prostitution' (hereafter 'the Statement').[88] As Seshu explains, the Statement was a reiteration of sex workers'

[84] Sonalkar, 'Translator's Introduction', 9–10.

[85] Conversation with Meena Seshu, above n 12. The event was called 'Speaking Tree, Womenspeak: Asia-Pacific Court of Women on the Violence of Development'. It was held in Bangalore on 28 January 1995. Asian Women's Human Rights Council (AWHRC) and Vimochana, *Speaking Tree, Womenspeak: Asia-Pacific Public Hearing on Crimes Against Women Related to the Violence of Development, 28 January 1995, Bangalore, India* (AWHRC and Vimochana, 1995).

[86] AWHRC and Vimochana, *Speaking Tree, Womenspeak*.

[87] Conversation with Meena Seshu, above n 12.

[88] VAMP, 'A Statement of Women in Prostitution', 28 January 1995, www.sangram.org/upload/resources/sangram-VAMP-statement-1995.pdf.

collective understanding of their own life and livelihood, arrived at through activism.[89] The document was written around the same time as the DMSC's *Sex Workers Manifesto*. It defines sex workers as dhandhewali, whereas the manifesto asserts that they are *workers*. The Statement argues (see Fig. 4.3):

> *We disagree* with the formulation that prostitution is a profession. We make a distinction between profession (vyavasay) and occupation/business (dhandha). For instance, if we are presently occupied by making money out of sex, then that is our occupation for a short span of time. The nature of the business itself is time-bound. Therefore, by using the term profession, we are necessarily being pushed into a category for a lifetime. We are women who are practicing this time-bound business of prostitution for a short and specific period in our lives. Please remember that when we are not making money out of sex, we are engaged in other income-generating activities.[90]

VAMP's articulation of the difference between sex work as *profession*, and sex work as *business*, ties back to women's desire for a non-governmental or non-regulatory organisational form. This has implications for our understanding of how the women in Sangli envisage their relationship with the state. For example, during our adda, Deshmukh argued that as a profession, sex work and the women who engaged in it would be subject to state regulation.[91] However, as business, sex work would be subject to individual and informal negotiations by its practitioners, leaving the state out of the matter.[92]

VAMP's articulation of sex work as dhandha/occupation, and the crafting of women's role in public life as dhandhewali/businesswomen, performs a twofold task. First, it crafts a reorganisation of sex workers' hierarchical social relations of gender, class and caste in Sangli. Second,

[89] Email correspondence with Meena Seshu as a follow-up to the conversation in person. In the email, Seshu mentions that it is on the basis of this statement that the sex workers were invited to attend the Fourth World Conference on Women held in Beijing in 1995. At the event in Bangalore, VAMP saw a complete rejection of the content of the statement. Email from Meena Seshu, 16 November 2015.

[90] VAMP, 'A Statement of Women in Prostitution', above n 88 (emphasis in original).

[91] Conversation with Kiran Deshmukh, above n 2. [92] Ibid.

SANGRAM

A STATEMENT OF WOMEN IN PROSTITUTION - **28 January 1995**

Prostitution is a way of life like any other. It is a survival strategy that is parallel to any other occupation. It is not created for the benefit of men, as is the common perception, rather it is primarily for the women who live off it. Women in prostitution make money out of sex and we are the breadwinners of our families.

We disagree with the formulation that prostitution is a profession. We make a distinction between profession (*vyavasay*) and occupation/business (*dhandha*). For instance, if we are presently occupied by making money out of sex, then that is our occupation for a short span of time. The nature of the business itself is time-bound. Therefore, by using the term profession, we are necessarily being pushed into a category for a lifetime. We are women who are practicing this time-bound business of prostitution for a short and specific period in our lives. Please remember that when we are not making money out of sex, we are engaged in other income-generating activities.

We believe that all occupations stereotypical to women adhere to so-called 'feminine values'. They capitalize upon qualities like tolerance, sympathy, tenderness, endurance, understanding, patience, forbearance and much more, be they housewives, typists, nurses, teachers, office assistants, receptionists, or women in prostitution. We believe that the socialization of the girl-child to accept such occupations as the only option is also a major reason for the perpetuation of sexual discrimination in the female work force. We believe that women in prostitution are no different.

We believe that we are more empowered than most women within male-dominated patriarchal structures are. For instance, within the family structure (which we know is the most oppressive), we are the breadwinners and the heads of our households. The relationships we share with the men in our families are more honest and equal because the purdah of double standards is not necessary.

1

Figure 4.3 A Statement of Women in Prostitution by VAMP.
Source: VAMP, Sangli.

Economic independence from men is a reality that we enjoy with pride and dignity. Brothel-owners, goons, the police and the self-appointed crusaders of morality in society harass us, try to curb our independence and are forever trying to douse our spirit. Control structures have a vested interest in criminalizing prostitution. What we demand is the de-criminalization of prostitution such that we can live safely and continue to choose to make money from sex without stigmatization. We demand the eradication of all laws concerning prostitution, which are oppressive and contribute to further criminalizing the trade.

We believe that making money from sex is only selling a part of our body, which is in no way different from selling our brains or physical labour. We protest against a society that deems our work contribution as less prestigious than other traditional forms of work. We believe that we challenge and undermine structures of power by using a part of our womanhood -our sexuality- as a source of our power and income.

We also protest against all laws and value systems that treat soliciting for sex as indecent while sanctioning other forms of sexual contracts from advertisements and exchanging gifts by marriage partners to dowry and bride price.

As people who experience violence as a part of our daily life, we are being more and more penalized by increasing violence in a society that is trying to order and control our lifestyles. As women in prostitution, we protest against a society that forces on us the violence of a judgmental attitude.

We believe that a woman's sexuality is an integral part of her as a woman, as varied as her mothering, domestic and such other skills. We do not believe that sex has a sacred space and women who have sex for reasons other than its reproductive importance are violating this space. Or that if they chose to make money from the transaction they are immoral or debauched.

We believe that child prostitution is child sexual abuse, molestation and child labor and that it exists in a society that is fraught with crimes of abduction, kidnap, rape, assault and violence against women. We believe that as comparable to poor, weak and

2

Figure 4.3 (*cont.*)

marginalized communities, we are unable to have a reasonable control of our lives and destinies. We share the same experiences of women who live in the Third World.

We believe that there is a distinction between trafficking, which is a criminal offence, and adult prostitution. While we agree that 'choice' is a cruel mirage for all women within capitalist patriarchy, we feel the need to acknowledge that adult prostitution as an option, exists. We also believe that women who are in prostitution, choose to continue to remain in business for many reasons.

We believe that when involuntary initiation into prostitution occurs, a process of socialization within the institution of prostitution exists whereby the involuntary nature of the business changes increasingly to one of active acceptance, not necessarily with resignation. This is not a coercive process. We believe that, despite living within a capitalist patriarchal society and having experienced the freedom of living outside the patriarchal system, it is almost impossible for us to contemplate entering such a system with its inherent double standard, lopsided value system and inequalities.

We protest against a society that deems us immoral and illegal mainly because we do not accept its mores, rules and governance. We protest against the various forces of mainstream society that deny us the right to liberty, security, and fair administration of justice, respect for our lives, discrimination, freedom of expression and association.

We also protest against a society that aggressively promotes objectification and commercialization of women and their sexuality. We protest against the sale of our sexuality in the international market by unscrupulous individuals and governments who reap huge profits off our bodies. We are in a business wherein the control has shifted from traditional members of our community to criminal syndicates. We were not for sale. In today's world, unfortunately we are sacrificed and commodified by vested interests, sometimes from within our own communities.

Globalization and economic liberalization is further breaking up our communities and forcing us to accept the sale of our bodies and the sale of our young in the urban industrial centers for prostitution. Movement in search of work is not new for us, the problem however is the criminalisation of the trade which is forcing us to turn to debt

3

Figure 4.3 (*cont.*)

bondage, forced labour and slavery-like practices. Consequently, we find ourselves in the trap of criminal syndicates in our search for work.

We believe that it is imperative that we must unite with each other to erase the stigmatization of women in prostitution and restore our dignity as workers and citizens of civil society. We must build alliances with other segments of society and together, we must struggle against the forces that have a vested interest in eroding the rights of all women.

This Statement was read at the
Speaking Tree, Womenspeak: Asia- Pacific Public Hearing on Crimes Against Women related to the violence of development 28 January 1995, Bangalore, India
by women in sex work from Sangli who collectivized in 1997 as
VESHYA ANYAY MUKTI PARISHAD (VAMP)

4

Figure 4.3 (*cont.*)

it positions women – socially and legally – as wilful actors who are capable of forming contractual relations based on individual needs and desires, and demands that the state trust them to be able to do so rationally and independently of state regulation.

Nivedita Menon, in an article where she maps 'the journeys made by the term gender in India', argues that although the category of gender is acknowledged as a contested feminist terrain, in India it is important to see how such a category has been shaped through contributions from sex workers.[93] According to Menon, the positioning of women as 'people in the prostitution business' has not only crafted a category of woman with relatively more power, it has also done something significant for the Indian feminist tradition.[94]

Indian feminism, Menon argues, conventionally understood the category of woman by looking at it through the heterosexual family, and understood prostitution only as a form of violence experienced by women.[95] The positioning of the sex worker, both female and transgender, within a category of 'woman' has worked to challenge the heteronormative conception of gender within the women's movement. Menon refers to sex workers' public assertions as 'counter-heteronormative' practices that emerge through a challenge to women's location within monogamous patriarchal marriage.[96] Menon's argument resonates with the claims made by the Statement, which argues that the dhandhewali is more empowered in comparison with other women who live within the traditional bounds of marriage.[97]

The Statement clearly defines the sex worker as a woman in relation not only to men, but to other (non–sex-working) women. According to the Statement, the sex worker is more 'empowered' in relation to other women, and their relations with the men in their families are more 'equal' compared to those of non–sex-working women. It argues:

> *We believe* that a woman's sexuality is an integral part of her as a woman, as varied as her mothering, domestic and such other skills. We do not believe that sex has a sacred space and women who have sex for reasons other

[93] Menon, 'Sexuality, Caste, Governmentality'. [94] Ibid., 102. [95] Ibid.
[96] Ibid., 98. [97] VAMP, 'A Statement of Women in Prostitution', above n 88.

> than its reproductive importance are violating this space. Or that if they chose to make money from the transaction they are immoral or debauched.[98]
>
> *We believe* that we are more empowered than most women within male-dominated patriarchal structures are. For instance, within the family structure (which we know is the most oppressive), we are the breadwinners and the heads of our households. The relationships we share with the men in our families are most honest and equal because the purdah of double standards is not necessary.[99]

The assertions in the Statement do not argue for sex workers' relative superiority over others. These assertions speak of a woman who is not a flattened, homogeneous category, but rather a layered, relational one. The Statement speaks of a woman who is not a product of abstract, hierarchical male/female social relations. Rather, she is grounded in women's particular lived experiences of activism in Sangli and produced in relation to law. For example, VAMP's activist practices perform a reorganisation of women's relations in Sangli with their children and their children's fathers. This has implications for the social and legal imperatives that are generally used to determine the meaning of family.

Pani mentioned that for women it was a very common experience to be asked who *their* child belongs to.[100] She noted that pregnant women were often asked about the child that she could be seen carrying in her womb, *kiska bacha hain?* (whose child is it?).[101] Seshu, who also spoke of this, argued that the source of this popular question was the authority attributed to the male figure around whom familial relations were organised in society, and belonging to whose lineage is signified through the use of his family name.[102] Speaking about this same experience, VAMP members point at the hierarchical organisation of women's familial relations in Sangli.

Durga Pujari, sex worker and member of VAMP, told me that sex workers did not consider the father's role to be of much significance as

98 Ibid (emphasis in original). 99 Ibid (emphasis in original).
100 Conversation with Kamlabai Pani, above n 1.
101 Ibid.; conversation with Meena Seshu, above n 12.
102 Conversation with Meena Seshu, above n 12.

far as their child's birth and rearing were concerned.[103] However, during childbirth the hospital authorities insist on seeing a man as the guardian of both the child and the mother to be able to include his name in the child's birth certificate.[104] In such situations, out of practical necessity, sex workers sometimes request a random male passerby, or a neighbour, to sign the form as their guardian, using a fictitious name. At times, women also pay a small amount of money to such people for doing this favour for them.[105]

What happens as a result is that sometimes all of their children have different family names, and the role of the surname is rendered absolutely inconsequential in determining their children's lineage.[106] Deshmukh told me that VAMP ensured that sex workers' children could be admitted in schools under the guardianship of their mother, so that children of sex workers were known by their mother's name.[107] This does not pose a problem until sex workers try to obtain a caste certificate for their children.[108] A caste certificate is a legal document authorised by the Government of India that certifies a person's belonging to a Scheduled Caste. This is the nomenclature used by the state to identify Dalits who are listed under a schedule appended to the Constitution of India as deserving of affirmative action as a constitutional right.[109] On the basis of this document, people can have access to certain entitlements, such as reservation of seats in government jobs and educational institutions, which are made available to them in order to help overcome inequalities historically experienced by members of such groups.[110]

An essential supporting document required for obtaining a caste certificate is the birth certificate. The birth certificate is the foremost official document on the basis of which one's existence and citizenship may be established. The Government of India stipulates, under the

[103] Conversation with Durga Pujari, sex worker and VAMP member, Karad, 9 December 2014.

[104] Ibid. The same was reiterated by Meena Seshu in my conversation with her; see above n 12.

[105] Conversation with Durga Pujari, above n 103.

[106] Ibid.

[107] Conversation with Kiran Deshmukh, above n 2.

[108] Ibid.

[109] See generally, Galanter, *Competing Equalities*.

[110] See generally, Deshpande, *Affirmative Action in India*.

Registration of Births and Deaths Act, 1969, that every event of birth must be registered with the concerned authorities. For birth certificates to be issued in the name of a child, the father's name is essential. For children of sex workers whose birth certificates often carry the names of fictional fathers, their family names do not belong to Scheduled Castes.

In some cases, the name of the father and his corresponding surname do not match the traditional naming practices of the community. Both of these things then work to negate the child's belonging to a Scheduled Caste even though the mother may be carrying a name that can certify the child's affiliation to the same. In 2013, sex workers tackled this problem by lobbying a senior state official.[111] The women convinced the district collector, an officer in the Indian Administrative Services in charge of local administration, to authorise the issue of caste certificates for children of sex workers in their mother's name.[112]

When one engages in conversations with sex workers at VAMP, caste appears to be a very palpable concern in terms of sex workers' familial and community relations. The women engage with caste on a daily basis, but it is not always expressly mentioned in their advocacy documents. For instance, the Statement highlights class and gender dimensions but is silent about women's experiences of caste. This is a noticeable pattern in almost all of VAMP's advocacy documents, barring a few exceptions such as donor reports.[113]

I consciously engaged in understanding the meaning of their silence on the issue of caste in some documents and not in others. To me, this silence seems a deliberate decision related to the crafting of women's role and responsibilities in public life as dhandhewali/businesswomen. The articulations of sex work in VAMP's activist texts that peg women's experiences mostly on a narrative of gender are linked to the tenuous

[111] Conversation with Kiran Deshmukh, above n 2.

[112] Conversations with Meena Seshu, above n 12; Kiran Deshmukh, above n 2.

[113] In documents that have been produced for purposes other than advocacy, such as Sangram's annual report, caste finds a mention. As noted in an annual report: 'A worrying aspect that backgrounds SANGRAM and its partner collectives in the past one year has been the increased violence and atrocities against people who are considered to be "lower caste" or dalits.' Sangram, *Annual Report, 1 April 2014–31 March 2015*, 3, www.sangram.org/upload/reports/annual-narrative-report-2014-2015-5.pdf.

relation that sex workers share with women's and feminist groups in Maharashtra.[114]

Seshu told me that in Maharashtra specifically, where there is a robust history of Dalit women's activism, conversations between mainstream women's groups and sex workers have been adversarial.[115] Sex workers' public positioning of themselves as women in prostitution is due to VAMP's conversations with the women's movement in Maharashtra. Seshu and women's rights activist Laxmi Murthy argue in the book *The Business of Sex* that sex workers and feminists have seldom been in conversation, and if they have, it has never been on friendly terms.[116] In their introductory chapter, Murthy and Seshu note, 'Feminists and sex workers in India have only recently begun to talk to each other; and the dialogue has been difficult. The awkwardness, hesitation and downright hostility from feminists towards sex workers and those working for their rights has been palpable.'[117]

Menon argues that sex workers' activist engagements have enriched the women's movement's discursive understanding and positioning of its subject, 'woman'.[118] Despite sex workers' contributions to feminisms in India, as Seshu and Murthy argue, sex workers are often not welcomed into feminist discourses as legitimate interlocutors or contributors.

The hostile sex worker–feminist relations that Murthy and Seshu refer to inform VAMP's public positioning of sex workers as women. Sex workers in their intra-group conversations prove to be vocal on the subject of their experiences of caste, as became evident in all my conversations at VAMP. However, in terms of assuming a public front, by crafting a role as dhandhewali/businesswomen, the women assert their gender over caste positions.

A conversation ensued between sex workers and the women's movement in early 2000 that is of relevance for understanding the significance of women's role as dhandhewali in terms of a feminist jurisprudence produced by VAMP. In 2006, the Bombay High Court struck down a ban

114 Menon, 'Sexuality, Caste, Governmentality', 102.

115 Conversation with Meena Seshu, above n 12.

116 See Seshu and Murthy, 'The Business of Sex', 1.

117 Ibid.

118 Menon, 'Sexuality, Caste, Governmentality'.

instituted by the Maharashtra government on dance bars.[119] Due to petitions filed by the bar owners and the bar girls' union, the court lifted the ban on dance bars by declaring it unconstitutional. The court affirmed that 'The right to dance has been recognized by the Apex Court as part of the fundamental right of speech and expression. If that be so, it will be open to a citizen to commercially benefit from the exercise of the fundamental right.'[120] The right to entertain through dancing came to be accepted as a livelihood option for women, but the decision also resulted in an affirmation of the separation of bar dancing from sex work.

For VAMP, while these events were taking place in Maharashtra, what proved to be of consequence were the conversations that started within feminist circles because of it.[121] It meant that issues relating to violence against women in the entertainment industry as well as among sex workers were gaining public visibility and were being seen as part of a feminist agenda.[122] Sex workers' particular experiences of womanhood, as they articulated and understood it, were thus entering into the conversations that constituted Indian feminist discourses.

The first-time presence of sex workers at the Seventh National Conference of Autonomous Women's Groups[123] held in Kolkata in

[119] I have already discussed this event in Chapter 1 while referring to the work of feminist lawyer and activist Flavia Agnes. See, generally, Utkarsh Srivastava, 'Maharashtra's Ban on Dance Bars Has Done More Harm than Good', *Wire*, 28 March 2016, https://thewire.in/gender/maharashtras-ban-on-dance-bars-has-done-more-harm-than-good.

[120] *Indian Hotel and Restaurants* ... v. *the State of Maharashtra through* ... 2006 (3) BomCR 705 (12 April 2006), https://indiankanoon.org/doc/1434517.

[121] Conversation with Meena Seshu, above n 12.

[122] Sangram/VAMP Team, *The VAMP/Sangram Sex Worker's Movement in India's Southwest*, above n 9, 13.

[123] The group defines its structure and workings thus: 'We are autonomous women's groups, formed in the late 1970s and early 1980s, which began their political journey with the anti rape, dowry murders and amniocentesis campaigns. We define autonomy in terms of maintaining institutional and ideological independence from political parties, governments and funding agencies. The National Conference is organised by a working group that is called the National Coordination Committee (NCC). It is not a registered or a permanent body but is re-convened prior to each conference and collectively inducts new members.' See National Conference of Women's Movements, http://openspace.org.in/node/173.

2006 bears testimony to this fact.[124] Feminist sociologist Meena Gopal, in a discussion on the women's conference, argues that the ban on dance bars triggered the entry of sex workers into Indian feminist discourse.[125] According to Gopal, sex workers' entry into the conversations happened via the emergent 'controversy' amongst feminists on the 'troubled connections' between 'sexuality, labour and caste' in India.[126]

With these events, sex workers may have become part of the more mainstream feminist conversations (the ones initiated by the Autonomous Women's Groups), but were relegated to a place of difference vis-à-vis other women, including bar dancers.[127] The bar dancers, who came closest to sex workers in terms of their professional designation, separated themselves from sex workers by publicly carrying placards that said 'we are not sex workers'.[128] VAMP abstained from participating in the anti-ban activisms that happened in their region because the bar dancers claimed their right to livelihood on the basis of their difference from sex work.[129] Thus, the bar dancers claimed that their work was legitimate precisely because bar dancing was *not* sex work.

In terms of a litigating strategy, it is understandable that, owing to the existence of the ITPA, which criminalises 'prostitution', not delineating bar dancing from sex work might go against the interests of bar dancers. And in this context, as Seshu argued, VAMP's show of solidarity with bar dancers would only put them at a disadvantage.[130] However, although this may have been a strategic move on the part of bar dancers, which made it possible for sex workers to enter mainstream feminist conversations, it was not necessarily useful for sex workers. The conversations arising from this event worked to further consolidate sex workers' position as different from other women. As a result of this, the crux of

[124] Sangram/VAMP Team, *The VAMP/Sangram Sex Worker's Movement in India's Southwest*, above n 9, 13.

[125] Meena Gopal, 'Caste, Sexuality and Labour: The Troubled Connection' (2012) 60(2), *Current Sociology*, 222, 223.

[126] Ibid.

[127] Prabha Kotiswaran, 'Sword or shield? The Role of the Law in the Indian Sex Workers' Movement' (2013) 15(4), *Interventions: International Journal of Postcolonial Studies*, 530, 532–33.

[128] Conversation with Meena Seshu, above n 12. [129] Ibid. [130] Ibid.

VAMP's activism and the crafting of women's role as dhandhewali comes to be founded on doing away with the *difference* accorded to them vis-à-vis other women.

As I was speaking with Kazi one afternoon and jotting down things in my notebook with a pen, she pointed at my writing and explained how my work as researcher was not very different from sex work. She argued:

> you can hold a pen so you write with it and earn a living. I cannot, so I use my hand to hold a penis and give a hand job. We both earn a living using our hands and head, but how will we ever make the state understand this, tell me?[131]

For Kazi, the distinctions between intellectual labour and bodily labour, whereby the former is attributed to the *mind* and the latter to the *body*, are blurred. Her interpretation of sex work dilutes the demarcations between my intellectual labour and the general perceptions of her work as a form of bodily labour that does not require the application of mind and reason. She describes the practices of both research and sex work as *mind-body* activities involving the conscious use of body parts as well as the capacity to think and judge for oneself. In her case, being a dhandhewali necessitates possessing business acumen along with the provision of sexual services.

Such a blurring of mind–body distinctions in the context of sex work was also articulated by VAMP in the Statement, which argues:

> *We believe* that making money from sex is only selling a part of our body, which is in no way different from selling our brains or physical labour. We protest against a society that deems our work contribution as less prestigious than other traditional forms of work. We believe that we challenge and undermine structures of power by using a part of our womanhood – our sexuality – as a source of our power and income.[132]

By taking on the role of dhandhewali – a woman who engages in sex work as an occupation and is capable of using her mind – the women

[131] 'Tumko pen pakad na ata hain is liye tum likhke kamate ho, mujhe nahin ata is liye main dimaag lagake haath madti hoon, par yeh sarkar ko kaise samajh ayega, bolo?' Conversation with Shabana Kazi, above n 25.

[132] VAMP, 'A Statement of Women in Prostitution', above n 88 (emphasis in original).

challenge hierarchical social relations in Sangli. Pani, while speaking to me about *devadasi* practices, to which many women and transgender sex workers at VAMP adhere, argued that women's relations with other people in their community became more equitable because they were dhandhewali.[133] These relations pertain to the specific relations of gender, class and caste experienced by the women in Sangli.

Pani told me that, in the religious devadasi tradition practised in some parts of Maharashtra and Karnataka, the disciples of the goddess Renuka Devi Yellamma dedicate young girls to the service (*dasi*) of the god/dess (*deva*).[134] For these girls, being dedicated to the goddess means that they cannot be married to a mortal, which then makes it easier for them to engage in sex work and live freely without the compulsion of adhering to the conventional social norms of marriage and family.[135]

Given that a devadasi cannot get married to a man, she often gets an equal share of her family property, which is otherwise usually denied to women.[136] Moreover, because devadasi women can earn a living through sex work, within their communities they are regarded as heads of households.[137] I learned from Pani that even though the caste system, which is highly prevalent in the region, prohibits inter-caste relationships, because they are sex workers women are able to challenge such prohibition.[138] This is because the rules of sexual purity do not apply to sex workers, and they can engage in sexual relations with men of upper castes.

The Statement notes that the woman's body is a resource that she can use as a form of capital in the business of sex for financial income.[139] This conviction is accompanied by an understanding that sex workers' use of the body as resource is permitted by the pre-existence of a social logic of male–female relations that supports this transaction. Therefore,

[133] Conversation with Kamlabai Pani, above n 1. Also noted by Seshu and Murthy, 'The Business of Sex', 35.

[134] Conversation with Kamlabai Pani, above n 1. [135] Ibid. [136] Ibid.

[137] Ibid. The same was reiterated by Durga Pujari, above n 103. This point is also noted by Seshu and Murthy, 'The Business of Sex', 35.

[138] Conversation with Kamlabai Pani, above n 1.

[139] VAMP, 'A Statement of Women in Prostitution', above n 88.

it becomes difficult for those not supported by this permissible logic, such as male sex workers as opposed to female and transgender sex workers, to make use of their bodies as a resource for this very same purpose.[140] The Statement explains:

> *We believe* that all occupations stereotypical to women adhere to so-called 'feminine values'. They capitalize upon qualities like tolerance, sympathy, tenderness, endurance, understanding, patience, forbearance and much more, be they housewives, typists, nurses, teachers, office assistants, receptionists, or women in prostitution. We believe that the socialization of the girl-child to accept such occupations as the only option is also a major reason for the perpetuation of sexual discrimination in the female work force. We believe that women in prostitution are *no different*.[141]

During our adda, Pandu, a transgender sex worker, explained that for her and other transgender people, the tradition of marriage with a divine entity was a practice of womanhood. Pandu, a 'jogappa',[142] is married to the goddess Renuka Devi Yellamma. She is also a sex worker who provides sexual services to men. She told me that her marriage with the goddess allows her to wear women's clothing, and being a sex worker allows her to have sexual relations with men.[143] According to Pandu, engaging in these activities publicly established her womanhood in the eyes of other people in the community, who would otherwise prohibit her conduct of gender and sexual relations.[144]

During my adda with a group of sex workers in Sangli, I asked them how they positioned transgender sex workers within VAMP, which is known as a women's collective (see Fig. 4.4). Nilawa, a sex worker, responded by saying, 'But they are women! Because they think of

[140] Conversation with Pandu, transgender sex worker and member of VAMP's partner organisation, Muskaan, Balajinagar, Sangli, 5 December 2014.

[141] VAMP, 'A Statement of Women in Prostitution', above n 88 (emphasis in original). Emphasis added at the end to point out how VAMP's activism is directed at countering the formulation of sex worker as an exceptional experience.

[142] 'Jogappa' refers to a male person at the service of the goddess, and *jogatin* or devadasi refers to a female person at the service of the goddess. See generally Ramberg, *Given to the Goddess*.

[143] Conversation with Pandu, above n 140. [144] Ibid.

Figure 4.4 Sangram's 2011 calendar portraying transgender sex workers as part of VAMP. *Source*: Sangram, Sangli.

themselves as women and also act and feel like women.'[145] According to Nilawa, the thoughts, actions and emotions of the transgender sex worker that tell her she is a woman are what make her so. Nilawa's articulation thus locates the woman within a *mind–body–heart* triad, the coordinates that shape a dhandhewali/businesswoman as a *thinking–acting–feeling* subject who categorically marks a departure from a popular perception of woman in a caste-based society.

The chaturvarna (four-caste) system classifies and categorises people on the basis of their labour practices. What underpins such classification is an assumption of hierarchy between the faculties of the mind and the body. Because of such a classification, those who perform intellectual labour, the Brahmins, are regarded as upper castes, while those who

[145] 'Par woh to mahila hi hain, mahila jaisa pheelings hain na, mahila hi sochti hain aur karti hain.' Conversation with Nilawa, sex worker and member of VAMP, Karad, 9 December 2014.

perform menial labour, Dalits, are considered lower castes. As Ambedkar argues, 'caste system is not merely division of labour. It is also a division of labourers.'[146] The hierarchical organisation of people is accompanied by a set of prohibitions, including prohibitions relating to the education of those who are ordained to perform bodily menial labour, such as Dalits and other lower castes.[147] Indeed, as Ambedkar asks with irony, 'Why need the Shudra brother take to education, when there is the Brahmin to whom he can go when the occasion for reading or writing arises?'[148] This caste-based ordering of social relations between men takes on a different form when it comes to women. Women's location within this schema, determined by marital relations with men, forms their status as equivalent to that of Shudras (servants), thus subservient to men.[149]

What becomes visible through adda with my interlocutors at VAMP is that women's crafting of a role in public life as dhandhewali, who can reason and use their sense of judgement, has implications for a feminist jurisprudence. Sex workers' thinking and practices of being 'woman' matter for their engagements with the social category of caste, and with the legal entity of the state that regulates their lives through criminal law. For instance, an assumption underlying the ITPA is that a woman engaged in sex work is incapable of taking decisions about her life. As discussed in the previous chapter, ITPA prohibits sex work by criminalising the activity and making women's consent completely irrelevant for the enforcement of these provisions.

To call sex work a profession would mean subjecting the organisation of these women's lives and their livelihood to the authority of that very state. It would mean a relegation of the decisions of community organisation and sex workers' well-being to an authority with which women share a hierarchical relation. As Deshmukh argued, calling sex work dhandha and crafting a role for women as dhandhewali, on the other hand, worked to perform the task of reducing state interference in women's

[146] Ambedkar, 'Annihilation of Caste', 263.
[147] Ibid., 282; Ambedkar, 'Castes in India', 241.
[148] Ambedkar, 'Annihilation of Caste', 281.
[149] See Urmila Pawar and Meenakshi Moon, *We Also Made History: Women in the Ambedkarite Movement* (Zubaan, 2008), chapter 1, 'Social Background', 53.

lives.[150] It works to place the decision-making authority with sex workers, whereby they are able to live their relations in accordance with the principles of collectivisation and perform a livelihood of their choice.

It seems contradictory that, despite adopting the organisational form of a society and a public trust under state-authorised rules, VAMP claims that it is reluctant to accept state regulation. However, the crafting of women's role as dhandhewali, and the subsequent demands for decriminalisation of sex work founded on such a role, worked as a means of calling the institutions of the state, and state-authorised law, into a somewhat mutual relationship with sex-working women in Sangli.

To do this, VAMP's activities are designed to minimise the state–sex worker interaction, even when it comes to holding state officials accountable for their acts and omissions.[151] One of VAMP's documents expressly states that the 'police and criminal gangs are major sources of violence. The power of the police lies in having the authority and institutional backing . . . In dealing with this violence, sex workers have been reluctant to turn to the State, but have resisted violence in their own ways.'[152]

Sex workers use community-based mechanisms such as *jan sunwai* (public hearings) to hold local politicians and government officials accountable. Shantilal Kale, an employee of Sangram and a close confidante of VAMP, explained that jan sunwai is an informal practice of listening to the grievances of people living in a particular locality.[153] This is a way of shaping public opinion and nurturing a shared sense of responsibility amongst people living in close proximity to undo the wrongdoing of members of their own community.[154] But the mechanism does not adopt punitive measures or subject wrongdoers to a fear of penalties. Rather, the processes are directed at making relations within a community more equitable.[155]

In 2013 and 2014, VAMP held a series of jan sunwais in the districts of Shirala and Kolhapur, where they invited the local people to share their experiences of discrimination encountered while accessing public health

[150] Conversation with Kiran Deshmukh, above n 2.

[151] Sangram/VAMP Team, *The VAMP/Sangram Sex Worker's Movement in India's Southwest*, above n 9, 13.

[152] Ibid. [153] Conversation with Shantilal Kale, above n 6. [154] Ibid. [155] Ibid.

facilities.[156] Deshmukh shared in our adda that by participating in the public hearings as dhandhewali, the women mobilised local political leaders, the media, government officials and local people. The women's aim was to create public pressure on these institutions and their office bearers and compel them to perform their duties.[157]

The participation of VAMP in these public hearings is in line with the Indian feminist tradition of women's courts (Nari Adalat) that were set up in the state of Gujarat in 1995 as an alternative community-based practice for seeking justice and holding wrongdoers accountable.[158] The women's courts were formed in response to the apathy of the legal system and state institutions towards women's experiences of violence and injustice. Abha Bhaiya argues that the public hearings conducted in the women's court were alternative practices of law directed at the redressal of grievances and seeking justice within communities.[159] For Bhaiya, these hearings initiated by a marginalised community of women were not legal but legitimate, although they operated parallel to the remit of formal law and official institutions.[160] This means that these hearings were in between legal and illegal by virtue of keeping state law and the judiciary out of a decision-making role in matters that should have conventionally been under their institutional jurisdiction.

Much like the women's courts, the jan sunwais organised by VAMP are deployed by sex workers for strengthening their belonging to the community, gaining public support and seeking justice through dispute resolution in matters pertaining to their own community.[161] However, as alternative practices of law, the most important function of jan sunwais,

[156] Full account of hearings available in Sangram, *Annual Report 2013–14*, 16, www.sangram.org/upload/reports/annual-narrative-report-2013-2014-4.pdf.

[157] Conversation with Kiran Deshmukh, above n 2. [158] Bhaiya, 'Legitimately Ours', 57.

[159] Ibid. [160] Ibid.

[161] While the mechanism of alternative dispute resolution as recognised by the Indian legal system requires that a procedure established by statutory regulations be followed, public hearings such as VAMP's jan sunwais do not. See Sylvia Vatuk, 'The "Women's Court" in India: An Alternative Dispute Resolution Body for Women in Distress' (2013) 45(1), *Journal of Legal Pluralism and Unofficial Law*, 76. On the activist tradition of jan sunwais in India, see Pradeep Ninan Thomas, 'Contentious Actions and Communication for Social Change: The Public Hearing (*Jan Sunwai*) as Process' (2017) 67(5), *Journal of Communication*, 719.

according to Kale, is to limit the authority of state and other formal institutions in sex workers' lives.[162] In comparison to the women at DMSC, the state is expressly more hostile towards sex workers in Sangli. In the states of Karnataka and Maharashtra, from where my interlocutors at VAMP come, sex workers' lives are regulated not just through ITPA but also through another set of state-authorised criminal laws.

A large number of women who practise sex work in this region are devadasis. On account of this, women's lives come within two inter-related state-authorised legal regulations that are anti-prostitution and anti-superstition. Thus, devadasi practices are made a criminal activity under the Maharashtra Devadasi System (Abolition) Act, 2005, and the Karnataka Devadasis (Prohibition of Dedication) Act, 1982. Both these statutes sanction the 'rescue' and 'rehabilitation' of devadasi sex workers by declaring it a criminal activity, much like the ITPA, and also negate the women's capacity to think rationally about their own well-being.[163]

Under ITPA, the police officers are invested with the power to enter and search the home of a sex worker and remove everyone who is found there.[164] A magistrate can authorise a police officer to remove a person from a brothel who is carrying out prostitution of her own volition, as well as a person who is being made to carry out prostitution by others.[165] The magistrate can also order a person who has been removed from a brothel to be sent to live in detention in a 'corrective institution' or a 'protective home'.[166] However, before sending a woman to any of these institutions, her wishes need not be heard by the magistrate in determining where she should be sent, even if the woman is an adult. Similarly, the Karnataka Devadasis (Prohibition of Dedication) Act, 1982, posits that 'the dedication of a woman as a devadasi ... whether she has consented to such dedication or not, is hereby declared unlawful'.[167]

Deshmukh shared her experience of being sent to a corrective home by the magistrate once when she had been 'rescued' by the police. She explained the irony of her situation thus: 'I can cast [a] vote and elect a

[162] Conversation with Shantilal Kale, above n 6.
[163] For example, Karnataka Devadasis (Prohibition of Dedication) Act, 1982, Sec. 3.
[164] ITPA, Sec. 15. [165] ITPA, Sec. 16. [166] ITPA, Sec. 17(4), 10A.
[167] Karnataka Devadasis (Prohibition of Dedication) Act, 1982, Sec. 3.

government, but I cannot tell what is good for me. I need correction at the age of 50 when I have already become a grandmother.'[168] Thus, although Deshmukh is deemed to have a capable mind for deciding her representative in the government, she is considered incapable of determining the course of her own life and in need of rehabilitation (see Figs. 4.5 and 4.6).

One of VAMP's advocacy documents, which they describe as a fact-sheet for understanding the decriminalisation demand, refers to one particular incident of rescue that took place in 2013.[169] The police raided a brothel in Kolhapur and sent ten adult sex workers to a corrective institution. Before sending the women away, the police asked them to produce their legal guardians or parents who would take charge of them. The women, who were almost all over the age of fifty, were unable to produce their guardians and so were forced to remain in an institution for two to three months. They were finally released on the condition that they would not engage in sex work anymore.[170]

A 2007 issue of VAMP's newsletter *Of Veshyas, Vamps, Whores and Women* quotes Revathi, a sex worker from Karnataka, on a similar experience of rescue and rehabilitation. Her experience, although it sounds like a joke, brings out the grim reality of sex workers' encounters with state-authorised rescue and rehabilitation programmes. She says:

> Since you are on rehabilitation, I must tell you about myself, as I was also a subject of rehabilitation. They gave me a buffalo. Well, I had this small room, which I now found myself sharing with the buffalo. You see the buffalo eats a lot, and as I was expected to stop sex work after rehabilitation, there was not much money. I didn't mind for myself, but I couldn't bear to see the buffalo wasting before my eyes. So soon I found myself doing twice the sex work to feed the buffalo and me. Well, now the buffalo was in heat, and I had to get her crossed. I was told that it would cost

[168] 'Main desh ka neta chun sakti hu par apne bare mein nahin soch sakta, mera pachas baras ho gaya ab mujhe sudharega, mera pota poti bhi ho gaya.' Conversation with Kiran Deshmukh, above n 2.

[169] VAMP, 'Understanding the De-criminalisation Demand: A Fact Sheet for Advocacy', http://feministlawarchives.pldindia.org/wp-content/uploads/Demanding-De-Criminalisation-of-Sex-Work-Fact-Sheet.pdf.

[170] Ibid., 2.

Figure 4.5 A VAMP pamphlet titled 'Rehabilitation Is Useless. We Want Our Rights'. *Source*: VAMP, Sangli.

100 rupees per attempt. So now there I was forced to do sex work to pay for the buffalo to have sex! That was enough. I decided I had enough with rehabilitation.[171]

[171] Sangram, 'Rehabilitation Against Their Will?' (June 2002) 1(2), *Of Veshyas, Vamps, Whores and Women*, 7.

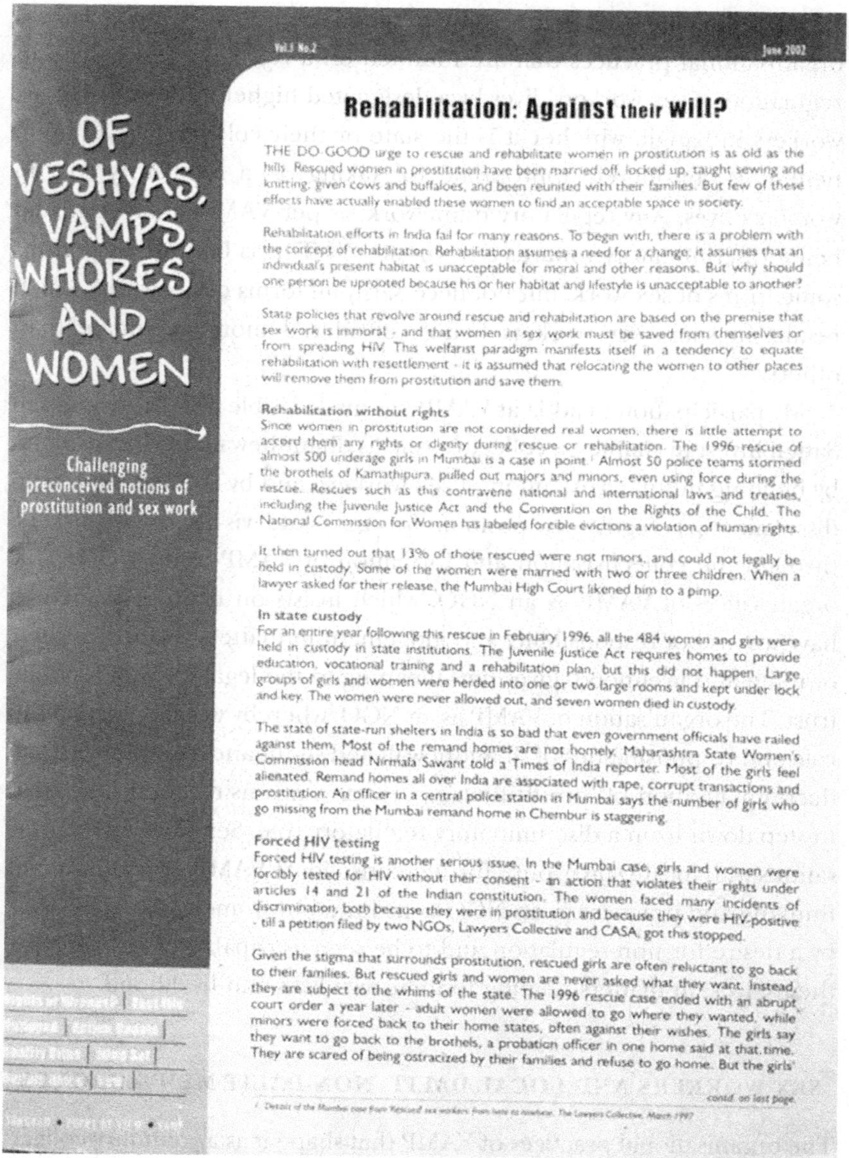

Vol.I No.2 June 2002

OF VESHYAS, VAMPS, WHORES AND WOMEN

Challenging preconceived notions of prostitution and sex work

Rehabilitation: Against their Will?

THE DO GOOD urge to rescue and rehabilitate women in prostitution is as old as the hills. Rescued women in prostitution have been married off, locked up, taught sewing and knitting, given cows and buffaloes, and been reunited with their families. But few of these efforts have actually enabled these women to find an acceptable space in society.

Rehabilitation efforts in India fail for many reasons. To begin with, there is a problem with the concept of rehabilitation. Rehabilitation assumes a need for a change; it assumes that an individual's present habitat is unacceptable for moral and other reasons. But why should one person be uprooted because his or her habitat and lifestyle is unacceptable to another?

State policies that revolve around rescue and rehabilitation are based on the premise that sex work is immoral - and that women in sex work must be saved from themselves or from spreading HIV. This welfarist paradigm manifests itself in a tendency to equate rehabilitation with resettlement - it is assumed that relocating the women to other places will remove them from prostitution and save them.

Rehabilitation without rights

Since women in prostitution are not considered real women, there is little attempt to accord them any rights or dignity during rescue or rehabilitation. The 1996 rescue of almost 500 underage girls in Mumbai is a case in point.[1] Almost 50 police teams stormed the brothels of Kamathipura, pulled out majors and minors, even using force during the rescue. Rescues such as this contravene national and international laws and treaties, including the Juvenile Justice Act and the Convention on the Rights of the Child. The National Commission for Women has labeled forcible evictions a violation of human rights.

It then turned out that 13% of those rescued were not minors, and could not legally be held in custody. Some of the women were married with two or three children. When a lawyer asked for their release, the Mumbai High Court likened him to a pimp.

In state custody

For an entire year following this rescue in February 1996, all the 484 women and girls were held in custody in state institutions. The Juvenile Justice Act requires homes to provide education, vocational training and a rehabilitation plan, but this did not happen. Large groups of girls and women were herded into one or two large rooms and kept under lock and key. The women were never allowed out, and seven women died in custody.

The state of state-run shelters in India is so bad that even government officials have railed against them. Most of the remand homes are not homely, Maharashtra State Women's Commission head Nirmala Sawant told a Times of India reporter. Most of the girls feel alienated. Remand homes all over India are associated with rape, corrupt transactions and prostitution. An officer in a central police station in Mumbai says the number of girls who go missing from the Mumbai remand home in Chembur is staggering.

Forced HIV testing

Forced HIV testing is another serious issue. In the Mumbai case, girls and women were forcibly tested for HIV without their consent - an action that violates their rights under articles 14 and 21 of the Indian constitution. The women faced many incidents of discrimination, both because they were in prostitution and because they were HIV-positive - till a petition filed by two NGOs, Lawyers Collective and CASA, got this stopped.

Given the stigma that surrounds prostitution, rescued girls are often reluctant to go back to their families. But rescued girls and women are never asked what they want. Instead, they are subject to the whims of the state. The 1996 rescue case ended with an abrupt court order a year later - adult women were allowed to go where they wanted, while minors were forced back to their home states, often against their wishes. The girls say they want to go back to the brothels, a probation officer in one home said at that time. They are scared of being ostracized by their families and refuse to go home. But the girls'

contd. on last page

1. Details of the Mumbai case from 'Rescued' sex workers: from here to nowhere, The Lawyers Collective, March 1997

Figure 4.6 VAMP's newsletter, *Of Veshyas, Vamps, Whores and Women* (July 2002). *Source.* VAMP, Sangli.

VAMP's demand for the decriminalisation of sex work follows from organisational practices that are founded on a rejection of any kind of regulation of sex workers' lives by a designated higher authority. For sex workers in Sangli, whether it is the state or their collective NGO itself, neither is considered appropriate for taking on a regulatory role in women's lives. Any regulatory framework, as per VAMP, always ends up being discriminatory towards sex workers.[172] This is because it 'permits some forms of sex work, but not necessarily all forms of sex work', which results in some sex workers being considered more legitimate than others.[173]

My participation in adda at VAMP has made visible how the women in Sangli invest in shaping a collective role as dhandhewali/businesswomen by building mutual trust amongst sex workers, and by authorising a non-discriminatory regulatory position for the state vis-à-vis sex workers, through the collectivisation and formation of VAMP as an NGO. This organisation of VAMP as an NGO, which insists on trusting women to have a sense of responsibility and judgement in matters relating to their own life and livelihood, gives new meaning to the legal form of a public trust. The organisation of VAMP as an NGO, whereby women take on the role and responsibilities of dhandhewali and simultaneously demand the decriminalisation of 'prostitution', works as a means of urging the state to step down from a discriminatory regulatory role. Sex workers' conversations with local Dalit groups further consolidate VAMP's organisational thinking and practices as an NGO constituted by women who are driven by a desire for non-regulation and to be seen as capable of deciding for themselves on matters relating to their own lives and livelihood.

SEX WORKERS AND LOCAL DALIT/NON-DALIT MEN'S GROUPS

The organisational practices of VAMP that shape it as a voluntary collective of sex workers constitute a form of Dalit activism based on women's experiences of collectivisation in Sangli. The women have shaped their organisation by drawing upon Ambedkarite anti-caste thinking on the mode of formation of a democratic collective life.

[172] VAMP, 'Understanding the De-criminalisation Demand', above n 169. [173] Ibid., 3.

The word 'dalit' literally means 'crushed' or 'broken'.[174] More generally, in the context of a Hindu religious way of life, the term refers to people who are untouchables because they lie outside the chaturvarna or the four-tiered caste system. The Dalit communities, in a sense, although born into the caste-based religious organisation of community life, carry the social status of outcasts.[175]

In 'The Annihilation of Caste', originally written as a speech addressing a group of Hindu social reformers in 1936, Ambedkar argues that the caste system is harmful for its practitioners.[176] According to Ambedkar, 'the effect of caste on the ethics of the Hindus is simply deplorable', preventing the followers of the Hindu religion from forming a sangathan (collective union).[177] The formation of a sangathan is hindered by the caste system because a 'Hindu's public is his caste. His responsibility is only to his caste.'[178] This works to divide people and create hierarchies, rather than uniting them by encouraging mutual cooperation amongst each other.

For Ambedkar, religion has two distinct meanings that are acquired through the ways in which it is lived by its practitioners. The duality of meaning, he argues, emerges through two distinct practices of Hinduism: religion practised as 'principles' and religion practised as 'rules'. It is religion in the form of rules, rather than principles, that hinders the realisation of a sangathan. Ambedkar argues:

> Not only do I make a distinction, but I say that this distinction is real and important. Rules are practical; they are habitual ways of doing things

[174] Human Rights Watch, *Broken People: Caste Violence Against India's 'Untouchables'*, 1999, www.hrw.org/reports/1999/india; Human Rights Watch, *'They Say We're Dirty': Denying an Education to India's Marginalized* (2014), www.hrw.org/report/2014/04/22/they-say-were-dirty/denying-education-indias-marginalized; Human Rights Watch, *India: 'Hidden Apartheid' of Discrimination against Dalits* (2007), www.hrw.org/news/2007/02/13/india-hidden-apartheid-discrimination-against-dalits. Despite the con-situational provision against discrimination, in order to tackle the issue a series of legislations have been passed in India: the Untouchability (Offences) Act, 1955; the Protection of Civil Rights Act, 1976; Scheduled Caste and Scheduled Tribe (Prevention of Atrocities) Act, 1989; and Rules, 1995.

[175] See generally, Anupama Rao, *The Caste Question: Dalits and the Politics of Modern India* (University of California Press, 2009).

[176] Ambedkar, 'Annihilation of Caste', 273. [177] Ibid., 275. [178] Ibid.

> according to prescription. But principles are intellectual; they are useful methods of judging things. Rules seek to tell an agent just what course of action to pursue. Principles do not prescribe a specific course of action.[179]

For Ambedkar, the distinction between 'rules' and 'principles' has significance for how the lives and relationships of their practitioners are organised. Those who live by 'principles' must consciously think about how to conduct themselves and relate with others, and are, therefore, able to take more responsibility for their own actions. People who organise their lives by 'rules' are told what to do and need not put conscious thought into their conduct. As a consequence, they are unable to take responsibility for what they do. Thus, in his own words, the 'difference between rules and principles makes the acts done in pursuit of them different in quality and in content'.[180]

Ambedkar demonstrates that sangathan may be formed by practices in which individuals use democratic principles to guide their thoughts and actions, and also to evaluate its uses and consequences. Democracy, he argues, 'is not merely a form of government. It is primarily a mode of associated living, of conjoint communicated experience. It is essentially an attitude of respect and reverence towards one's fellow men.'[181]

The meaning that sex workers attribute to the formation of a volunteer-based NGO resonates with Ambedkar's view that sangathan may be formed through democratic principles that aid mutual and collective living at a place. However, it became clear during our adda at VAMP that even though sex workers are greatly influenced by Ambedkar, they neither share an easy relationship with his worldview, nor can they claim affiliation to him very readily.

At Miraj, the women jointly recounted their experiences of being denied participation in the celebration of Ambedkar Jayanti (Ambedkar's birth anniversary), which is observed every year on 14 April.[182] The women noted that Ambedkar Jayanti was an important day for publicly marking sex workers' presence within the Dalit community in Sangli, and showing solidarity with the values of social equality

[179] Ibid., 298. [180] Ibid. [181] Ibid., 276.

[182] Group discussion with ten sex worker members of VAMP at Miraj, Sangli, 4 December 2014.

Figure 4.7 VAMP hoarding to mark Ambedkar's birth anniversary on 14 April 2014. *Source*: VAMP, Sangli.

that Ambedkar represents.[183] The women further explained that local Dalit groups once got violent when the women took out a public rally to pay homage to Ambedkar's statue.[184] Deshmukh told me that the women fought back as they understood this to be a violation of their right to claim affiliation with the local Dalit community and with the Ambedkarite Dalit tradition.[185] Due to this reason, Deshmukh added, irrespective of their religion, every year sex workers gathered from across the region to make sure they participated in public celebrations of the life and contributions of Ambedkar (see Fig. 4.7).[186]

Deshmukh clarified that conflicts between local Dalit groups and sex workers arose on the basis of an assumption held by these groups that sex-working women perpetuated caste-based discriminations by demanding the decriminalisation of sex work.[187] Such accusations against sex workers arose from a belief that women who did sex work belonged to lower castes or Dalit devadasi communities, which made sex

[183] See Sangram's annual report on the celebration of Ambedkar's birth anniversary by sex workers in Sangli. Sangram, *Annual Report, 1 April 2014–31 March 2015*, above n 113, 19.

[184] Group discussion, above n 182.

[185] Conversation with Kiran Deshmukh, above n 2.

[186] Ibid.

[187] Ibid.; see generally Sharmila Rege, *Against the Madness of Manu: B. R. Ambedkar's Writings on Brahminical Patriarchy* (Navayana, 2013).

work essentially a caste-based practice.[188] Thus, according to these other Dalit groups, by demanding sex workers' rights VAMP upholds the caste system, causing a setback to the anti-caste Dalit movement.[189]

The book *We Also Made History: Women in the Ambedkarite Movement*, written by two Dalit feminist writers, Urmila Pawar and Meenakshi Moon, bears testimony to Dalit women's uneasy relationship with Dalit men's activist groups in Maharashtra.[190] It demonstrates that Dalit women's experiences of anti-caste struggle have historically been excluded from male-dominated narratives about Dalit activism. Pawar and Moon write a counter-history by tracing an account of the Ambedkarite movement through a reading of biographies and interviews of women who were involved in anti-caste struggles from 1920 to 1956, when Ambedkar himself was providing leadership.[191] They document this history of women's role in anti-caste struggles to assert women's inheritance of the Ambedkarite tradition.[192]

Feminist writer Wandana Sonalkar, who has translated the book from Marathi to English, notes that Dalit women had a positive relationship with Ambedkar and his worldview.[193] Ambedkar was one of the first people to have considered that Dalit women's education and participation in public life were crucial for the liberation of Dalit people.[194] For Ambedkar, religious practices, like the devadasi practice through which a large number of Dalit women took up prostitution, were also a signifier of Dalit women's caste status. That is why Ambedkar urged Dalit women to give up prostitution, even if it caused them economic difficulties.[195] At a conference held in Mumbai in 1936,[196] Ambedkar directly addressed devadasis and other women who practised religious prostitution and said:

> You are the cause of shame for our community. Women should be the jewels of the community. Every society gives great importance to the question of women's moral character ... Recall the example of Draupadi from the *Mahabharata*. Just as Draupadi suffered a life of poverty

[188] Conversation with Kiran Deshmukh, above n 2.
[189] Ibid.; Group discussion, above n 182. [190] Pawar and Moon, *We Also Made History*.
[191] Sonalkar, 'Translator's Introduction', 6. [192] Ibid. [193] Ibid., 31. [194] Ibid.
[195] Ibid. [196] Conference of Devadasis, Damodar Hall, Parel, Bombay, 13 June 1936.

> with her husband while in exile, so you too will have to suffer. Character is more important than wealth.[197]
>
> Give up prostitution and live a moral life. We are not afraid of poverty; it is with us from our birth. So don't take up this profession for fear of poverty.[198]

The contemporary inheritance of the Ambedkarite anti-prostitution stand, which was developed in the particular historical context of the 1930s, by the local community in Sangli hinders sex workers' participation in a Dalit community life. Alongside this inheritance, in non-Dalit communities, there is also an existing caste-based prejudice that tends to segregate sex-working women from a community life in general. Seshu shared that in 2002, sex workers of VAMP bought a property in Nipani, a small town in Karnataka. The women wanted it to be used as VAMP's own office space for conducting meetings and providing HIV/AIDS prevention services to sex workers. However, a local real estate builder ordered the women to stop holding meetings, or to do it in a manner that did not 'offend the respectability of … upper-caste women'.[199] Sex workers were told they could hold their meetings, but 'not on the side facing the street … [and] VAMP members should only enter their building through the back with their heads covered'.[200] The women, Seshu told me, did not get much support from the police or other state officials to tackle the matter, but they protested on their own and disregarded these caste-based prohibitions.

This community-wide opposition to sex-working women, Pani told me, originated from an incorrect understanding of the meanings of sex work and devadasi practices.[201] Pani, a devadasi sex worker herself, explained that sex work allowed her to earn a living through which she, a Maang (Dalit), was able to match the economic status of higher-caste

197 Pawar and Moon, *We Also Made History*, 100.

198 Ibid., 161. In anti-caste scholar and activist Gail Omvedt's account of this incident, in response to Ambedkar's speech, the women at the conference staged a walkout in protest: 'there was an uproar, and the women poured into the streets, cursing and yelling'. Gail Omvedt, *Ambedkar: Towards an Enlightened India* (Penguin, 2004), 64.

199 Human Rights Watch, 'Abuses Against HIV/AIDS Outreach Workers' (2002), <www.hrw.org/reports/2002/india2/india0602–05.htm#P276_42340>.

200 Ibid. 201 Conversation with Kamlabai Pani, above n 1.

Patils (upper-caste village chiefs) who were traditionally meant to be served by members of her caste.[202] She asserted that in Sangli, even though it was impossible for the men of her caste to earn as much as Patils, she was able to earn as much. By doing sex work, according to Pani, she was able to overcome the discriminations she experienced in relation to both upper- and lower-caste men living in her own community. With this money, she was able to have access to healthcare, children's education and financial security for her old age. Pani noted that although these resources were necessary for one's well-being, they were denied to Dalit women living in her community.[203] She argued that she would never be able to have access to such resources if she was a *gharghuti aurat*, a woman living within the bounds of a traditional marriage under the domestic authority of her husband.[204]

As a devadasi sex worker, despite her caste and gender affiliations, Pani shared that she was able to live more freely compared to other married women.[205] As a statement of her rejection of the caste-based practices that ordain Dalit women to wear only jewellery made of base metals, a signifier of the women's subservient position within the community, Pani took pride in wearing gold jewellery. She told me that these were ornaments that she had purchased with her own earnings from sex work.[206] Pani's account of her own experience illustrated a claim made by VAMP in its earliest organisational documents: '*Economic independence* from men is a reality that we enjoy with pride and dignity.'[207]

Sonalkar writes that Ambedkar had made an appeal to Dalit women to give up all external signifiers of their caste status, which were actually 'markers of inferiority' and made them distinguishable from people of upper castes.[208] The way in which some sex workers at Sangli drape the saree, women's traditional attire, bears imprints of this Ambedkarite

[202] Ibid. According to Kamlabai, in Sangli, Mahars do the work of drying the skins that have been removed from dead animals by members of the Maang community. The Mahars also rear and feed the animals owned by Patils who are the village heads.

[203] Ibid. [204] Ibid. [205] Ibid.

[206] Ibid.; also mentioned in Seshu, 'Kamala Maushi', above n 10. See also Pawar and Moon, *We Also Made History*, 31.

[207] VAMP, 'A Statement of Women in Prostitution', above n 88, 2.

[208] Sonalkar, 'Translator's Introduction', 31.

worldview. Devadasi and Dalit sex workers Shaalan and Suvarna told me that they refused to adhere to the indignity of wearing the saree in a way that designated their caste affiliation.[209] They explained to me that Dalit women were meant to drape the saree around their waist and between their legs because it made movement easier for those who performed menial labour. But they wore it like any other non-Dalit woman in order to make their assertion of dignity as Dalit women and dhandhewali publicly visible.[210]

Through my adda with VAMP members, I was able to understand the meaning and significance of a distinct sex worker jurisprudence that was birthed through women's collectivisation in Sangli as dhandhewali/businesswomen. The formation of VAMP as an NGO is a means of reorganising women's interlinked social relations of caste, class and gender in Sangli, as well as keeping the state out of a regulatory role in matters pertaining to women's lives and livelihood.

In this chapter and the ones before this – that is Chapters 3 and 4 – I am interested in working out the diverse forms of mutual law–life relations that are accounted for in the sex worker feminist jurisprudence that inhabits the activist literatures produced by DMSC and VAMP. The specific learning from my engagement with VAMP's activism is that, first, the formation of VAMP was informed by sex workers' conversations with a non–sex worker women's organisation called Sangram, Dalit and non-Dalit feminist groups in Maharashtra, and Dalit and non-Dalit men's groups in Sangli. These conversations led to the formation of VAMP as an NGO under the SRA and the BPTA, and consolidated a collective role for the sex-working women in Sangli as dhandhewali, or women in the business of prostitution.

Second, by understanding sex work as business (dhandha), and subsequently crafting a collective role in public life as dhandhewali/businesswomen, the women in Sangli facilitated the formation of VAMP as a voluntary organisation. The dhandhewali is a woman inflected by sex workers' understanding and reorganisation of their caste, class and

209 Conversation with Shaalan and Suvarna, sex workers and VAMP members, Miraj, Sangli, 8 December 2014.

210 Ibid.

gender relations within a specific community of people in Sangli. The meaning and responsibilities that the women attached to their role of dhandhewali by undertaking activism involved the non-regulation of their lives by the state, the community of people in Sangli and even the sex workers' own collective. The women achieved this by developing mutual trust amongst themselves, and in their capacities of rational decision-making and judgement in relation to matters concerning their own lives and livelihood, including whether or not and how much to participate in collective activism.

Third, by crafting a role for women as dhandhewali, VAMP presented a new subject position from which the sex workers at Sangli could engage with the state. As dhandhewali, the women reorganised their hierarchical relations with the state, which considered them as criminals under ITPA, and as irrational/unable to decide in matters relating to their own life and livelihood under the Maharashtra Devadasi System (Abolition) Act, 2005, and the Karnataka Devadasis (Prohibition of Dedication) Act, 1982.

Moving on, in the next chapter I engage with the diverse experiences of mutual law–life relations that found academic feminist jurisprudence. I will engage with scholarly texts authored by legal academics Upendra Baxi and Ratna Kapur, which they have co-produced along with other legal academics. I will ground my performance of adda within the location of legal academia where these scholarly texts were written. I will draw out a specific set of conversations that have informed the writing of these texts through a shaping of the collective thoughts and practices of their co-authors. In doing so, I will illustrate that these academic scholarly practices, like sex workers' collectivisations, are also formations of mutual law–life relations, which shape the field of Indian feminist jurisprudence.

CHAPTER 5

Academic Feminist Jurisprudence

Upendra Baxi and Ratna Kapur

> In relations, differences of opinion do not turn into animosities: that was one of the great pedagogies that we all imbibed during the Open Letter movement.[1]
>
> [W]e are brown and white, but the collaboration was so not like that. The intellectual default position for Brenda [Cossman] was not that let me go out and do some good in the Third World ... it was a learning experience for her ... I wasn't playing the role of a native informant, or a nationalist ... none of those categories could describe me ... we were in that in-between in our lives and that is why we could talk.[2]

In this chapter, I shift my performance of adda from the locations of sex workers' collectives and place it within the context of Indian legal academia. The adda, which I now ground within the university, shows that there are continuities between the sex workers' collectivisations and the collective productions of scholarship by legal academics.

I focus on two specific texts by the legal academics Upendra Baxi and Ratna Kapur, as opposed to their entire repertoire of scholarship. These are not single-authored texts, but works that they have collectively authored with other legal academics. Even though I focus on the writing of two specific texts by Kapur and Baxi and my discussions with them revolve only around these, I do refer to their other works wherever it is necessary for clarifying certain ideas put forth in the texts that I focus on here.

[1] Email correspondence with Upendra Baxi, 25 August 2018.

[2] Skype conversation with Ratna Kapur, Geneva, 18 January 2016.

There are two texts that are of consequence for the discussions that will follow from here: 'An Open Letter to the Chief Justice of India' (1979) written by Upendra Baxi, Vasudha Dhagamwar, Raghunath Kelkar and Lotika Sarkar; and *Subversive Sites: Feminist Engagements with Law in India* (1996) written by Ratna Kapur and Brenda Cossman. I show how these collectively written texts by Baxi and Kapur inhabit their experiences of conversations with other people located at particular places and times. These located conversations shape the formation of collective thoughts and practices that inform the ways in which the legal academics call the discipline of law into mutual relations with their professional lives. These collective scholarly writings by the legal academics are examples of the diverse experiences and locations of mutual law–life relations that contribute to the productions of a field of Indian feminist jurisprudence.

The Open Letter and *Subversive Sites* are different not only in terms of their specific times and places of production, but also their form and content. This is the reason why I choose these materials, and for them to be read together, because the texts speak directly to diverse forms of academic practice. Another interrelated reason for focusing on these two texts is the fact that these are collectively authored. The act of collective authorship would have demanded that the academics relate their ways of thinking with one another, which makes the relationships amongst the people who wrote these texts central to the act of writing them.

I engage with the texts through the performance of my method, adda. As I have explained earlier, adda is an act, and an activity, for engaging and relating with the disparate practices of feminist jurisprudential knowledge production in India. I perform adda as an actual *activity* of interpreting texts, and of engaging in meaning making, through reciprocal conversations with their authors; and as an imaginative *act* of relating life and law.

I perform reciprocal conversations with Baxi and Kapur about the meanings and significance of the contents of their texts and the experiences of writing them. In case of the Open Letter, Baxi is the only surviving author, for which reason I speak with him alone. In the case of *Subversive Sites*, I speak only with Ratna Kapur. Kapur, even though she is not permanently stationed in India, has a continued and prolonged relationship with the place through her ongoing academic work, which is not the case for Cossman. I am – in this chapter – particularly interested in learning how the authors reflect on the writing of their texts, and their engagements with law, from the locus of their sustained experiences of living and working in the Indian post-colonial context.

By performing adda, I draw out a key set of conversations that inform the formation of the collective thoughts and practices of the legal academics that shape each of the texts in terms of their form and content. I show how, through the writing of these texts, Baxi and Kapur craft a role and responsibilities for themselves in public life. Such roles and responsibilities are formed in relation to the academic discipline of law and the institutions within which they are located, and also in relation to the people with whom they are engaged in conversations through the activity of writing the texts, including with their co-authors. It is in this way that the legal academics shape mutual law–life relations.

I organise my discussion of the conversations that inhabit the writing of the texts in two parts. In the first part, I discuss three sets of conversations that embodied the writing of the Open Letter in the context of late 1970s post-Emergency India. I discuss conversations between Baxi and his co-authors. These conversations directly informed the ideas put forth in the text. They also informed, and were informed by, the individual role and responsibilities that Baxi crafted for himself as a 'feminist law teacher' of the post-Emergency era. I show how the conversations that took place between Baxi and his co-authors attained a collective form in the writing of the text. In their collective voice, the authors also drew the chief justice of India, to whom the letter is addressed, into conversation. A conversation between the law teachers and a tribal girl called Mathura on whose behalf the Open Letter was written is another dimension in the Open Letter that I highlight. All of these conversations consolidated the professional role and responsibilities of feminist law teacher that Baxi worked out for himself in/through the collective writing of the Open Letter. Simultaneously, by crafting such a role in public life, he reorganised his privileged position of a man in relation to law.

In the second part of the chapter, I discuss a set of two interrelated conversations that took place in the context of early 1990s post-liberalisation India, which embody the writing of *Subversive Sites.*[3] I discuss Kapur's conversations with her friend and co-author Brenda Cossman, and conversations between Kapur and the Indian women's movement. Both these conversations informed the writing of the book through which Kapur worked out her role and responsibilities as a post-colonial feminist legal scholar. Simultaneously, by crafting such a role, Kapur reorganised an existing form of racialised intellectual hierarchy between brown and white women, while expressly addressing the question of what constitutes a feminist mode of engagement with law in an Indian post-colonial context.

'AN OPEN LETTER TO THE CHIEF JUSTICE OF INDIA' (1979)

The Open Letter is a five-page letter addressed to the chief justice of India. It was written, as noted in the text, for drawing 'judicial attention' and creating 'public debate' on the Supreme Court's decision in *Tukaram* v. *State of Maharashtra.*[4] The decision pertained to an incident of the rape of a tribal girl named Mathura, a minor, by two policemen, Ganpat and Tukaram, inside a police station. The apex court's decision, which became public knowledge in 1979, prompted the collective writing of the Open Letter by four law professors, Upendra Baxi, Vasudha Dhagamwar, Raghunath Kelkar and Lotika Sarkar.[5]

The Open Letter holds a significant place in terms of its contributions to the field of feminist jurisprudence in the Indian context. The text played a major role in consolidating a women's movement in India around the question of rape law reform. Feminist scholar Radha Kumar characterises the Open Letter as a facilitator for the Indian

[3] The 1990s post-liberalisation era is the same period during which the sex workers of DMSC and VAMP started to collectivise.

[4] *Tukaram* v. *State of Maharashtra* (1979) 2 SCC 143.

[5] The rape was committed in 1972. The case came up for hearing in 1974 in the sessions court, which let off the two accused policemen, Tukaram and Ganpat. In 1976, on appeal, the Bombay High Court convicted the accused. In 1978, on further appeal, the Supreme Court reversed the high court's decision and upheld the decision of the sessions court. See, generally, Kannabiran and Menon, *From Mathura to Manorama.*

women's movement.[6] Kumar argues that the publication of the document worked as a catalyst for getting 'isolated' campaigns on the issue of rape by women's groups in the country to finally join forces.[7] As a result of this, women's groups in Delhi jointly filed a petition in the Supreme Court demanding that it review the Mathura decision. However, the petition was eventually denied by the Court on the ground that the women's groups did not have the *locus standi* to legally act on behalf of the aggrieved woman, Mathura.[8]

Pratiksha Baxi, in her account of the 'rape trials in India', describes the Open Letter as a feminist intervention that 'questioned the judicial interpretation of consent'.[9] For Nandita Haksar, too, the 'main focus of the Open Letter is the interpretation of "consent" in the law of rape'.[10] Haksar believes that the document set the stage for feminist human rights lawyering and the evolution of a jurisprudence that is particularly relevant for the question of people's rights in India.[11]

What is of consequence for us is not only the significance of the content of the Open Letter in terms of how it shapes a legal feminism in India. Rather, the focus of my method is on the feminist jurisprudential insights that the text carries in terms of being an illustration of how scholarship is a collective means of experiencing mutual life–law relation, at a specific time and place.

My method of engaging with the text shows the processes of the formation of the Open Letter. It illuminates the way in which the writing of the text is tied to how Upendra Baxi shaped his role and responsibilities in public life as a male feminist law teacher, for *his own* engagements with other people and with law. Moreover, my method of engaging with the text also makes explicit how, through the writing of the Open Letter, Baxi shaped his role and responsibilities as a male feminist law teacher by undertaking it as a collective activity in conversations with others.

[6] Kumar, *The History of Doing*, 127–38. [7] Ibid., 129.

[8] Nandita Haksar, 'Human Rights Lawyering: A Feminist Perspective', in Mala Khullar (ed.), *Writing the Women's Movement: A Reader* (Zubaan, 2005), 133; P. Baxi, *Public Secrets of Law*, 17.

[9] P. Baxi, *Public Secrets of Law*, 16. [10] Haksar, 'Human Rights Lawyering', 132.

[11] Ibid.

A LAW TEACHER AND HIS CO-AUTHORS

The 1970s in India were an especially troubled decade for a country only a few years into the birth of a new constitutional order. During 1975–77, India's first woman prime minister, Indira Gandhi, proclaimed a nationwide Emergency backed by the judiciary. Ordering the imposition of President's Rule resulted in people's fundamental rights being suspended, press freedom being muzzled and leaders of opposition parties being imprisoned. All of this took place through the judicial imprimatur of the Supreme Court of India.[12] The Emergency shook public faith in the rule of law in a post-colonial democracy.[13]

In the post-Emergency period, the Supreme Court, which is the highest authority in the Indian adjudicatory system, worked hard to undo its own contribution to the legitimisation of the Emergency by challenging the spread of unbridled executive powers. By virtue of its adjudication in two landmark constitutional cases, the 1967 case of *Golak Nath*[14] and the 1973 case of *Kesavananda Bharati,*[15] the Constitution became the ground on which the state administration battled for the exercise of its powers over the lives of Indian people. In contrast, as Baxi argues in 'Taking Suffering Seriously: Social Action Litigation in the Supreme Court of India', the judiciary began to emerge as a 'people-oriented' institution that was interested in exercising its authority for 'social action'.[16] By acting on behalf of ordinary people and addressing their

[12] Gyan Prakash, *Emergency Chronicles: Indira Gandhi and Democracy's Turning Point* (Princeton University Press, 2019).

[13] See, generally, Coomi Kapoor, *The Emergency: A Personal History* (Penguin, 2016); Prashant Bhushan, *The Case That Shook India: The Verdict That Led to the Emergency* (Penguin, 2017).

[14] The Supreme Court's decision in this case declared that it was beyond the scope of the parliament to amend part III of the Constitution, which consists of the Fundamental Rights. *Golak Nath* v. *State of Punjab* 1967 AIR (SC) 1643.

[15] The Supreme Court's decision in this case declared that it was beyond the scope of the parliament to amend the Constitution so as to alter its basic structure, a set of inviolable principles within the framework of the Constitution. The decision also outlined the Basic Structure Doctrine, which gives power to the judiciary to review and also do away with parliamentary amendments that are in conflict with the Constitution's basic structure. *His Holiness Kesavananda Bharati Sripadagalvaru and Ors* v. *State of Kerala and Anr* (1973) 4 SCC 225.

[16] Upendra Baxi, 'Taking Suffering Seriously' (1985) 4, *Third World Legal Studies,* 107, 111.

experiences of social inequality, Baxi notes, the judiciary came to expose the 'lawlessness of the Indian state'.[17]

Parallel to these events, around the same time as the Indian people's relationships with their state and judiciary were being defined through government processes, another landmark event took place. In 1971, the Ministry of Education and Social Welfare passed a resolution to set up the Committee on the Status of Women in India. The task of the committee was to prepare a report on women's status and rights in India.[18] As mentioned in Chapter 1, in 1974, after undertaking a countrywide study, the members of the committee prepared a historic report called *Towards Equality*.[19] Lotika Sarkar, one of the signatories of the Open Letter, was a co-author of this report.[20]

During the mid 1970s, women's lives, and particularly their status in society, received considerable attention from the United Nations. The United Nations General Assembly declared 1975 as the first International Women's Year and organised the World Conference on Women in Mexico.[21] The *Towards Equality* report was sent to the World Conference on Women in Mexico as the official document for reporting on the status of women in India. The report heavily criticised the government for failing to secure the rights of its female citizens.[22]

[17] Upendra Baxi, *Courage, Craft and Contention: The Indian Supreme Court in the Eighties* (N. M. Tripathi, 1985), viii.

[18] John, *Women's Studies in India*, 3.

[19] The other members of the committee were: Phulrenu Guha, Maniben Kara, Savitri Shyam, Neera Dogra, Vikram Mahajan, Leela Dube, Sakina A. Hasan, Urmila Haksar and Vina Mazumdar.

[20] Sarkar was the first Indian woman to graduate from Cambridge and receive a PhD in law from there. In 1953, she was also the first female lecturer in law at the University of Delhi's Law Faculty. See generally Amita Dhanda, 'RIP Lotika Sarkar: Pioneering Feminist and Lawyer but Teacher Foremost', *Legally India*, 8 March 2013, www.legallyindia.com/Legal-opinions/lotika-sarkar-obituary.

[21] Since Mexico, the UN has held three other conferences on women: Copenhagen (1980), Nairobi (1985) and Beijing (1995). The Beijing Conference, which was the Fourth World Conference on Women, was a significant event that produced the Beijing Declaration and the Platform for Action, a document that considerably shaped the global agenda for gender equality.

[22] John, *Women's Studies in India*, 3.

But Gandhi's administration sent the report to a global forum without editing its content. Feminist and women's studies scholar Mary John argues that the Indian government's act of sending an unedited report to a global audience was intended to give an impression of its commitment to the improvement of women's lives.[23] Back home, however, John notes, the state machinery emerged as a brutal force against constitutional values.[24] A plausible explanation for the state's hypocritical action may be the perception common at the time that the subject of women's deplorable status and condition in society was generally of a non-threatening nature on account of it not being considered a political issue.[25]

Thus, the post-colonial Indian state of the 1970s was experienced as non-caring and abusive towards ordinary people – whether men or women. The activities of Gandhi's administration pointed at the failure of the government, but also at the fact that institutionally, the state machinery with its executive and legislative powers was completely malleable in the hands of a ruling party. In 1976, in the case of *ADM Jabalpur* v. *Shivkant Shukla*, the Supreme Court aided the state in this process of gaining more and more political currency.[26] The Supreme Court held that during an emergency, a detained person could not file a habeas corpus petition seeking release from the unlawful custody of the state.[27] In doing so, the Supreme Court conferred more power on the state machinery.

Many jurists argue that the post-Emergency phase of adjudication by the Supreme Court involved deliberate attempts at correcting its own failures in the delivery of justice in instances such as *ADM Jabalpur*.[28] During this period, the Supreme Court made a concerted effort to act in

[23] Ibid., 5. [24] Ibid. [25] Ibid.

[26] *ADM Jabalpur* v. *Shivkant Shukla* AIR 1976 SC 1207.

[27] Habeas Corpus, Art. 32 of the Constitution, Fundamental Right to Constitutional Remedies. See, generally, Nayar, *The Judgement*.

[28] The Supreme Court's decision in *Maneka Gandhi* v. *Union of India* is understood to be the corrective action for *ADM Jabalpur*. See U. Baxi, 'Taking Suffering Seriously', 111; also, see generally Zia Mody, *10 Judgements That Changed India* (Penguin, 2013); S. P. Sathe, *Judicial Activism in India* (Oxford University Press, 2002); Sudhir Krishnaswamy, *Democracy and Constitutionalism in India: A Study of the Basic Structure Doctrine* (Oxford University Press, 2010).

ways that sought to redeem itself in the eyes of the people.[29] Upendra Baxi characterises this phase of adjudication by the Supreme Court as 'social action litigation', or a form of judicial activism to restore the values of the Constitution within Indian social life.[30]

With the Emergency as the backdrop, a considerable volume of Baxi's writings up to the mid 1980s are invested in reflecting on the institutional formation of the judiciary, its jurisdictional contestations with the state, and its relationship with people's lives.[31] His writings on the adjudicatory practices of the Supreme Court speak of his faith in the judiciary and its abilities to pave the way for, as he writes, 'a truly homespun, swadeshi jurisprudence'.[32]

In the post-Emergency period, when anger against the lawlessness of the state was still alive in the minds of Indian people, and the Supreme Court was taking on its role as a champion of constitutional values, the writing of the Open Letter took place. At the time, Upendra Baxi, the primary and now the only surviving author of the Open Letter, was teaching law at the University of Delhi.[33] He started teaching there in 1973 after returning from Australia, where he had taught law at Sydney University.[34]

Baxi shared during our adda that he had always been a systematic follower of the decisions of the Supreme Court.[35] He recounted that one evening, while reading a copy of the judgement reporter *Supreme Court Cases,* he encountered the Supreme Court's decision that reversed the judgement of the Bombay High Court in *Tukaram* v. *State of Maharashtra.*[36] Two police constables, Tukaram and Ganpat, who had been convicted for the rape of a tribal girl named Mathura, were let off

[29] Mody, *10 Judgements That Changed India*, 31. [30] U. Baxi, 'Taking Suffering Seriously'.

[31] Upendra Baxi, *The Indian Supreme Court and Politics* (1980); U. Baxi, *Courage, Craft and Contention*; U. Baxi, 'Taking Suffering Seriously'.

[32] U. Baxi, *Courage, Craft and Contention*, vii.

[33] Upendra Baxi, 'Violence Against Women in the Labyrinth of Law', in *Inhuman Wrongs and Human Rights: Unconventional Essays* (Har-Anand Publications, 1994), 70.

[34] Upendra Baxi, 'Teaching as Provocation', in Amrik Singh (ed.), *On Being a Teacher* (Konark Publishers, 1990), 150–58, 152, http://upendrabaxi.in/documents/On%20being%20a%20teacher.pdf; U. Baxi, 'Violence Against Women', 69.

[35] Conversation with Upendra Baxi, Karkarduma, New Delhi, 25 January 2017; also noted in U. Baxi, 'Violence Against Women', 70; U. Baxi, 'Unlearning the Law with Lotika Sarkar'.

[36] Conversation with Upendra Baxi, above n 35; also noted in U. Baxi, 'Violence Against Women', 70.

by the Supreme Court on the ground that there was no evidence to convict them for the crime. The Court decided that there was no evidence that Mathura had resisted her perpetrators or shouted for help, which was then read as Mathura's consent to having sex with the men.[37] Acting on such a presumption of consent, the Supreme Court concluded that even if there might have been a sexual encounter between Mathura and the two constables, there was no rape.

Baxi recalled that he was enraged at reading about the decision and spent that whole night drafting a letter of protest.[38] The next day, he spoke about the letter with Lotika Sarkar, his friend and colleague at Delhi University and an author of the *Towards Equality* report.[39] Having recently drafted the report, and as a professor of criminal law and evidence, Sarkar readily saw the decision as anomalous.[40] Baxi also discussed the letter with his friend Vasudha Dhagamwar, who taught law at the University of Poona.[41] Both Sarkar and Dhagamwar promptly agreed to come on board as signatories.[42]

Baxi told me that to Sarkar, Dhagamwar and himself, the Supreme Court's decision represented a sacrifice of the human rights of women under the law and the Constitution.[43] According to them, there was patriarchy in the law, and that patriarchy was unjust to women.[44] This was because it conferred more power on men, which made women's status, despite being citizens, unequal in society. What united the three law professors against the decision was their shared position that the standing of both men and women, within law and in society, ought to be equal. This, however, was not the common ground on the basis of which Kelkar joined in the conversation with the three academics.

[37] *Tukaram* v. *State of Maharashtra* above n 4.

[38] Conversation with Upendra Baxi, above n 35; also noted in Baxi, 'Violence Against Women', 70.

[39] Conversation with Upendra Baxi, above n 35. I have discussed the *Towards Equality* report in Chapter 1.

[40] U. Baxi, 'Violence Against Women', 70.

[41] The university has been renamed as Savitribai Phule Pune University.

[42] Conversation with Upendra Baxi, above n 35. [43] Ibid.

[44] Upendra Baxi, interview with Janaki Nair, video recording available as part of the P. C. Joshi Archives on Contemporary History, Jawaharlal Nehru University; video #1 at 8:00 mins.

Kelkar, a professor of criminal law and criminal procedure at the University of Delhi, came on board as a signatory after being persuaded by Sarkar.[45] Unlike Sarkar, Dhagamwar and himself, Baxi observed, Kelkar did not identify as a feminist.[46] Kelkar was, in fact, rather uncomfortable with the entire activity, but was sympathetic to his colleagues' discomfort with an act of injustice.[47] For Kelkar, the Supreme Court's decision committed a wrong not necessarily due to its non-recognition of women's experiences of injustice, but rather due to the incorrect application of criminal and procedural law in the determination of a crime.[48]

Thus, Kelkar came on board as the result of a conversation between his understanding of criminal law and the others' understanding of women's experiences of social inequality and the existence of patriarchy in the law. This conversation can be evidenced in the form of the text, where a gender-based conception of 'consent' is made to join with the legal one that is posited under Section 375 of the Indian Penal Code:

> We ... find it surprising that the Supreme Court should have only focused on the third component of Section 375 of the Indian Penal Code, which applies when rape is committed with the woman's consent, when 'her consent has been obtained by putting her in fear of death or hurt'. But the second component of Section 375 is when rape occurs without her consent.
>
> There is a clear difference in law, and common sense, between 'submission' and 'consent'. Consent involves submission; but the converse is not necessarily true. Nor is absence of resistance necessarily indicative of consent. It appears from the facts as stated by the Court and its holdings that there was submission on the part of Mathura. But where was the finding on the crucial element of consent?[49]

The Open Letter works to present a feminist account of consent that is based on women's lived experiences without the mention of the term 'feminism' anywhere in the text. The articulation of the authors'

[45] Upendra Baxi noted this in his conversation with Janaki Nair. See ibid.
[46] Conversation with Upendra Baxi, above n 35. [47] Ibid. [48] Ibid.
[49] Baxi et al., 'An Open Letter to the Chief Justice of India'.

concerns with the Supreme Court's decision – and its alternative account of consent – is formulated squarely as a legal one. The authors present their concerns by arguing that the decision was lacking in its attention to precedent,[50] application of the appropriate provision in criminal law[51] and proper use of evidentiary information.[52]

By considering women's experiences of injustice, the Open Letter posits a feminism that is based on an understanding of woman that comprises varied experiences of caste, class and gender. Most significantly, it informs a feminism that contains an understanding of the hierarchies between men and women, as well as amongst women on the basis of their class and caste affiliations. In the Open Letter, the authors draw attention to the judges' differential treatment of a poor tribal woman, Mathura, and the two men who raped her. The authors argue that in two of its previous decisions – *Nandini Satpathy*[53] and *Maneka Gandhi*[54] – the Supreme Court was more understanding of women's experiences, unlike in the case of Mathura. According to them, this speaks of the Supreme Court's differential treatment of

[50] 'The Court stated in *Nandini* that it "is quite probable that the very act of directing a woman to come to the police station in violation of Section 160(1) CrPC may make for tension and negate 'voluntariness'." This observation was made in the context of the right against self-incrimination; 'is it any the less relevant to situations of "rape" or, as the Court wishes to put it, "intercourse" in a police station?' Ibid.

[51] 'We also find it surprising that the Supreme Court should have only focused on the third component of Section 375 of the Indian Penal Code, which applies when rape is committed with the woman's consent, when "her consent has been obtained by putting her in fear of death or hurt". But the second component of Section 375 is when rape occurs without her consent.' Ibid.

[52] 'The fact remains that she was asked to remain in the police station even after her statement was recorded and her friends and relations were asked to leave. Why? The fact remains that Tukaram did nothing whatsoever to rescue the girl from Ganpat. Why? The Court says in its narration of facts, presumably based on the trial Court records, that Tukaram was intoxicated. But this is not considered material either. Why? Why were the lights put off and doors shut?' Ibid.

[53] *Nandini Satpathy* v. *Dani (P.L.) and Anr* 1978 SCR (3) 608 is a 1978 constitutional case that strengthened the rights of the accused, particularly of women, against self-incrimination; https://indiankanoon.org/doc/1938988.

[54] *Maneka Gandhi* v. *Union of India* 1978 SCR (2) 621 is a 1978 case that expanded the provision on the right to life and liberty in Article 21 of the Indian Constitution to include the right to travel abroad; https://indiankanoon.org/doc/1766147.

'urban affluent women' who, unlike Mathura, were not poor or tribal.[55]

In the view of the authors of the Open Letter, as stated in the text, the Supreme Court's decision not only caused injustice to women like Mathura, but also had far-reaching consequences in terms of how it caused 'constitutionalism [to be] at stake'.[56] It sacrificed a value system based on equal social relations that ought to constitute the contemporary lives of people in order to distinguish it from a 'pre-constitutional Indian fate'.[57] Thus, on the one hand, the Open Letter argues that the decision committed injustice against a tribal woman by invalidating her experiences of discrimination. On the other hand, it argues that the actions of the judiciary granted impunity to the state by not holding its representatives, the police, accountable to their duties.[58] Moreover, it also shows how the Supreme Court's decision failed to deliver on the constitutional promise that the post-colonial Indian society would be composed of equal relations of caste, class and gender.[59]

Baxi recounted that once the authors were able to agree upon their position on the Mathura decision, and were sure of how the Open Letter would be worded, difficulty arose in determining what to do with the

[55] 'The Supreme Court, speaking through Justice Krishna Iyer, condemned the practice of calling women to police stations in gross violation of Section 160(1) of the Criminal Procedure Code. Under that provision, a woman shall not be required to attend the police investigation at any other place than her place of residence.' Baxi et al., 'An Open Letter to the Chief Justice of India'.

[56] Ibid. [57] Ibid.

[58] 'There is not a single word condemning the very act of calling Mathura, and detaining her at the police station in gross violation of the law of the land made by Parliament and so recently reiterated by the Supreme Court. Nor is there a single word in the judgment condemning the use of the police station as a theatre of rape or submission to sexual intercourse. There is no direction to the administration to follow the law. There are no strictures of any kind.' Ibid.

[59] Article 15 of the Indian Constitution lays down the grounds for non-discrimination on the basis of gender, and Article 14 promises the right to equality. In para. 4 of the Open Letter, the authors write, 'The Court, under your leadership, has taken great strides for civil liberties in cases involving affluent urban women (e.g. Mrs. Maneka Gandhi and Mrs. Nandini Satpathy). Must illiterate, labouring, politically mute Mathuras of India be continually condemned to their pre-constitutional Indian fate?' Ibid.

text.[60] The authors were concerned about whether or not its writing by law teachers constituted a lawful act.[61] Baxi, in particular, believed that 'criminal law decisions by courts, extending to guilt and punishment, should not yield to public sentiment or opinion'.[62] Thus, for him, judicial decision-making was a domain of specialised knowledge pertaining to the official role of judges.[63] But he believed that the evaluation and criticism of judicial decision-making, especially when it concerned the 'exploitation and oppression of women', was a duty imposed by the Constitution on each one of its citizens, including law teachers.[64]

Baxi recounted that, although the authors were sure that they wanted to put the Open Letter out in the public domain, they couldn't be sure about how they would do so.[65] There was no precedent that laid down how teachers of law, seeking to generate critical thinking on a decision that they considered unjust and detrimental for public life, should initiate a conversation on the same.[66] However, 'should law professors send an open letter [to the Chief Justice]?'[67] In the absence of a precedent, the authors' self-questioning yielded an answer in the affirmative. Alongside the intent 'to focus judicial attention' on the Mathura decision, the authors also intended to generate 'public debate' on the same, for which reason the text was sent for publication in newspapers.[68]

The law professors took on a pedagogical role outside of their classrooms, and in relation to the judiciary, after having somewhat consolidated a collective mode of thinking and acting as law teachers. The authors performed such a pedagogical role collectively by means of the conversation they engaged in with the chief justice of India through the writing and publication of the Open Letter.

60 Conversation with Upendra Baxi, above n 35. 61 Ibid.

62 Ibid.; Baxi has also mentioned this in U. Baxi, 'Unlearning the Law with Lotika Sarkar'.

63 Conversation with Upendra Baxi, above n 35.

64 U. Baxi, 'Unlearning the Law with Lotika Sarkar'.

65 Conversation with Upendra Baxi, above n 35.

66 Ibid.; U. Baxi, interview with Janaki Nair, above n 44, video #1 at 24:00 mins: 'Nowhere in the common law world such a letter was written.'

67 U. Baxi, 'Violence Against Women', 70.

68 Conversation with Upendra Baxi, above n 35.

LAW TEACHERS AND A JUDGE

The Open Letter is addressed to 'your lordship'[69] with whom the authors initiated a public conversation owing to his official role as the chief presiding officer of the Indian judiciary. Baxi told me that because the authors intended to generate a public debate on the Mathura decision through their letter, he took the initiative to send the text for publication to various newspapers in the country.[70] He typed out several copies of the text on a typewriter, because those were not the days of computers, and personally mailed the Open Letter through the daily post to almost every national newspaper.[71] However, Baxi recounted, none of these newspapers published it, until about four months later when the Open Letter suddenly appeared in *Dawn*, a leading newspaper in Pakistan.[72] *Dawn*'s reasons for publishing the Open Letter, Baxi noted, were unknown to him, but he would like to believe that it was published because a feminist ally in the neighbouring country found its content and the issues at stake to be worthy of public knowledge.[73]

The newspapers in India where Baxi had sent the Open Letter refused to publish it on the grounds 'that it was not "news"!' and that 'the open letter bordered on the contempt of court'.[74] Baxi added, however, that once the letter was published in Pakistan, India's geopolitical adversary, it came to the attention of the judicial and journalist communities in India, and the authors' actions received some very negative responses.[75] The Bar Council of India was enraged and objected to the public criticism of the Court's decision.[76] Commenting on the response of the Bar Council, Baxi has argued that the Open Letter was viewed as an encroachment on the Bar's '*natural right* to judge [the] judges; a *guild* right which constitutes their privileged space', and that they did not wish to democratise.[77]

[69] Baxi et al., 'An Open Letter to the Chief Justice of India'.

[70] Conversation with Upendra Baxi, above n 35. [71] Ibid. [72] Ibid. [73] Ibid.

[74] Ibid.; also mentioned in U. Baxi, 'Violence Against Women', 71.

[75] Conversation with Upendra Baxi, above n 35. [76] Ibid.

[77] 'The Bar was justified to a point. They were objecting to the public criticism of the Court; so far, such criticism was their turf! The Bar in India has always claimed a natural right to judge [the] judges; a guild right which constitutes their privileged space. Judicial process was not to be understood by all and sundry and the responsible mode of criticism was

Baxi shared that the authors of the Open Letter did not encroach upon the judges' role or transgress their own as law teachers.[78] The authors did not ask for any specific remedy in the Mathura case and merely entreated the court to 'review this decision *suo motu*'.[79] The authors of the Open Letter, in fact, only intended to hold the Supreme Court accountable for its own decisions, but did not want to encroach upon its function.[80] That is why, Baxi told me, when the women's movement filed a petition in the Supreme Court asking it to review its decision in the Mathura rape case, Baxi and the other authors did not join them.[81] The women's groups had requested Baxi and Sarkar to join the petition. But they refused to participate in the petition because they did not think it was their prerogative as law teachers to direct the judges about how they should conduct their legal role and duties.[82]

As I gather from my adda with Baxi, his decision to disengage from the review petition filed by the women's groups was tied to his conscious experiences of shaping his role in public life, collectively with others, as a feminist law teacher.[83] In the text of the Open Letter, the authors drew a line at the point of educating the court about the social impact of its decision and requesting the Supreme Court to review such a decision *suo motu* – that is, to figure out a way in which to perform its legal task on its own accord without external directives. This power to review cases *suo motu* was already available to the Supreme Court, which meant that in making such a plea the authors worked within the limits of their role as law teachers.[84]

Baxi observed that the Open Letter engaged the chief justice of India in a conversation because it attempted to hold Supreme Court judges accountable to an official role that they had fashioned for themselves in

known only to those initiated by the black coat and the gown (and affluence).' U. Baxi, 'Violence Against Women', 72.

78 Conversation with Upendra Baxi, above n 35.

79 'We can only appeal, in conclusion, to have the case reheard, as an unusual situation, by a larger bench, and if necessary by even the Full Court.' Baxi et al., 'An Open Letter to the Chief Justice of India'.

80 Conversation with Upendra Baxi, above n 35. 81 Ibid. 82 Ibid. 83 Ibid.

84 Ibid.; also mentioned in U. Baxi, 'Violence Against Women', 73.

post-Emergency India.[85] This becomes explicitly evident in the text itself, where the authors demand that the Supreme Court fulfil its role as an arbiter of human rights and justice:

> My Lord, your distinguished colleagues and yourself have earned a well-merited place in contemporary Indian history for making preservation of democracy and human rights a principal theme of your judicial and extra-judicial utterances, especially after March, 1977. But a case like this with its cold-blooded legalism snuffs out all aspirations for the protection of human rights of millions of Mathuras in the Indian countryside. Why so?[86]

Baxi recounted that whether law teachers remained within the boundaries of their pedagogic role in publicly demanding this kind of accountability from the Supreme Court was a bone of contention amongst the authors.[87] In *Courage, Craft and Contention: The Indian Supreme Court in the Eighties,* Baxi argues, 'The idea of a "judge" was a part of the common heritage of humankind. But what judges were expected to do, varied across time, place and circumstance.'[88] This means that, according to Baxi, the legal role and duties of adjudication is contextual. There is a need for rethinking adjudicatory roles in relation to the particular social and historical context in which such duties are meant to be performed. In the same vein, Baxi told me, the role of the law teacher, on which question he has pondered in some of his writings, is also particular to a time, place and circumstance.[89]

In *Socio-legal Research in India: A Programschrift,* Baxi reflects on the question of the role of law teachers in India.[90] The desired role for

85 U. Baxi, 'Violence Against Women', 73.

86 Baxi et al., 'An Open Letter to the Chief Justice of India'.

87 Conversation with Upendra Baxi, above n 35; also mentioned in U. Baxi, 'Violence Against Women', 71.

88 U. Baxi, *Courage, Craft and Contention,* 4.

89 Conversation with Upendra Baxi, above n 35; also mentioned in U. Baxi, 'Teaching as Provocation', 154; Upendra Baxi, *Socio-legal Research in India: A Programschrift,* ICSSR Occasional Monograph (Indian Council of Social Science Research, 1975), 4.

90 In 1975, the Indian Council of Social Science Research (ICSSR) entrusted Baxi with the task of writing a paper with suggestions for the development of programmatic institutional research in the area of law and social change. Baxi delivered on his task by writing a monograph; see U. Baxi, *Socio-legal Research in India,* 4.

lawyers and law teachers that emerges from Baxi's account is not one that is limited to producing skilled legal technicians or expanding the disciplinary knowledge base within academic institutions alone. Baxi suggests a political role for the educator of law in relation to the particular society within which such a person is situated, by which he means a role which is founded on an active engagement with the question of power as it operates in specific social relations.[91]

For Baxi, 'teaching' and 'learning' are forms of action in which the life of the mind and the life of the body converge.[92] In other words, for him, a law teacher is a conduit for calling law into relation with life, including one's own, through the act of teaching and learning. In 'Teaching as Provocation', Baxi writes, 'To my mind, teaching and learning are *acts* of social intervention and they are complete when knowledge accumulated the erudite way is enriched by knowledge earned through encounters which interrogate tyranny, injustice and exploitation enacted before our own eyes even as we "teach" and "learn".'[93]

As is evident from the essay, Baxi's idea of teaching entails two distinct actions – saying and doing – that are related, yet not the same. He urges his students, 'Do not merely look at what I say; look at what I *do* with what I say.'[94] According to Baxi, the doing of law is a practice through which 'conviction' is established in what is spoken about law.[95] Thus, according to him, the role and responsibilities of a law teacher are a combination of both what is said and what is done by such a person, in relation to what law is or how it might be lived. Baxi further notes that the practices that lead to the learning of law do not happen in abstraction either, as 'one learns something always in context'.[96] So, the conceptual and technical

[91] Baxi writes, 'In a way, we also emphasize study of movements of social change through the law by recourse to "direct action" or civil disobedience.' Ibid., 18.

[92] In the way in which Baxi describes the interrelated practices of teaching and learning, I hear resonances with sex workers' jurisprudence that is structured on their articulation of sex work as a mind-body activity, which I discussed at length in Chapters 3 and 4.

[93] U. Baxi, 'Teaching as Provocation', 154. [94] Ibid.

[95] Baxi writes, 'I simply cannot carry conviction about what I say to young minds unless they see that I mean what I say about the rule of law, human rights, human dignity.' Ibid., 154.

[96] U. Baxi, 'Unlearning the Law with Lotika Sarkar'.

teaching of law that produces learning is also intimately related to the context in which a society and its institutions and people exist and function.[97]

A law teacher in a post-colonial society assumes a particular pedagogic role in Baxi's own account. It was a cognisance of one's historical relations to law, as well as of the unequal social relations within which one was situated, which led to the formation of a pedagogic role appropriate for the Indian post-colonial location.[98] He added that, in the Indian context, where the society was stratified to such grave extents on the basis of gender, caste and class, a law teacher could not perform their role by remaining distant from such realities. In the vastly unequal Indian society, a person who performed legal pedagogy was required to respond to injustice and also act outside the bounds of an academic institution to transform unequal social relations with the knowledge of law when needed, through 'civil disobedience'.[99] Regarding the question of how to arrive at a decision whether 'civil disobedience' is an appropriate mode of action, Baxi asserts that in situations where it concerns the suffering of women, the feminist position must succeed and disobey all others to undo experiences of injustice.[100]

The way in which Baxi imagined and shaped his role and responsibilities as a feminist–law teacher is tied to the thinking practised by Mohandas Gandhi and B. R. Ambedkar, two key jurists in India.[101] In the context of colonial rule in India, Gandhi believed that an unjust order passed by any authority was unlawful.[102] The passing of an unjust order by a colonial authority imposed an obligation on Indians to disobey the lawgivers. So he devised his method of *satyagraha* as an act of non-violent non-cooperation with injustice, or the peaceful conduct of a public duty to violate unjust laws.[103] Ambedkar, on the other hand, was

[97] 'While labels [of legal concepts] can be borrowed, history cannot be.' U. Baxi, 'Taking Suffering Seriously', 108.

[98] Conversation with Upendra Baxi, above n 35.

[99] Ibid.; also mentioned in U. Baxi, *Socio-legal Research in India*, 18.

[100] Upendra Baxi, 'Towards the Liberation of Women's Studies', in *Inhuman Wrongs and Human Rights: Unconventional Essays* (Har-Anand Publications, 1994), 68.

[101] Conversation with Upendra Baxi, above n 35.

[102] M. K. Gandhi, *The Story of My Experiments with Truth* (Maple Press, 2011).

[103] Ibid.

especially concerned with the hierarchies of caste that constituted the relations amongst the colonised Hindus, and which he saw as a hindrance to the constitution of a just post-colonial Indian society.[104] Ambedkar believed that non-discrimination on the basis of caste was an essential moral value for constituting an equitable post-colonial society and for instituting a democratic mode of governance.

The contents of the Open Letter, and how Baxi shaped his professional role and responsibilities as a feminist law teacher through its collective writing, echo both Ambedkar and Gandhi.[105] Baxi and his co-authors refused to accept the orders of the Supreme Court as just, and so they wrote the Open Letter in which they argued that the non-recognition of Mathura's experiences of sexual violence by the Supreme Court was owing to her gender, caste and class status, which was a violation of her constitutional right to non-discrimination.[106] In doing so, the authors performed an act of civil disobedience, as opposed to contempt of court, through a public criticism of the Supreme Court's decision.[107]

In keeping with the Ambedkarite tradition, the Open Letter is acutely mindful of the social, and of the experiences underlying its unequal formation, which, as Ambedkar has argued, was a hindrance for post-colonial democratic state-making in independent India.[108] The Open Letter speaks of Mathura's experiences in relation to the role of the Indian judiciary in ensuring the establishment of a post-colonial

[104] Ambedkar, 'Annihilation of Caste', 273.

[105] On Baxi's inheritance of both Ambedkar and Gandhi, see Sundhya Pahuja and Adil Hasan Khan, 'The Southern Jurist as a Teacher of Laws: An Interview with Upendra Baxi' (2018) 9(2), *Jindal Global Law Review*, 351. For another discussion of Baxi's inheritances of life and law, see generally Arvind Narrain, Lawrence Liang, Sitharamam Akarala and Sruti Chaganti, *Of Law and Life: Upendra Baxi in Conversation* (Orient Blackswan, 2024).

[106] The Constitution ascribes to certain tribes the status of castes by enlisting them as Scheduled Tribes. See Scheduled Caste and Scheduled Tribe (Prevention of Atrocities) Act, 1989.

[107] The adjudication of contempt in India is carried out as per the Contempt of Courts Act, 1971, https://indiankanoon.org/doc/1396751.

[108] As Ambedkar had famously remarked during the Constituent Assembly Debates, 'Democracy in India is only a top-dressing on an Indian soil, which is essentially undemocratic.' *Constituent Assembly Debates*, volume 7, page 38.

sovereign state machinery that is accountable to its people as well as invested in a just organisation of society.[109] Simultaneously, in a Gandhian tradition of civil disobedience, the Open Letter by citizen law teachers ends by respectfully seeking a public apology from the chief justice of India thus:

> ... you will no doubt forgive us for this impertinence of writing an open letter to you. But the future of judicial protection of human rights at grassroots level in India at the turn of the century, a concern we all share as citizens and as lawmen, leaves us with no other and better alternative.[110]

In writing the Open Letter, Baxi collectively shaped his role in public life as a feminist law teacher by engaging in a conversation with his co-authors and also by drawing the judiciary into the same conversation. The Open Letter simultaneously drew into conversation the tribal girl named Mathura, whose experiences the authors publicly and legally spoke about and represented in/through the text. This conversation primarily makes visible the consolidation and undertaking of a particular role and responsibilities by Baxi as a male feminist. He is conscious of his gendered privilege in relation to women, and decides to speak against it in/through law.

LAW TEACHERS AND MATHURA

Baxi shared with me during our discussions that he identified himself as a feminist.[111] But being a man, he noted, it was not always easy for him to take on this role in public.[112] He recollected how, after the Open Letter had been written and published, his co-author Lotika Sarkar had asked him to go with her to an event organised by the Indian feminist

[109] See above n 58. The Open Letter also notes, 'Maybe on re-examination Ganpat and Tukaram may stand acquitted for better reasons than those now available. But what matters is a search for liberation from the colonial and male-dominated notions of what may constitute the element of consent, and the burden of proof, for rape which affect many Mathura's on the Indian countryside.' Baxi et al., 'An Open Letter to the Chief Justice of India'.

[110] Ibid.

[111] Conversation with Upendra Baxi, above n 35; also mentioned in U. Baxi, 'Violence Against Women', 69.

[112] Conversation with Upendra Baxi, above n 35.

anthropologist Leela Dube. At this event, where many women's groups were present, when Sarkar introduced Baxi as the author of the Open Letter, the audience refused to listen to him speak because he was a man. They only wanted to hear a woman speak about the Open Letter.[113] When Sarkar and Dube tried to press upon them the fact that Baxi had actually penned its content, the group expressed disbelief at the fact that Upendra Baxi was not a woman.[114]

Baxi told me that for him this experience was a first-hand learning in the dichotomy between biology and culture.[115] Although biologically male, his education and culture had made him aware of women's experiences and also the privileges he carried as a man.[116] However, as Baxi writes in an article, he was 'not quite at home with the reality of [his] being a "pertinent effect" of determinately dominant structures'.[117] He decided that as a practitioner of law, for him, 'a revisitation of the androcentric tradition of knowledge and theories of power, state and the law must be a prime task'.[118] In formulating such a task, he shaped his role as a feminist who not only worked towards the transformation of a gendered society through law, but was also engaged in a rethinking of his disciplinary location as a male law teacher.

In the acknowledgement section of his book *The Crisis of the Indian Legal System*, published in 1982, Baxi notes that female domestic labour is an integral part of male intellectual production.[119] According to him, this aspect, however, is seldom adequately accounted for by male intellectuals. The act of merely acknowledging the contributions of 'wife and children' in male intellectual productions, according to Baxi, is inadequate. Drawing on the work of Australian feminist author Anne Summers, he notes that such acknowledgement practices are, in fact, a manifestation of patriarchy.[120] Speaking in the context of the women's

[113] Ibid. [114] Ibid. [115] Ibid. [116] Ibid.

[117] U. Baxi, 'Violence Against Women', 69.

[118] U. Baxi, 'Towards the Liberation of Women's Studies', 63.

[119] Upendra Baxi, *The Crisis of the Indian Legal System: Alternatives in Development Law* (Vikas, 1982).

[120] Baxi quotes Anne Summers from her book *Damned Whores and God's Police: The Colonization of Women in Australia* (1975) thus: 'I would have ended acknowledgements with appreciation of the help by my wife Prema, and children (Pratiksha and Viplav).

studies centres that were set up in the 1970s, and the practice of feminism within Indian academia, Baxi is particularly self-critical. He writes:

> The struggle would also be within us, against a part of ourselves and would require, whether as men or women, us to combat the 'micro-fascism' which we are able to practise with impunity even as we celebrate our roles as feminists … Even as innovators of state and society, we also reflect, and are bearers of the very modes of repression we seek to combat through scholarship and struggle. This must be so as long as scholarship is in itself *not* an act of struggle.[121]

It is evident from Baxi's writings, more generally, how he struggled with the realisation of his own gendered and privileged position vis-à-vis his professional legal intellectual labour and women's experiences of marginalisation. In relation to his role and performance of intellectual labour in the field of feminist legal knowledge productions, Baxi carried out a complex interweaving of his gendered experiences as a male legal scholar with his intellectual legal productions. Some of his writings, such as the Open Letter, are directly about law and gender. In some of his other works where he does not directly write about gender, Baxi often includes sexual and gendered metaphors in his texts. For instance, in 'Teaching as Provocation', while describing his role as law teacher he posits that he 'impregnated' problems of the future with knowledge learnt in the past.[122] Similarly, in the essay 'Violence Against Women in the Labyrinth of Law', he asserts that he was seeking to engage with law in a manner that was not 'replete with its *seminal* [derived from semen] ideas, *penetrating* [peno-vaginal penetration] insights, or *bodies* of knowledges'.[123] As a feminist law teacher and legal scholar, in this way Baxi writes gendered experiences into his legal texts.

But Anne Summers has convinced me now that such appreciation is merely a manifestation of a "sexist culture". I conclude by adopting her statement: "The traditional two-line acknowledgement: 'To my wife, without whom etc. …' is a nauseatingly jejune recompense which disguises what is often the absolute truth … The wives and children of writers contribute more than is ever acknowledged to the getting out of a book."' Ibid., xiii.

121 U. Baxi, 'Towards the Liberation of Women's Studies', 56.

122 U. Baxi, 'Teaching as Provocation', 153.

123 U. Baxi, 'Violence Against Women', 69.

The Open Letter crafts a feminism that speaks *for* women and represents their experiences of violence and suffering in/through law. Baxi shared how Mathura was 'politically mute', which was why her experience of suffering needed to be represented within public and legal discourses by the law teachers.[124] However, although the authors spoke on Mathura's behalf, seeking to represent her cause and ameliorate her suffering, they did not do so in consultation with her.[125] The authors' representation was determined not by the individual who experienced suffering, but the authors' own collective understanding of what Mathura's suffering was.

Feminist historian Janaki Nair raises concerns about the fact that the Open Letter, which worked to shape a legal notion of 'consent' informed by feminist ideas, did not consider it necessary to seek Mathura's consent before publicly articulating a demand on her behalf.[126] Feminist lawyer and activist Flavia Agnes also raises a similar concern. Agnes asks why, although Mathura was turned into an 'icon' for the women's movement in the 1980s through the writing of the Open Letter, the law teachers did not think it necessary to obtain her permission before writing such a letter.[127] Baxi told me that a media correspondent from *Hindustan Times*, a leading daily, alleged that Mathura became a victim of sex trafficking when her husband came to know about the incident because it was publicised by the law teachers.[128] On hearing this, Baxi and his co-authors who were troubled by such an accusation, sent an acquaintance to verify the information; the latter confirmed that nothing like that had happened.[129] While reflecting on the criticisms against the writing of the

[124] 'Must illiterate, labouring, politically mute Mathuras of India be continually condemned to their pre-constitutional Indian fate?' Baxi et al., 'An Open Letter to the Chief Justice of India'.

[125] Echoing Spivak (as I discussed in Chapter 2), where she talks about how, often when critical thinkers speak on behalf of subaltern women, they work to alienate women's subjectivity from their own experiences.

[126] U. Baxi, interview with Janaki Nair, above n 44, video #1 at 40 mins.

[127] Flavia Agnes, 'Transgressing Boundaries of Gender and Identity' (2002) 36(37), *Economic and Political Weekly*, 3696.

[128] Conversation with Upendra Baxi, above n 35.

[129] '[B]ut perhaps the greatest challenge came from Krishen Mahajan who in a Sunday edition of *Hindustan Times* (of which he was a legal correspondent) criticised us for not

Open Letter, Baxi notes that 'any activist intervention that tends to *revictimize* the victims is morally wrong and the concerned activist must bear full responsibility for atonement if that happens'.[130] He writes that a learning from this experience for him was that the 'scope of activist intervention stands diminished, even though when it occurs it is full of passionate intensity'.[131]

The writing of the Open Letter, as feminists have pointed out, was a practice in which the 'lawmen' or 'teachers of law' wielded the authority to speak on behalf of a suffering woman like Mathura. The woman herself wielded no authority in terms of whether or not, or how, she desired her experiences to be represented in law. By writing about Mathura's experiences and making it public knowledge, Baxi told me, he and his co-authors took the responsibility of causing women's experiences of injustice to enter the disciplinary bounds of law and not remain outside as a non-issue.[132] For Baxi, as a law teacher, this responsibility specifically included the task of creating an 'archive of [women's] suffering'[133] and making gender-based experiences a part of institutional forms of legal knowledge, including the kind arising from the judges' jurisprudence.

Baxi shared during our adda that while writing the Open Letter, he and his co-authors were explicitly interested in two things.[134] First, they were interested in making an intervention into the judicial understanding and interpretation of consent in relation to women's experiences of sexual violence by educating the members of the judiciary.[135] The authors were interested in activating a dialogue between academic legal

reaching out to Mathura, upon whom the impact on her was most lethal. She was, it was alleged, in [a] sex traffic network having been spurned by her husband on hearing about the case. Lot was most upset because Krishen never raised the matter with her; she expected her former student such a discourtesy, even when she respected his freedom of speech. At any rate, Dada Chitale of the AIR at Nagpur was kind enough to respond to my urgent call and send a law reporter to Chanderpur to verify the story: we learnt that contrary to newspaper report; Mathura was accepted by husband and was relatively leading a peaceful life.' U. Baxi, 'Unlearning the Law with Lotika Sarkar'.

130 U. Baxi, 'Violence Against Women', 75. 131 Ibid.

132 Conversation with Upendra Baxi, above n 35.

133 U. Baxi, 'Towards the Liberation of Women's Studies', 59.

134 Conversation with Upendra Baxi, above n 35. 135 Ibid.

institutions and the judiciary of post-Emergency times, which had made an implicit promise to undo the inequalities and injustices experienced by people living in the society within which the institution functioned and performed its role. Secondly, as Baxi told me, the authors were intent upon drawing societal attention to the issue of rape and state impunity by generating discussions and debates about it amongst common people.[136] In light of the authors' intent, Baxi notes, the Open Letter was not meant for speaking on behalf of Mathura as much as it was about speaking against a misrepresentation of her social experiences of suffering in/through law by the judiciary.[137] Thus, the authors were interested in building a legal consciousness around social experiences, and the injustices that were responsible for the organisation of an unequal post-colonial society.

My method of reading and interpreting the text of the letter through reciprocal conversations with Baxi helps understand how, in speaking about Mathura, the Open Letter correlates her experiences with those of a range of other people, and with law and legal institutions in India. My method also helps understand how the process of writing the text was consciously experienced by Baxi as a means through which he related his own life with his academic discipline of law collectively, in conversations with others, by assuming a role and responsibility in his public life as a feminist law teacher.

In terms of both its content and form, the text speaks to the repertoire of sex workers' activist literature that I engaged with in Chapters 3 and 4. The Open Letter is in continuity with the sex workers' activist genre of writing and mode of knowledge production. The Open Letter is, in a sense, a predecessor of sex workers' literature, the bulk of which is in the nature of personalised communications, as in the case of the letter, and includes subjective accounts by sex workers about their experiences of law. Likewise, the Open Letter locates its discursive productions in the subjective – it is an explicit act of public speaking by Baxi and his colleagues from their locus of 'law teachers'. Additionally, my

[136] Ibid.

[137] Ibid.; Upendra Baxi also noted this in his conversation with Janaki Nair. See U. Baxi, interview with Janaki Nair, above n 44.

mode of engagement with sex workers' texts and the Open Letter through the performance of adda helps understand how these texts inhabit a specific set of conversations between their authors and others, conversations that are related to particular places and times.

Adda, as a method, also makes visible how the Open Letter is a precursor to the scholarly literature that constitutes the field of Indian feminist jurisprudence as a socio-legal body of knowledge and scholarship. As shown in Chapter 1, Indian feminist jurisprudence is primarily constituted of a body of literature that establishes the field in terms of law's relationship with the social experiences of gender, caste, class, sexuality and religion. The content of the Open Letter speaks to a large body of literature, produced through the 1980s, 1990s and up until the present, as it attempts to relate and create an understanding of people's social experiences of life and law in India.

Following from the writing and publication of the Open Letter, throughout the 1980s and early 1990s, the Indian women's movement came to devote considerable attention to law reform.[138] Agnes argues that even when the women's movement was able to institute 'new legislations', the assertions of women's equal status in formal law yielded no reformation of the lived inequalities in women's lived conditions.[139] Agnes charts how, starting with 'rape law (1983)', the women's movement engaged with issues such as 'dowry (1984–86)', 'domestic violence (1983–86)', 'prostitution (1986)', 'indecent representation of women (1986)', the self-immolation of young widows or 'sati (1987)' and 'sex determination tests (1988)'.[140] However, none of these was able to bring about the substantive changes that the women's movement desired to see in women's actual lives. This period of legislative overdrive led to the writing of *Subversive Sites*, which I will discuss now in the second part of the chapter through my adda with Ratna Kapur.

SUBVERSIVE SITES: FEMINIST ENGAGEMENTS WITH LAW IN INDIA (1996)

Subversive Sites is a 352-page book written by Indian feminist legal scholar Ratna Kapur and Canadian feminist legal scholar Brenda

[138] See generally Agnes, 'Protecting Women Against Violence?' [139] Ibid. [140] Ibid.

Cossman.[141] The co-authored book was published in India by Sage Publications, New Delhi, in 1996. At a broader level, the book, with five chapters and an introduction, looks at what it means to engage with law for the transformation of women's lives in an Indian society from an expressly feminist standpoint. *Subversive Sites*, Kapur told me during our adda, responds to the disjunction between the experiences of a decade of law reform led by the Indian women's movement in the 1980s and the lack of corresponding substantive gains in women's lives.[142]

The book's central contention is that law is a complex and contradictory site of meaning making about the world.[143] The authors argue that 'law needs to be reconceptualised as a site of discursive struggle, where competing visions of the world, and of women's place therein, have been and continue to be fought out'.[144] That means, law needs to be seen as a site of contestations and interactions between rival visions of life, how it may be lived and women's roles in it, and a feminist vision is but one of these. According to Kapur and Cossman, within a feminist project that is interested in women's equality, law must not be conceived only as a site of loss or victory. Rather, it must be seen as a process of engagement that can open up 'democratic space for women's participation in political, social, economic and cultural life'.[145]

In the same year that *Subversive Sites* was published, Indian jurist and constitutional law scholar S. P. Sathe wrote a review of the book. Sathe begins his review piece by stating that the book breaks away from 'the dichotomous description of law either as sustainer and legitimiser of oppression of women or an instrument of social change'.[146] Sathe argues that the 'main thrust of the book is to reveal how legal regulation of women is informed by an ideology, which the authors call familial ideology'.[147]

[141] For discussions on the enduring legacy of *Subversive Sites*, see generally, Ratna Kapur and Brenda Cossman, '*Subversive Sites* 20 Years Later: Rethinking Feminist Engagements with Law' (2018) 44(2), *Australian Feminist Law Journal*, 265; Oishik Sircar, 'The Fraught Terrain of Law and Feminism: 20 Years of *Subversive Sites*' (2016) 12(1), *Socio-legal Review*, 133.

[142] Conversation with Ratna Kapur, above n 2.

[143] Kapur and Cossman, *Subversive Sites*, 40. [144] Ibid., 12. [145] Ibid., 285.

[146] S. P. Sathe, 'Law and Women' (1996) 31(41–42), *Economic and Political Weekly*, 2804.

[147] Ibid.

Sathe notes that for Kapur and Cossman, 'familial ideology' refers to 'the set of norms, values and assumptions' that have attained a universal status because they have become a dominant part of how the family is commonly thought about.[148] From the perspective of legal knowledge production in India, in Sathe's view, the book is 'a very good effort to study law as one of the inputs of the process of social change'.[149] Simultaneously, Sathe considers that *Subversive Sites* carries 'a very positive view of law'.[150] This is because, he clarifies, the book acknowledges that law creates gendered subjects that support women's social subordination, and yet at the same time law is a site at which women's social roles are contested and where they are reconstructed as persons through a realisation of their human rights.[151]

In 1997, Prabha Kotiswaran also wrote a review of *Subversive Sites*. The stated aim of this review is to 'assess the value of *Subversive Sites* in the Indian context and in furthering the aspirations of feminist legal theory'.[152] Kotiswaran argues that it is the 'first Indian book of its kind that articulates the experiences of the Indian women's movement in explicit terms of feminist legal theory'.[153] Not only that, for Kotiswaran, the book is also an important contribution to legal scholarship in India per se because, up until then, legal scholarship had not 'addressed issues of legal theory from a political perspective ... [or] drawn from non-legal disciplines'.[154] In her view, *Subversive Sites* exemplifies that 'collaborative' feminist projects can draw on feminists' wide-ranging experiences from around the world and demonstrate that a 'solidarity of cause' is possible across cultural differences.[155] Kotiswaran further notes that an important aspect of the North American–Indian feminist collaboration in *Subversive Sites* is that 'it recognizes Third World differences without treating Third World women as a homogenous category of long-suffering victims of patriarchy'.[156]

In her review article, Kotiswaran also comments on the form of intellectual production in *Subversive Sites*. She draws from the scholarship of American legal scholar D. Kelly Weisberg to make a distinction

[148] Ibid. [149] Ibid. [150] Ibid. [151] Ibid.

[152] Prabha Kotiswaran, 'Rumblings of a New Beginning: The Case of Feminist Legal Scholarship in India' (1997) 20, *Harvard Women's Law Journal*, 313, 341.

[153] Ibid., 350. [154] Ibid., 351. [155] Ibid. [156] Ibid.

between 'feminist legal theory' and 'feminist jurisprudence'.[157] Kotiswaran notes that according to Weisberg, feminist legal theory is a way of applying feminist theory to the analysis of concrete areas of law, whereas feminist jurisprudence is a way of analysing the relationship between law and gender.[158] For Kotiswaran, *Subversive Sites* simultaneously belongs to both traditions.[159] The book is a work of feminist jurisprudence 'in its espousal of postmodern feminist theory' as well as a work of feminist legal theory for 'its detailed analysis of judicial pronouncements of women's rights'.[160] In belonging to both traditions of thought so successfully, *Subversive Sites* demonstrates that for feminists, working across both traditions is both desirable and inevitable.[161]

Both Kotiswaran and Sathe engage with the substantive legal issues that are addressed in *Subversive Sites.* They argue that the book makes significant contributions to feminist legal scholarship from the perspective of women's lived experiences in India. I engage with *Subversive Sites* and the processes of its formation through my participation in adda with Ratna Kapur. I read and interpret the text in reciprocal conversations with Ratna Kapur, whereby I learn about her experiences of co-authoring the book with Brenda Cossman.

I draw out how the writing of the book by Kapur and Cossman inhabits conversations between the authors, and Kapur's conversations with the Indian women's movement, in the context of 1990s post-liberalisation India. I demonstrate how both of these conversations are conscious experiences through which Kapur works out her role and responsibilities as a post-colonial feminist legal scholar. By crafting such a role, Kapur performs a reorganisation of an existing racialised form of intellectual hierarchy between brown and white women, while expressly addressing the question of what constitutes a feminist mode of engagement with law in an Indian post-colonial context.

A BROWN AND A WHITE FEMINIST LEGAL SCHOLAR

In 1996 when *Subversive Sites* was published, Kapur recounts, within the Indian women's movement law was understood solely as a functional tool

[157] Ibid., 356n15. [158] Ibid. [159] Ibid., 351. [160] Ibid. [161] Ibid.

for either women's oppression or social upliftment.[162] Thus, when Kapur and Cossman co-authored the book, their intent was to show that law was not one or the other; it was a site of contestations that, in fact, offered possibilities for a feminist project to work with law as a useful, although limited, site of engagement.[163]

The early half of the 1990s, the years through which the research, writing and the publication of the book were done, saw a major restructuring of people's political, social, economic and cultural life in India.[164] In 1991, the government of India, influenced by the Bretton Woods Institutions, adopted the New Economic Policy (NEP).[165] As a result, the Indian economy was officially opened up to foreign and private capital and goods. The state loosened its regulatory authority on markets and India became part of a consolidation of global economies.[166] Although 1991 marked the official onset of the new economic order, it was merely a culmination of a process that had started much earlier. The period thus ushered in an era of formal economic reforms 'which intensified India's encounter with global capital' on account of the NEP.[167]

In 1993, the Indian Association for Women's Studies brought out a collection of papers about the harmful effects of economic restructuring on women's lives.[168] The papers showed how development projects initiated through the NEP had impacted the lives of female workers in the informal sector and how such impact might be tackled.[169] The NEP, characterised by liberalisation, privatisation and globalisation, also had

162 Kapur and Cossman, *Subversive Sites*, 12.

163 Conversation with Ratna Kapur, above n 2.

164 *Economic and Political Weekly, Quarter Century of Liberalization in India.*

165 Jason A. Kirk, *India and the World Bank: The Politics of Aid and Influence* (Anthem Press, 2011).

166 Baldev Raj Nayar, *Globalization and India's Economic Integration* (Georgetown University Press, 2014).

167 Rupal Oza, *The Making of Neoliberal India: Nationalism, Gender, and the Paradoxes of Globalisation* (Routledge, 2006), 2.

168 Indian Association for Women's Studies (eds), *The New Economic Policy: A Collection of Background Papers to Sixth National Conference* (IAWS, 1993), http://iaws.org/wp-content/themes/pdf/publications/NCF06.3-The_New_Economic_Policy_And_Women,1993.pdf.

169 Ibid.

far-reaching consequences for the shaping of law as a new kind of academic discipline in the country.[170] Legal education and legal scholarship at the time, including the materialisation of *Subversive Sites*, were intertwined with India's economic restructuring.

When Kapur and Cossman wrote *Subversive Sites*, they were based at the National Law School of India University in Bangalore, an institution that was the first outcome of the restructuring of legal education in India. The Bar Council of India introduced the five-year integrated law degree as a professional course, unlike the erstwhile law courses to offer a 'liberal (academic) learning of law'.[171] A formal process was also set in motion for the establishment of autonomous residential law schools, such as the National Law School of India University, with financial support from the Ford Foundation, an international funding organisation.[172]

Upendra Baxi argues that this new phenomenon of setting up national law schools with Ford Foundation funds was a foreign import.[173] Not denying that these institutions opened up spaces for innovative legal research and learning, Baxi saw these changes as a 'fulfillment of the vision of some US founders of "modern" legal education', rather than something which evolved out of local processes.[174] For him, these shifts in legal education represented an 'unfortunate Ford Foundation

170 There is a lot of feminist literature that looks at the harmful effects of this economic restructuring on women's lives that primarily resulted from the development projects initiated by the government of India during this period. See, e.g., Karin Kapadia, *The Violence of Development: The Politics of Identity, Gender and Social Inequalities in India* (Zed Books, 2003).

171 As described by Madhava Menon, who has been credited with revolutionising law education in India. See N. R. Madhava Menon, *Turning Point (The Story of a Law Teacher)* (Universal Law Publishing, 2012), 47.

172 For an account of this process, see generally Madhava Menon, *Turning Point*; Jayanth K. Krishnan, 'Professor Kingsfield Goes to Delhi: American Academics, the Ford Foundation, and the Development of Legal Education in India', Maurer School of Law, Indiana University, 2004, www.repository.law.indiana.edu/cgi/viewcontent.cgi?referer=https://www.google.com/&httpsredir=1&article=1347&context=facpub.

173 Baxi documents such processes that he was part of in U. Baxi, 'Enculturing Law?', 19n39.

174 Ibid., 14.

transferral of the American agendum of pursuing "diversity" in Indian legal education'.[175]

Kapur evaluates this occurrence differently. She shared that the National Law Schools, and the financial support they received from the Ford Foundation, opened up a much-needed institutional space for doing legal research that was explicitly of the feminist kind.[176] For her, the setting up of the National Law School in Bangalore in the early 1990s worked to open up some institutional avenues for feminist research to secure a place within legal academia. It enabled the feminist standpoint to become a legitimate locus from where law could be engaged with, particularly in the Indian post-colonial context.[177]

Kapur's conversations with Cossman, which resulted in the co-authorship of *Subversive Sites*, started while she was living in Canada, during the period of the 'sex wars' in late 1970s and 1980s North America.[178] During this time in Canada, the authors' public presence together always elicited a discriminatory response from people. Cossman would often point out to her whenever the authors went out together in public how, in other people's perceptions, they were only seen as 'brown' and 'white' and their experiences were considered vastly different.[179] Moreover, due to their differences, Cossman was considered intellectually superior to Kapur.[180]

In 1991, Kapur and Cossman jointly published the article 'Trespass, Impasse, Collaboration: Doing Research on Women's Rights in India', where they wrote about their experiences of undertaking intellectual collaborations across their cultural differences.[181] They wrote that as individuals, they shared certain common experiences on account of being 'feminist, women-identified, university educated, middle-class, unmarried, urban'.[182] Simultaneously, the authors also experienced certain identifiable differences based on their race and cultural affiliations

175 Ibid., 18n32. 176 Conversation with Ratna Kapur, above n 2. 177 Ibid.

178 Ibid.; see, generally, Lisa Duggan and Nan D. Hunter, *Sex Wars: Sexual Dissent and Political Culture* (Taylor & Francis, 2006).

179 Conversation with Ratna Kapur, above n 2. 180 Ibid.

181 Brenda Cossman and Ratna Kapur, 'Trespass, Impasse, Collaboration: Doing Research on Women's Rights in India' (1991) 2(2), *Journal of Human Justice*, 99.

182 Ibid.

as 'brown/white, Indian/Canadian, "third" world/"first" world, Hindu/Jew'.[183]

Kapur shared that despite the authors' shared experiences of similarities *and* differences, public perceptions of their racial identities often worked to negate the relationship of equals that existed between them. Their racial difference and hierarchy, Kapur noted, created assumptions of the cultural superiority of the white, western woman and hierarchised their intellectual partnership. Kapur recounts that in her experience at the time, it was as if only the white, western woman had the wisdom to teach the brown woman, who had everything to learn from her but nothing to teach.[184]

In India too, Kapur's experiences of public perceptions of her intellectual relationship with Cossman were discriminatory, and she realised how the stereotypes played out on both sides of the North/South divide.[185] Kapur recounted that, at the time, certain prejudicial ideas prevailed in the minds of people who were part of women's rights activist circles about white feminists and also those who belonged to the Indian diaspora.[186] They were understood as 'alien' and 'western', and therefore lacking in authenticity and the authority to speak about the experiences of Indian women.[187] So, when the authors decided to collaborate on a book project, their worry was that 'any touch of whiteness [might] stigmatise the book, any touch of brownness would put it in area studies'.[188]

When the authors considered writing a book together, Kapur told me, they intended to displace these dominant public discourses that were shaped through hierarchical notions of race and culture.[189] By writing as 'we' in *Subversive Sites*, the authors worked out a way of bringing to fruition an intellectual project that they had started together in the early 1990s of 'learning how to speak together'.[190] As stated in the book, an important aspect of the authors' collaborative intellectual project for law was to craft a feminist position from where they could speak collectively by avoiding 'the false objectivism of the detached author, and to capture

[183] Ibid. [184] Conversation with Ratna Kapur, above n 2. [185] Ibid. [186] Ibid.
[187] Ibid. [188] Ibid. [189] Ibid.
[190] Cossman and Kapur, 'Trespass, Impasse, Collaboration', 100.

the sense of perspective, location and participation that is essential for scholarship and for the resolution of the dilemmas that confront all of us who endeavor to use law to advance progressive social movements'.[191]

Thus, through the activity of writing *Subversive Sites*, the authors carved out a practice of speaking *with* each other and invoked law as a 'discursive site', a site which enabled them to dialogue across their racial and cultural locations. *Subversive Sites* attained its material form within the institutional location of the National Law School with a grant from the Ford Foundation, which had also provided financial support to the Indian government to set up the national law schools.[192] The Ford Foundation grant, along with some additional finances that Cossman was able to get from the International Research Council in Ottawa, Canada, made provisions for the authors to travel in India and conduct research for their book.[193] The authors' only obligation to the Ford Foundation as their grantee was to teach at the law school once it was properly set up.[194]

Once they were able to secure financial support, both Kapur and Cossman came to India and began researching for their book. They began their research by studying the experiences of the women's movement. In order to get to know about women's organisations that were part of the movement, they conducted legal trainings for grassroots women's groups and attended women's conferences that were being organised in the country.[195] The authors' aim, Kapur told me, was to gather information about the issues that were relevant to the lives of Indian women, and how women's groups addressed these issues through their engagements with law.[196]

I learned through my adda with Kapur how, as she began her collaborative research with Cossman, she simultaneously worked out her professional role as a post-colonial feminist legal scholar.[197] Such a role was shaped through a mutual reciprocation of ideas and experiences across racial and cultural locations, and by undertaking scholarly

[191] Kapur and Cossman, *Subversive Sites*, 14.

[192] Conversation with Ratna Kapur, above n 2; the Ford Foundation is thanked in the acknowledgements of *Subversive Sites*, 9.

[193] Conversation with Ratna Kapur, above n 2. [194] Ibid. [195] Ibid. [196] Ibid.

[197] Ibid. During my conversations with her, Kapur insisted that she be called as such.

responsibilities in a certain way. Post-colonial feminist legal scholarship and research, Kapur observed, was distinct from undertaking a women-oriented study of law.[198] Broadly speaking, based on what I gathered through our adda, the distinction lies in the different methodological vantage points from which these modes of scholarship fashion an engagement with law. The former is based on the use of gender as an analytical framework for engaging with the nature of law and thinking about its relationship with women's lives. This theoretical framework is shaped by correlating law with women's contemporary lived experiences, and India's specific historical context and experiences of colonial encounter in the past. A women-oriented study of law, in contrast, is simply a way of thinking about law that is based on women's lived experiences.

Kapur shared that the authors formulated their analytical lens of post-colonial feminist legal theory primarily by combining two different academic feminist traditions of scholarship.[199] This included legal writings by feminist historians in India and legal theory produced by feminists in North America.[200] Kapur recounted that the 1980s and 1990s had seen an emerging body of scholarship by Indian historians who looked into how the question of women's rights had been taken up in law during colonial rule, and how that impacted legal interventions post-independence.[201] Among these historians were academics such as Tanika Sarkar, Lata Mani, Janaki Nair, Prem Chowdhry, Kumkum Sangari and Sudesh Vaid.[202] This cluster of scholarly insights pertained to women's experiences of law in colonial India.[203]

On women's experiences of law in post-colonial India, the authors drew from scholarship by feminist authors like Flavia Agnes, Archana

198 Ibid. 199 Ibid. 200 Ibid. 201 Ibid.

202 Tanika Sarkar, *Hindu Wife, Hindu Nation: Community, Religion, and Cultural Nationalism* (Indiana University Press, 2002); Mani, 'Contentious Traditions'; Nair, *Women and Law in Colonial India*; Prem Chowdhry, 'Conjugality, Law, and State: Inheritance Rights as Pivot Control in Northern India', in S. Basu (ed.), *Dowry and Inheritance* (Zed Books, 2005); Kumkum Sangari and Sudesh Vaid, *Recasting Women: Essays in Indian Colonial History* (Rutgers University Press, 1990).

203 This body of scholarship involved feminist interrogations of questions of tradition and modernity from the perspective of the colonial experience.

Parashar, Rajeswari Sunder Rajan and Bina Agarwal.[204] A primary source for the feminist legal theory component of their analytical tool, which was concerned with the relationship between law and women's lives, was drawn from North American feminist scholars. This included the scholarship of feminists such as Patricia Williams, Martha Minow, Mary Joe Frug, Susan Boyd, Angela Harris, Janine Brodie, Shelley Gavigan and Jane Jenson.[205] Post-colonial theory developed in North America by Indian feminist literary thinkers such as Gayatri Chakravorty Spivak, Chandra Talpade Mohanty and Ania Loomba also played a major role in shaping the theoretical position adopted in *Subversive Sites.*[206]

In *Subversive Sites,* although the authors' understanding of law is predominantly shaped by legal theory developed in the west, they state that they did not intend to simply lift and apply it as an explanatory framework in the Indian context.[207] They draw on western legal scholarship because it provides a rich resource for 'revisioning feminist engagement with law in India'.[208] Kapur recounted that because both authors were trained in the discipline of law, using North American feminist legal theory for doing a conceptual analysis of Indian statutes and judgements was not difficult. But enabling a systematic interaction between legal and historical scholarship was especially challenging and the most important element of the book for the authors.[209]

[204] See, generally, Agnes, *Law and Gender Inequality*; Parashar, *Women and Family Law Reform in India*; Sunder Rajan, *The Scandal of the State*; Bina Agarwal, *A Field of One's Own: Gender and Land Rights in South Asia* (Cambridge University Press, 1995).

[205] See generally, Patricia Williams, *The Alchemy of Race and Rights* (Harvard University Press, 1992); Martha Minow, *Feminist Legal Theories* (Routledge, 1997); Mary Joe Frug, *Postmodern Legal Feminism* (Routledge, 1993); Susan Boyd, *Challenging the Public/Private Divide: Feminism, Law, and Public Policy* (University of Toronto Press, 1997); Harris, 'Race and Essentialism in Feminist Legal Theory'; Shelley A. M. Gavigan, *Hunger, Horses and Government Men: Criminal Law on the Aboriginal Plains, 1870–1905* (University of British Columbia Press, 2012); Jane Jenson, 'Writing Women Out, Folding Gender In' (2008) 15(2), *Social Politics*, 131.

[206] See generally, Gayatri Chakravorty Spivak, *The Post-colonial Critic: Interviews, Strategies, Dialogues* (Routledge, 1990); Chandra Talpade Mohanty, *Feminism Without Borders: Decolonizing Theory, Practicing Solidarity* (Duke University Press, 2003); Ania Loomba, *Colonialism/Postcolonialism* (Routledge, 2016).

[207] Kapur and Cossman, *Subversive Sites*, 14. [208] Ibid.

[209] Conversation with Ratna Kapur, above n 2.

Kapur recounted that it was very challenging for her and Cossman to engage with the historical scholarship, and many of their conversations pertained to making sense of these writings. A majority of the authors' conversations pertained to how the historical scholarship could be effectively drawn into conversation with law and feminist legal theory.[210] At the time, from the disciplinary location of law, Kapur told me, no systematic scholarly engagement had been undertaken that looked at the rich repertoire of feminist writing that was being produced from a post-colonial context.[211] So, Kapur and Cossman decided that their priority would be to revisit this scholarship and engage with it carefully in order to build a post-colonial feminist theory of law.[212]

Kapur told me that while one half of the authors' theoretical framework was based on Indian feminist historical scholarship, the other half was built by drawing on Canadian feminist writers.[213] The feminist scholarship on law and feminism published in Canada in the 1990s proved particularly useful for developing the authors' understanding and analysis of law.[214] Amongst these was scholarship produced by political scientists Janine Brodie and Jane Jenson, and also legal scholar Shelley Gavigan. These scholars informed the authors' conception of law as a discursive site.[215] Along with these Canadian writers, the scholarship of British sociologist Carol Smart helped Kapur and Cossman be mindful of law's power to construct the experiences and meanings of women's lives through its discourses.[216]

Drawing on this kind of scholarship that identified law as inseparable from politics, Kapur told me, helped the authors think about legal discourses as also a site of politics, because of the contestations of power over the meanings of women's lives carried out at this site.[217] However, while the authors drew from these feminists, they also differed from them in the understanding that law could not be equated with the political struggles over women's lives.[218] The authors argue in *Subversive*

[210] Ibid. [211] Ibid. [212] Ibid. [213] Ibid.

[214] Ibid.; Kapur and Cossman, *Subversive Sites*, 40.

[215] Conversation with Ratna Kapur, above n 2; Kapur and Cossman, *Subversive Sites*, 40.

[216] Kapur and Cossman, *Subversive Sites*, 40.

[217] Conversation with Ratna Kapur, above n 2.

[218] Kapur and Cossman, *Subversive Sites*, 42.

Sites that law has its own discourse and institutional structures, within which the political contestations are entrenched.[219] Therefore, according to the authors, 'the focus of feminist legal studies' must be to look into law's distinctive nature and the ways in which it works as a site of discursive and political struggles.[220]

Kapur recalled that at the time, feminist legal scholarship was largely centred in the western world, while critical legal education was mostly shaped by white and male scholarly thinking.[221] So, for her and Cossman, their particular post-colonial feminist legal intervention into these conversations on feminism and law carried a specific obligation to show that critical legal wisdom can also originate from a non-western location.[222] Kapur noted that it was mainly the combined insights from the works of Indian feminist legal history and Canadian feminist legal scholarship that helped them undertake and perform this obligation through the collaborative writing of *Subversive Sites*.[223]

With reference to the Indian women's movement, Kapur and Cossman argue in the book that it is important for the movement to understand that law is a shape-shifting discourse.[224] The central thesis of *Subversive Sites* is that there is no uniform logic that governs law and judicial pronouncements. Being devoid of a unified, singular logic makes the inherent nature of law contradictory and prone to contesting views. This is, in fact, what potentially makes law a site for the realisation of women's rights and subverting discriminatory authority that creates their subordinate position in society.[225]

Kapur recounted that when she began her research with Cossman, they realised that dedicated institutional spaces for a systematic feminist engagement with law were scarce in India.[226] The setting up of women's studies departments had worked to secure the place of 'woman' as a subject of disciplinary study since the mid 1970s.[227] The relationship between 'women and law' became a much-studied area and some law schools even offered a subject by that name. But, a place for public

[219] Ibid. [220] Ibid. [221] Conversation with Ratna Kapur, above n 2. [222] Ibid.
[223] Ibid. [224] Kapur and Cossman, *Subversive Sites*, 12. [225] Ibid.
[226] Conversation with Ratna Kapur, above n 2.
[227] See generally Yogesh Atal (ed.), *Sociology and Social Anthropology in India* (Pearson, 2009), 306.

articulation and study of how feminist theory and practice informed by women's lived experiences in a post-colonial location challenged the foundations of the legal discipline, had not been secured in the same vein.[228]

Kapur further explained that while 'woman' had attained considerable legitimacy as a subject of study within the university, in common perception, the term 'feminist' carried a 'negative connotation' on account of being understood as a foreign import.[229] As Kapur engaged the discourses of the Indian women's movement while researching for *Subversive Sites*, she realised that a similar understanding of feminism was harboured by those who were a part of the movement.[230] It is Kapur's experiences of engaging in a conversation with the Indian women's movement that consolidated her understanding of the role and responsibilities of a post-colonial feminist legal scholar, which she crafted through her collaboration with Cossman and the writing of *Subversive Sites*.

A POST-COLONIAL FEMINIST LEGAL SCHOLAR AND THE WOMEN'S MOVEMENT IN INDIA

In 1991, the conference 'Religion, Culture, and Politics' was organised in Kolkata by the Indian Association for Women's Studies (IAWS).[231] The IAWS is a network of academics, researchers and activists who came together in the aftermath of the publication of the *Towards Equality* report and the consolidation of a women's movement in India in the 1970s.[232] At this event, she witnessed a tension amongst the participants as they debated whether to use the term 'feminist' to describe the IAWS network. Many of the participants who identified as feminists were concerned that calling the group 'feminist' was not a feasible idea because then it might not be able to accommodate certain women-oriented positions.[233] What underpinned this logic was the worry of letting

[228] Conversation with Ratna Kapur, above n 2. [229] Ibid. [230] Ibid.

[231] IAWS, 'Religion, Culture and Politics', www.iaws.org/conferences/national-conferences/1991-kolkata-religion-culture-and-politics.

[232] IAWS, http://iaws.org. [233] Conversation with Ratna Kapur, above n 2.

themselves turn into an exclusionary group, rather than one encompassing and speaking for an entire gamut of women's experiences.[234]

Kapur disagreed with this argument because it worked to deny legitimacy to feminist politics.[235] Moreover, according to her, such attempts at uniting varied, and often also opposing, political agendas under the umbrella term of 'woman' were not a useful endeavour for another reason. She believed that women spoke, and were spoken about, from various positions. Not all of them were necessarily beneficial for the realisation of women's equality and so could not be called feminist.[236] Therefore, such voices did not need to be represented in women's studies.[237]

Kapur told me that her thinking on this subject was informed by the Shah Bano case and the debates around the Uniform Civil Code and rights of Muslim women amongst women's rights activists in the late 1980s.[238] As these events were unfolding, Kapur was able to see how the debates in the women's movement started to resemble the agenda of the religious Hindu groups.[239] Although the interest of these groups lay in forwarding a communal agenda and not women's rights, in the ways in which events unfolded, the women's movement and these groups appeared to speak in one voice.[240]

The 'Shah Bano controversy', as Kapur and Cossman write in *Subversive Sites*, gave rise to 'a campaign for the reform of personal laws through a Uniform Civil Code'.[241] The Shah Bano case pertained to a matter in which the Supreme Court adjudicated on whether divorced Muslim women had a right to seek maintenance under the Criminal Procedure Code (CrPC) of 1973, or whether they were ruled only by Muslim personal laws when it came to such matters.[242] The Supreme Court held that Muslim women were entitled to claim their rights under

[234] Ibid. [235] Ibid. [236] Ibid. [237] Ibid. [238] Ibid.

[239] Ibid.; see also Kapur and Cossman, *Subversive Sites*, 63.

[240] Conversation with Ratna Kapur, above n 2; see also Kapur and Cossman, *Subversive Sites*, 63.

[241] Kapur and Cossman, *Subversive Sites*, 63; see also Upendra Baxi, 'The Shah Bano Reversal: Coup Against Constitution', in *Inhuman Wrongs and Human Rights: Unconventional Essays* (Har-Anand Publications, 1994), 89.

[242] *Mohammad Ahmed Khan* v. *Shah Bano Khan* AIR 1985 SC 945.

Section 125 of the CrPC, and that it would not interfere with the authority of Muslim personal laws. In the course of the judgement, the Supreme Court also made certain remarks about the Quran that led to much outrage amongst the Muslim community.[243] The legislature reacted to such uproar by passing the Muslim Women's (Protection of Rights on Divorce) Act, 1986, which declared that Section 125 of the CrPC was not applicable to divorced Muslim women.[244] This left Muslim women with the option of claiming maintenance only under personal laws for the period of *iddat*, or for the three months after divorce.[245]

The women's movement, which was outraged at the consequent outcome of these developments in the lives of Muslim women, made demands for a secular Uniform Civil Code. As noted in *Subversive Sites*, in their demands, the women's movement was joined by the Hindu Right groups. Even though the Hindu Right's motivation was in 'attacking the rights of minorities and the Muslim community in particular',[246] they had somehow managed to coalesce with voices that were advocating for a rival agenda of freeing women from patriarchal family laws through the enactment of a secular law.[247]

Kapur told me that at the IAWS conference in Kolkata where she had witnessed a resistance towards the use of the term 'feminist' to describe the activities of the women's movement, another significant incident had taken place.[248] Feminist lawyer and activist Flavia Agnes had openly pointed out that Muslim women, as opposed to Hindu women, were more susceptible to violence because of the way religious discourses were being shaped in the country at that time.[249] Based on her experience of working with Muslim women, Agnes pointed out that they chose to rely on their religious community more, rather than seeking support and solidarity outside of it in the women's movement.[250] According to Agnes,

[243] Kapur and Cossman, *Subversive Sites*, 63. [244] Ibid.

[245] For a detailed discussion of the case, see Agnes, *Law and Gender Inequality*.

[246] Kapur and Cossman, *Subversive Sites*, 64.

[247] Kapur and Cossman note that at the time of the independence struggle, the Hindu right had vehemently opposed women's demand for a Hindu Code Bill. Kapur and Cossman, *Subversive Sites*, 64.

[248] Conversation with Ratna Kapur, above n 2.

[249] Agnes, 'Women's Movement within a Secular Framework'.

[250] Conversation with Ratna Kapur, above n 2.

Kapur told me, the women's movement had failed in creating a solidarity base amongst women belonging to minority religious groups, which in turn meant that it had failed to represent the cause of women other than those who were Hindu.

Kapur recounted that, to her, Agnes's point of view suggested that the group, which wanted to be seen as inclusive and speaking for *all* women, was being accused of being exclusionary and carrying a religious bias.[251] For Kapur, this posed a challenge in her work of theorising law and its relations with women's lives: how would law need to be theorised by a feminist in order to reflect the reality of minority women in a post-colonial location? Did a feminist notion of equality, embedded in secular values of the Constitution, indeed carry a religious connotation?[252]

These questions, Kapur told me, necessitated serious reflection on what this accusation meant for a post-colonial feminist scholar who was speaking about secular law from a location where women's subject positions were deeply marked by not just gender, caste and class, but also religion.[253] Yet again, Kapur deeply felt the need for an institutional home where specific questions facing law from a post-colonial feminist standpoint could be explored.[254]

Connected to this question of the lack of institutional space for feminist projects was Kapur's experience of interactions with women's rights activists in India.[255] In the perceptions of many of those in the Indian women's movement, activism and scholarship were understood as two conflicting activities and not complementary, and activism was regarded as more virtuous.[256] Kapur told me that as a feminist and a lawyer, her primary realisation was that for the women's movement, whenever there was a question of engaging with law, they believed in doing things very quickly, so much so that no quality time was then spent in carefully reflecting on how to engage with law or what could be the consequences of a certain mode of engagement.[257] Given such a realisation, Kapur came to an understanding that the women's movement's interventions in relation to law had considerably disadvantaged the feminist project in India.[258] Moreover, Kapur felt the acute necessity of

[251] Ibid. [252] Ibid. [253] Ibid. [254] Ibid. [255] Ibid. [256] Ibid. [257] Ibid.
[258] Ibid.

a designated institutional space for addressing women's experiences of law through feminist debates and discussions.

To respond to this exigency, which was not being met by the law schools in India, she started the Centre for Feminist Legal Research (CFLR). Kapur set up CFLR as a research organisation for feminists and legal researchers along with her academic friends in the fields of the arts, law and the humanities.[259] It was meant to be a space for feminist legal researchers, mostly a transient group of people, who intended to bring conceptual feminist rigour to the study of law. It was also meant to be a space for exploring the intersections between law and feminist theory and practice.[260]

Kapur told me that she felt that there was no academic institutional space for engaging with law in a way that helped to build an understanding of the more fundamental role that law played in the imaginations of life as/of women.[261] The CFLR was thus formed for reclaiming public space and for boldly declaring that there was a feminist position from where one could engage with law. Moreover, the intent of setting up CFLR was also to assert, through the activity of feminist legal research, that women need not have been conceived solely as oppressed victim subjects. Open to western and non-western researchers alike, the setting up of CFLR by Kapur and her feminist friends created a site of knowledge production and co-learning for Southern and western scholars in a post-colonial location.

Kapur explained that before she set up CFLR, she had spent a considerable amount of time studying in the United States while the so called 'sex wars' were in full swing.[262] During this time, she was highly influenced by Catharine MacKinnon's feminist jurisprudence, which taught her that objective reason in law was but a patriarchal rationality.[263] That law could be theorised by formulating a feminist position of analysis was new to her. However, Kapur also became aware of the limits

[259] The membership of CFLR included feminist academics such as filmmaker and film scholar Shohini Ghosh; feminist lawyer Sara Hossain; and feminist historian Tanika Sarkar.

[260] Conversation with Ratna Kapur, above n 2.

[261] Ibid.

[262] Kapur did an LLM from Harvard Law School.

[263] Conversation with Ratna Kapur, above n 2.

of MacKinnon's theory of law that posited that women's sexuality was the root cause of their oppression.[264] This limitation was shown to her by the sex-positive feminism of queer scholars such as Pat Califia, Carol Vance, Gayle Rubin and Annie Sprinkle, who talked about sex and women's sexuality as not just a source of their victimhood but also as integral to their being and self-expression.[265] Through this learning, Kapur realised the harmful effects of MacKinnon's work on racial and sexual minorities. MacKinnon's ideas, Kapur thought, could cause the erasure of the diverse experiences of gender and sexuality, if 'woman' was taken to mean one single, stable category.[266]

Kapur found a lot of similarities between her experiences in the US and what she experienced in India while attending women's studies conferences.[267] A similar lack of space for taking note of the plurality of women's experiences of gender and sexuality also existed in India. The CFLR thus started to organise seminars that brought together people with very diverse lived experiences, such as sex workers, gay puppeteers, grassroots women's rights groups, academics and so on.[268] The reason for bringing these diverse groups of people into conversation was to think about an engagement with law that was built on people's diverse experiences of gender and sexuality.[269]

Kapur recounted that the institutional spaces opened up by women's studies provided avenues for exploring law's relationship with women, but did not provide an institutional location from where law could be conceived beyond its functional role in women's lives.[270] Although an understanding of the links between law and women's lived experiences had been established within academic institutions, attention was paid primarily to achieving formal equality.[271] The knowledge about law that was produced through feminist scholarship and the activism of the women's movement was too positivist and was entirely focused on the state.[272] This resulted in a dearth of research that would enable the

[264] MacKinnon, *Toward a Feminist Theory of the State.*

[265] Pat Califia, *Macho Sluts: Erotic Fiction by Pat Califia* (Alyson Books, 1994); Carol Vance, *Pleasure and Danger: Exploring Female Sexuality* (Rivers Oram Press, 1993); Gayle Rubin, *Deviations: A Gayle Rubin Reader* (Duke University Press, 2011); Annie Sprinkle, *Hardcore from the Heart: The Pleasures, Profits and Politics of Sex in Performance* (A&C Black, 2006).

[266] Ibid. [267] Ibid. [268] Ibid. [269] Ibid. [270] Ibid. [271] Ibid. [272] Ibid.

women's movement to develop a thinking around law beyond the formal legal institutions of the state and judiciary.[273] Legal discourse was heavily influenced by social and political theory, and law played a functional role in such scholarship.[274] Within such discourses, law was almost synonymous with the state, and the state structure was perceived either as the oppressor and/or as the formal structure that could address social oppression. This view of law, according to Kapur, left activists in the Indian women's movement completely unprepared and ill-equipped to respond to the Bhopal Gas Tragedy, a case of mass atrocity perpetrated by entities other than the state, but in collaboration with the state.[275]

The Bhopal Gas Tragedy was an incident that took place in 1984 as a result of a gas leak in a pesticide plant in Bhopal, Madhya Pradesh. The plant was owned by Union Carbide India Limited, a private corporate entity.[276] The leak exposed residents in the nearby locality to a toxic substance that killed thousands of people and subjected thousands of others to injuries that caused permanent disabilities. Both civil and criminal cases were instituted against the Union Carbide Corporation that jointly held majority ownership of the plant along with the Indian state. Legal proceedings were also initiated against Union Carbide's chief executive officer at the time, to hold him culpable.

Kapur recounted that in the aftermath of the incident, social rights activists undertook litigation to pin responsibility on the corporation, but the judicial process proved to be useless for the victims of the tragedy.[277] The activists failed to gain compensation for the victims, as well as to impose culpability on those whose negligence caused the tragedy.[278] The frustrations experienced by activists in this case had resonances with the experiences of the women's movement. The activists' inability to get

[273] Ibid. [274] Ibid. [275] Ibid.

[276] See generally, Suroopa Mukherjee, *Bhopal Gas Tragedy: The Worst Industrial Disaster in Human History* (Tulika Books, 2002).

[277] Conversation with Ratna Kapur, above n 2.

[278] For a detailed account of this process, see generally Upendra Baxi and Thomas Paul (eds), *Mass Disasters and Multinational Liability: The Bhopal Case* (N. M. Tripathi, 1986); Upendra Baxi, 'Introduction: Towards the Revictimization of the Bhopal Victims', in Baxi and Paul, *Mass Disasters and Multinational Liability*; Upendra Baxi, 'The Bhopal Victims in the Labyrinth of the Law: An Introduction', in Baxi and Paul, *Mass Disasters and Multinational Liability*.

justice for the victims of Bhopal through the process of litigation, and the failures experienced by the women's movement in their attempts to attain equality for women through law reform, pointed at the inherent contradictions in law.[279]

The judicial process, Kapur observed, was largely intermingled with ideologies that caused obstructions in the delivery of justice.[280] It was only when one engaged in the production of an expressly feminist discourse of law that it became visible that law, by virtue of being subject to interpretation, was mediated by patriarchal ideologies.[281] Law's ability to be subjected to interpretation based on ideologies was what caused a lack of uniformity in its application and made law a site of contradictions. The fact that there could be contradictions, according to Kapur, was what offered both possibilities and limitations for a feminist project.[282]

In India, at that time, starting with the *Towards Equality* report and the Open Letter, feminist thought as well as the activism of the women's movement drew heavily on constitutional equality. Both the *Towards Equality* report and the Open Letter were critical of the non-application of the constitutional provision of equality. They were not critical of such provisions per se.

Through *Subversive Sites*, Kapur and Cossman point out that the very formulation of the constitutional provisions on equality disadvantages women. This means that women's inequality arises not only from a lack of proper application of the equality provisions in the Constitution, but is written into the text of such provisions itself. Kapur and Cossman argue in *Subversive Sites* that the constitutional principle of equality, which, to be 'neutral' and 'objective', advocates for 'likes being treated alike', ends up being discriminatory towards women in the process.[283] The authors make this argument in another article that they wrote together in 1993, much before the publication of the book. In this article, titled 'On Women, Equality and the Constitution: Through the Looking Glass of Feminism', Kapur and Cossman first draw a distinction between formal

[279] Conversation with Ratna Kapur, above n 2. [280] Ibid. [281] Ibid. [282] Ibid.
[283] Kapur and Cossman, *Subversive Sites*, 175–80.

and substantive equality.[284] They put forth the idea that the notion of equality contained in Articles 14, 15 and 16 of the Indian Constitution potentially disadvantages women. This is because the foundational logic of the equality provisions, which is that *likes are to be treated alike*, opens up the possibility of women's inequality in law. Women can be regarded as unlike men, because the premise of the equality provision potentially allows for translating the differences between men and women into grounds for treating them as unequal.[285]

Kapur and Cossman argue in *Subversive Sites* that their 'feminist engagement with law in India' is able to show how the question of women's equality is embedded in a discourse of rival worldviews and is linked to competing agendas.[286] In doing so, they demonstrate two things: first, that women's issues are not a part of a feminist agenda alone; and second, that a woman-oriented claim is not necessarily equivalent to a claim for women's equality.[287] According to the authors, most discourses that speak about improving women's lives, or about women's equality, essentialise a notion of Indian womanhood. This notion constructs women primarily as subordinate beings due to their economic dependence on the father, or husband, within the family.[288]

As noted in *Subversive Sites*, both during colonial times and in the postcolonial present, attempts at law reform *for* the transformation of women's lives have been initiated not just by the women's movement but also by other actors.[289] Social reformers during colonial rule, and the Hindu right in contemporary India, have sought to bring about law reform for improving women's status and conditions.[290] The authors

[284] Ratna Kapur and Brenda Cossman, 'On Women, Equality and the Constitution: Through the Looking Glass of Feminism' (1993) 1, *National Law School Journal*, 1. These notions of formal and substantive equality are further developed in *Subversive Sites*.

[285] Ibid. [286] Kapur and Cossman, *Subversive Sites*, 12.

[287] A similar point is made by Janet Halley in *Split Decisions*. Halley argues that speaking for women is not equivalent to representing women's interests. Janet Halley, *Split Decisions: How and Why to Take a Break from Feminism* (Princeton University Press, 2006).

[288] Kapur and Cossman, *Subversive Sites*, chapter 3, 173–231. [289] Ibid., chapter 1, 19–86.

[290] See ibid., 43–72, for an elaboration of this point. *Subversive Sites* defines the Hindu right thus: 'The Hindu Right refers to the contemporary political movement in India, informed by the ideology of the Hindutva which seeks to establish a Hindu Rashtra (Hindu State).' Ibid., 234.

argue in *Subversive Sites* that a systematic study of judgements and the various statutes that have resulted from these demands and have been 'designed to benefit women'[291] show that in the garb of objectivity, law has, in fact, been governed by a patriarchal rationality, what the authors call 'familial ideology'.[292] These judgements and statutes informed by 'familial ideology' work to sustain the construction of the 'Indian woman' in law essentially as duty-bound to the family in the role of 'mother' and 'wife', and as a 'naturally different and subordinate subject'.[293]

Thus, according to Kapur and Cossman, 'familial ideology' constructs the 'family as a private sphere'[294] within which 'the honour of good women – chaste wives, virgin daughters – is held sacred'.[295] Such ideology, the authors argue, also acts as the basis for a false 'public/private distinction' in women's lives that 'undermine[s] the effective enforcement of laws designed to intervene within this private realm'[296] and advance women's equality.[297] The authors also argue that the private/public distinction is not made uniformly within law, which speaks to its contradictory nature. It is these contradictions within law that make it a useful site for subverting women's experiences of inequality. According to Kapur and Cossman, for this reason, law should neither be uncritically accepted nor renounced by feminists at any given time.[298]

Nivedita Menon, in her book *Recovering Subversion*, also argues against the renunciation of law by feminists.[299] However, according to Menon, it is not a question of whether and how feminists should or should not renounce law. Feminists simply cannot renounce law, because in modern systems of democratic governance, law is deeply entrenched in the constructions of women's identities.[300] For Menon, every aspect of a woman's identity, including her religion or caste or gender, is defined by the state and legal procedures for the regulatory purposes of

[291] Ibid., 118. [292] Ibid., chapter 2, 87–172. [293] Ibid., 74. [294] Ibid., 118.
[295] Ibid., 119. [296] Ibid., 118. [297] Ibid., chapter 2, 87. [298] Ibid., 18.
[299] Menon, *Recovering Subversion*.
[300] Ibid., 236–37. 'The option of abdicating the law is not a viable one, for the law will not abdicate us – the only permissible identities in modern democracies are those put in place by the law. We are inextricably implicated in state and legal procedures – every aspect of my identity is legally established – as woman, as Hindu, as upper caste.' Ibid.

governance. Thus, she argues, 'precisely for this reason, because the regulating and defining force of the law is directed towards the creating and naturalising of specific, governable identities, the law cannot be a "subversive site"'.[301]

For Menon, the task for a feminist is to think outside the conventional and established legal framework, because, for her, law is primarily a technology for governance and it belongs to the state. Because the state is such a powerful entity, feminists can never wield any authority over/in law even if they want to.[302] The post-colonial feminist theory of law that Kapur and Cossman develop in *Subversive Sites* is contrary to the position taken by Menon. Kapur and Cossman imagine law also as a site for gaining a positive social value and meaning for women, as opposed to only being a constellation of state-authorised rules and regulations for governance that marginalise them. For them, law is a discursive site, which leaves it open to being a discourse of governance as well as one of women's emancipation from the discriminatory legal and social regulation of their lives.

Kapur told me during our adda that, to her, the inseparability of the colonial encounter and law became visible as a result of being a part of the debates in the Indian women's movement during the early 1990s, and having also experienced a life in North America.[303] These experiences helped her think about the importance of writing *Subversive Sites* and shaping a feminist project for law that carried a 'historical consciousness'[304] of women's experiences, and its diversity, in the post-colonial location. Moreover, as she noted in our discussions, her experiences of the conversations in India and those in the west, a very different historical context, helped her understand the importance of collaborative projects across experiential and historical divides.

As I understand from my engagement with *Subversive Sites* through a performance of adda, for Kapur, the thoughts and practices of a post-colonial feminist legal scholar are not based on some abstract and universal notion of 'law' and 'women'; neither are they only learnt from

[301] Ibid. [302] Ibid. [303] Conversation with Ratna Kapur, above n 2.

[304] Chela Sandoval, 'US Third-World Feminism: The Theory and Method of Oppositional Consciousness in the Post Modern World' (1991) 10, *Genders*, 1.

the west. Rather, they are premised on an understanding that the experiences of the colonial encounter in the past continue to inform the normative imaginations of women's lives in the post-colonial present, and that the same is carried and reflected in/through law.[305] It is through such an understanding of a situated relationship between law and feminism – informed through conversations experienced at different places and times and with different people – that Kapur shaped her role and responsibilities as a post-colonial feminist legal scholar. In doing so, she crafted a mutual relationship between her professional life as a legal academic and the academic discipline of law. Moreover, my method helps us recognise what I have already noted in Chapter 1. The writing of *Subversive Sites* is an example of how conversations across 'different spatio-temporal locations' inform and inhabit the thoughts and practices that shape the field of Indian feminist jurisprudence in a post-colonial context.[306]

Both of the texts that I engaged with in this chapter – the Open Letter and *Subversive Sites* – are co-authored texts that Baxi and Kapur wrote together with other legal academics. The performance of adda in this chapter has entailed the reading and interpretation of the texts through reciprocal conversations with Baxi and Kapur. This means that I have carried out the task of understanding the significance of the contents of these texts through a direct exchange of meanings in conversations with the authors, which I have grounded in the context of their location in Indian legal academia in particular time periods.

I did this by asking the academics to reflect on how their specific experiences of being in an academic location, in the late 1970s and 1990s respectively, informed their decisions to co-author the texts with other people, as well as the formation of the contents of these texts. In doing so, I was able to understand how Baxi and Kapur publicly positioned themselves and shaped their roles and responsibilities as legal academics in relation to their discipline and with other people. Simultaneously, I was also able to relate the discursive content of the texts with the authors' experiences of writing them, and the time and place of their

305 Conversation with Ratna Kapur, above n 2.

306 Menon, 'Sexual Violence and the Law in India', 209.

production. By conducting adda in this way, I have drawn out the following two things in relation to the legal academics' collective mode of scholarship and their contributions to the production of a field of Indian feminist jurisprudence.

First, the acts of writing the Open Letter and *Subversive Sites* inhabit particular sets of conversations between the legal academics and other people. In the case of the Open Letter, the contents and writing of the text inhabit Baxi's conversations with his co-authors Lotika Sarkar, Vasudha Dhagamwar and Raghunath Kelkar, which shaped a collective of law teachers who jointly published the text; the conversations between a collective of law teachers and the chief justice of India to whom the Open Letter is addressed; and conversations between the law teachers and the tribal girl called Mathura on whose behalf the Open Letter is written. These specific sets of conversations took place in the context of Indian legal academia in late 1970s post-Emergency India.

In the case of *Subversive Sites*, the conversations that inhabit the book took place in the context of Indian legal academia in mid-1990s post-liberalisation India, a decade and a half after the writing of the Open Letter. The writing of *Subversive Sites* is informed by Kapur's conversations with her friend and co-author Brenda Cossman; and Kapur's conversations with the Indian women's movement. Kapur's conversations with Cossman, which resulted in many intellectual collaborations including *Subversive Sites*, started when Kapur was living in Canada. This was the period when the so-called feminist debates of the late 1970 and 1980s called the 'sex wars' were in full swing in North America, a time and place that was different from the context in which *Subversive Sites* was written. Kapur's experiences of conversations with Cossman, which are central to the writing of *Subversive Sites*, were caused by the authors' existence in, and mobility across, two distinct temporalities and locations. This was not the case for the authors of the Open Letter or the sex workers' activist documents discussed in Chapters 4 and 5.

Second, in writing the Open Letter and *Subversive Sites*, both Baxi and Kapur crafted their individual roles and responsibilities in public life, which, however, they formed collectively with others through the means of co-authored scholarship. Baxi crafted his role and responsibilities as a 'feminist law teacher'. For Baxi, taking on such a role in public life, in the way that my engagement with the writing of the Open Letter makes evident, meant that he made use of his gender-privileged position as a male legal academic and extended his disciplinary pedagogic responsibilities beyond the bounds of academia by attempting to educate the judiciary. In doing so, he made the understanding and knowledge of law inseparable from women's experiences of gender- and caste-based social discriminations and suffering, also raising questions about state accountability in the process.

Through the writing of *Subversive Sites*, Kapur shaped her role and responsibilities as a 'post-colonial feminist legal scholar'. For Kapur, the taking up of such a role in public life entailed the responsibilities of creating the post-colonial location as a site of feminist legal theory production; and the formulation of a feminist legal theory, a systematic mode of conceptualisation and analysis of law that was explicitly informed by women's diverse social experiences in relation to their specific location in the context of India's history of colonialism. Through her intellectual collaboration with Cossman in *Subversive Sites*, Kapur reorganised the perceived intellectual hierarchy and differences existing between brown and white women.

Thus, the collective scholarly practices of the legal academics are conscious experiences that enable their roles and responsibilities in public life to be shaped as both social and legal formations. It is so on account of such roles being formed in relation to academic legal institutions and the discipline of law, as well as the gendered modes of legal knowledge production and social life. Therefore, adda helps us understand how, through their scholarship, the academics draw their legal discipline into mutual relations with their own lives, by exploring two distinct examples of academics' experiences of mutual law–life relations that are located at different times and places, which have contributed to the productions of a field of Indian feminist jurisprudence. With this, I draw my performances of adda, which I began in Chapter 3, to a close.

CHAPTER 6

Towards a Feminist Jurisprudence of Conversations

THE BOOK DRAWS ITS METHODOLOGICAL TOOLS from an intellectual tradition that sees knowledge production as a way of being in the world and accounting for the ways in which we conduct our role and relationships towards others ethically. Adda – a jurisprudence of conversations – enables an enactment of that ethos and sensibility.

Jurisprudence (and by extension law), understood in conventional ways, is predicated upon a validating authority or source like the sovereign or the scholar. This book is focused on the question of how authority is accounted for within legal knowledge by the scholar as researcher. In adda, the way I have performed it as method, scholarly authority is performed by consciously shaping my role and responsibilities in relation to a field of feminist jurisprudence and those who participate in its productions. Adda, then, is not just what we say to others by way of good conduct or proper social etiquette or righteous behaviour. It is about the relationships formed with others in adda through attention to our own role and responsibilities towards them. Adda is two-way. It has to do with how we perform our responsibilities towards others as we speak with them for the purposes of knowledge production. Simultaneously, it is about making ourself receptive to how others take up their role and responsibilities in relationships with and within law. This, in turn, determines the nature and quality of the relationships we form with others and what we get to learn about how they relate with law, life and feminism. Adda is, therefore, an orientation and a practice requiring continuous cultivation and attention to one's own place and relationships.

Through my cultivation and practices of adda, I set out to show how life, law and feminism were lived relationally and in diverse ways through conversations grounded in place and time. I showed how reciprocal relations amongst people and between people's lives and law, experienced in conversations, contributed to the productions of feminist jurisprudence in a post-colonial context. In pursuit of this goal, I joined and built on the conventions and ongoing discourses within the field. I demonstrated that Indian feminist jurisprudence is a diverse body of knowledge that is not solely the domain of legal academics, but is developed in relationship with non-lawyer activists. In doing so, I argued that diverse experiences of mutual law–life relations, at varied locations, have produced a feminist jurisprudence in contemporary post-colonial India.

By way of demonstration and as examples to locate my research, I focused on the collective activism of the sex worker groups, DMSC and VAMP, and the collective scholarly practices of the legal academics, Upendra Baxi and Ratna Kapur. I read a select set of texts authored by these sex workers' collectives and legal academics. To engage with my materials, I developed a localised practice of adda – an activity of reciprocal conversations – as a methodology. What were the motivations for developing this new method, what has its performances entailed, what has it contributed towards the advancement of my argument, and what are its implications for feminist jurisprudence?

In undertaking the methodological task in this book, I had two aims: First, to address the question of the caste-based, hierarchical organisation of the field of intellectual labour in India that creates a structural disparity with respect to who can be counted as knowledgeable, and by speaking from which location. Second, to account for a body of knowledge within the field of Indian feminist jurisprudence that has resulted from people's diverse experiences of life and law in an Indian post-colonial context. These specific aims were motivated by a conscious attempt to think about my own place as a researcher and how to take on a particular role and responsibilities vis-à-vis: my academic disciplinary location in law; my interlocutors, drawing on whose wisdom I have built this discourse; and the location of this book in the contemporary historical context of India where much of the experience of our disciplinary knowledge continues to be informed by caste, gender and colonialism.

I began by situating my methodological project in relation to the field of Indian feminist jurisprudence; and laid the ground for the performance of my method by illuminating its relevance and significance. Adda refers to the everyday action or activity of engaging in reciprocal conversations (as verb), and a meeting place (as noun). I joined insights from the works of scholars who are located within the disciplines of law and/or the humanities to think about how to adapt this everyday cultural practice in vernacular to a scholarly methodology for law. By drawing on and weaving together ideas and practices from post-colonial, feminist and jurisprudential thought, I imbibed a way of performing adda as a living act and activity of reciprocal conversations for relating people's experiences of life and law.

I staged my methodology to demonstrate how it helped to account for the diverse experiences and locations of mutual law–life relations. In this regard, my performances of adda entailed three interrelated aspects. First, it involved a practice of reading and interpretation of selected texts authored by the sex worker activist groups DMSC and VAMP, and legal academics Upendra Baxi and Ratna Kapur. I practised my reading and interpretation of scholarly and activist texts reciprocally in actual conversations with the authors. Through such shared activity I derived an understanding of the contents, meanings and significance of these texts. Second, in these conversations, my engagement involved learning about authors' experiences of writing the texts, the thoughts and practices that were contained in the texts, and the place and time at which the texts were produced. I paid particular attention to how the legal academics and sex workers thought about the correlations between law and the social experiences of gender/class/caste/sexuality/religion. Third, I paid attention to how my interlocutors consciously shaped their own distinct role and responsibilities in life, and for law, when they spoke about the relationships between their lives and law.

The adda were reported by presenting them as a series of conjoined conversations between me and the authors and between the authors and other people, in conversations with whom the authors developed the ideas and practices that inhabit their texts. By presenting adda in this manner, I made visible how the sex workers' practices of collective activism and the legal academics' practices of collective scholarship exist in a continuum of conversations between diverse actors and across times and places. I made visible how the practices of collectivisation and scholarship are diverse forms of similar experiences of conversations. Through these conversations, the sex workers and the legal academics shaped mutual relations between their lives and law, from their own specific temporality and locations within Indian legal academia and collective organisations respectively.

In terms of both form and substance, the experiences of mutual law–life relations consciously practised by my interlocutors through their activism and scholarship are distinct. Thus, there are four diverse ways of forming mutual law–life relations that have been made visible in this book. In all four instances, the relationships of mutuality involved a reorganisation of existing relations of hierarchy in public life.

For example, DMSC envisaged and materialised sex workers' mutual relations with law by way of a reorganisation of the state–sex worker relationship through 'cooperation' and 'reinhabitation' within a community in Kolkata. Sex workers initiated this reorganisation in the post-liberalised India of the 1990s. Through 'cooperation' and 'reinhabitation', sex workers of DMSC shaped their collective role and responsibilities in public life as jouno kormi/sex workers to present a new subject in and for legal engagements. The organisation of the Durga Puja or the formation of Self-Regulatory Boards by sex workers in Kolkata are illustrations of how women have worked out a means of entering into dialogue with the state, to call its institutions into this other relation by taking on a new role. Similarly, the formation of DMSC through a codification of its rules and principles of collectivisation or, for that matter, the implementation of an elaborate electoral system, gives it a state-like but self-regulatory authoritative form. In this regard, DMSC's demands for the legalisation of sex work reflect the women's desire for drawing the state into a dialogue with sex workers, holding its institutions accountable to the women, and securing institutionalised representation of the women's interests in state-authorised laws and policies. The organisational form of DMSC as a cooperative society is therefore meant to act as a liaison between the sex-working women in Kolkata and the state and its institutions, and establishing channels of communication between the women and the Indian state.

In the case of VAMP, the formation of mutual law–life relation is also materialised through a reorganisation of the sex worker–state relationship, albeit differently from the approach and practices of DMSC. Like in the case of DMSC, VAMP's reorganisation was also initiated right after the Indian economy was liberalised in the 1990s. The collectivisation and formation of VAMP in Sangli as an NGO was essentially an attempt to keep the state away from any involvement in sex workers' lives and choice of livelihood, including in the capacity of a regulatory authority vested with the power to make decisions about women's lives. My performance of adda made visible how VAMP presented a new subject in and for legal engagements by shaping women's collective role and responsibilities in public life as dhandhewali/businesswomen, to cause a reorganisation of women's relations with the state. Thus, VAMP is meant to act as an interface or a means of separation between the state and the women. Unlike the women at DMSC, sex workers at VAMP made a conscious choice to institutionalise their collective organisation *not* as a state-like regulatory authority, but as a non-governing association of like-minded people who do not believe in undermining individual interests for the consolidation of a collective. The demands of VAMP for decriminalisation are in line with this impulse to curb state interference and give importance to sex workers' individual interests, which is how the sex-working women in Sangli implemented and shaped their mutual relations with law.

In the case of Baxi, my engagement with his collective scholarly practice revealed that he approached the question of law by shaping his role and responsibilities in public life as a feminist law teacher. Taking on such a role and responsibilities, which he shaped collectively in conversations with other people, Baxi presented a new subject for legal engagements within the academic institution of law and reorganised the relationship between the educator of law and the post-colonial Indian society. This reorganisation was carried out by Baxi in the context of the post-Emergency India of the late 1970s. Baxi formed mutual relations with law by extending his disciplinary pedagogic responsibilities beyond the institutional bounds of legal academia. By attempting to educate members of the judiciary about women's experiences of suffering through his writing and teaching, Baxi expanded the role of the law teacher and the institutional function of legal education in Indian post-colonial society. Thus, Baxi materialised his mutual relations with law by making the understanding and pedagogy of law inseparable from the social context in which these activities existed, as well as by accounting for women's experiences of suffering in his writing and teaching of law.

Kapur approached law by shaping her role and responsibilities in public life as a post-colonial feminist legal scholar. She materialised her mutual relations with law by reorganising the perceived intellectual hierarchy and differences existing between brown and white women. This reorganisation, like in the cases of DMSC and VAMP, was carried out by Kapur in the context of the post-liberalisation India of the 1990s. Kapur worked to make the Indian post-colonial location a recognisable site for the origin of legal wisdom, or the production of legal knowledge, and not let it remain a recipient of legal thought from the western world. For Kapur, this meant the development of a systematic analysis of law based on women's diverse social experiences that were informed by people's history and experiences of colonialism in India.

What does a jurisprudence of conversations offer feminist projects in law? This book is a scholarly experiment. It explores the development of an imaginative methodological exercise for learning about how a field of feminist jurisprudence comes to be through the combined work of disparate groups of people. As a methodology, the performances of adda provide a mode of thinking about how, as feminists, we can relate with law and, more importantly, how we can infuse life into law and give it meanings through the ways in which we consciously decide to conduct our relations. The performance of adda and the formations of mutual law–life relations that it helps to uncover, shows how the representations and relations of law take new shapes across different locations and experiences of meaning. Thinking relationally, and particularly in terms of how our own accounts of law are formed based on our conduct of life and relations with other people, helps to recognise that the experiences of life and law are interlinked and can attain meaning through our conscious thoughts and practices. Adda helps to uncover how we authorise meanings to law through our determinations and conduct of roles and responsibilities in our lived relationships. Such a recognition of the life of law accounts for a feminist jurisprudence, which is an embodied and agential practice of reciprocal relationship making both within life and discourse.

Reciprocity, in this sense, does not mean an absence of conflict or disagreements. It refers to a formation of ties across divergences that can enrich feminist legal discourses, by making visible through them the specific and collective nature of the experiences of life and law. As a methodology, adda helps to recognise how knowledge making through joint invocations of law and feminism is thus an ongoing performance of reciprocal relations that is always a collective work-in-progress. It requires thinking through disagreements and dilemmas, and even a careful reworking of discursive and daily relations with others through mutual conversations. That is why, through this book, I have argued for a feminist jurisprudence that is founded on a reciprocity between life and law through a shared practice of adda. My methodological project and its attention to reciprocal relations is *not* meant to transcend hierarchies. My participation in adda helps to address hierarchies in/of life and law, and facilitate a mode of thinking about how to live and work responsibly with them.

APPENDICES

Sex Workers' Manifesto

FIRST NATIONAL CONFERENCE OF SEX WORKERS IN INDIA 14–16 NOVEMBER 1997, CALCUTTA

A new spectre seems to be haunting the society. Or maybe those phantom creatures who have been pushed into the shades for ages are taking on human form – and that is why there is so much fear. The sex workers' movement for last few years has made us confront many fundamental questions about social structures, life sexuality, moral rights and wrongs. We think an intrinsic component of our movement is to go on searching for the answers to these questions and raise newer ones.

WHAT IS THE SEX WORKERS' MOVEMENT ALL ABOUT?

We came together as a collective community through our active involvement as health workers, the Peer Educators, in a HIV/STD Control Project which has been running in Sonagachhi since 1992. The Project provided the initial space for building mutual support, facilitating reflection and initiating collective action among us, sex workers. Very early in the life of the Sonagachhi Project, we, with the empathetic support of those who had started the Project, clearly recognised that even to realise the very basic Project objectives of controlling transmission of HIV and STD it was crucial to view us in our totality – as complete persons with a range of emotional and material needs, living within a concrete and specific social, political and ideological context which determine the quality of our lives and our health, and not see us merely in terms of our sexual behaviour.

To give an example, while promoting the use of condoms, we soon realised that in order to change the sexual behaviour of sex workers it was not enough to enlighten them about the risks of unprotected sex or to improve their communication and negotiation skills. How will a sex worker who does not value herself at all think of taking steps to protect her health and her life? Even when fully aware of the necessity of using condoms to prevent disease transmission, may not an individual sex worker feel compelled to jeopardise her health in fear of losing her clients to other sex workers in the area unless it was ensured that all sex workers were able to persuade their clients to use condoms for every sexual act? Some sex workers may not even be in a position to try negotiate safer sex with a client as they may be too closely controlled by exploitative madams or pimps. If a sex worker is starving, either because she does not have enough custom or because most of her income goes towards maintaining a room or meeting the demands of madams, local power-brokers or the police, can she be really in a position to refuse a client who can not be persuaded to use condoms?

And what about the client? Is a man likely to be amenable to learn anything from a woman, particularly an uneducated 'fallen' woman? For him does not coming to a prostitute necessarily involve an inherent element of taking risk and behaving irresponsibly? In which case are not notions of responsibility and safety completely contradict his attitude towards his relationship with a prostitute? Does not a condom represent an unnecessary impediment in his way to 'total' pleasure?

In most case this male client himself may be a poor, displaced man. Is he in a position to value his own life or protect his health?

Then again why does not a sex worker who is ready to use condom with her client, would never have protected sex with her lover or husband? What fine balance between commercial transaction and love, caution and trust, safety and intimacy engender such behaviour? How do ideologies of love, family, motherhood influence our every sexual gesture?

Thus, thinking about such an apparently uncomplicated question – whether a sex worker can insist on having safe sex, made us realise that the issue is not at all simple. Sexuality and the lives and the movement of sex workers are intrinsically enmeshed in the social structure we live within and dominant ideology which shapes our values.

Like many other occupations, sex work is also an occupation, and it is probably one of the 'oldest' profession in the world because it meets an important social demand. But the term 'prostitute' is rarely used to refer to an occupational group who earn their livelihood through providing sexual services, rather it is deployed as a descriptive term denoting a homogenised category, usually of women, who poses threats to public health, sexual morality, social stability and civic order. Within this discursive boundary we systematically find ourselves to be targets of moralising impulses of dominant social groups, through missions of cleansing and sanitising, both materially and symbolically. If and when we figure in political or developmental agenda, we are enmeshed in discursive practices and practical projects which aim to rescue, rehabilitate, improve, discipline, control or police us. Charity organisations are prone to rescue us and put us in 'safe' homes, developmental organisations are likely to 'rehabilitate' us through meagre income generation activities, and the police seem bent upon to regularly raid our quarters in the name of controlling 'immoral' trafficking. Even when we are inscribed less negatively or even sympathetically within dominant discourses we are not exempt from stigmatisation or social exclusion. As powerless, abused victims with no resources, we are seen as objects of pity. Otherwise we appear as self-sacrificing and nurturing supporting cast of characters in popular literature and cinema, ceaselessly ready to give up our hard-earned income, our clients, our 'sinful' ways and finally our lives to ensure the well-being of the hero or the society he represents. In either case we are refused enfranchisement as legitimate citizens or workers, and are banished to the margins of society and history.

The kind of oppression that can be meted out to a sex worker can never be perpetrated against a regular worker. The justification given is that sex work is not real work – it is morally sinful. As prostitution is kept hidden behind the facade of sexual morality and social order, unlike other professions there is no legitimacy or scope for any discussion about the demands and needs of the workers of the sex industry.

People who are interested in our welfare, and many are genuinely concerned, often can not think beyond rehabilitating us or abolishing prostitution altogether. However, we know that in reality it is perhaps impossible to 'rehabilitate' a sex worker because the society never allows to erase our identity as prostitutes. Is rehabilitation feasible or even desirable?

In a country where unemployment is in such gigantic proportions, where does the compulsion of displacing millions of women and men who are already engaged in an income-earning occupation which supports themselves and their extended families, come from? If other workers in similarly exploitative occupations can work within the structures of their profession to improve their working conditions, why can not sex workers remain in the sex industry and demand a better deal in their life and work?

WHAT IS THE HISTORY OF SEXUAL MORALITY?

Like other human propensities and desires, sexuality and sexual need are fundamental and necessary to the human condition. Ethical and political ideas about sexuality and sexual practices are socially conditioned and historically and contexually specific. In the society as we know it now, ideologies about sexuality are deeply entrenched within structures of patriarchy and largely misogynist mores. The state and social structures only acknowledges a limited and narrow aspect of our sexuality. Pleasure, happiness, comfort and intimacy find expression through sexuality. On one hand we weave narratives around these in our literature and art. But on the other hand our societal norms and regulations allow for sexual expression only between men and women within the strict boundaries of marital relations within the institution of the family.

Why have we circumscribed sexuality within such a narrow confine, ignoring its many other expressions, experiences and manifestations?

Ownership of private property and maintenance of patriarchy necessitates a control over women's reproduction. Since property lines are maintained through legitimate heirs, and sexual intercourse between men and women alone carry the potential for procreation, capitalist patriarchy sanctions only such couplings. Sex is seen primarily, and almost exclusively, as an instrument for reproduction, negating all aspects of pleasure and desire intrinsic to it. Privileging heterosexuality, homosexuality is not only denied legitimacy, it is considered to be undesirable, unnatural, and deviant. Thus sex and sexuality are given no social sanction beyond their reproductive purpose.

Do we then not value motherhood? Just because our profession or our social situation does not allow for legitimate parenthood, are we trying to claim motherhood and bearing children is unworthy and unimportant for women? That is not the case. We feel that every woman has the right to bear children with if she so wishes. But we also think that through trying to establish motherhood as the only and primary goal for a woman the patriarchal structures try to control women's reproductive functions and curb their social and sexual autonomy. Many of us sex workers are mothers – our children are very precious to us. By social standards these children are illegitimate – bastards. But at least they are ours and not mere instruments for maintaining some man's property or continuing his genealogy. However, we too are not exempt from the ideologies of the society we live in. For many of us the impossible desire for family, home and togetherness is a permanent source of pain.

DO MEN AND WOMEN HAVE EQUAL CLAIMS TO SEXUALITY?

Societal norms about sex and sexuality do not apply similarly to men and women. If sexual needs are at all acknowledged beyond procreation, it is only for men. Even if there are minor variations from community to community and if in the name of modernity certain mores have changed in some place, it is largely men who have had enjoyed the right to be polygamous or seek multiple sexual partners. Women have always been expected to be faithful to a single man. Beyond scriptural prohibitions too, social practices severely restricts the expression of female sexuality. As soon as a girl reaches her puberty her behaviour is strictly controlled and monitored so as not to provoke the lust of men. In the name of 'decency' and 'tradition' a woman teacher is prohibited from wearing the clothes of her choice to the University. While selecting a bride for the son, the men of the family scrutinise the physical attributes of a potential bride. Pornographic representations of women satisfy the voyeuristic pleasures of millions of men. From shaving cream to bathroom fittings are sold through attracting men by advertisements depicting women as sex objects.

In this political economy of sexuality there is no space for expression of women's own sexuality and desires. Women have to cover up their bodies from men and at the same time bare themselves for male gratification. Even when women are granted some amount of subjecthood by being represented as consumers in commercial media, that role is defined by their ability to buy and normed by capitalist and patriarchal strictures.

IS OUR MOVEMENT ANTI-MEN?

Our movement is definitely against patriarchy, but not against all individual men. As it so happens, apart from the madams and landladies almost all people who profit from the sex trade are men. But what is more important is that their attitudes towards women and prostitution are biased with strong patriarchal values. They generally think of women as weak, dependent, immoral or irrational – who need to be directed and disciplined.

Conditioned by patriarchal gender ideologies, both men and women in general approve of the control of sex trade and oppression of sex workers as necessary for maintaining social order. The power of this moral discourse is so strong that we prostitutes too tend to think of ourselves as morally corrupt and shameless. The men who come to us as clients are victims of the same ideology too. Sometimes the sense of sin adds to their thrill, sometimes it leads to perversion and almost always it creates a feeling of self loathing among them. Never does it allow for confident, honest sexual interchange.

It is important to remember that there is no uniform category as 'men'. Men, like women are differentiated by their class, caste, race and other social relations. For many men adherence to the dominant sexual norm is not only impracticable but also unreal. The young men who look for sexual initiation, the married men who seek the company of 'other' women, the migrant labourers separated from their wives who try to find warmth and companionship in the red light area can not all be dismissed as wicked and perverted. To do that will amount to dismissing a whole history of human search for desire, intimacy and need. Such dismissal creates an unfulfilled demand for sexual pleasure, the burden of which though shared by men and women alike, ultimately weighs more heavily on women. Sexuality – which can be a basis of an equal, healthy relationship between men and women, between people, becomes the source of further inequality and stringent control. This is what we oppose.

Next to any factory, truckers check points, market there has always been red light areas. The same system of productive relations and logic of profit maximisation, which drives men from their homes in villages to towns and cities, make women into sex workers for these men.

What is deplorable is that this patriarchal ideology is so deeply entrenched, and the interest of men as a group is so solidly vested in it, that women's question hardly ever find a place in mainstream political or social movements. The male workers who organise themselves against exploitation rarely address the issues of gender oppression, let alone the oppression of sex workers. Against the interest of women these radical men too defend the ideology of the family and patriarchy.

ARE WE AGAINST THE INSTITUTION OF FAMILY?

In the perception of society we sex workers and in fact all women outside the relation of conjugality are seen as threats to the institution of family. It is said that enticed by us, men stray from the straight and narrow, destroy the family. All institutions from religion to formal education reiterate and perpetuate this fear about us. Women and men too, are the victims of this all pervasive misogyny.

We would like to stress strongly that the sex workers movement is not against the institution of family. What we challenge is the inequity and oppression within the dominant notions of an 'ideal' family which support and justify unequal distribution of power and resources within the structures of the family. What our movement aims at is working towards a really humanitarian, just and equitable structure of the family which is perhaps yet to exist.

Like other social institutions the family too is situated within the material and ideological structures of the state and society. The basis of a normative ideal family is inheritance through legitimate heirs and therefore sexual fidelity. Historically, the structures of families in reality have gone through many changes. In our country, by and large joint families are being replaced by nuclear ones as a norm. In fact, in all societies people actually live their lives in many different ways, through various social and cultural relations – which deviate from this norm, but are still not recognised as the ideal by the dominant discourses.

If two persons love each other, want to be together, want to raise children together, relate to the social world it can be a happy, egalitarian, democratic arrangement. But does it really happen like that within families we see, between couple we know? Do not we know of many, many families where there is no love, but relations are based on inequality and oppression. Do not many legal wives virtually live the life of sex slaves in exchange for food and shelter? In most cases women do not have the power or the resources to opt out of such marriages and families. Sometimes men and women both remain trapped in empty relations by social pressure. Is this situation desirable? Is it healthy?

THE WHORE AND THE MADONNA – DIVIDE AND RULE

Within the oppressive family ideology it is women's sexuality that is identified as the main threat to conjugal relationship of a couple. Women are pitted against each other as wife against the prostitute, against the chaste and the immoral – both represented as fighting over the attention and lust of men. A chaste wife is granted no sexuality, only a de-sexed motherhood and domesticity. At the other end of the spectrum is the 'fallen' woman – a sex machine, unfettered by any domestic inclination or 'feminine' emotion. A woman's goodness is judged on the basis of her desire and ability to control and disguise her sexuality. The neighbourhood girl who dresses up can not be good, models and actresses are morally corrupt. In all cases female sexuality is controlled and shaped by patriarchy to reproduce the existing political economy of sexuality and safeguard the interest of men. A man has access to his docile home-maker wife, the mother of his children and the prostitute who sustain his wildest sexual fantasies. Women's sexual needs are not only considered to be important enough, in most cases its autonomy is denied or even its existence is erased.

Probably no one other than a prostitute really realises the extent of loneliness, alienation, desire and yearning for intimacy that brings men to us. The sexual need we meet for these men is not just about mechanical sexual act, not an momentary gratification of 'base' instincts. Beyond the sex act, we provide a much wider range of sexual pleasure which is to with intimacy, touch and companiability – a service which we render without any social recognition of its significance. At least men can come to us for their sexual needs – however prurient or shameful the system of prostitution may be seen as. Women hardly have such recourse. The autonomy of women's sexuality is completely denied. The only option they have is to be prostitutes in the sex industry.

WHY DO WOMEN COME TO PROSTITUTION?

Women take up prostitution for the same reason as they may take up any other livelihood option available to them. Our stories are not fundamentally different from the labourer from Bihar who pulls a rickshaw in Calcutta, or the worker from Calcutta who works part time in a factory in Bombay. Some of us get sold into the industry. After being bonded to the madam who has bough us for some years we gain a degree of independence within the sex industry. A whole of us end up in the sex trade after going through many experiences in life – often unwillingly, without understanding all the implications of being a prostitute fully.

But when do most of us women have access to choice within or outside the family? Do we become casual domestic labourer willingly? Do we have a choice about who we want to marry and when? The choice is rarely real for most women, particularly poor women.

Why do we end up staying in prostitution? It is after all a very tough occupation. The physical labour involved in providing sexual services to multiple clients in a working day is no less intense or rigorous than ploughing or working in a factory. It is definitely not fun and frolic. Then there are occupational hazards like unwanted pregnancy, painful abortions, risk of sexually transmitted diseases. In almost all red light areas housing and sanitation facilities are abysmal, the localities are crowded, most sex workers quite poor, and on top of it there is police harassment and violence from local thugs. Moreover, to add to the material condition of deprivation and distress, we have to take on stigmatisation and marginalisation – the social indignity of being 'sinful', being mothers of illegitimate children, being the target of those children's frustrations and anger.

DO WE ADVOCATE 'FREE SEX'?

What we advocate and desire is independent, democratic, non-coercive, mutually pleasurable and safe sex. Somehow 'free sex' seems to imply irresponsibility and lack of concern for other's well-being, which is not what we are working towards. Freedom of speech, expression or politics all come with obligations and need to acknowledge and accommodate other's freedom too. Freedom of sexuality should also come with responsibility and respect for other's needs and desires. We do want the freedom to explore and shape a healthy and mature attitude and practice about sex and sexuality – free from obscenity and vulgarity.

We do not yet know what this autonomous sexuality will be like in practice – we do not have the complete picture as yet. We are working people not soothsayers or prophets. When for the first time in history when workers agitated for class equity and freedom from capitalist exploitation, when the blacks protested against white hegemony, when feminists rejected the subordination of women they too did not know fully what the new system they were striving for would exactly be like. There is no exact picture of the 'ideal' future – it can only emerge and be shaped through the process of the movement.

All we can say in our imagination of autonomous sexuality men and women will have equal access, will participate equally, will have the right to say 'yes' or 'no', and there will be no space for guilt or oppression.

We do not live in an ideal social world today. We do not know when and if ever an idea social order will come into place. In our less than ideal world if we can accept the immorality of commercial transaction over food, or health why is sex for money so unethical and unacceptable. Maybe in an ideal world there will be no need for any such transactions – where material, emotional, intellectual and sexual needs of all will be met equitably and with pleasure and happiness. We do not know. All we can do now is to explore the current inequalities and injustices, question their basis and confront, challenge and change them.

WHICH WAY IS OUR MOVEMENT GOING?

The process of struggle that we, the members of Mahila Samanwaya Committee are currently engaged in has only just begun. We think our movement has two principal aspects. The first one is to debate, define and re-define the whole host of issues about gender, poverty, sexuality that are being thrown up within the process of the struggle itself. Our experience of Mahila Samanwaya Committee shows that for a marginalised group to achieve the smallest of gains, it becomes imperative to challenge an all encompassing material and symbolic order that not only shapes the dominant discourses outside but, and perhaps more importantly, historically conditions the way we negotiate our own locations as workers within the sex industry. This long term and complex process will have to continue.

Secondly, the daily oppression that is practised on us with the support of the dominant ideologies, have to be urgently and consistently confronted and resisted. We have to struggle to improve the conditions of our work and material quality of our lives, and that can happen through our efforts towards us, sex workers, gaining control over the sex industry itself. We have started the process – today in many red light areas in cities, towns and villages, we sex workers have come to organise our own forums to create solidarity and collective strength among a larger community of prostitutes, forge a positive identity for ourselves as prostitutes and mark out a space for acting on our own behalf.

MALE PROSTITUTES ARE WITH US TOO

The Durbar Mahila Samanwaya Committee was originally formed by women sex workers of Sonagachhi and neighbouring red light areas, and initially for women prostitutes. However, within two years of our coming into existence male sex workers have come and joined as at their own initiative. These male sex workers provide sexual services to homosexual men primarily. As our society is strongly homophobic, and in fact, the penetrative sexual act even between consenting adult men can still be legally penalised, the material and ideological status of male sex workers is even more precarious. We therefore had welcomed them in our midst as comrades in arms and strongly believe that their participation will make the sex workers' movement truly representative and robust.

Sex workers movement is going on – it has to go on. We believe the questions about sexuality that we are raising are relevant not only to us sex workers but to every men and women who question subordination of all kinds – within the society at large and also within themselves. This movement is for everyone who strives for an equal, just, equitable, oppression free and above all a happy social world. Sexuality, like class and gender after all makes us what we are. To deny its importance is to accept an incomplete existence as human beings. Sexual inequality and control of sexuality engender and perpetuate many other inequalities and exploitation too. We're faced with situation to shake the roots of all such injustice through our movement. We have to win this battle and the war too – for a gender just, socially equitable, emotionally fulfilling, intellectually stimulating and exhilarating future for men, women and children.

Box A.1 A Statement of Women in Prostitution – 28 January 1995

Figure A.1

Prostitution is a way of life like any other. It is a survival strategy that is parallel to any other occupation. It is not created for the benefit of men, as is the common perception, rather it is primarily for the women who live off it. Women in prostitution make money out of sex and we are the breadwinners of our families.

We disagree with the formulation that prostitution is a profession. We make a distinction between profession (*vyavasay*) and occupation/business (*dhandha*). For instance, if we are presently occupied by making money out of sex, then that is our occupation for a short span of time. The nature of the business itself is time-bound. Therefore, by using the term profession, we are necessarily being pushed into a category for a lifetime. We are women who are practicing this time-bound business of prostitution for a short and specific period in our lives. Please remember that when we are not making money out of sex, we are engaged in other income-generating activities.

We believe that all occupations stereotypical to women adhere to so-called 'feminine values'. They capitalize upon qualities like tolerance, sympathy, tenderness, endurance, understanding, patience, forbearance and much more, be they housewives, typists, nurses, teachers, office assistants, receptionists, or women in prostitution. We believe that the socialization of the girl-child to accept such occupations as the only option is also a major reason for the perpetuation of sexual discrimination in the female work force. We believe that women in prostitution are no different.

We believe that we are more empowered than most women within male-dominated patriarchal structures are. For instance, within the family structure (which we know is the most oppressive), we are the breadwinners and the heads of our households. The relationships we share with the men in our families are more honest and equal because the purdah of double standards is not necessary.

Figure A.2

Economic independence from men is a reality that we enjoy with pride and dignity. Brothel-owners, goons, the police and the self-appointed crusaders of morality in society harass us, try to curb our independence and are forever trying to douse our spirit. Control structures have a vested interest in criminalizing prostitution. What we demand is the decriminalization of prostitution such that we can live safely and continue to choose to make money from sex without stigmatization. We demand the eradication of all laws concerning prostitution, which are oppressive and contribute to further criminalizing the trade.

We believe that making money from sex is only selling a part of our body, which is in no way different from selling our brains or physical labour. We protest against a society that deems our work contribution as less prestigious than other traditional forms of work. We believe that we challenge and undermine structures of power by using a part of our womanhood – our sexuality – as a source of our power and income.

We also protest against all laws and value systems that treat soliciting for sex as indecent while sanctioning other forms of sexual contracts from advertisements and exchanging gifts by marriage partners to dowry and bride price.

As people who experience violence as a part of our daily life, we are being more and more penalized by increasing violence in a society that is trying to order and control our lifestyles. As women in prostitution, we protest against a society that forces on us the violence of a judgmental attitude.

We believe that a woman's sexuality is an integral part of her as a woman, as varied as her mothering, domestic and such other skills. We do not believe that sex has a sacred space and women who have sex for reasons other than its reproductive importance are violating this space. Or that if they chose to make money from the transaction they are immoral or debauched.

We believe that child prostitution is child sexual abuse, molestation and child labor and that it exists in a society that is fraught with crimes of abduction, kidnap, rape, assault and violence against women. We believe that as comparable to poor, weak and marginalized communities, we are unable to have a reasonable control of our lives and destinies. We share the same experiences of women who live in the Third World.

Figure A.3

We believe that there is a distinction between trafficking, which is a criminal offence, and adult prostitution. While we agree that 'choice' is a cruel mirage for all women within capitalist patriarchy, we feel the need to acknowledge that adult prostitution as an option, exists. We also believe that women who are in prostitution, choose to continue to remain in business for many reasons.

We believe that when involuntary initiation into prostitution occurs, a process of socialization within the institution of prostitution exists whereby the involuntary nature of the business changes increasingly to one of active acceptance, not necessarily with resignation. This is not a coercive process. We believe that, despite living within a capitalist patriarchal society and having experienced the freedom of living outside the patriarchal system, it is almost impossible for us to contemplate entering such a system with its inherent double standard, lopsided value system and inequalities.

We protest against a society that deems us immoral and illegal mainly because we do not accept its mores, rules and governance. We protest against the various forces of mainstream society that deny us the right to liberty, security, and fair administration of justice, respect for our lives, discrimination, freedom of expression and association.

We also protest against a society that aggressively promotes objectification and commercialization of women and their sexuality. We protest against the sale of our sexuality in the international market by unscrupulous individuals and governments who reap huge profits off our bodies. We are in a business wherein the control has shifted from traditional members of our community to criminal syndicates. We were not for sale. In today's world, unfortunately we are sacrificed and commodified by vested interests, sometimes from within our own communities.

Globalization and economic liberalization is further breaking up our communities and forcing us to accept the sale of our bodies and the sale of our young in the urban industrial centers for prostitution. Movement in search of work is not new for us, the problem however is the criminalisation of the trade which is forcing us to turn to debt bondage, forced labour and slavery-like practices. Consequently, we find ourselves in the trap of criminal syndicates in our search for work.

Figure A.4

We believe that it is imperative that we must unite with each other to erase the stigmatization of women in prostitution and restore our dignity as workers and citizens of civil society. We must build alliances with other segments of society and together, we must struggle against the forces that have a vested interest in eroding the rights of all women.

This Statement was read at the

Speaking Tree, Womenspeak: Asia- Pacific Public Hearing on Crimes Against Women related to the violence of development 28 January 1995, Bangalore, India by women in sex work from Sangli who collectivized in 1997 as

VESHYA ANYAY MUKTI PARISHAD (VAMP)

AN OPEN LETTER TO THE CHIEF JUSTICE OF INDIA

Your Lordship,

We, as Indian citizens and teachers of law, take the liberty of writing this open letter to focus judicial attention and public debate over a decision rendered by the Supreme Court on September 15, 1978, which has been recently reported. The decision was rendered by Justice Jaswant Singh, Kailasam and Koshal in *Tukaram* v. *State of Maharashtra*, (1979) 2 SCC 143.

The facts of the case briefly are as follows. Mathura, a young girl of the age 14–16, was an orphan who lived with her brother, Gama, both of them labourers. Mathura developed a relationship with Ashok, the cousin of Nushi at whose house she used to work, and they decided to get married. On March 26, 1972, Gama lodged a report that she was kidnapped by Nushi, her husband and Ashok. They were all brought to the police station at 9 p.m. when their statements were recorded. When everyone started to leave the police station, around 10.30 p.m., Tukaram, the head constable and Ganpat, a constable, directed that Mathura remain at the police station.

What happened thereafter is best described in the words of Justice Koshal, who wrote the decision of the Court:

> Immediately thereafter Ganpat . . . took Mathura . . . into latrine situated at the rear of the main building, loosened her underwear, lit a torch and started at her private parts. He then dragged her to a chhapri . . . In the chhapri he felled her to the ground and raped her in spite of her protests and stiff resistance on her part. He departed after satisfying his lust and then Tukaram . . . who was seated in the cot nearby, came to the place where Mathura . . . was and fondled her private parts. He also wanted to rape her but was unable to do so for the reason that he was in a highly intoxicated condition.

There was natural anxiety outside the police station as the lights were put off and doors bolted. They shouted for Mathura but to no avail. A crowd collected; shortly after, Tukaram emerged to announce that Mathura had already left. Mathura then emerged and announced that she had been raped by Ganpat. The doctor to whom people approached advised them to file a report with the police. Head Constable Baburao was brought from his home to the station, by the fear of the restive crowd, and first information report was lodged.

Mathura was examined by the doctor on March 27. She had no injury. Her hymen revealed old reptures. Other aspects of physical examination revealed that she had had intercourses in the past. Presence of semen was detected on her clothes and the pyjama of Ganpat.

The Sessions Judge found this evidence insufficient to convict the accused. The farthest he would go was to hold that Mathura had sexual intercourse with Ganpat! But sexual intercourse cannot be equated with rape; there was 'a world of difference', in law, between the two. He feared that Mathura had cried 'rape' in order to prove herself 'virtuous' before the crowd which included her lover. He was also not sure that the semen on her clothes was from intercourse with Ganpat; and although he was disinclined to accept Ganpat's claim that semen on his trousers was due to habitual nocturnal discharges, he entertained the possibility that the semen stains on his clothes may well be due to the possibility of his having intercourse 'with persons other than Mathura'.

The Bombay High Court (Nagpur Bench) reversed the finding and sentenced Tukaram to rigorous imprisonment for one year and Ganpat for five years. Its grounds for reversal were that since both these 'gentlemen' were perfect strangers to Mathura, it was highly unlikely that 'she would make any overtures or invite the accused to satisfy her sexual desires'. Nor could she have resisted her assailants. The High Court came to the conclusion that the policemen had 'taken advantage of the fact that Mathura was involved in a complaint filed by her brother, and she was alone in the dead hour of the night' in a police station. This proved that she could not, in any probability, have consented to intercourse.

Your Court, Your Lordship, *reversed* the High Court verdict. The reasons given by Justice Koshal are as follows. First, Justice Koshal held that as there were no injuries shown by the medical report, the story of 'stiff resistance having been put up by the girl is all false' and the 'alleged intercourse was a peaceful affair'. Second, the Court disbelieves the testimony of the girl that she shouted 'immediately after her hand was caught by Ganpat'; that she was not allowed to shout when she was taken to latrine and 'that she had raised the alarm even when the underwear was loosened and Ganpat was looking at her private parts with the aid of a torch'.

The Court holds that the 'cries and alarms are, of course, a concoction on her part'. This is said because when she was leaving the police station with her brother, Ganpat had caught her by the arm and she made no attempt to resist it then. The Court says, 'If that be so, it would be preposterous to suggest that although she was in the company of her brother ... she would be so overawed by the fact of appellants being persons in authority or the circumstance that she was just emerging from a police station that she would make no attempt at all to resist.' Third, the Court holds that under Section 375 of the Penal Code, only the 'fear of death or hurt' can vitiate consent for sexual intercourse. There was no such finding recorded. The circumstantial evidence must be such also as to lead to 'reasonable evidence of guilt'.

While the High Court thought there was such reasonable evidence, the Supreme Court did not. Tukaram too was held not guilty because Mathura had in her deposition attributed far more serious things to him and later attributed these acts to Ganpat instead. The fact that Tukaram was present when the incident took place and that he left it soon after the incident, says the Court, is 'not inculpatory and is capable of more explanations than one'. But these other explanations are not at all indicated by Justice Koshal in his judgment.

Your Lordship, this is an extraordinary decision sacrificing human rights of women under the law and the Constitution. The Court has provided no cogent analysis as to why the factors which weighed with the High Court were insufficient to justify conviction for rape. She was in the police station in the 'dead hour of night'. The High Court found it impossible to believe that she might have taken initiative for intercourse.

The fact remains that she was asked to remain in the police station even after her statement was recorded and her friends and relations were asked to leave. Why? The fact remains that Tukaram did nothing whatsoever to rescue the girl from Ganpat. Why? The Court says in its narration of facts, presumably based on the trial Court records, that Tikaram was intoxicated. But this is not considered material either. Why? Why were the lights put off and doors shut? Your Lordship, does the Indian Supreme Court expect a young girl 14–16 years old, when trapped by two policemen inside the police station, to successfully raise alarm for help? Does it seriously expect the girl, a labourer, to put up such stiff resistance against well-built policemen so as to have substantial marks of physical injury? Does the absence of such marks necessarily imply absence of stiff resistance? If anything it is Ganpat's body which would have disclosed marks of such resistance by Mathura, like clawing and biting.

Maybe, the evidence of shouts for help and 'stiff resistance' is all 'a tissue of lies'. But does the absence of shouts justify an easy inference of consensual intercourse in a police station? (Incidentally, what would be the Court's reaction if the victim was dumb or gagged?) In any event, how could the fact of shouting within closed doors of a police station be established in such cases?

In restoring the decision of the Sessions Judge, does the Supreme Court of India really believe with him that Mathura had 'invented' the story of rape, and even the confinement in the police station, in order to sound 'virtuous' before Ashok? Does the Court believe that Mathura was so flirtatious that even when her brother, her employer and her lover were waiting outside the police station, she could not let go the opportunity of having fun with two policemen and that too in the area adjoining a police station latrine? Does it believe with the Sessions Judge that Mathura was 'habituated to sexual intercourse' to such an extent? And therefore further think that the semen marks on Mathura's clothing could have come from further sexual activities between the police incident and the next morning when she was medically examined? What about semen marks on Ganpat's trousers? Why this double standard? Ganpat's sexual habits give him the benefit of doubt of having 'raped' Mathura; her sexual habits make the Court disbelieve the story of the rape altogether!

We also find it surprising that the Supreme Court should have only focused on the third component of Section 375 of the Indian Penal Code, which applies when rape is committed with the woman's consent, when 'her consent has been obtained by putting her in fear of death or of hurt'. But the second component of Section 375 is when rape occurs without her consent. There is a clear difference in law, and common sense, between 'submission' and 'consent'. Consent involves submission; but the converse is not necessarily true. Nor is absence of resistance necessarily indicative of consent. It appears from the facts as stated by the Court and its holdings that there was submission on the part of Mathura. But where was the finding on the crucial element of consent?

It may be that in strict law Ganpat was charged with rape on the third component of description of rape. In that case, the issue before the Court was simply whether the act was committed with her consent, under fear of death or hurt. But still the question whether there was 'consent' was quite relevant; indeed, it was crucial. From the facts of the case, all that is established is *submission,* and not consent. Could not their Lordships have extended their analysis of 'consent' in a manner truly protective of the dignity and right of Mathura? One suspects that the Court gathered an impression from Mathura's liaison with her lover that she was a person of easy virtue. Is the taboo against pre-marital sex so strong as to provide a licence to Indian police to rape young girls? Or to make them submit to their desires in police stations?

My Lord, the ink is hardly dry on the decision in *Nandini Satpathy*, (1978) 2 SCC 424 when the Supreme Court, speaking through Justice Krishna Iyer, condemned the practice of calling women to police stations in gross violation of Section 160(1) of the Criminal Procedure Code. Under that provision, a woman shall not be required to attend the police investigation at any other place than her place of residence. The Court stated in *Nandini* that it 'is quite probable that the very act of directing a woman to come to the police station in violation of Section 160(1) CrPC may make for tension and negate "voluntariness"'. This observation was made in the context of the right against self-incrimination; is it any the less relevant to situations of 'rape' or, as the Court wishes to put it, 'intercourse' in a police station?

Certainly, the hope expressed by Justice Krishna Iyer that 'when the big fight forensic battles the small gain by victory' has been belied. The law made for Nandini Satpathy does not, after all, apply to the helpless Mathuras of India.

There is not a single word condemning the very act of calling Mathura, and detaining her at the police station in gross violation of the law of the land made by Parliament and so recently reiterated by the Supreme Court. Nor is there a single word in the judgment condemning the use of the police station as a theatre of rape or submission to sexual intercourse. There is no direction to the administration to follow the law. There are no strictures of any kind.

The Court gives no consideration whatsoever to the socio-economic status, the lack of knowledge of legal rights, the age of victim, lack of access to legal services, and the fear complex which haunts the poor and the exploited in Indian police stations. May we respectfully suggest that yourself and your distinguished colleagues visit incognito, wearing the visage of poverty, some police stations in villages adjoining Delhi?

My Lord, your distinguished colleagues and yourself have earned a well-merited place in contemporary Indian history for making preservation of democracy and human rights a principal theme of your judicial and extra-judicial utterances, especially after March, 1977. But a case like this with its cold-blooded legalism snuffs out all aspirations for the protection of human rights of millions of Mathuras in the Indian countryside. Why so?

No one can seriously suggest that all policemen are rapists. Despite massive evidence of police maltreatment of women in custody which rocked the State of Madhya Pradesh in 1977–78 and Andhra Pradesh in *Rameeza Bee case* not too long ago, we would agree with the Court were it to say it explicitly that the doctrine of judicial notice cannot be used to negative the presumption of innocence, even in such type of cases. But must presumption of innocence be carried so far as to negative all reasonable inference from circumstantial evidence?

Mathura, with all her predicaments, has been fortunate that her problem reached the High Court and your Court. But there are millions of Mathuras in whose situations even the first information reports are not filed, medical investigations are not made in time, who have no access to legal services at any level and who rarely have the privilege of vocal community support for their plight.

The Court, under your leadership, has taken great strides for civil liberties in cases involving affluent urban women (e.g. Mrs. Maneka Gandhi and Mrs. Nandini Satpathy). Must illiterate, labouring, politically mute Mathuras of India be continually condemned to their pre- constitutional Indian fate?

What more can we say? We can only appeal, in conclusion, to have the case reheard, as an unusual situation, by a larger bench, and if necessary by even the Full Court. This may appear to your Lordship as a startlingly unconventional, and even a naive suggestion. But nothing short of protection of human rights and constitutionalism is at stake. Surely, the plight of millions of Mathuras in this country is as important as that of Golak Nath, and His Holiness Kesavananda Bharti challenging the validity of restriction on the right to property as a fundamental right, whose cases were heard by a full court.

Maybe on re-examination Ganpat and Tukaram may stand acquitted for better reasons than those now available. But what matters is a search for liberation from the colonial and male- dominated notions of what may constitute the element of consent, and the burden of proof, for rape which affect many Mathuras on the Indian countryside.

You will no doubt forgive us for this impertinence of writing an open letter to you. But the future of judicial protection of human rights at grassroots level in India at the turn of the century, a concern we all share as citizens and as lawmen, leaves us with no other and better alternative.

With best regards and greetings, we remain[1]

Delhi,
September 16, 1979.

[1] Upendra Baxi, Raghunath Kelkar and Lotika Sarkar teach at the University of Delhi; Vasudha Dhagamwar teaches at the University of Poona.

Bibliography

ACADEMIC SOURCES

Abrams, Kathryn. 'Feminist Lawyering and Legal Method' (1991) 16, *Law and Social Inquiry*, 373.

Agarwal, Bina. *A Field of One's Own: Gender and Land Rights in South Asia* (Cambridge University Press, 1995).

Agnes, Flavia. 'Protecting Women against Violence: Review of a Decade of Legislation, 1980–89' (1992) 27(17), *Economic and Political Weekly*, WS19.

'Women's Movement within a Secular Framework' (1994) 29(19), *Economic and Political Weekly*, 1123.

State, Gender and the Rhetoric of Law Reform (Research Centre for Women's Studies, Shreemati Nathibai Damodar Thackersey Women's University, 1995).

'Transgressing Boundaries of Gender and Identity' (2002) 36(37), *Economic and Political Weekly*, 3696.

'Hypocritical Morality: Mumbai's Ban on Bar Dancers' (2005) 149, *Manushi*, www.bitly.com.

'The Bar Dancer and the Trafficked Migrant: Globalisation and Subaltern Existence', in Sibaji Pratim Basu (ed.), *The Fleeing People of South Asia: Selections from Refugee Watch* (Anthem, 2009), 355–66.

Family Law, vol. II: Marriage, Divorce and Matrimonial Litigation (Oxford University Press, 2012).

'Law and Gender Inequality: The Politics of Women's Rights in India', in Flavia Agnes, Sudhir Chandra and Monmayee Basu, *Women and Law in India* (Oxford University Press, 2016). https://academic.oup.com/book/9051.

Ambedkar, Bhimrao Ramji. 'Castes in India: Their Mechanism, Genesis, and Development', *Dr. Babasaheb Ambedkar: Writings and Speeches*, vol. 1 (Education Department, Government of Maharashtra, 1979), 3–22, www.columbia.edu/itc/mealac/pritchett/00ambedkar/txt_ambedkar_castes.html.

BIBLIOGRAPHY

Ambedkar, B. R. 'Annihilation of Caste', in Valerian Rodrigues (ed.), *The Essential Writings of B. R. Ambedkar* (Oxford University Press, 2010), 263–305.

'Castes in India', in Valerian Rodrigues (ed.), *The Essential Writings of B. R. Ambedkar* (Oxford University Press, 2010).

Atal, Yogesh (ed.). *Sociology and Social Anthropology in India* (Pearson, 2009).

Ayyar, Varsha. 'Caste-Gender Matrix and the Promise and Practice of Academia' (2017) 52(50), *Economic and Political Weekly*, www.epw.in/engage/article/caste-gender-matrix-and-promise-and-practice-academia.

Balagopal, K. 'This Anti-Mandal Mania' (1990) 25(40), *Economic and Political Weekly*, 2231.

Banerjee, Sumanta. *Dangerous Outcast: The Prostitute in Nineteenth Century Bengal* (Seagull Books, 1998).

Bartlett, Katharine T. 'Feminist Legal Methods' (1990) 103(4), *Harvard Law Review*, 829.

Basu, Srimati. *She Comes to Take Her Rights: Indian Women, Property, and Propriety* (SUNY Press, 1999).

The Trouble with Marriage: Feminists Confront Law and Violence in India (University of California Press, 2015).

Baxi, Pratiksha. 'Feminist Contributions to Sociology of Law: A Review' (2008) 43(43), *Economic and Political Weekly*, 79.

Public Secrets of Law (Oxford University Press, 2014).

Baxi, Upendra. *Socio-legal Research in India: A Programschrift*, ICSSR Occasional Monograph (Indian Council of Social Science Research, 1975).

The Indian Supreme Court and Politics (Eastern Book Company, 1980).

The Crisis of the Indian Legal System: Alternatives in Development Law (Vikas, 1982).

Courage, Craft and Contention: The Indian Supreme Court in the Eighties (N. M. Tripathi, 1985).

'Taking Suffering Seriously' (1985) 4, *Third World Legal Studies*, 107.

'The Bhopal Victims in the Labyrinth of the Law: An Introduction', in Upendra Baxi and Thomas Paul (eds), *Mass Disasters and Multinational Liability: The Bhopal Case* (N. M. Tripathi, 1986), i–lxix.

'Introduction: Towards the Revictimization of the Bhopal Victims', in Upendra Baxi and Thomas Paul (eds), *Mass Disasters and Multinational Liability: The Bhopal Case* (N. M. Tripathi, 1986), 1–34.

'Teaching as Provocation', in Amrik Singh (ed.), *On Being a Teacher* (Konark Publishers, 1990), 150–58, http://upendrabaxi.in/documents/On%20being%20a%20teacher.pdf.

'The Shah Bano Reversal: Coup against Constitution', in *Inhuman Wrongs and Human Rights: Unconventional Essays* (Har-Anand Publications, 1994), 89–94.

'Towards the Liberation of Women's Studies', in *Inhuman Wrongs and Human Rights: Unconventional Essays* (Har-Anand Publications, 1994), 55–68.

'Violence against Women in the Labyrinth of Law', in *Inhuman Wrongs and Human Rights: Unconventional Essays* (Har-Anand Publications, 1994), 67–88.

'Emancipation as Justice: Babasaheb Ambedkar's Legacy and Vision' in Upendra Baxi and Bhikhu Parekh (eds), *Crisis and Change in Contemporary India* (Sage, 1995), 122–49.

'From Human Rights to the Right to Be a Woman', in Amita Dhanda and Archana Parashar (eds), *Engendering Law: Essays in Honour of Lotika Sarkar* (Eastern Book Company, 1999), 275–90.

'Enculturing Law? Some Unphilosophic Remarks', in Sitaram Kakarala and Mathew John (eds), *Enculturing Law: New Agendas for Legal Pedagogy* (Tulika Books, 2007), 2–21.

'Postcolonial Legality: A Postscript from India' (2012) 45(2), *Law and Politics in Africa, Asia and Latin America,* 178.

'Unlearning the Law with Lotika Sarkar', Lotika Sarkar Memorial Lecture (2014) 2, *Journal of the Campus Law Centre,* 1, http://clc.du.ac.in/JCLC/JCLC%20Vol_2.pdf.

Baxi, Upendra, and Thomas Paul (eds). *Mass Disasters and Multinational Liability: The Bhopal Case* (N. M. Tripathi, 1986).

Berg, Peter, and Raymond F. Dasmann. 'Reinhabiting California', in David Pepper, Frank Webster and George Revill (eds), *Environmentalisms: Critical Concepts* (Routledge, 2002), vol. 2, 231–36.

Bhaiya, Abha. 'Legitimately Ours: The Parallel Systems of Feminist Jurisprudence', in Poonam Kathuria and Abha Bhaiya (eds), *Indian Feminisms: Individual and Collective Journeys* (Zubaan, 2018), 46–64.

Bhowmik, Sharit Kumar. 'Ideology and the Co-operative Movement: Worker Co-operatives in the Tea Industry' (1988) 23(51), *Economic and Political Weekly,* 2703.

Bhuimali, Anil. *Rural Cooperative and Economic Development* (Sarup & Sons, 2003).

Bhushan, Prashant. *The Case That Shook India: The Verdict That Led to the Emergency* (Penguin, 2017).

Blumm, Michael C. 'The Public Trust Doctrine: A Twenty-First Century Concept' (2010) 16, *Hastings West-Northwest Journal of Environmental Law and Policy,* 105.

Boyd, Susan. *Challenging the Public/Private Divide: Feminism, Law, and Public Policy* (University of Toronto Press, 1997).

Bradford, Nicholas J. 'Transgenderism and the Cult of Yellamma: Heat, Sex, and Sickness in South Indian Ritual', in Gary David Comstock and Susan E. Henking (eds), *Que(e)rying Religion: A Critical Anthology* (A&C Black, 1997), 294–310.

Brown, Wendy. 'Introduction', in Talal Asad, Wendy Brown, Judith Butler and Saba Mahmood, *Is Critique Secular? Blasphemy, Injury, and Free Speech* (University of California Press, 2009), 7–19.

Butler, Judith. *Giving an Account of Oneself* (Fordham University Press, 2005).

Cavarero, Adriana. *Relating Narratives: Storytelling and Selfhood* (Routledge, 2014).

Chakrabarty, Dipesh. *Provincializing Europe: Postcolonial Thought and Historical Difference* (Princeton University Press, 2008).

Chakraborty, Mridula Nath. 'Being Bengali: At Home and in the World: Some Speculations', in Mridula Nath Chakraborty (ed.), *Being Bengali: At Home and in the World* (Routledge, 2016), 1–10.

Chakravorty, Swapan, Suzana Milevska and Tani E. Barlow. *Conversations with Gayatri Chakravorty Spivak* (Seagull Books, 2006).

Chaudhuri, Maitrayee. 'Feminism in India: The Tale and Its Telling' (2019) 1(209), *Revue Tiers Monde,* 19, www.cairn.info/revue-tiers-monde-2012-1-page-19.htm.

Chowdhry, Prem. 'Conjugality, Law, and State: Inheritance Rights as Pivot Control in Northern India', in S. Basu (ed.), *Dowry and Inheritance* (Zed Books, 2005), 171–93.

Contentious Marriages, Eloping Couples: Gender, Caste, and Patriarchy in Northern India (Oxford University Press, 2009).

Cossman, Brenda, and Ratna Kapur. 'Trespass, Impasse, Collaboration: Doing Research on Women's Rights in India' (1991) 2(2), *Journal of Human Justice,* 99.

Secularism's Last Sigh? Hindutva and the (Mis)rule of Law (Oxford University Press, 2001).

Darian-Smith, Eve (ed.). *Ethnography and Law* (Routledge, 2017).

Das, Veena. 'Public Good, Ethics, and Everyday Life: Beyond the Boundaries of Bioethics' (1999) 128(4), *Daedalus,* 99.

'Ethics, the Householder's Dilemma, and the Difficulty of Reality' (2014) 4(1), *HAU: Journal of Ethnographic Theory,* 487.

'What Does Ordinary Ethics Look Like?', in Michael Lambek, Veena Das, Didier Fassin and Webb Keane, *Four Lectures on Ethics: Anthropological Perspectives* (University of Chicago Press, 2015).

'Ethics, Self-Knowledge, and Life Taken as a Whole' (2018) 8(3), *HAU: Journal of Ethnographic Theory,* 537.

Davies, Margaret. 'Ethics and Methodology in Legal Theory: A (Personal) Research Anti-Manifesto' (2002) 6, *Law Text Culture,* 7–26.

Asking the Law Question, 3rd ed. (Thomson Lawbook Co., 2008).

Davies, Margaret, and Vanessa E. Munro (eds). *The Ashgate Companion to Feminist Legal Theory* (Routledge, 2013).

Davis, Jr, Donald R. 'Introduction', in Patrick Olivelle and Donald R. Davis (eds), *Hindu Law: A New History of Dharmasastra* (Oxford University Press, 2017), 1–14.

Deshpande, Ashwini. *Affirmative Action in India*, Oxford India Short Introductions (Oxford University Press, 2013).

Dhanda, Amita. 'RIP Lotika Sarkar: Pioneering Feminist and Lawyer but Teacher Foremost', *Legally India*, 8 March 2013, www.legallyindia.com/Legal-opinions/lotika-sarkar-obituary.

Dhanda, Amita, and Archana Parashar (eds). *Decolonisation of Legal Knowledge* (Routledge, 2009).

Dirks, Nicholas B. *Castes of Mind: Colonialism and the Making of Modern India* (Princeton University Press, 2002).

Dorsett, Shaunnagh, and Shaun McVeigh. *Jurisdiction* (Routledge-Cavendish, 2012).

Doucet, Andrea, and Natasha S. Mauthner. 'Feminist Methodologies and Epistemology', in C. D. Bryant and D. L. Peck (eds), *Handbook of 21st Century Sociology* (Sage, 2006), 26–32.

Drakopoulou, Maria. 'Revisiting Feminist Jurisprudence: A Rehabilitation' (2013) 3(2), *Feminists@Law.*

Duggan, Lisa, and Nan D. Hunter. *Sex Wars: Sexual Dissent and Political Culture* (Taylor & Francis, 2006).

Dutta, Debolina. 'Brushstrokes: The Sound of Laughter', *In Plainspeak*, 18 January 2016, www.tarshi.net/inplainspeak/brushstrokes-the-sound-of-laughter.

Dutta, Debolina, and Oishik Sircar. 'From Entertainment Worker to Sex Worker: Strategic Politics of DMSC' (2008) 4(3), *Global South*, 3–5.

'India's Winter of Discontent: Some Feminist Dilemmas in the Wake of a Rape' (2013) 39(1), *Feminist Studies*, 293.

Economic and Political Weekly. *Quarter Century of Liberalisation in India: Essays from Economic & Political Weekly* (Oxford University Press, 2018).

Eslava, Luis. *Local Space, Global Life: The Everyday Operation of International Law and Development* (Cambridge University Press, 2015).

Felsci, Rita. *The Limits of Critique* (University of Chicago Press, 2015).

Foucault, Michel. 'Practicing Criticism', in *Politics, Philosophy, Culture: Interviews and Other Writings, 1977–1984* (A. Sheridan et al., trans., L. D. Kritzman, ed., Routledge, 1988), 152–58.

Frug, Mary Joe. *Postmodern Legal Feminism* (Routledge, 1993).

Galanter, Marc. *Competing Equalities: Law and the Backward Classes in India* (University of California Press, 1984).

Gandhi, M. K. *The Story of My Experiments with Truth* (Maple Press, 2011).

Gangoli, Geetanjali. 'Sex Work, Poverty and Migration in Eastern India', in Sadhna Arya and Anupama Roy (eds), *Poverty, Gender and Migration* (Sage, 2006), 214–35.

Indian Feminisms: Law, Patriarchies and Violence in India (Routledge, 2007).

Gavigan, Shelley A. M. *Hunger, Horses and Government Men: Criminal Law on the Aboriginal Plains, 1870–1905* (University of British Columbia Press, 2012).

Genovese, Ann. 'Inheriting and Inhabiting the Pleasures and Duties of Our Own Existence: *The Second Sex* and Feminist Jurisprudence' (2013) 38(1), *Australian Feminist Law Journal*, 41.

'On Australian Feminist Tradition: Three Notes on Conduct, Inheritance, and the Relations of Historiography and Jurisprudence' (2014) 38(4), *Journal of Australian Studies*, 430.

Genovese, Ann, and Shaun McVeigh. 'Nineteen Eighty-Three: A Jurisographic Report on *Commonwealth v Tasmania*' (2015) 24(1), *Griffith Law Review*, 68.

Genovese, Ann, and Margaret Thornton. 'On *The Liberal Promise*: A Conversation' (2015) 41(1), *Australian Feminist Law Journal*, 3.

Ghosh, Anjan. 'Spaces of Recognition: Puja and Power in Contemporary Calcutta' (2000) 26(2), *Journal of Southern African Studies*, 289–99.

Ghosh, Shohini. 'Decriminalizing Sex Work' (March 2008), 583, *Seminar*, www.india-seminar.com/2008/583/583_shohini_ghosh.htm.

Ghosh, Swati. 'Elusive Choice and Agency: A Feminist Re-reading of the Sex Workers' Manifesto', in Rohini Sahni, V. Kalyan Shankar and Hemant Apte (eds), *Prostitution and Beyond: An Analysis of Sex Workers in India* (Sage, 2008), 54–72.

Gopal, Meena. 'Caste, Sexuality and Labour: The Troubled Connection' (2012) 60(2), *Current Sociology*, 222.

Graycar, Regina, and Jenny Morgan. *The Hidden Gender of Law* (Federation Press, 2nd ed., 2002).

Guru, Gopal. 'Dalit Women Talk Differently' (1995) 30(41–42), *Economic and Political Weekly*, 2548.

'Egalitarianism and the Social Sciences in India', in Gopal Guru and Sundar Sarukkai, *The Cracked Mirror: An Indian Debate on Experience and Theory* (Oxford University Press, 2017).

Guru, Gopal, and V. Geetha. 'New Phase of Dalit-Bahujan Intellectual Activity' (2000) 35(3), *Economic and Political Weekly*, 30.

Guru, Gopal, and Sundar Sarukkai. *The Cracked Mirror: An Indian Debate on Experience and Theory* (Oxford University Press, 2017).

Hadot, Pierre. *Philosophy as a Way of Life: Spiritual Exercises from Socrates to Foucault* (Wiley-Blackwell, 1995).

Haksar, Nandita. *De-mystification of Law for Women* (South Asia Books, 1996).

'Human Rights Lawyering: A Feminist Perspective', in Mala Khullar (ed.), *Writing the Women's Movement: A Reader* (Zubaan, 2005).

Halley, Janet. *Split Decisions: How and Why to Take a Break from Feminism* (Princeton University Press, 2006).

Halley, Janet, Prabha Kotiswaran, Rachel Rebouché and Hila Shamir. *Governance Feminism: An Introduction* (University of Minnesota Press, 2018).

Hammersley, Martin. 'On Feminist Methodology' (1992) 26(2), *Sociology*, 187.

Harasym, Sarah (ed.). *Gayatri Chakravorty Spivak: The Post-colonial Critic – Interviews, Strategies, Dialogues* (Routledge, 1990).

Harding, Sandra (ed.). *Feminism and Methodology* (Indiana University Press, 1988).

Harris, Angela P. 'Race and Essentialism in Feminist Legal Theory' (1990) 42(3), *Stanford Law Review*, 581.

Hasan, Zoya. *Politics of Inclusion: Castes, Minorities, and Affirmative Action* (Oxford University Press, 2011).

Ilaiah, Kancha. *Why I Am Not a Hindu: A Shudra Critique of Hindutva Philosophy, Culture and Political Economy* (Bhatkal & Sen, 2005).

Indian Association for Women's Studies (eds). *The New Economic Policy: A Collection of Background Papers to Sixth National Conference* (IAWS, 1993), http://iaws.org/wp-content/themes/pdf/publications/NCF06.3-The_New_Economic_Policy_And_Women,1993.pdf.

Jaffrelot, Christophe. *India's Silent Revolution: The Rise of the Lower Castes in North India* (C. Hurst & Co., 2003).

Jain, Chirayu, Spadika Jayaraj, Sanjana Muraleedharan, Harjas Singh and Marc S. Galanter. 'The Elusive Island of Excellence: A Study on Student Demographics, Accessibility and Inclusivity at National Law School 2015–16' (2016), https://papers.ssrn.com/sol3/papers.cfm?abstract_id=2788311.

Jaising, Indira (ed.). *Men's Laws, Women's Lives: A Constitutional Perspective on Religion, Common Law and Culture in South Asia* (Women Unlimited, 2005).

Jayaraman, Raja. 'Personal Identity in a Globalized World: Cultural Roots of Hindu Personal Names and Surnames' (2005) 38(3), *Journal of Popular Culture*, 476.

Jenson, Jane. 'Writing Women Out, Folding Gender In' (2008) 15(2), *Social Politics*, 131.

Jodhka, Surinder S. *Caste* (Oxford University Press, 2013).

Caste in Contemporary India (Routledge, 2014).

John, Mary (ed.). *Women's Studies in India: A Reader* (Penguin India, 2008).

Kannabiran, Kalpana (ed.). *Women and Law: Critical Feminist Perspectives* (Sage, 2013).

Kannabiran, Kalpana, and Vasanth Kannabiran. *De-eroticizing Assault: Essays on Modesty, Honour and Power* (Popular Prakashan, 2002).

Kannabiran, Kalpana, and Ritu Menon. *From Mathura to Manorama: Resisting Violence Against Women in India* (Women Unlimited, 2007).

Kapadia, Karin. *The Violence of Development: The Politics of Identity, Gender and Social Inequalities in India* (Zed Books, 2003).

Kapoor, Coomi. *The Emergency: A Personal History* (Penguin, 2016).

Kapur, Ratna. 'Sexcapades and the Law' (2001) 505, *Seminar*, http://cscs.res.in/dataarchive/textfiles/textfile.2012-03-12.1317951631/file.

Erotic Justice: Law and the New Politics of Postcolonialism (Routledge-Cavendish, 2005).

'India', in *Collateral Damage: The Impact of Anti-trafficking Measures on Human Rights Around the World* (Global Alliance Against Traffic in Women, 2007).

Kapur, Ratna, and Brenda Cossman. 'On Women, Equality and the Constitution: Through the Looking Glass of Feminism' (1993) 1, *National Law School Journal*, 1.

Subversive Sites: Feminist Engagements with Law in India (Sage, 1996).

'*Subversive Sites* 20 Years Later: Rethinking Feminist Engagements with Law' (2018) 44(2), *Australian Feminist Law Journal*, 265.

Kirk, Jason A. *India and the World Bank: The Politics of Aid and Influence* (Anthem Press, 2011).

Kotiswaran, Prabha. 'Rumblings of a New Beginning: The Case of Feminist Legal Scholarship in India' (1997) 20, *Harvard Women's Law Journal*, 313.

'Born Unto Brothels: Toward a Legal Ethnography of Sex Work in an Indian Red-Light Area' (2008) 33(3), *Law and Social Inquiry*, 579.

Dangerous Sex, Invisible Labor: Sex Work and the Law in India (Princeton University Press, 2011).

'Sword or Shield? The Role of the Law in the Indian Sex Workers' Movement' (2013) 15(4), *Interventions: International Journal of Postcolonial Studies*, 530.

'Governance Feminism in the Postcolony', in Janet Halley, Prabha Kotiswaran, Rachel Rebouché and Hila Shamir, *Governance Feminism: An Introduction* (University of Minnesota Press, 2018), 75–148.

(ed.). *Sex Work* (Women Unlimited, 2010).

Krishnan, Jayanth K. 'Professor Kingsfield Goes to Delhi: American Academics, the Ford Foundation, and the Development of Legal Education in India', Maurer School of Law, Indiana University, 2004, www.repository.law.indiana.edu/cgi/viewcontent.cgi?referer=www.google.com/&httpsredir=1&article=1347&context=facpub.

Krishnaswamy, Sudhir. *Democracy and Constitutionalism in India: A Study of the Basic Structure Doctrine* (Oxford University Press, 2010).

Kumar, Radha. *The History of Doing: An Illustrated Account of Movements for Women's Rights and Feminism in India, 1800–1990* (Zubaan, 1993).

Loomba, Ania. *Colonialism/Postcolonialism* (Routledge, 2016).

MacKinnon, Catharine A. 'Feminism, Marxism, Method, and the State: An Agenda for Theory' (1982) 7(3) *Signs* 515.

MacKinnon, Catharine. *Toward a Feminist Theory of the State* (Harvard University Press, 1989).

Mallick, Ross. *Development Policy of a Communist Government: West Bengal since 1977* (Cambridge University Press, 2007).

Mani, Braj Ranjan. *Debrahminising History: Dominance and Resistance in Indian Society* (Manohar, 2005).

Mani, Lata. 'Contentious Traditions: The Debate on Sati in Colonial India' (1987) 7, *Cultural Critique*, 119.

Marx, Karl. 'Theses on Feuerbach', in Robert C. Tucker (ed.), *The Marx-Engels Reader*, 2nd ed. (W.W. Norton and Co., 1978), 143–45.

McDaniel, June. *Offering Flowers, Feeding Skulls: Popular Goddess Worship in West Bengal* (Oxford University Press, 2014).

McVeigh, Shaun. 'Afterword: Office and the Conduct of the Minor Jurisprudent (2015) 5, *University of California Irvine Law Review*, 499.

'Conditions of Carriage: Finding a Place' (2017) 21, *Law Text Culture*, 165.

'Reciprocal Relations: Formations of the Office of Legal Scholar' (2018) 9(2), *Jindal Global Law Review*, 231–38.

McWilliam, Erica. 'Performing between the Posts: Authority, Posture, and Contemporary Feminist Scholarship', in William G. Tierney and Yvonna S. Lincoln (eds), *Representation and the Text: Re-framing the Narrative Voice* (SUNY Press, 1997), 219–32.

Menon, Nivedita. 'Foucault and Indian Scholarship: History, Governmentality, Modernity', in Franson Manjali (ed.), *Trajectory of French Thought* (Rupa, 2004), 63–81.

Recovering Subversion: Feminist Politics Beyond the Law (University of Illinois Press, 2004).

'Between the Burqa and the Beauty Parlour? Globalization, Cultural Nationalism, and Feminist Politics', in Ania Loomba, Jed Esty, Antoinette Burton, Matti Bunzl and Suvir Kaul (eds), *Postcolonial Studies and Beyond* (Duke University Press, 2005), 206–29.

'Outing Heteronormativity: Nation, Citizen, Feminist Disruptions', in Nivedita Menon (ed.), *Sexualities* (Women Unlimited, 2007), 3–51.

'Sexuality, Caste, Governmentality: Contests over "Gender" in India' (2009) 91, *Feminist Review*, 94.

'Is Feminism about "Women"? A Critical View on Intersectionality from India' (2015) 50(17), *Economic and Political Weekly*, 37.

'Sexual Violence and the Law in India', in Robin West and Cynthia Grant Bowman (eds), *Research Handbook on Feminist Jurisprudence* (Elgar, 2019), 184–212.

Menon, N. R. Madhava. *Turning Point (The Story of a Law Teacher)* (Universal Law Publishing, 2012).

Minow, Martha. *Feminist Legal Theories* (Routledge, 1997).

Mody, Zia. *10 Judgements That Changed India* (Penguin, 2013).

Mohanty, Chandra Talpade. *Feminism Without Borders: Decolonizing Theory, Practicing Solidarity* (Duke University Press, 2003).

Mukherjee, Suroopa. *Bhopal Gas Tragedy: The Worst Industrial Disaster in Human History* (Tulika Books, 2002).

Murthy, Laxmi, and Meena Seshu (eds). *The Business of Sex* (Zubaan, 2014).

Nag, Moni. 'Sex Workers in Sonagachi' (2005) 40(49), *Economic and Political Weekly*, 5151.

Nair, Janaki. *Women and Law in Colonial India: A Social History* (Kali for Women, 1996).

Narain, Vrinda. *Reclaiming the Nation: Muslim Women and the Law in India* (University of Toronto Press, 2008).

Narayan, Badri. 'Margins and Politics: Introduction', in *The Making of the Dalit Public in North India: Uttar Pradesh, 1950–Present* (Oxford University Press, 2016), xvi–xxxviii.

Nayar, Baldev Raj. *Globalization and India's Economic Integration* (Georgetown University Press, 2014).

Nayar, Kuldip. *The Judgment: Inside Story of the Emergency in India* (Vikas, 1977).

Nedelsky, Jennifer. *Law's Relations: A Relational Theory of Self, Autonomy, and Law* (Oxford University Press, 2013).

Oksala, Johanna. 'In Defense of Experience' (2014) 29(2), *Hypatia*, 388.

Olivelle, Patrick, and Donald R. Davis (eds). *Hindu Law: A New History of Dharmasastra* (Oxford University Press, 2017).

Olsen, Frances E. *Feminist Legal Theory I: Foundations and Outlooks* (New York University Press, 1995).

Feminist Legal Theory II: Positioning Feminist Theory Within Law (New York University Press, 1995).

Ovichegan, Samson K. *Faces of Discrimination in Higher Education in India: Quota Policy, Social Justice and the Dalits* (Routledge Research in Educational Equality and Diversity) (Routledge, 2015).

Oza, Rupal. *The Making of Neoliberal India: Nationalism, Gender, and the Paradoxes of Globalisation* (Routledge, 2006).

Pahuja, Sundhya, and Adil Hasan Khan. 'The Southern Jurist as a Teacher of Laws: An Interview with Upendra Baxi' (2018) 9(2), *Jindal Global Law Review*, 351.

Parashar, Archana. *Women and Family Law Reform in India: Uniform Civil Code and Gender Equality* (Sage, 1992).

'Feminism in Indian Legal Education', in Amita Dhanda and Archana Parashar (eds), *Engendering Law: Essays in Honour of Lotika Sarkar* (Eastern Book Company, 1999), 89–116.

Parashar, Archana, and Amita Dhanda. 'Introduction', in Amita Dhanda and Archana Parashar (eds), *Engendering Law: Essays in Honour of Lotika Sarkar* (Eastern Book Company, 1999), 1–32.

Parmar, Pooja. *Indigeneity and Legal Pluralism in India: Claims, Histories, Meanings* (Cambridge University Press, 2015).

Pawar, Urmila, and Meenakshi Moon. *We Also Made History: Women in the Ambedkarite Movement* (Zubaan, 2008).

Prakash, Gyan. *Emergency Chronicles: Indira Gandhi and Democracy's Turning Point* (Princeton University Press, 2019).

Prasad, Rajendra. *A Conceptual-Analytic Study of Classical Indian Philosophy of Morals*, vol. 12, part I (Concept Publishing Company, 2008).

Ramamirthammal, Muvalur, Kalpana Kannabiran and Vasanth Kannabiran (eds). *Web of Deceit: Devadasi Reforms in Colonial India* (Kali for Women, 2003).

Ramberg, Lucinda. *Given to the Goddess: South Indian Devadasis and the Sexuality of Religion* (Duke University Press, 2014).

Rao, Anupama (ed.). *Gender and Caste* (Zed Books, 2005).

The Caste Question: Dalits and the Politics of Modern India (University of California Press, 2009).

Rathore, Aakash Singh, and Garima Goswamy. *Rethinking Indian Jurisprudence: An Introduction to the Philosophy of Law* (Routledge, 2018).

Ray, Raka. *Fields of Protest: Women's Movements in India* (University of Minnesota Press, 1998).

Reddy, Gayatri. *With Respect to Sex: Negotiating Hijra Identity in South India* (University of Chicago Press, 2005).

Rege, Sharmila. 'Dalit Women Talk Differently: A Critique of "Difference" and Towards a Dalit Feminist Standpoint Position' (1998) 33(44), *Economic and Political Weekly*, WS39.

'Education as "Trutiya Ratna": Towards Phule-Ambedkarite Feminist Pedagogical Practice' (2010) 45(44–45), *Economic and Political Weekly*, 88.

Against the Madness of Manu: B. R. Ambedkar's Writings on Brahminical Patriarchy (Navayana, 2013).

Restakis, John. *Humanizing the Economy: Co-operatives in the Age of Capital* (New Society Publishers, 2010).

Riles, Annelise. 'An Ethnography of Abstractions?' (2000) *Cornell Law Faculty Publications*, 781, https://scholarship.law.cornell.edu/facpub/781.

The Network Inside Out (University of Michigan Press, 2001).

Collateral Knowledge: Legal Reasoning in the Global Financial Markets (University of Chicago Press, 2011).

Rocher, Ludo. *Studies in Hindu Law and Dharmasastra*, ed. Donald R. Davis (Anthem Press, 2013).

Rose, Deborah Bird. *Hidden Histories: Black Stories from Victoria River Downs, Humbert River and Wave Hill Stations* (Aboriginal Studies Press, 1991).

Reports from a Wild Country: Ethics for Decolonisation (UNSW Press, 2004).

Roy, Anupama. *Gendered Citizenship: Historical and Conceptual Explorations* (Orient BlackSwan, 2013).

Rubin, Gayle. *Deviations: A Gayle Rubin Reader* (Duke University Press, 2011).

'Thinking Sex: Notes for a Radical Theory of the Politics of Sexuality', in *Deviations: A Gayle Rubin Reader* (Duke University Press, 2011), 137–81.

Sagade, Jaya. *Child Marriage in India: Socio-legal and Human Rights Dimensions* (Oxford University Press, 2012).

Sahni, Roshni, V. Kalyan Shankar and Hemant Apte (eds). *Prostitution and Beyond: An Analysis of Sex Workers in India* (Sage, 2008).

Samaddar, Ranabir. *Passive Revolution in West Bengal, 1977–2011* (Sage, 2013).

Sandoval, Chela. 'US Third-World Feminism: The Theory and Method of Oppositional Consciousness in the Post Modern World' (1991) 10, *Genders*, 1.

Sangari, Kumkum, and Sudesh Vaid. *Recasting Women: Essays in Indian Colonial History* (Rutgers University Press, 1990).

Sarkar, Lotika. 'Rape: A Human Rights Versus a Patriarchal Interpretation' (1994) 1(1), *Indian Journal of Gender Studies*, 69.

Sarkar, Tanika. *Hindu Wife, Hindu Nation: Community, Religion, and Cultural Nationalism* (Indiana University Press, 2002).

Sathe, S. P. 'Is a National Law School Necessary?' (1974) 9(39), *Economic and Political Weekly*, 1643.

'Law and Women' (1996) 31(41–42), *Economic and Political Weekly*, 2804.

Judicial Activism in India (Oxford University Press, 2002).

Scales, Ann C. 'Towards a Feminist Jurisprudence' (1981) 56, *Indiana Law Journal*, 375.

Scott, Joan. 'The Evidence of Experience' (1991) 17(4), *Critical Inquiry*, 773.

Sedgwick, Eve. 'Paranoid Reading and Reparative Reading', in *Touching Feeling: Affect, Pedagogy, Performativity* (Duke University Press, 2003), 123–52.

Sen, Amartya. *The Idea of Justice* (Harvard University Press, 2011).

Sen, Samita. 'Toward a Feminist Politics? The Indian Women's Movement in Historical Perspective', Policy Research Report on Gender and Development, Working Paper Series No. 9, World Bank, Development Research Group/Poverty Reduction and Economic Management Network, April 2000, http://unpan1.un.org/intradoc/groups/public/documents/apcity/unpan051009.pdf.

Sen, Satyendra Nath. *Cooperative Movement in West Bengal* (Bookland, 1966).

Seshu, Meena Saraswathi, and Laxmi Murthy. 'The Business of Sex: An Introduction', in Laxmi Murthy and Meena Seshu (eds), *The Business of Sex* (Zubaan, 2014), 1–7.

Shukla, Rakesh. 'A Walk Through the Labyrinths of Sex Work Law', in Laxmi Murthy and Meena Seshu (eds), *The Business of Sex* (Zubaan, 2014), 212–42.

Singh, Kriti. *Separated and Divorced Women in India: Economic Rights and Entitlements* (Sage, 2013).

Sircar, Oishik. 'The Fraught Terrain of Law and Feminism: 20 Years of *Subversive Sites*' (2016) 12(1), *Socio-legal Review*, 133.

Sircar, Oishik, and Debolina Dutta. 'Beyond Compassion: Children of Sex Workers in Kolkata's Sonagachi' (2011) 18(3), *Childhood*, 333.

Smart, Carol. *Feminism and the Power of Law* (Routledge, 2002).

'Shifting Horizons: Reflections on Qualitative Methods' (2009) 10(3), *Feminist Theory*, 295.

Smart, C., J. Hockey and A. James (eds). *The Craft of Knowledge: Experiences of Living with Data* (Palgrave Macmillan, 2014).

Smith, Linda Tuhiwai. *Decolonizing Methodologies: Research and Indigenous Peoples* (Zed Books, 2012).

Solanki, Gopika. *Adjudication in Religious Family Laws: Cultural Accommodation, Legal Pluralism, and Gender Equality in India* (Cambridge University Press, 2011).

Sonalkar, Wandana. 'Translator's Introduction', in Urmila Pawar and Meenakshi Moon (eds), *We Also Made History: Women in the Ambedkarite Movement* (Zubaan, 2008), 1–37.

Spivak, Gayatri. 'Feminism and Critical Theory' (1978) 1(3), *Women's Studies International Quarterly*, 241.

Spivak, Gayatri Chakravorty. 'Can the Subaltern Speak?', in Cary Nelson and Lawrence Grossberg (eds), *Marxism and the Interpretation of Culture* (University of Illinois Press, 1988), 271–313.

The Post-colonial Critic: Interviews, Strategies, Dialogues (Routledge, 1990).

'An Interview with Gayatri Chakravorty Spivak: New Nations Writers Conference in South Africa', by Leon de Kock (1992) 23(3), *Ariel: A Review of International English Literature*, 29.

'An Interview with Gayatri Spivak' by Sara Danius, Stefan Jonsson and Gayatri Chakravorty Spivak (1993) 20(2), *boundary 2*, 24.

'Echo', in Gayatri Chakravorty Spivak, *The Spivak Reader*, ed. Donna Landry and Gerald MacLean (Routledge, 1996), 175–202.

'Subaltern Talk: Interview with the Editors', in Gayatri Chakravorty Spivak, *The Spivak Reader*, ed. Donna Landry and Gerald MacLean (Routledge, 1996), 287–308.

The Spivak Reader, ed. Donna Landry and Gerald MacLean (Routledge, 1996).

A Critique of Postcolonial Reason: Toward a History of the Vanishing Present (Harvard University Press, 1999).

'Envisioning an Aesthetic Education in the Era of Globalisation', TLHEC8: Workshop with Prof. Gayatri Spivak, Teaching & Learning TV by UTLO (2014), www.youtube.com/watch?v=iMTzutBH5eM&feature=youtu.be.

Sunder Rajan, Rajeswari. *The Scandal of the State: Women, Law and Citizenship in Postcolonial India* (Duke University Press, 2003).

Tambe, Ashwini. *Codes of Misconduct: Regulating Prostitution in Late Colonial Bombay* (Zubaan, 2009).

Teltumbde, Anand. *The Persistence of Caste: The Khairlanji Murders and India's Hidden Apartheid* (Zed Books, 2010).

Thomas, Pradeep Ninan. 'Contentious Actions and Communication for Social Change: The Public Hearing (*Jan Sunwai*) as Process' (2017) 67(5), *Journal of Communication*, 719.

Thornton, Margaret. 'The Development of Feminist Jurisprudence' (1998) 9(2), *Legal Education Review*, 171.

Van Inwagen, Peter, and Meghan Sullivan. 'Metaphysics', *Stanford Encyclopedia of Philosophy*, ed. Edward N. Zalta (Spring 2018), https://plato.stanford.edu/entries/metaphysics.

Vanita, Ruth, and Madhu Kishwar. 'Using Women as a Pretext for Repression: The Indecent Representation of Women (Prohibition) Bill' (1987) 37, *Manushi*, http://manushi.in/docs/882.%20Law-Using%20Women%20As%20aPretext%20for%20Repression%20-37.pdf.

Vatuk, Sylvia. 'The "Women's Court" in India: An Alternative Dispute Resolution Body for Women in Distress' (2013) 45(1), *Journal of Legal Pluralism and Unofficial Law*, 76.

Wacks, Raymond. *Philosophy of Law: A Very Short Introduction* (Oxford University Press, 2014).

Walkowitz, Judith R. *Prostitution and Victorian Society: Women, Class and the State* (Cambridge University Press, 1980).

Warner, Michael. '*Uncritical Reading*', in Jane Gallop (ed.), *Polemic: Critical or Uncritical* (Routledge, 2004), 13–38.

Weiss, Penny. 'Conversation as Method', in *Conversations with Feminism: Political Theory and Practice* (Rowman & Littlefield, 1998).

West, Robin. 'Women in the Legal Academy: A Brief History of Feminist Legal Theory' (2018) 87(3), *Fordham Law Review*, 977.

Wickramasinghe, Maithree. *Feminist Research Methodology* (Zubaan, 2015).

Williams, Patricia. *The Alchemy of Race and Rights* (Harvard University Press, 1992).

ACTIVIST SOURCES: DMSC AND VAMP

DMSC (Durbar Mahila Samanwaya Committee). By-laws of Usha Multipurpose Co-operative Society Limited (n.d.) (on file with author).

DMSC (Durbar Mahila Samanwaya Committee). *Codes of Conduct for Durbar Leaders and Members* (pamphlet published by DMSC, n.d., on file with author).

DMSC (Durbar Mahila Samanwaya Committee). 'Durbar Mahila Samanwaya Committee (DMSC) & The Usha Multipurpose Cooperative Society Ltd.' (n.d.), www.nswp.org/sites/nswp.org/files/DMSC%20short%20history.pdf.

DMSC (Durbar Mahila Samanwaya Committee). *Sex Workers' Durga Puja Will Now Reach Your Neighbourhood from Sonagachi. Are You with Us?* (DMSC pamphlet, n.d.) (on file with author).

DMSC (Durbar Mahila Samanwaya Committee). *Smarakpatra,* 17 (on file with author).

DMSC (Durbar Mahila Samanwaya Committee). *Sex Workers' Manifesto,* First National Conference of Sex Workers in India, 14–16 November 1997 (published by DMSC for distribution at the conference) (on file with author), www.nswp.org/sites/nswp.org/files/Sex%20Workers%20Manifesto%20-%20Meeting%20in%20India.pdf.

DMSC (Durbar Mahila Samanwaya Committee). Secretary's Address, Third State Conference of Sex Workers (report published by DMSC, May 2005) (on file with author).

DMSC (Durbar Mahila Samanwaya Committee). *All India Conference of Entertainment Workers* (pamphlet published by DMSC, March 2007) (on file with author).

DMSC (Durbar Mahila Samanwaya Committee). *Self Regulatory Board: A Rolling Success in Anti-trafficking Program, Lessons Learnt from DMSC* (Durbar Prakashani, 2007) (on file with author).

DMSC (Durbar Mahila Samanwaya Committee). *Durbar: A Brief Profile* (Durbar Prakashani, 2011, 4th ed.).

DMSC (Durbar Mahila Samanwaya Committee). *Community Led Anti Trafficking and Child Protection Program* (Durbar Prakashani, 2013) (on file with author).

DMSC (Durbar Mahila Samanwaya Committee). '20 Years of USHA Multipurpose Cooperative Society' (January 2015) (on file with author).

Jana, Smarajit. 'Editorial', *Durbar Bhavna,* nos 5–6 (Durbar Prakashani, September–October 2014).

Sangram. *Sangram Bill of Rights,* www.sangram.org/resources/sangram_billof_rights.pdf.

Of Veshyas, Vamps, Whores and Women, www.sangram.org/upload/resources/of_veshyas_vamps_whores_and_women_part_I.pdf.

Of Veshyas, Vamps, Whores and Women, www.sangram.org/upload/resources/Of_veshyas_vamp_whore_and_women_II.pdf.

'Rehabilitation against Their Will?' (June 2002) 1(2) *Of Veshyas, Vamps, Whores and Women.*

Annual Report 2013–14, www.sangram.org/upload/reports/annual-narrative-report-2013-2014-4.pdf.

Annual Report, 1 April 2014–31 March 2015, 3, www.sangram.org/upload/reports/annual-narrative-report-2014-2015-5.pdf.

Sangram/VAMP Team, *The VAMP/Sangram Sex Worker's Movement in India's Southwest,* AWID, www.awid.org/sites/default/files/atoms/files/changing_their_world_2_-_vamp_-sex_workers_movement_in_indias_southwest.pdf.

Seshu, Meena. 'Kamala Maushi: Salute to a Proud Devadasi', 15 February 2015, www.sangram.org/resources/Kamala-Maushi-Salute-to-a-proud-Devadasi.pdf.

VAMP (Veshya Anyay Mukti Parishad). 'Understanding the De-criminalisation Demand: A Fact Sheet for Advocacy', http://feministlawarchives.pldindia.org/wp-content/uploads/Demanding-De-Criminalisation-of-Sex-Work-Fact-Sheet.pdf.

VAMP (Veshya Anyay Mukti Parishad). 'A Statement of Women in Prostitution', 28 January 1995, www.sangram.org/upload/resources/sangram-VAMP-statement-1995.pdf.

MEDIA SOURCES

Dhar, Sujoy. 'RIGHTS-INDIA: Sex Workers Draw the Line on Religious Rites', *Inter Press Service,* 5 September 2002, www.ipsnews.net/2002/09/rights-india-sex-workers-draw-the-line-on-religious-rites.

Donthi, Praveen. 'How Caste Shaped the Experience of Rohith Vemula and Other Students at the University of Hyderabad', *Caravan*, 24 August 2016, https://caravanmagazine.in/vantage/caste-shaped-experience-rohith-vemula-students-university-hyderabad.

Dutta, Debolina, and Oishik Sircar. 'Sex, Work and Pleasure', *Times of India*, 10 April 2007, http://timesofindia.indiatimes.com/edit-page/Sex-work-and-pleasure/articleshow/1881189.cms.

Hosain, Alamgir. 'Caste Bar on Puja Festivity', *Telegraph*, 16 October 2010, www.telegraphindia.com/1101016/jsp/bengal/story_13063416.jsp.

IANS (India Abroad News Service). 'Finally, Kolkata Sex Workers Get Their Own Durga Puja', *Business Standard* (online), 9 October 2013, www.business-standard.com/article/news-ians/finally-kolkata-sex-workers-get-their-own-durga-puja-113100900907_1.html.

IANS (India Abroad News Service). 'Durga Puja Pandals to Touch Upon Controversial Global Issues', *Hans India*, 3 October 2015, www.thehansindia.com/posts/index/National/2015-10-03/Durga-Puja-pandals-to-touch-upon-controversial-global-issues/178993.

India Today. 'Kolkata Durga Puja Harps On Various Social Issues with Theme Puja', 19 October 2015, http://indiatoday.intoday.in/education/story/durga-puja-pandals/1/502282.html.

Outlook. 'Kolkata Sex Workers Host Their First Own Durga Puja', 11 October 2014, http://test.outlookindia.com/newswire/story/kolkata-sex-workers-host-their-first-own-durga-puja/813238.

PTI (Press Trust of India). 'Kolkata: Sex Workers Complain About Police Harassment, Stop Holding Durga Puja', *Indian Express*, 7 October 2016, http://indianexpress.com/article/india/india-news-india/sex-workers-in-kolkata-stop-holding-durga-puja-3070859.

Scroll.in. '2016 Una Flogging Incident: Dalit Victim Writes to President, Asks for Mercy killing', 28 November 2018, https://scroll.in/latest/903757/2016-una-flogging-incident-dalit-victim-writes-to-president-asks-for-mercy-killing.

Sengupta, Gopal. 'Meaning of Durga Puja', *Daily Star*, 6 October 2011, http://archive.thedailystar.net/newDesign/news-details.php?nid=205286.

Spivak, Gayatri Chakravorty. 'Envisioning an Aesthetic Education in the Era of Globalisation', TLHEC8: Workshop with Prof. Gayatri Spivak, Teaching & Learning TV by UTLO (2014), www.youtube.com/watch?v=iMTzutBH5eM&feature=youtu.be.

Srivastava, Utkarsh. 'Maharashtra's Ban on Dance Bars Has Done More Harm than Good', *Wire*, 28 March 2016, https://thewire.in/gender/maharashtras-ban-on-dance-bars-has-done-more-harm-than-good.

Telegraph. 'What Are Little Girls Made Of? Nightmares on Celluloid', Letters to the Editor, 15 March 2005, www.telegraphindia.com/opinion/letters-to-editor-15-03-2005/cid/1022371.

'VAMP Protests against *Prostitutes of God*', https://directorsnotes.com/2010/10/12/vamp-protests-against-prostitutes-of-god (VAMP protest video against the documentary film *Prostitutes of God*).

DOCUMENTARY AND FEATURE FILMS

Dutta, Debolina, and Oishik Sircar (dir.). *We Are Foot Soldiers* (PSBT India, 2015), www.youtube.com/watch?v=Bfm06qBo4c4.

Ghosh, Shohini (dir.). *The Tales of the Nightfairies* (Mediastorm Collective, 2002), www.youtube.com/watch?v=Ystke5m8now&t=168s.

Ray, Satyajit (dir.) *Agantuk* (NDFC, 1991).

REPORTS: GOVERNMENTAL AND NON-GOVERNMENTAL

Asian Women's Human Rights Council (AWHRC) and Vimochana. *Speaking Tree, Womenspeak: Asia-Pacific Public Hearing on Crimes Against Women Related to the Violence of Development, 28 January 1995, Bangalore, India* (AWHRC and Vimochana, 1995).

Baxi, Upendra, Vasudha Dhagamwar, Raghunath Kelkar and Lotika Sarkar. 'An Open Letter to the Chief Justice of India', 16 September 1979, http://pldindia.org/wp-content/uploads/2013/03/Open-Letter-to-CJI-in-the-Mathura-Rape-Case.pdf.

Government of India. *Towards Equality: Report of the Committee on the Status of Women in India* (Ministry of Education and Social Welfare, Department of Social Welfare, New Delhi, December 1974), http://pldindia.org/wp-content/uploads/2013/04/Towards-Equality-1974-Part-1.pdf.

Human Rights Watch. *Broken People: Caste Violence Against India's 'Untouchables'*, 1999, www.hrw.org/reports/1999/india.

Human Rights Watch. 'Abuses Against HIV/AIDS Outreach Workers' (2002), www.hrw.org/reports/2002/india2/india0602–05.htm#P276_42340.

Human Rights Watch. *India: 'Hidden Apartheid' of Discrimination Against Dalits* (2007), www.hrw.org/news/2007/02/13/india-hidden-apartheid-discrimination-against-dalits.

Human Rights Watch. *'They Say We're Dirty': Denying an Education to India's Marginalized* (2014), www.hrw.org/report/2014/04/22/they-say-were-dirty/denying-education-indias-marginalized.

Sarkar, Lotika, and Vina Mazumdar. 'Note of Dissent by Lotika Sarkar and Vina Mazumdar', in Government of India, *Towards Equality: Report of the Committee on the Status of Women in India* (Ministry of Education and Social Welfare, Department of Social Welfare, New Delhi, December 1974), 355–57.

CASE LAW

ADM Jabalpur v. *Shivkant Shukla* AIR 1976 SC 1207.

Golak Nath v. *State of Punjab* 1967 AIR (SC) 1643.

His Holiness Kesavananda Bharati Sripadagalvaru and Ors v. *State of Kerala and Anr* (1973) 4 SCC 225.

Indian Hotel and Restaurants ... v. *the State of Maharashtra through ...* 2006 (3) BomCR 705 (12 April 2006), https://indiankanoon.org/doc/1434517.

Maneka Gandhi v. *Union of India* 1978 SCR (2) 621, https://indiankanoon.org/doc/1766147.

Mohammad Ahmed Khan v. *Shah Bano Khan* AIR 1985 SC 945.

Nandini Satpathy v. *Dani (P. L.) and Anr* 1978 SCR (3) 608, https://indiankanoon.org/doc/1938988.

State of Maharashtra v. *Indian Hotel and Restaurants Association* WP No. 2450/2005 (Bombay High Court), https://indiankanoon.org/doc/38033723.

State of West Bengal & Ors v. *Durbar Mahila Samanwaya Committee & Ors*, M. A. T. 1493 of 2013, High Court of Calcutta Appellate Side, Banerjee HJ and Chaudhuri HJ, 26 September 2013, https://indiankanoon.org/doc/63503501.

Tukaram v. *State of Maharashtra* (1979) 2 SCC 143.

FICTION AND NON-FICTION SOURCES

Ali, Saiyad Mujtaba. 'Adda', in *Rachanaboli: Saiyad Mujtaba Ali*, vol. 1, 81–89, https://www.banglabooks.in/bangla-ebooks/saiyad-mujtaba-ali/rachanabali-saiyad-mujtaba-ali-vol-1-to-11-in-pdf.

Bose, Buddhadeva. 'Adda' (Rosinka Chaudhuri, trans.), in Amit Chaudhuri (ed.), *Memory's Gold: Writings on Calcutta* (Penguin Viking, 2008), 271–76.

Califia, Pat. *Macho Sluts: Erotic Fiction by Pat Califia* (Alyson Books, 1994).

Das, Samarendranath (ed.). *Kolkatar Adda* (Gangchil, 2015).

Sprinkle, Annie. *Hardcore from the Heart: The Pleasures, Profits and Politics of Sex in Performance* (A&C Black, 2006).

Tagore, Rabindranath. *The Co-operative Principles* (Visva-Bharati, 1963) (originally published in Bangla in 1928 as *Samabaya Niti*).

The Home and the World (Penguin, 2005).
'Samabyay', *Durbar Bhavna*, nos 5–6 (Durbar Prakashani, September–October 2014).
Vance, Carol. *Pleasure and Danger: Exploring Female Sexuality* (Rivers Oram Press, 1993).

Index

INDEX

Printed by Integrated Books International,
United States of America